Interpretation

PROFESSIONAL INTERPRETING IN THE REAL WORLD
Series Editor: Diane Teichman, *Linguistic Services, Houston, Texas, USA*

This series includes books ranging from resource texts which help both interpreters in training and practising interpreters to better prepare for their assignments, to training materials and instruction manuals for instructors of interpreters.

Full details of all the books in this series and of all our other publications can be found on http://www.multilingual-matters.com, or by writing to Multilingual Matters, St Nicholas House, 31–34 High Street, Bristol BS1 2AW, UK.

Interpretation

Techniques and Exercises

Second Edition

James Nolan

MULTILINGUAL MATTERS
Bristol • Buffalo • Toronto

Library of Congress Cataloging in Publication Data
Nolan, James
Interpretation : techniques and exercises / James Nolan. — 2nd ed.
Professional Interpreting in the Real World: 4
Includes bibliographical references and index.
1. Translating and interpreting. I. Title.
P306.N586 2012
418'.02–dc23 2012022010

British Library Cataloguing in Publication Data
A catalogue entry for this book is available from the British Library.

ISBN-13: 978-1-84769-810-0 (hbk)
ISBN-13: 978-1-84769-809-4 (pbk)

Multilingual Matters
UK: St Nicholas House, 31–34 High Street, Bristol BS1 2AW, UK.
USA: UTP, 2250 Military Road, Tonawanda, NY 14150, USA.
Canada: UTP, 5201 Dufferin Street, North York, Ontario M3H 5T8, Canada.

The policy of Multilingual Matters/Channel View Publications is to use papers that are natural, renewable and recyclable products, made from wood grown in sustainable forests. In the manufacturing process of our books, and to further support our policy, preference is given to printers that have FSC and PEFC Chain of Custody certification. The FSC and/or PEFC logos will appear on those books where full certification has been granted to the printer concerned.

Typeset by Techset Composition Ltd., Salisbury, UK.
Printed and bound in Great Britain by the MPG Books Group.

Contents

Acknowledgments   ix
Preface to the Second Edition   xi

Introduction: Frequently Asked Questions   1
     Why This Book?   1
     How to Use This Book   1
     What Is Interpretation?   2
     How Does Interpretation Differ From Translation?   2
     What Is the Difference Between Consecutive
        Interpretation and Simultaneous Interpretation?   3
     Is it Useful to Specialize in a Particular Subject Area?   4
     Are Some Languages More Important Than Others
        for Translation and Interpretation?   5
     Are There Any Formal Professional Requirements?   6
     Is it Advantageous to Be Bilingual?   6
     Is Simultaneous Interpretation a Stressful Occupation?   7

1   Speaking   8
     Exercises   9

2   Preparation/Anticipating the Speaker   17
     Exercises   18

3   Complex Syntax/Compression   24
     Exercises   24

4   Word Order/Clusters   44
     Exercises   45

5   General Adverbial Clauses   51
     Exercises   52

6   Untranslatability   55
     Exercises   58

7   Figures of Speech   64
     Exercises   65

8   Argumentation   111
     Exercises   111

9   Diction/Register   121
     Exercises   122

10 Formal Style   162
     Exercises   163

11 A Policy Address   180
     Exercises   181

12 Quotations/Allusions/Transposition   205
     Exercises   207

13 Political Discourse   211
     Exercises   211

14 Economic Discourse   225
     Exercises   225

15 Humor   245
     Exercises   248

16 Latinisms   262
     Exercises   263

17 Numbers   272
     Exercises   272

18 Note-taking   278
     Exercises   282

     Annex I: Additional Reformulation Strategies   288
       Using Appositives to Combine, Shorten and Clarify Sentences 288
       Using the Gerund to Create a Concise Subject Phrase   289

Avoiding Nominalizations   290
Avoiding Strings of Prepositional Phrases   291
Keeping Modifiers Close to the Words They Modify   292

Annex II: Memory Drill   294

Annex III: Patterns in Speech   296
    Cause and Effect   296
    General to Specific (deductive)   297
    Specific to General (inductive)   297
    Simple Listing   297
    Chronological   298
    Classification   298
    Comparison/Contrast   299
    Thesis – example   299
    Problem – solution   299

Annex IV: Political Discourse – Additional Exercise   301
    Europe Divided Over Palestinian State, by Julio Godoy   301

Bibliography   304
    Works Consulted   304
    Illustrative Materials Used   304
    Resources   307
    Internet Resources   316

Index   325

Acknowledgments

I am much indebted to Mr Bruce Boeglin, training officer of the United Nations Interpretation Service and director of the Marymount Manhattan College certificate program in interpretation, for his encouragement. Useful comments on some of the exercises in this book also came from my students at Marymount Manhattan College and New York University. Mr Jean-Luc Rostan's careful proofreading of the manuscript and Diane Teichman's editorial guidance are highly appreciated. And no words can express my gratitude to my wife Adele, without whose patience and moral support this book would not have been written.

Preface to the Second Edition

Interpretation can be defined in a nutshell as conveying understanding. Its value stems from the fact that a speaker's meaning is best expressed in his or her native tongue but is best understood in the languages of the listeners.

In the art of interpretation several complex interrelated processes make it possible to convey the semantic and emotive contents of a message from one language and culture to another. The complex interaction of these processes and the difficulty of coordinating them simultaneously in the oral/aural mode require alertness, sensitivity, intense concentration and mental agility. In some ways, training for interpreting resembles training for musicianship: the most fruitful approach is guided practice; individual aptitudes and skills are important; talent needs to be nurtured and encouraged; performance is improved by awareness of audience expectations; intuition plays a role; and there may be several valid ways of interpreting a particular passage. The skills required for interpretation, especially simultaneous interpretation,

Table 1 The interpreting process

Listening	
Comprehension/receptivity/empathy	Memorizing
Processing	
Analysis/visualization	Thinking
Reformulation/mimicry	
Inference/extrapolation/deduction	
Speaking/expression	
Reproduction of meaning	Remembering
Articulation, enunciation	
Meaning modulated by tone, intonation	
Emotion conveyed by tone, intonation	

must be developed through practice to the point where they become automatic.

The world has come to rely on interpretation for cross-cultural communication in real time. Although interpretation is not always perfect, if it is performed by professionals with training and a high degree of proficiency in their working languages the result is always better than the alternative method of cross-cultural communication, which consists of asking speakers of various languages to speak a single so-called 'international' language in which they may have limited proficiency.

A second advantage of interpretation is that the respect shown by addressing an interlocutor in that person's own language is conducive to successful diplomacy or negotiation. Learning a foreign language represents a major investment of time and effort, and not all statesmen, diplomats or executives have the time, energy or linguistic talent to master the language of each party with whom they must speak. The interpreter helps these speakers to discharge their duty to make themselves understood and helps listeners to satisfy their need to understand what is being said.

A third advantage of interpretation is that it supports specialization and thus enhances the quality of multinational meetings and deliberations. Where interpretation is available, it is not necessary to take knowledge of a particular language into consideration when deciding who will attend the meeting; consequently, it is easier to select delegates or spokesmen solely on the basis of their qualifications and abilities.

A further advantage of interpretation is that it serves as a psychological equalizer between participants in discussions that are adversarial or controversial. A delegate at an international assembly who is speaking his own language just as he would at home does not feel he is making undue concessions or giving in to pressures from others. Sovereign equality in the use of languages puts all speakers on equal footing.

Finally, interpretation serves as a buffer between different sides in an adversarial discussion, making it possible to use the interpreter as a messenger to convey ideas and positions: it is sometimes possible to say things through a 'linguistic intermediary' that one would hesitate to say directly in one's own language or the language of an adversary.

Because of these advantages, conducting multilateral diplomatic and economic relations in the multilingual mode has become the standard way to do business. But there has been a parallel development: the rate at which speeches are delivered at international meetings has increased dramatically, for several reasons. There are now 196 independent countries in the world and, among the 6000+ languages spoken today, the number of languages being used as a medium of international communication is growing in parallel with the recognition of people's right to use their native languages. The European Union, for example, now uses 24 languages. Electronic and digital technologies have created an expectation that communication should normally be instantaneous, taking place in real time regardless of geographical and cultural distances. Consequently, there are a growing number of interlocutors on the world scene speaking a growing number of different languages and making their statements in the expectation of being immediately understood. And they all have a great deal to say about a growing number of pressing issues. But for practical and logistical reasons there are still only a limited number of hours in the day that can be used as conference time and those hours must be equitably shared among the many speakers vying for the microphone. The result is that spokesmen inevitably resort to speaking faster and faster during their all-too-brief turn on the world stage, further complicating the interpreter's already difficult task.

Introduction: Frequently Asked Questions

Why This Book?

Over recent decades the explosive growth of globalization and regional integration has fueled parallel growth in multilingual conferences. Although conference interpreting has come of age as a profession, interpreter training programs have had varied success, pointing to the need for an instructional manual which covers the subject comprehensively. This book seeks to fill that need by providing a structured syllabus and an overview of interpretation accompanied by exercises, developed for the classroom, in the main aspects of the art. It is meant to serve as a practical guide for interpreters and as a complement to interpreter training programs, particularly those for students preparing for conference interpreting in international governmental and business settings.

It is assumed that students have mastered their active and passive working languages and the fundamentals of translation. Those exercises which deal with lexicon focus on expanding the student's range of expression in order to build vocabulary to the level needed for conference interpreting.

The texts used in the exercises have been selected both to illustrate various aspects of translation and interpretation and to introduce the student to the wide range of topics and perspectives that arise in the international fora where conference interpreters work.

How to Use This Book

Interpretation cannot be learned from a book alone, but only through a combination of study and steady practice. However, it is hoped that the exercises in this book will help the student interpreter determine what techniques she or he needs to concentrate on. Although interpretation is an oral skill, it contains an element of composition. Consequently, the writing exercises in this book should not be overlooked.

For the sake of brevity, the treatment of subjects and techniques in this book is somewhat arbitrarily divided and some subjects are treated together in one chapter. The chapters need not be followed strictly in sequence and can be taken up in any order that the instructor or student finds appropriate, although it is strongly recommended that none be omitted from a comprehensive introductory course. The skills introduced earlier in the book (e.g. developing confidence as a public speaker) are those which are most necessary to a professional interpreter or which usually take longer for most students to master; those presented later in the book (e.g. transposing literary allusions) are techniques which are less often needed in practice or which interpreters can gradually acquire outside the classroom through experience and study. Most of the exercises can be done in class and/or as homework. Some require the use of tape recorders. Although the working languages used in these exercises are English, French and Spanish, most of the exercises can be adapted for other languages. Exercises for other languages may also be accessed through the internet resources and links listed in the final section of the Bibliography.

What Is Interpretation?

Interpretation can be defined in a nutshell as conveying understanding. Its usefulness stems from the fact that a speaker's meaning is best expressed in his or her native tongue but is best understood in the languages of the listeners.

In addition, the respect shown by addressing an interlocutor in that person's own language is conducive to successful diplomacy or negotiation. For example, US President John F. Kennedy undertook the task of mastering French specifically with a view toward negotiating with French President Charles de Gaulle. But not all statesmen and diplomats have the time, energy or linguistic talent for mastering the language of each party with whom they must speak. By bridging the gap between languages, the interpreter helps speakers discharge their duty to make themselves understood and helps listeners to satisfy their need to understand what is being said.

How Does Interpretation Differ From Translation?

A translator studies written material in one language (the 'source language') and reproduces it in written form in another language (the 'target language'). An interpreter listens to a spoken message in the source language and renders it orally, consecutively or simultaneously, in the target language. Both the translator and the interpreter must have a thorough mastery of the target language, as well as a very good passive understanding of the source language or languages with which they work. For most interpreters, the target language will be his or her native tongue.

The translator relies mainly on thorough research with background materials and dictionaries in order to produce the most accurate and readable written translation possible. The interpreter relies mainly on the ability to get the gist of the message across to the target audience on the spot.

No translation is ever 'perfect' because cultures and languages differ. However, in practice, the translator is usually held to a higher standard of accuracy and completeness (including the ability to reproduce the style of the original), while the interpreter is expected to convey the essence of the message immediately.

The translator's activity is more like that of a writer, while the interpreter's performance is more like that of an actor. A good translator will spend much time searching for the correct technical term or the right choice of words, but a good interpreter must immediately come up with a satisfactory paraphrase or a rough equivalent if *le mot juste* does not come to mind, in order not to keep the audience waiting. Some people are able to do both translation and interpretation. Others find that, for reasons of temperament and personality, they cannot do one or the other. Generally, some experience as a translator provides a good foundation for becoming an interpreter.

What Is the Difference Between Consecutive Interpretation and Simultaneous Interpretation?

A consecutive interpreter listens to the speaker, takes notes, and then reproduces the speech in the target language. Depending on the length of the speech, this may be done all at one go or in several segments. The consecutive interpreter relies mainly on memory, but good note-taking technique is an essential aid.

A simultaneous interpreter, usually sitting in a soundproof booth, listens to the speaker through earphones and, speaking into a microphone, reproduces the speech in the target language as it is being delivered in the source language. Because the simultaneous interpreter cannot fall too far behind, this method requires considerable practice and presence of mind.

Consecutive interpretation was long the standard method, until simultaneous interpretation was first tried out on a large scale, and found to be workable, at the Nuremberg trials. Thanks to that breakthrough and to modern sound equipment, simultaneous interpretation has now become the most widely used method, in every type of meeting from business conventions to summit conferences, and can even be done via remote communications links. It is much less time consuming and enables a multilingual conference, with participants speaking a number of languages, to proceed without interruption. However, consecutive interpretation is still preferred in certain situations, such as one-on-one interviews, confidential hearings, brief public appearances by prominent persons or some legal proceedings. It has the advantage of not requiring much equipment.

Occasionally, interpreters may be asked to do 'whispering' or 'chuchotage', which consists of sitting behind a participant at a meeting and simultaneously interpreting the proceedings *sotto voce* only for that person.

Simultaneous interpreters normally work in teams of two per booth, taking turns in shifts of about 30 minutes each for a maximum of about three hours at a time, which has been found to be the maximum average time during which the necessary concentration and accuracy can be sustained. They generally work only into their 'A' (best) language, or their mother tongue. In certain situations (e.g. in a meeting where one language largely predominates), a single team of three people, known as a 'petite équipe', will work both ways, rather than two booths of two people each. The number of languages spoken at the meeting may also determine the make-up of the team. In the United Nations, for example, the standard 'English booth' team consists of two interpreters, one of whom interprets from Russian, one of whom interprets from Spanish, and both of whom can interpret from French. For certain language combinations, relay, or two-step, interpretation is also sometimes used: a speaker will be interpreted in one booth from language A into language B, and then in another booth from language B into language C.

Is it Useful to Specialize in a Particular Subject Area?

Yes. It is easier to translate or interpret with an understanding of the subject. Some translators, for example, specialize in medical translation and obtain regular work from pharmaceutical manufacturers. Some translation agencies specialize in technical, business or legal translation and rely on translators and interpreters with expertise in those areas. Specialist translators can usually command higher fees.

Many translators and interpreters make an effort to keep abreast of certain fields in which their language combination is useful. However, most translators and interpreters are of necessity generalists, since it is not possible to be an expert in every field in which there is a demand for translation. Accordingly, translators and interpreters must cultivate the ability quickly to assimilate the basic issues and vocabulary that go with a particular assignment.

Among conference interpreters, the usual practice is to obtain background materials from the conference organizer prior to the meeting and study the materials to gain a basic understanding of the subject and the specialized vocabulary. A translator or interpreter who works regularly for a particular organization or client will soon become familiar with the subject and its jargon.

Are Some Languages More Important Than Others for Translation and Interpretation?

It depends on the market. There is more work to be found in the 'major' world languages that are most widely spoken and written, but there is also more competition. On the other hand, a translator or interpreter who knows a 'rare' or 'exotic' language in a particular market is harder to find and can often command higher fees even though there may be fewer work opportunities.

Most institutional employers, like multinational corporations and governmental or intergovernmental agencies, use a specific set of languages in their operations and will often test the applicant's knowledge of those languages. The United Nations, for example, has six 'official languages' (English, French, Spanish, Chinese, Arabic and Russian) and requires most applicants to know at least two of these in addition to their native tongue. Some court systems in America regularly employ interpreters with a knowledge of certain Asian languages, like Vietnamese, or certain indigenous languages, like Navajo. Some corporations, like multinational banks, operate mainly in English but hold their board meetings and publish their annual reports in two or more languages and hire interpreters and translators for that purpose. Some national governments conduct official business and issue official publications in two or more languages, for example Canada (English and French), Switzerland (French, German, Italian and Romansh) and India (Hindi, English and 14 other languages).

Are There Any Formal Professional Requirements?

There is no single, uniform accreditation process to become a translator or interpreter. Each employer has different standards and requirements. Book publishers generally employ translators based on their academic credentials. Court systems will usually administer a formal interpretation exam and certify those who pass. Corporate employers and translation agencies will sometimes administer an entrance test or require a college degree or diploma from a translation school. Governmental and intergovernmental employers will usually administer a competitive examination and/or require a college degree in languages or a diploma from a recognized translation school. An MA in conference interpreting is now offered by several universities. The European Union administers a competitive general knowledge exam as well as language tests. The United Nations holds periodic worldwide competitive examinations for translators and places the highest-scoring candidates' names on a roster from which applicants are recruited as vacancies occur. At the UN, freelance interpreters must pass a test and staff interpreters are recruited through a formal exam before a panel.

Some professional associations, such as the American Translators' Association (ATA), the American Association of Language Specialists (TAALS), the Association Internationale des Interprètes de Conférence (AIIC) and the National Association of Judiciary Interpreters and Translators (NAJIT), also administer tests to their members in order to grant certifications or list them in their yearbooks according to language competences.

Some employers, because of the nature of their workload, will require staff linguists to do both translation and interpretation, for example the UN International Civil Aviation Organization (ICAO) or the UN Food and Agriculture Organization (FAO). Other employers may require applicants to do both simultaneous and consecutive interpretation (e.g. court systems) or may require more than one active language (e.g. the World Trade Organization).

Most international organizations, and the languages they use, are listed in a large directory entitled *Yearbook of International Organizations*, which can be consulted at major libraries.

Is it Advantageous to Be Bilingual?

Only if one is truly bilingual, that is thoroughly conversant with both languages, sensitive to the differences between them, and able to use both equally well as a medium of expression. Few people are truly bilingual. Early exposure to two or more languages is helpful because it trains the ear to recognize the sounds of both languages, to grasp difficult accents and to recognize nuances and idiomatic expressions. However, without additional study and training, it is usually not sufficient to enable a translator or interpreter to use both languages actively at a professional level.

Is Simultaneous Interpretation a Stressful Occupation?

Yes. The sustained alertness and concentration required to perform this job well have been compared with those required to be an air traffic controller. However, for that very reason, interpreters' associations have developed standards governing workload, team strength and equipment, based on medical studies, which are intended to keep the workload and cumulative stress within reasonable limits. At the UN, for example, simultaneous interpreters are usually required to cover a maximum of seven three-hour meetings per week, except during peak periods. The average workload at the European Union is somewhat heavier.

1 Speaking

Public speaking is an important part of training to become an interpreter for several reasons. First, many people studious enough to have acquired a thorough grasp of two or more working languages tend to be of a somewhat shy and retiring disposition and, when faced with an audience, may freeze up and develop mental blocks. Second, interpretation assignments – especially the better ones – often require interpreters to perform before large audiences of important people, which can be rather intimidating even for those of us who are not especially shy. But stage fright can be overcome by the same method that student actors use: rehearsal. Last but not least, an interpreter, like an actor, a talk-show host or a news announcer, must learn how to use his or her voice.

In order to understand the kind of language used by public speakers and at international conferences, interpreters should appreciate how it differs from everyday speech. We use language in our daily lives primarily to communicate information and express feelings. But the main function of language as used by public speakers such as diplomats, officials and corporate executives, who are usually acting as spokesmen for groups, is advocacy. A campaign speech by a candidate for office is designed to win the listeners' votes. A speaker praising a public figure is seeking to persuade listeners of that person's merits. An official making a public explanation or apology for an error or embarrassment is trying to persuade the public to forgive and forget. A diplomat making a lengthy policy statement is trying to persuade other diplomats to support her positions by striving to portray her country and its policies in a favorable light. Even a speaker using expository language to relate facts or report information is often doing so in order to support a particular viewpoint, thesis or proposal.

Public speakers have usually acquired some proficiency in the art of persuasion, and interpreters must be able to mirror that skill. So, interpreters should strive to be good public speakers. An important step in becoming an effective public speaker is to learn not only to use one's skill at expository and descriptive speech but also to draw on one's own powers of persuasion. Enhancing this skill will also help the interpreter to acquire greater confidence and thus overcome stage fright.

Exercises

(1) Write an imaginary letter to a public official urging that a law be passed to remedy what you consider to be a serious social problem. What arguments would you use? Read the letter aloud as a speech, record it, listen to it at a later time and consider what you could have said to make it more convincing.

(2) Think of someone you know who would disagree with you about an important question. What arguments could you use to change that person's mind? Suit your arguments to what you know about that person's psychology.

(3) (a) Choose a significant event from a newspaper and write a 200-word speech commenting on it. Read out the speech into your tape recorder, then listen to it. Was it convincing? Could the speech be improved by changing your delivery, intonation, organization or diction (choice of words)? If your speech were a broadcast editorial, would listeners pay attention?

      (b) Listen to the speech again. This time, cast yourself in the role of the opponent or 'devil's advocate', and write a brief rebuttal speech arguing against what you have just heard.

(4) Write a short speech in praise of a public figure whom you admire. Read it out into your tape recorder and listen to it. Would it be convincing to a listener who did not know that public figure?

(5) The following statements of opinion on various issues are calculated to be controversial and to spark debate. Choose one of the positions presented and defend that point of view to an imaginary audience of skeptical listeners, first in your mother tongue and then in your other working languages. Then repeat the exercise, taking the opposite point of view.

      (a) Se debería prohibir la transmisión por televisión de deportes violentos. El boxeo y la lucha libre, por ejemplo, embrutecen al ser humano. Y las corridas de toros exaltan la crueldad para satisfacer los instintos más frívolos del público. (Read the article 'Bullfighting Makes a Comeback' in Chapter 15, pp. 254–257.)

      (b) Las carreras de coches son un despilfarro de dinero y de hidrocarburos en una época en que la escasez de petróleo inclusive ha ocasionado guerras. Son un riesgo para la vida de los pilotos. Tienen poco que ver con el espíritu deportivo, y son más bien una muestra del grado de locura de nuestra civilización.

(c) No es justo gravar más la gasolina que el tabaco. La gasolina es un bien necesario para la sociedad actual, mientras que el tabaco es una droga que contribuye a causar el cáncer. Este debe estar gravado con más impuestos que aquélla. ((a), (b) and (c) are adapted from the practice test for the *Diploma de Español como Lengua Extranjera*, 1995.)

(d) Un certain 'populisme' est de rigueur actuellement des deux côtés de l'Atlantique. Mais, alors que les populistes Américains réduisent carrément les impôts des riches et les prestations sociales des pauvres, les Français se sentent obligés de tenir un discours contraire. Ils dénoncent 'l'exclusion', tout en ménageant les intérêts des classes aisées. Les hommes politiques devraient avoir le courage de déclarer sans ambages leurs véritables intentions, afin que les électeurs sachent à quoi s'en tenir. (Adapted from Singer, 1995)

(e) Le désarmement complet est un idéal qui ne sera pas atteint de notre vivant, car les forces qui engendrent les conflits armés ont plutôt tendance à augmenter qu'à décroître, et aucun pays ne peut donc se permettre le luxe de mettre sa sécurité en péril. En fait, ce sont les pays de moindre taille, non pas les grandes puissances, qui ont le plus besoin d'armements de haute technologie. La prolifération de telles armes est donc inévitable.

(f) L'emploi d'une seule langue dans les relations internationales n'est ni possible ni souhaitable, et le multilinguisme s'impose donc par la force des choses. Imposer aux diplomates la corvée supplémentaire de s'exprimer dans une langue étrangère serait un retour à la Tour de Babel et donnerait lieu à des malentendus et des frictions à n'en plus finir. L'interprétation s'avère donc moins coûteuse qu'elle ne paraît de prime abord, car elle contribue de beaucoup à nous épargner cette espèce d'anarchie linguistique où chacun chercherait à imposer sa propre langue comme langue 'universelle'.

(6) Use the topics in (5) above for a session of classroom debates, choosing a 'pro' and 'con' speaker for each topic by random drawing. Conduct at least one debate in each language. Ask students from the audience to summarize the 'pro' and 'con' statements of each debate in a different language.

(7) Choose any one of the propositions offered below and prepare a three-minute speech, to be given in class, arguing either for or against the proposition you have selected. You may use outlines or notes, but your speech should not be written out and read verbatim to the class. Use both logic and emotion to make your points. Maintain eye contact with

your audience. After your speech, another student will be called on at random to briefly recapitulate what you have said; another will be called on at random to briefly critique your delivery; then the rest of the class will be invited to ask you questions about any points in your speech that did not seem clear; finally, anyone in class who wishes to offer a brief rebuttal of your speech will be invited to do so.

(a)   The Global Biodiversity Assessment, based on the work of 1500 scientific experts from all over the world, indicates that almost three times as many species became extinct from 1810 to the present (112 species) as between 1600 and 1810 (38 species). But protecting endangered species can hamper economic growth, and a 1995 Harris opinion poll of 1007 adults indicated that only 42% believed that government had struck the right balance between protecting the environment and protecting jobs.

Once a species is gone, it is gone for good. So, preserving biological diversity is more important than promoting industrial progress and creating jobs, and endangered species should be protected by law against the spread of industry and pollution even if jobs are lost in the process.

(b)   Economic prosperity cannot be sustained unless everyone in the population has access to health care. If private insurance coverage does not provide such access, health care should be made a public service funded by public revenues.

(c)   Free trade fosters prosperity and understanding by promoting the flow of goods, people and ideas across borders. Therefore, exerting political pressure on countries by a trade embargo is counterproductive. Economic sanctions should be used only to punish serious violations of international law.

(d)   Computers are useful tools, but the widespread use of automated word processing programs in schools will eventually make people illiterate, as students will no longer feel any need to learn rules of spelling or grammar.

(e)   Exploring the far reaches of outer space is a waste of precious resources which could be put to better use alleviating poverty or promoting economic development here on Earth.

(f)   The city of Portland, Oregon is considering an 'anti-panhandling' municipal ordinance which would make it illegal for people to sit on sidewalks, but not to sit at a sidewalk café. This proposal unfairly discriminates against the poor.

(g)   In order to keep the French language alive, Quebec was right to declare it the official language of the province and to require its use in public spaces and on storefront signs, even if that restricts the rights of those who speak English or other languages.

(h) Companies should not be allowed indefinitely to keep off the market any useful invention they have patented, such as a break-through drug. If they do not promptly manufacture the invention and make it available for use by the public, the patent should be revoked and awarded to a different company.

(i) When armed conflicts cause severe suffering among civilians, the international community should intervene to help even without the consent of the belligerent forces or the governments involved in the conflict.

(j) The practice of 'warehousing' (keeping dwellings off the market until real-estate prices and rents go up) is anti-competitive. It should be prohibited when housing is in short supply and many are homeless. Landlords who engage in this practice should be fined or required to rent vacant properties at a fair market price.

(8) Translate the topics in (7) above into Spanish, French or your other working languages, and repeat the exercise.

(9) In the international fora where interpreters work, the fundamental tension is that between international cooperation and national sovereignty. It is important to understand this overarching (often implicit) debate, because it sheds light on speakers' intent and often renders intelligible positions and statements that may otherwise not be clear. The following are brief presentations of the arguments for and against 'neutrality' or 'isolationism'. Prepare a brief speech (two or three minutes) to be given in class, based on one of these two positions. Use any additional arguments or facts you wish. When all class members have spoken, decide by a show of hands which side was more convincingly argued.

The 'Unilateralist' Argument

A great nation should stand on its own record and assert its own identity in international affairs. More is to be gained by leadership, hard-earned prestige, statesmanship and independent judgment than by alliances. Multilateral diplomacy is a treacherous minefield into which wise leaders should not venture lightly. National security demands that we keep our options open and avoid 'entangling alliances'. Many nations, such as Switzerland, have prospered for centuries by maintaining scrupulous neutrality and staying aloof from the world's quarrels. Why should that prudent attitude be labeled 'isolationism' when it is practiced, for example, by the United States?

The 'Multilateralist' Argument

One of our time's great poets, the Syrian-born Adonis, has found a simple way of describing the United States and its present foreign policy: 'What strikes me about the States is the richness of American society on the one hand and, on the other, the smallness of its foreign policy.' The struggle in the UN Security Council, when America opposed the International Criminal Court, evoked George Orwell's novel 'Animal Farm', in which some of the farm's inhabitants claim that 'we are all equal but some are more equal than others'. The compromise reached in the Security Council was based on the fact that an overwhelming majority of the UN member states saw the ICC (International Criminal Court) as a new and vital centerpiece of international law, worth fighting for. How does a superpower wield its power in an interdependent world? Democratic power needs legitimacy. 'For us or against us' is not the best way to attract allies and friends. 'If you elect the wrong leader' – Salvador Allende in Chile or Yasser Arafat in Palestine – 'it will have consequences' is another disturbing line. That kind of gunboat diplomacy leads to banana-republic democracy. History teaches that cooperation and integration are more successful in achieving positive results than confrontation and unilateralism. Post-war Germany chose to become Gulliverized within European networks and structures. It has even given up the mighty Deutschmark for the sake of the euro and Europe. Post-Communist Russia renounced the ambition of trying to become a superpower. Instead it has chosen integration and cooperation, even with former archenemies within NATO. The United States possesses powers and riches never seen before in the world. But to tackle the global challenges of the 21st century and its new security threats, you need a global strategy and a global network. And only the United Nations can provide the necessary legitimacy and sustainability for worldwide common action. Fortress Europe, Fortress USA? That is not only an outdated model, it is also hopelessly counterproductive. The United States is neither a Goliath nor a benign Gulliver, but the essential partner that we want to see, and that we need, in our common quest for global peace, development and democracy. So the United States should think again and let the International Criminal Court prove its worth. It was designed to constrain, prevent, deter and punish the actions of would-be criminals, not of peacekeepers. (Schori, 2002: 6 (excerpt))

(10) (a) Read the following argument advocating greater 'isolationism' or 'unilateralism' by France vis-à-vis Algeria. Evaluate the strength of

the argument in light of the conclusions you have reached on this issue in the previous exercise. Does the author use any additional or new arguments that you find persuasive?

Algeria: At Arm's Length

'Algeria is France.' That was the byword forever repeated by French political leaders – including François Mitterrand, and excepting General de Gaulle – until 1957. Today, in 1995, 38 years later, Algeria is no longer France. And yet, despite independence, despite the massive, and now complete, departure of the French from Algeria, public opinion is still galvanized by Algeria's turmoil: hostage-taking incidents, murders of foreigners on Algerian soil, terrorist attacks in France, acrimonious exchanges and canceled meetings between leaders – all conveying the feeling that Algeria will never find its way out of the tunnel.

That deep concern is due to an attitude that has unreasonably outlived its usefulness among certain political and media circles, an attitude which amounts to conferring a unique quality on relations between France and Algeria, making them somehow different from those which normally exist between independent states: a 'special relationship', and a posture of 'non-interference'. It is the result of keeping permanently alive a climate of political post-colonialism.

There is no other way out of this bind than to look the facts squarely in the eye: Algeria is not France. Algeria and France are two independent countries, different in their history and culture, two countries which have no common borders and no imperialistic designs on each other.

When I went to Algiers in 1957, as the first French President to visit an independent Algeria, I was trying to consolidate that normalization, that release from post-colonial feelings of regret and remorse in the wake of the war of independence. The words were followed by events, and our relations did become normal, that is to say good when we were in agreement, as when we launched the North–South dialogue together, and bad when we disagreed, as when the problem of the former Spanish Sahara arose. That is how international affairs are ordinarily conducted, with each acting according to his obligations and interests, without trying to make other people's decisions for them. . . .

Algeria has been governed by the same group of people for 38 years. ... That group has shown itself incapable of responding to the fundamental needs of Algerians: the desire for a recognized national identity, a halt to runaway population growth, and the need for economic development to stem unemployment, which, by official figures, has reached 25 per cent! And yet, Algeria did have assets on which to capitalize: good infrastructure, efficient agriculture, and profits flowing in from the two oil shocks. Hence the profound frustration felt by the Algerian people at a government that has failed them. ...

Keeping Algeria's problems at arm's length will not dispel the risk of terrorist incidents, but it will give us a solid basis for fighting them. The unanimity across the political spectrum about fighting terrorism requires a political foundation: France will not intervene in other countries' choices; it is ready, with its European Union partners, to support genuinely democratic developments. And it will steadfastly protect the safety of its citizens at home against any acts conceived abroad. That is the only way to keep the maelstrom from sweeping up two large communities, one French and one foreign, here in France: the French Moslems who came from Algeria, and the Algerians residing in France. (Giscard d'Estaing, 1995 (excerpts); trans. James Nolan)

(b) Pretend that you are President Valéry Giscard d'Estaing and that you have been asked to record the above opinion piece for the radio. Read the article aloud and record your reading on your tape recorder. Give your delivery as much conviction as possible, giving the tone and inflections of your voice the proper force and emphasis. Relax and take your time. Think through each sentence before you speak. Do not declaim or use an 'artificial voice'; rather, make the most of the positive natural qualities of your own voice. Speak clearly and distinctly, but do not use more volume than necessary. Use the voice you use when you are speaking on the telephone and saying something important to the other party.

Play back your recording and listen to it carefully and critically. What could you do with the natural range of your voice that would make it more interesting, more clear or more pleasant to listen to? Are there any points where your pronunciation is indistinct? Was the pace of your delivery too fast to be clear, or too slow to be interesting?

(c)   Make a recording of a news program by your favorite news commentator or announcer on television. Compare it with the recording of your reading of the above article. What does the announcer do with his or her voice that you did not do with yours? Repeat the exercise until you feel the two performances are comparable.

There is a temptation, in speaking publicly, to declaim, to speak too loudly and to 'playact'. That temptation must be resisted, for using your natural voice is very important. By reducing strain, it will increase your endurance as an interpreter. It will sound more genuine and persuasive. Remember that a simultaneous interpreter works in a soundproof booth, where he or she has no way to reproduce the speaker's gestures or body language other than with the range and emphasis of his voice, and the only way to do this is by learning how to modulate the natural timber, pitch and volume of your own voice. Listen to yourself through one ear as you are interpreting. Also remember that by speaking fairly close to the microphone you can speak much more softly and be heard just as clearly (modern microphones are extremely sensitive). Consider the following description of Gandhi's soft-spoken yet powerful oratorical style by his contemporary, Nehru:

> this voice was somehow different from all the others. It was quiet and low, and yet it could be heard above the shouting of the multitude; it was soft and gentle, and yet there seemed to be steel hidden away somewhere in it; it was courteous and full of appeal, and yet there was something grim and frightening in it; every word was full of meaning and seemed to carry a deadly earnestness. Behind the language of peace and friendship there was power and the quivering shadow of action.

(11) Using the topics in (5) and (7) above drawn by lot, or other timely topics, assign each student in class to give a brief speech extemporaneously and without notes.

2   Preparation/Anticipating the Speaker

Consistently good performance in conference interpreting depends on sustained mental alertness. An interpreter must maintain attention and concentration through many hours of meetings and absorb the contents of lengthy discussions on many subjects. This means keeping fit, notably by getting enough sleep and following good habits of nutrition and exercise.

An interpreter must also adopt an attitude of intellectual modesty and willingness to learn, keeping up with changes in his or her languages as well as current events and the related jargon. Interpreters must be able to understand and clearly state a wide range of possible ideas and arguments representing different sides of any issue, even arguments which may seem implausible, or with which they may strongly disagree. Gaining familiarity with the subject matter to be discussed at an upcoming assignment is important, and attending a meeting in advance will be especially helpful to get a grasp of procedural rules and terms. Careful observation of speakers' gestures and demeanor, as well as the reactions of listeners, will provide additional clues to the intent behind the words. Knowing the specific themes of a conference in advance and obtaining a copy of the agenda, background documents, list of speakers and any prepared speeches available can also be very helpful. Many speakers prepare their speeches well in advance of delivery and will gladly give or send a copy to an interpreter who takes the trouble to ask for it. Copies of formal speeches and policy statements by public officials can often be readily obtained from their offices or looked up on their internet websites. Sometimes a translation of the speech to be delivered will also be made available by the speaker or his institution (known among interpreters as 'a Van Doren') and can be read out by the interpreter if the translation is of good quality.

Yet, despite these elementary precautions, every speech still has its surprises. A speaker may change his or her mind at the last minute, discard or amend prepared remarks and say something quite unexpected. (Be especially alert to this when the speech is marked 'Check Against Delivery'.) And even an experienced interpreter can be caught off guard by a novel idea, an unusual turn of phrase, a breakthrough in the debate, an eccentric speaker, a spur-of-the-moment argument, an impenetrable accent, a mispronounced key word, a halting delivery, poor sound quality, an obscure reference or acronym, or a deliberately ornate way of saying a perfectly simple thing.

Overcoming problems of that kind involves a certain amount of intuition. Although an interpreter should avoid wild guesses, it is often possible, relying on the context, to 'fill in the blanks' of a statement when an element of it is unclear or indistinctly heard. It can be helpful if one tries, by an effort of imagination, to anticipate what the speaker is likely to say, how he or she is likely to say it and how it can be made comprehensible to the audience for which one is interpreting.

Exercises

(1) The next time you plan to hear a public figure make a speech on television or radio, write out beforehand a rough outline of your 'best guess' about what the speaker is likely to say, based on what you know about the person, the circumstances of the speech, the current issues and the occasion. Then listen to the actual speech and compare it with your notes to see how close your guesses were.

(2) Formulate each of the speeches suggested below in your mind. Then deliver it aloud, to a listener or to a mirror. If you have trouble, try writing out your speech or speaking from notes. Time yourself. Finally, record your speech, listen to it and consider possible improvements in your arguments, diction, and speed and rhythm of delivery.

(a) You are the spokesperson of an environmental group. You have been allowed to address a legislative panel considering a law to ban all plastic beverage containers. You have 10 minutes.

(b) Make the same speech as in (a) above, but to an audience of high-school students at a symposium on environmental issues.

(c) You are the trade representative of a Central American country at an international conference to promote tourism. In as few words as possible, convince the Air Travel Committee (which is made up mostly of West Indian delegates) that the whole Caribbean region should take a common stand against rising air fares.

(d) The World Association of Modern Art Museums plans to give a large endowment to the university which best promotes the teaching of fine arts. You have been asked by the Rector to address the association's annual meeting and win the endowment for your school. You have five minutes.

(e) Your country, Catatonia, stands accused of massive human rights violations. The Provisional Head of State of Catatonia, General Cornelius Crunch, has named you Ambassador to the World Assembly. If you do not convince the assembly to lift economic sanctions against Catatonia this year, General Crunch will be disappointed with you. Persons with whom General Crunch is disappointed have been known to vanish without a trace. You have five minutes to convince an audience of seasoned diplomats from 190 countries that all of the prisoners in Catatonia's jails are common criminals, vagrants or dangerous subversives. Your voice should not betray nervousness.

(f) Your non-governmental organization, the World League for Animal Rights, has finally gotten its one and only chance to speak to the International Commission on Ocean Resources to argue for a ban on drift-net fishing in order to protect an endangered species of dolphin. A UN Food and Agriculture Organization study indicates that 70% of the world's fish stocks are fully exploited, overexploited, depleted or slowly recovering. Moreover, you have solid scientific evidence that dolphins have an IQ comparable to that of humans.

Unfortunately, half the members of the commission come from countries that are dependent on fishing, who argue that dolphin-safe netting practices are sufficient, and the other half come from land-locked countries where dolphins are unfamiliar creatures. The chairman of the commission is Ambassador Hook from Catatonia, whose navy is using dolphins experimentally to develop new sonar for its nuclear submarine fleet. Without antagonizing your audience, convince them that dolphins are sentient beings and an essential part of the world's biological and genetic heritage. You have five minutes.

(g) After a prolonged constitutional crisis, a separatist movement in southern Catatonia is threatening to declare independence and nationalize all mineral resources in the south. You, Ambassador Hook, have been asked by General Crunch to convince the Global Bank Committee on Resource Development Credits that the situation will soon return to normal and that any suspension of credits to Catatonia would only make things worse. Today's telex from Catatonia reads: 'Our diplomats are soldiers in the service of the Nation. Failure is no excuse! Crunch.' You have five minutes in which to convince the Committee.

(h)   You are the foreign trade minister of Begonia, a small tropical island country that earns all of its foreign exchange by exporting flowers to major cities in the industrialized countries. To reach florists while still fresh, flowers must be shipped by air. The international air-freight cartel is about to adopt a decision doubling air-freight rates. This will bankrupt your country. The only way to prevent it is to convince the assembly of the Global Air Transport Organization that air-freight rates affecting mono-crop-developing island states must be subject to international regulation. But the cartel argues that only deregulation of air-freight rates can save beleaguered airlines from bankruptcy. You have 10 minutes in which to refute the cartel's argument and save Begonia from a recession.

(i)   The year is 2070. The Global Standardization Organization has finally decided to promulgate a worldwide standard for electric plugs. If the worldwide standard specifies American-type flat prongs, all of the European manufacturers will have to re-tool. If the worldwide standard specifies European-type round prongs, all of the American manufacturers will have to re-tool. In either case, all manufacturers of electric plug adapters will go out of business.

   (i)   You are the spokesman for the American manufacturers. In five minutes, convince the GSO assembly that flat prongs are best.

   (ii)   You are the spokesman for the European manufacturers. In five minutes, convince the GSO assembly that round prongs are best.

   (iii)   You are the spokesman for the adapter manufacturers. In five minutes, convince the GSO assembly that there is no need to standardize electric plugs.

(3)   There are times when 'words fail'. But an interpreter does not have the luxury to pause, catch her breath and grope for another word. At such times, one way out is to convey the main thrust of the intended message not through words but through intonation. To sharpen your sense of how your own voice carries different feelings, read out the 'neutral' sentences from Table 2.1 into your tape recorder, coloring the statement with each of the feelings listed beside it; take a short break, then listen to your performance and consider how well the feeling was conveyed. Keep repeating the exercise until the feeling comes across convincingly.

(4)   Pretend that you are interpreting the following excerpt of a speech and that a number of words have been obscured by bad pronunciation,

Table 2.1 Exercise

'The cat is on the windowsill.'	angry / satisfied / frustrated / puzzled / skeptical
'The bus is at the corner.'	relieved / annoyed / pleased / despairing
'I have bought the newspaper.'	apologetic / amused / solemn / cheery / weary
'The bed has been made.'	overjoyed / admonitory / irate / defensive
'The phone is out of order.'	overawed / despondent / emphatic / uncertain

conference-room noise or poor sound quality. Read out the speech into your tape recorder and, relying on the context, fill in the gaps in a way that does not distort the meaning of the sentence as a whole. Try your best to complete every sentence. When you have finished your recording, check your performance against the full text of the speech, given in Chapter 11, pp. 181–202. Were your guesses close enough to the original?

Mr Ouellet: It is a great _____ to represent Canada here today as we celebrate the fiftieth anniversary of the United Nations during this general debate.

M. Ouellet: Alors que nous célébrons le cinquantième anniversaire des Nations Unies durant ce débat général, c'est un insigne _____ pour moi de représenter le Canada aujourd'hui dans cette enceinte.

Canada has always been among the strongest supporters of the United Nations, not only in word but also in _____. In 1945 we were, through Canadian _____ Minister Mackenzie King, an original signatory of the United Nations Charter. Ambassador John Humphreys helped _____ the 1948 United Nations Universal Declaration of Human Rights. Successive Canadian Ambassadors to the United Nations have distinguished themselves in the _____ of the Organization, as have countless Canadian negotiators in ___ ranging from disarmament to trade to development. In addition, Lester B. Pearson won a _____ Peace Prize for his contribution to the success of the United Nations in establishing the first peace-_____ operation, in 1956.

Notre pays a toujours été l'un des plus ardents défenseurs de l'ONU, en paroles comme en _____. En 1945, le Canada, en la personne du _____ Ministre canadien, Mackenzie King, a été l'un des premiers pays signataires de la Charte des Nations Unies. L'Ambassadeur John Humphreys a participé à la _____ de la Déclaration universelle

des droits de l'homme de l'ONU, en 1948. Les ambassadeurs succes-
sifs du Canada auprès de cette organisation se sont distingués dans
leur travail au _____ de l'Organisation, tout comme l'ont fait
d'innombrables négociateurs canadiens dans des _____ allant du
désarmement au commerce et au développement. M. Lester B.
Pearson, quant à lui, s'est vu décerner le prix _____ de la paix
pour avoir contribué au succès de la première opération de maintien
montée _____ par l'ONU en 1956.

All these Canadians had a unifying purpose: to promote progress
in _____ the United Nations Charter, which enshrines the commitment of the people of the United Nations to the _____ of
humanity.

Tous ces Canadiens avaient un objectif commun: promouvoir le
progrès en _____ la Charte des Nations Unies, laquelle
exprime la volonté des peuples des Nations Unies à s'employer à
favoriser _____ de l'humanité.

Of course, there have been criticisms of the Organization; many
are legitimate and require _____. It is clear, however, that the
international _____ remains committed to the goals of the
Charter and to the United Nations as the primary instrument for
global problem _____.

Bien sûr, l'Organisation a fait l'objet de critiques. Un grand nombre
d'entre elles sont fondées et méritent qu'on leur _____. Il est clair
cependant que la _____ internationale demeure résolue à atteindre
les buts de la Charte et voit dans l'ONU un excellent instrument
pour _____ les problèmes mondiaux.

The United Nations deserves our continued support. If we look at
the _____ of just the last few years, the United Nations has conducted _____ peacekeeping operations in Cambodia, Mozambique
and Haiti. Thanks to the United Nations, in this decade alone
5 million children will grow up normally, children who would
have _____ been paralyzed by polio. This year the United Nations
is _____, as it does every year, to ensure a better life for the almost
23 million refugees in the world.

Les Nations Unies méritent que nous continuions de leur accorder
notre soutien. Si l'on fait seulement le _____ des dernières années,

on constate que l'Organisation a mené des opérations de maintien de la paix _____ au Cambodge, au Mozambique et en Haïti. Dans cette seule décennie, cinq millions d'enfants grandiront normalement, alors que _____ ils auraient été paralysés par la polio. En 1995, l'ONU _____ pour offrir à près de 23 millions de réfugiés dans le monde une meilleure vie. (Statement by the Honourable André Ouellet, Minister of Foreign Affairs of Canada, UN General Assembly, Official Records, A/50/PV7)

(5) Repeat the above exercise with other speeches (e.g. those presented in Chapter 10, pp. 162–179), as follows. Make a photocopy of the speech. With a black marker, blot out key words in each paragraph of the photocopy. Lay the speech aside overnight. Then do a sight-translation of the photocopy of the speech, trying to 'fill in the blanks', and record your performance. Check yourself against the original.

(6) Repeat the exercise again with a new photocopy. This time, blot out the final words of key sentences in each paragraph. When you do the sight-translation, try to finish the sentences in a way that makes sense without altering the main thrust of the sentence. Check yourself against the original. In those cases where you were not able to reconstruct the original meaning intended, consider whether it would have been better to take an educated guess or to drop the entire sentence rather than risk getting it wrong. This depends on your judgment and on the context in which the sentence appears.

(7) Additional Cloze exercises may be found in the final section of the Bibliography.

3   Complex Syntax/Compression

When speakers use short, declarative sentences and speak at moderate speed, the interpreter's task is made easier. More complex sentences can also be interpreted without too much difficulty if spoken at moderate speed. However, when speakers use long, complex structures and deliver them at high speed, the interpreter's task is greatly complicated. A lag of a single sentence or phrase can lead to an omission and inability to catch up. This chapter presents several strategies interpreters use to help cope with the combined difficulty of complexity and speed. Additional reformulation strategies are presented in Annex I.

Exercises

(1) *Complex syntax.* In interpreting a speech, especially a fast speech, it is usually a good strategy to 'simplify the syntax as you go along', breaking up any long and convoluted sentences into shorter ones, identifying whole ideas or units of meaning, clarifying the relationship between the sentences (for yourself as well as for the audience), deleting superfluous and/or ambivalent conjunctions and organizing lists of items by means of parallel constructions. This is particularly true when interpreting into English, because clarity, concision and parallelism are positive stylistic values in English. There is nothing 'elegant' about a complicated run-on sentence in English, especially if the meaning gets muddled because the speaker or the interpreter has lost track of the syntax. It is better to get the meaning – or at least most of it – across, even if some 'elegant flourishes' are lost in the process.

For example, this sentence appeared in a speech given by a Latin-American speaker:

(*Spanish original*): La intensa y permanente actividad desarrollada por el Embajador X durante el ejercicio de su mandato, ha reflejado la importancia del grupo de los 77 como ente coordinador de las posiciones de los países en desarrollo, en la vasta complejidad de temas económicos, sociales, ambientales, **de la** cooperación y asistencia para el desarrollo, así como en el proceso de reforma de las Naciones Unidas en el campo económico y social, que por **su** índole global **son** centro de interés y prioridad de la comunidad mundial y, consecuentemente, objeto de examen permanente en los esfuerzos para mejorar las relaciones económicas de los estados orientándolos hacia el establecimiento de un nuevo oren económico internacional.

(*French version*): L'activité intense déployée par l'Ambassadeur X pendant la durée de son mandat, reflète l'importance du Groupe des 77 en tant qu'entité coordinatrice des positions des pays en voie de développement, dans le vaste ensemble de questions économiques, sociales, écologiques, de la coopération et de l'assistance au développement, ainsi que dans le processus de réforme des Nations Unies dans le domaine économique et social, qui par sa nature globale constitue le centre d'intérêt et de priorité de la communauté mondiale et, par conséquent, l'objet d'examen constant dans les efforts visant à améliorer les relations économiques des états en les dirigeant vers l'établissement d'un nouvel ordre économique international.

The main problem in interpreting this passage is that some of the key syntactic words (marked in bold) are ambiguous. For example, does the word 'son' refer back to 'las Naciones Unidas' or to 'cooperación y asistencia'? The answer is not clear even when one reads the passage at leisure, much less when one hears it at high speed. Consequently, if we try to interpret this into English as a single sentence, tracking the structure of the original, we are liable to get lost half way through the sentence and become tongue tied, end up with a hopelessly confused run-on sentence, or miss whatever comes next while we are struggling to sort out this sentence.

On the other hand, if we tackle this long sentence piece by piece, taking each complete unit of meaning as it comes, we are more likely to get at least some of it right. Notice that, although the sentence as a whole is very complex, each of the different ideas it contains is fairly simple and the connections are fairly obvious. In other words, those troublesome ambiguous links are not essential and need not necessarily be translated. If each idea is stated in a separate sentence one at a time, it is fairly clear how they all fit together. (It may also be clear to listeners familiar with the subject even if it is unclear to the interpreter.) Moreover, once you have gotten one idea out of the way, your mind is then free to focus the next idea.

Reduced to its bare essentials, the sentence above contains the following ideas:

(a)   Ambassador X has been very busy.
(b)   He has been very busy coordinating the work of the G-77.
(c)   The Group of 77 plays an important role.
(d)   The Group of 77 has positions on many issues.
(e)   Those issues are very important to the international community.
(f)   Those issues are being continuously discussed as part of an effort to establish a new international economic order.
(g)   Those issues include economic, social, environmental, aid, development and institutional reform issues.

If, due to the speaker's speed, you managed to interpret all of these ideas except (c), that would be a minor omission, because (c) so obviously flows from the rest that it is almost a superfluous statement of the obvious. The same applies to idea (d). On the other hand, if the entire sentence and *all* of the ideas got lost or garbled because you were struggling to make sense of the ambiguous syntactic links, that would be a more serious error.

Try to translate the above sentence as a single unit. Next, try to translate it using the 'piece by piece' strategy. Then compare the two translations and ask yourself: (a) Which approach yielded the better result? (b) Which took longer? (c) Which is more complete? (d) Which is more accurate? (e) Which is stylistically superior?

(2)   In order to improve your skill at using the 'piece by piece' strategy with complex structures, try to decide which syntactic cues in the original statement are *logically necessary* and which are not. For example, in 'I fell down the stairs and **therefore** have a broken leg' is the word **therefore** logically necessary? Isn't the causal link just as obvious if I say 'I fell down the stairs and have a broken leg'? When the logical links between the parts of a complex structure are self-evident from the meaning of the parts, you are only slowing yourself down and running the risk of muddling the message if you try to translate all of them.

In this regard, it is important to remember what assumptions you can safely make about the knowledge of your audience and what actually needs to be spelled out for them. If I am interpreting a speech to an audience of professional physicists and I hear 'the theory of relativity, **which was formulated by** Einstein', do I need to treat the words **which was formulated by** as a logically necessary syntactic cue? 'Einstein's theory of relativity' will do just as well, will save time and will actually sound less patronizing. On the other hand, I might want to spell it out if the audience consisted of schoolchildren.

Once you have mastered the 'piece by piece' strategy, you will sometimes find it easier to interpret complex structures all in one piece, because you will be more accustomed to deciphering the parts of the whole puzzle and how they are supposed to fit together, and better able to supply the necessary syntactic cues in the target language.

(3) The following sentences appeared in a statement by a Latin-American speaker. Identify the main idea and the secondary or qualifying ideas in each sentence; then try to translate them by forming one sentence containing the main idea and separate, short sentences containing the secondary, supporting or qualifying ideas:

Las restricciones unilaterales y arbitrarias impuestas recientemente a mi país por distintos Estados industrializados, sobre sus exportaciones de banano, flores y productos del mar, son clara muestra de que los esfuerzos nacionales que llevan adelante los países en desarrollo por diversificar sus exportaciones y fortalecer los sectores más competitivos de sus economías, son insuficientes si se mantiene el actual entorno económico internacional, en especial si no se llevan acciones en favor de un reordenamiento de los mercados internacionales.

Un reordenamiento de la acción de los organismos de Bretton Woods en la provisión de recursos adicionales y estables para los proyectos de desarrollo llevados adelante por los Estados y las agencias especializadas, sobre la base de directrices y políticas acordadas por la comunidad internacional en el ECOSOC, tras las consultas del caso, es una iniciativa que permitiría hacer frente a las exigencias de la magnitud que el momento requiere.

(4) (a) The following sentence appeared in a statement by an African delegate:

Si, en ce qui concerne le premier aspect des engagements pris dans le cadre de cet important accord, la responsabilité du gouvernement est quasi-exclusive, il n'en va pas de même en ce qui concerne le deuxième aspect.

First, translate the sentence following the original order of phrases. Then divide it into two sentences, the first beginning with 'En ce qui concerne . . .' and the second beginning with 'Il n'en va pas de meme . . .' Which version is clearer? Was it necessary to translate the word 'Si . . .'?

(b) The following sentence is from the same speech:

La situation au Libéria vient de connaître, après une série d'initiatives ayant abouti à la mise en place du nouveau conseil d'état, une évolution positive réelle.

First, translate the sentence following the original order of phrases. Then translate it again, starting with 'Après une série ...' (the longest phrase). Which version is clearer?

Notice that, even if the syntactic link 'après' is not translated at all, the causal relationship is still quite clear: 'A series of initiatives has led to the creation of a new council of state. The situation in Liberia has really changed for the better.'

(c)   The following sentence is from the same speech:

> Mon pays, qui avait favorablement accueilli la pression militaire exercée sur les Serbes par notre organisation et l'OTAN au mois de Septembre dernier, salue chaleureusement les dernières initiatives de paix, conduites par les Etats Unis d'Amérique, qui tendent vers le retour de la paix dans cette région.

First, translate the sentence following the original order of phrases. Then translate it again as follows: Delete 'qui' (the third word); start a new sentence with 'salue' by repeating the subject ('Le Niger' or 'Nous'). Are the two translations the same in meaning? Which is clearer?

(5) The following passage is from a statement by a Latin-American delegate:

> Reiteramos la necesidad de establecer al desarrollo alternativo como elemento prioritario de cualquier enfoque. Dicha estrategia, orientada a prevenir y solucionar los problemas generados por los cultivos ilícitos, propone, no solo la sustitución de cultivos sino que, en esencia, busca la plena incorporación de los grupos sociales involucrados en esta actividad a una economía lícita, a través de planes y programas que pongan en marcha un sistema de desarrollo socio-económico de naturaleza integral, que tenga especialmente en cuenta a los actores centrales del problema, en un marco ambientalmente sustentable y con el apoyo de mercados mundiales, transparentes y menos restrictivos.
>
> (*English version*): We reiterate the need to establish alternative development as a priority component of any approach. That strategy, geared to preventing and solving the problems created by illicit crops, comprises not only crop substitution but, essentially, pursues the full involvement of the social groups devoted to that activity into a legal economy, through plans and programs that set in motion a system of socio-economic development that is comprehensive in character, which especially takes into account the central

actors in the problem, in an environmentally sustainable framework and with the support of transparent and less restrictive world
markets.

(a)   In one sentence, state the central theme of the passage.
(b)   Isolate and list separately the distinct ideas in the passage, stating
each as concisely as possible.
(c)   Break up the passage into as many simple sentences as possible,
making a separate sentence out of any general adverbial clause that
can stand alone. (see Chapter 5.)
(d)   Recombine those simple sentences which logically fit together.
(e)   Using the above structural approach, translate the passage into each
of your languages.
(6)   Repeat the previous exercise with the following passages:

Han variado sustancialmente de naturaleza las condiciones que sos-
tienen el difícil tejido de la seguridad internacional. En este escenario
de grandes transformaciones es indispensable que la Organización
de las Naciones Unidas, si quiere mantenerse fiel a los postulados y
principios que le dieron vida, y, en consecuencia constituir un instru-
mento útil para la paz y el desarrollo armónico del planeta, y no una
institución meramente figurativa, emprenda una renovación pro-
funda de sus estructuras a fin de lograr la eficiencia que todos los
países del mundo, obviamente, reclaman.

(*English version*): There has been a substantive change in the nature
of the conditions that determine the complex fabric of international
security. In this scenario of great changes, if the United Nations
wishes to remain faithful to the purposes and principles that presided over its birth and thus constitute a useful instrument of peace
and harmonious development for the planet, rather than a merely
symbolic institution, the Organization will undertake a profound
renewal of its structures in order to achieve the efficiency that all
countries of the world are clearly calling for. (Statement by the
President of Peru; trans. James Nolan)

Igualmente, y siendo consciente de la necesidad de que nuestros
Gobiernos, y también nuestras opiniones públicas, dispongan de la
necesaria información sobre los trabajos que se dearrollan en las
Naciones Unidas, mi Delegación considera que tanto los servicios de
archivo y biblioteca como los bancos de datos de la Organización
deben poder ser consultados en todos los idiomas oficiales.
(Statement by representative of Spain)

(*English version*): Also aware of the need for our governments as well as public opinion in our countries to have the necessary information about the work of the United Nations, my delegation believes that archive and library services as well as data banks in our Organization should be available for use in all official languages.

Pido respetuosamente a todas las estimables delegaciones que consideren esta iniciativa que compartimos varios estados miembros y que transmitan a sus respectivas capitales ese deseo de transformar el año 1996 en un año decisivo y trascendental en la lucha contra la pobreza extrema, dando un paso hacia adelante en el cumplimiento de este primer Compromiso de la Cumbre Social y estableciendo, a la vez, según los propios mecanismos de decisión interna, las bases operativas para avanzar, en forma integral y como expresión de un esfuerzo compartido por todas las fuerzas y sectores que integran las respectivas realidades nacionales, hacia el cumplimiento efectivo de los 10 Compromisos de la Cumbre Social.

(*English version*): I respectfully request distinguished delegations to consider this initiative that several member states share and transmit to their capitals this wish to make 1996 a banner year in the fight against extreme poverty, taking a step forward in the fulfillment of this first Commitment of the Social Summit and, at the same time, in keeping with internal decision-making mechanisms, establishing the operational foundations needed to move ahead, in an integrated fashion and through the joint efforts of all forces and sectors making up the reality of our respective nations, toward the effective fulfillment of the 10 Commitments of the Social Summit.

(7) *Ambivalent conjunctions*. Ambivalent conjunctions placed at the beginning of a sentence can create problems in interpretation. If the interpreter ascribes the wrong meaning to the conjunction, the interpretation of the rest of the sentence will turn out wrong and there will usually be no way to correct it because there will not be time.

  For example, the word 'since' may mean (a) from the time when, or (b) due to the fact that. How is a Spanish interpreter to know whether to begin his sentence with 'Desde que ...' or 'Puesto que ...'? Rather than take a 50% chance of being wrong, it is better to delete the initial conjunction and insert the needed concept at a later point in the sentence:

* **Since** my government began making contributions to this program 20 years ago, we will not stop supporting it now. = Mi gobierno

comenzó a contribuir a este programa hace 20 años; **por con-siguiente**, no cesaremos de hacerlo hoy.

- **Since** my government began making contributions to this program 20 years ago, it has scored many successes. = Mi gobierno comenzó a contribuir a este programa hace 20 años; **desde entonces** el programa ha registrado muchos logros.

(a) Translate the following sentences without translating the initial 'since', and dividing them into more than one sentence if it seems desirable for ease or clarity:

  ○ **Since** the Middle East peace process was set in motion by the Madrid Peace Conference in 1991, the Republic of Korea has consistently held the view that peace cannot be whole without reconciliation between Israel and Syria, and between Israel and Lebanon.

  ○ **Since** the Thai Government has long supported the Middle East peace process, the termination of the state of war between Jordan and Israel, announced in Washington in July this year, following last year's historic agreement between Israel and the PLO, gives all of us reason to rejoice.

  ○ **Since** the success of this first meeting, the ASEAN Regional Forum has become a viable forum for the promotion of trust as well as political and security cooperation within the Asia-Pacific region.

(b) In the example given above ('Since my government began making contributions ...'), is the word 'since' a *logically necessary* syntactic cue? Would the meaning be sufficiently clear if the ambivalent conjunction were omitted altogether or replaced by a simple 'and'? Consider the following:

  ○ My government began making contributions to this program 20 years ago. We will not stop supporting it now.

  ○ My government began making contributions to this program 20 years ago, and we will not stop supporting it now.

  ○ My government began making contributions to this program 20 years ago. It has scored many successes.

  ○ My government began making contributions to this program 20 years ago, and it has scored many successes.

(c) Is the 'since' in the three sentences given in (a) above logically necessary in each case?

(d) The French word 'si', which can mean either 'if' or 'although', presents a similar problem, which can be tackled by the same strategy.

What other ambivalent conjunctions can you think of in each of your working languages?

(8)   *Enumerations.* A structure that can pose problems in both translation and interpretation is the 'shopping list'. The problem arises because the speaker may or may not use parallel construction in rattling off a long list of items, or because not all of the items may be translatable in the same parallel grammatical form, for example, with verbs, nouns or gerunds, in the target language. The interpreter struggling to maintain the grammatical parallelism of an enumeration delivered at high speed can easily be thrown off.

It is important to recall that parallelism is only a stylistic requirement and does not necessarily affect meaning. But the fact remains that, at least in English, failure to observe parallelism produces a very awkward-sounding result. An item in a list that is not grammatically parallel to the others 'sticks out like a sore thumb', for example:

Our agricultural plan includes several new projects:
- building dams
- increasing arable land area
- to build more grain storage silos
- producing more irrigation equipment.

There are several ways to handle shopping lists. Although the main concern is to make sure you translate all of the items, the translator or interpreter should, ideally, try to preserve parallelism in the target language even if it is missing from the original. This can often be done, especially when the speaker announces in advance that he is about to give a list of items, for example, 'In the next five years my company will shoot for the following seven goals' or 'During the Decade to Combat Desertification, my government will introduce the following five programs'.

The introductory sentence or 'chapeau' should make it clear that what follows is a list of items. Then the interpreter will have some freedom to maneuver and can, if possible, maintain parallelism or, if it is not possible, rephrase the list as necessary. If the parallelism breaks down half-way through the list, the interpreter can (if time permits) repeat the introductory construction or resort to using a new sentence or phrase for each item.

In the following example, notice that there is no dramatic difference in meaning between the various ways of handling a list, so that any of these ways which permits you to keep up with the speaker and cover all of the items mentioned would be acceptable:

Mi gobierno tiene planificadas varias iniciativas para lograr nuestras metas en la esfera de la educación: la formación de más efectivos docentes, la construcción de más escuelas, el suministro de becas adicionales, la ayuda a familias de zonas rurales que carecen de escuelas, la edición de libros escolares económicos, y el mejoramiento de la programación educativa en los canales de televisión.

- My government's plans for education include: training more teachers, building more schools, providing more scholarships, helping families in rural areas lacking schools, publishing affordable textbooks and improving educational television programs.
- To improve education, my government plans: to train more teachers, to build more schools, to provide more scholarships, to help families in rural areas lacking schools, to publish affordable textbooks and to improve educational programs.
- My government's plans for education include training of more teachers, building of more schools, provision of more scholarships, help to families in rural areas lacking schools, publication of affordable textbooks and improvement of educational television programs.
- To improve education my government will train more teachers, build more schools, provide more scholarships, help families in rural areas lacking schools, publish affordable textbooks and improve educational television programs.
- My government's education plans include more teacher training, more schools construction, more scholarships, helping rural families far from schools, publication of affordable textbooks and educational television improvement.
- More teacher training, more school construction, more scholarships, help to rural families far from schools, publication of affordable textbooks, better educational television: these are some of the ways in which my government is meeting its educational goals.
- My government's educational goals include more teacher training, school construction and scholarships, as well as help to rural families far from schools, publication of affordable textbooks and better educational TV programs.

(a)   From the options suggested above, choose the one which most fully respects parallelism. Choose the one which is clearest. Choose the one which is shortest. Which one would you use if the speaker's delivery was very slow? Which one would you use if his delivery was extremely fast?

(b) Consider the following paragraph, which contains a 'surprise' (unannounced) shopping list of seven items:

> En base a esos principios todos los países seremos sujetos activos de la comunidad mundial, capaces de hacer posible el desarrollo sustentable; capitalizar y crear empresas para responder a los desafíos de nuestra época; erradicar el consumo y el tráfico de sustancias nocivas; liberar la humanidad del armamentismo y el peligro atómico; consolidar la estabilidad política y la democracia participativa; respetar la pluralidad cultural y étnica; y crear condiciones reales para que los hombres y las mujeres, ancianos, jóvenes y niños, vivan mejor en un mundo verdaderamente solidario. (Statement by representative of Bolivia)

The English interpreter, who was asked to translate this speech in advance, rendered the shopping list as follows:

> Based upon those principles all countries will be active members of the world community, capable of making sustainable development possible, of capitalizing and creating enterprises to respond to the challenges of the day, of eradicating consumption and trafficking of harmful substances, of releasing mankind from the arms spiral and nuclear peril, of consolidating political stability and participatory democracy, of respecting cultural and ethnic diversity, and of creating real conditions for all men and women, the elderly, youth and children, to live in a better world of true solidarity.

> However, the list could also be handled by repeating the phrase 'we can' for each item, or by starting with 'we will be able to ...' and then repeating the word 'to ...' for each item.

(c) Translate the above passage in each of these two ways, and then compare the result, for clarity and brevity, with the translation above.

(d) Translate the following passage into English, French or another working language, preserving parallelism, first by means of gerunds and then by means of infinitives:

> La acción del estado supone esfuerzos simultáneos en varios frentes a fin de consolidar la nueva imagen social de la mujer, revirtiendo prejuicios subsistentes; incorporándola en la toma de decisiones y promoviendo su participación en los espacios de poder; propiciando la igualdad; brindándoles mayores oportunidades para una mejor calificación educativa destinada a una

adecuada y justa inserción en el mercado laboral; eliminando todas las formas de violencia y discriminación contra la mujer; e incorporando los temas que condicionan la situación de la mujer en las políticas publicas a fin de superar su postergación. (Statement by representative of Peru)

(e) Translate the following passage into Spanish, French or other working languages, preserving parallelism, first by means of gerunds and then by means of infinitives:

> The activities of the state imply making efforts on several fronts in order to consolidate the new social image of women, rolling back the remaining prejudices; involving women in decision-making and promoting their participation in positions of power; supporting equality; offering greater opportunities for improved educational training designed for an appropriate and just entry to the labor market; eliminating all forms of violence and discrimination against women; and encompassing topics affecting the status of women under public policies with a view to overcoming their disadvantaged position.

(f) Translate the following shopping list into English, French or other working languages, by starting with a general statement and then making each and every item into an independent sentence with its own verb:

> Los diferentes seguros sociales pueden diferir en algún punto, pero sus elementos principales son:
> - financiación mediante cotizaciones, por lo común tanto de los trabajadores como de los empleadores, y a menudo con participación del Estado;
> - afiliación obligatoria;
> - ingreso de cotizaciones en cajas especiales con cargo a las cuales se satisfacen las prestaciones;
> - inversión de los excedentes para obtener mayores ingresos;
> - garantía de las prestaciones sobre la base del historial contributivo personal, independientemente de los recursos económicos (por ejemplo, los ingresos y el patrimonio);
> - cotizaciones y prestaciones muy a menudo proporcionales a los ingresos del afiliado;
> - en general, la financiación de las prestaciones de accidentes del trabajo y enfermedades laborales suele estar únicamente a cargo de los empleadores. (ILO, 1995: 7)

(g) Translate the following passage into English, Spanish or other working languages, preserving parallelism to the extent possible:

> Notification du transit de missiles à portée intermédiaire ou à plus courte portée ou de lanceurs de tels missiles, ou du déplacement de missiles d'entraînement ou de lanceurs d'entraînement pour missiles à portée intermédiaire ou à plus courte portée, au plus tard 48 heures après son achèvement, notamment:
>
> (i) Le nombre de missiles ou de lanceurs;
> (ii) Le point, la date et l'heure de départ et d'arrivée;
> (iii) Le mode de transport utilisé;
> (iv) L'emplacement et l'heure à cet emplacement au moins une fois tous les quatre jours durant la période de transit. (Treaty on intermediate-range missiles between the US and the USSR of 8 December, 1987–1988: 209 (excerpt))

(h) Translate the following passage into French, Spanish or other working languages, preserving parallelism to the extent possible:

> The ozone layer, a fragile shield which protects the Earth from the harmful portion of the rays of the sun (namely, excess solar UV-B radiations) is being damaged by man-made chemicals released on Earth. The main danger from the weakening of this shield is that it could lead to a rising intensity of the ground level UV-B radiation. This in turn could lead to increased rates of skin cancer and eye cataracts, to stunted agricultural production and to the possible disappearance of phytoplankton – organisms which form the base of the marine food chain. The main chemicals involved are CFCs (used in refrigeration, aerosols and as cleaners in many industries), halons (used in fire extinguishers), methyl bromide (used mainly for soil fumigation in agriculture) and some industrial solvents. Because CFCs and other chemicals remain in the atmosphere for decades, the ozone layer will be at its most vulnerable over the next decade. The most important and effective measure included in the Montreal Protocol is the commitment to limit the use of, and to gradually phase out, all of these man-made chemicals (known as ozone depleting substances, or ODSs) ... Activities expected to take place in countries all over the world as part of the celebration of the

second International Day for the Preservation of the Ozone
Layer include:

- ○ Honouring industries which are phasing out ODSs, and sharing their experience with others;
- ○ Honouring individual scientists, technologists, media persons and administrators who are assisting in the phase-out of ODSs;
- ○ Broadcasting television and radio programmes related to the protection of the ozone layers;
- ○ Publication of articles on the International Ozone Day in the printed media;
- ○ Organization of scientific and technological conferences, meetings and workshops to discuss the ozone layer . . .;
- ○ Organization of competitions for schools on the awareness of the ozone problem; and
- ○ Involving non-governmental organizations (NGOs) in these activities. (UNEP News Release, 1996 (excerpt))

(9) *De-verbalization.* The first step in good interpreting is to 'get beyond the words'. The words are nothing more than a container for the ideas. The interpreter must pour those ideas into a new container: the target language. A useful term coined by Spanish interpreters to refer to this mental process is *desverbalización*, which might be translated as 'de-verbalizing' or 'de-wording' the speech.

Another way of describing this mental process is to say that interpreting a speech involves two translations: first, the words of the original are translated into a mental image; then the mental image is translated into the words of the target language. So, the accuracy of the translation depends on how accurate a mental image one can form from the original meaning. As Boileau observed:

> Ce que l'on conçoit bien s'énonce clairement, Et les mots pour le dire arrivent aisément.

The second step in this three-step process is, in a sense, non-verbal. One way to practice de-verbalizing is to practice going from a verbal mode of communication to a non-verbal mode, or vice versa.

(a) Close your eyes and form a mental image of what you did this morning. Write out a few brief sentences describing what you did. Then translate each sentence into a rough sketch on a separate sheet of paper. Then translate each picture back into the sentence that inspired it, but in a different language.

(b)   From a photo album choose some photos that portray group gatherings or interaction. Try to remember what the people actually did
and said to each other on that occasion. Write out a brief narrative,
with dialogue, for each photo, on a separate sheet of paper. Then
repeat the exercise, but in a different language.

(c)   Watch a television program in which you know the characters.
Wait for a dialogue. Turn off the sound during the dialogue and try
to preserve the image of the situation in your mind's eye. Finish
the dialogue in your mind as you think the characters would have
finished it.

(d)   The next time you overhear a group of people talking in a public
place, try to remember the scene and the dialogue you heard. Later
on, write out a narrative of the scene and the dialogue in a different
language.

(e)   Choose an interesting news story from a newspaper. Read it carefully and form a mental picture of the people and events reported.

Without referring to the original story, recreate a report of your
own from your mental picture, in another language, trying to preserve as many details as possible. Later, check your story's completeness and accuracy against the original.

(10) *Compression.* Human speech can attain speeds of 200 or 300 words per
minute and remains comprehensible even at 500 words per minute.
Generally, only excited sportscasters or auctioneers reach such a rate of
delivery, but many normal speakers do tend to speak very fast in certain
situations, for example when they have several important points to make
and are up against a strict time limit. At these inordinate speeds, it is
important for an interpreter to do everything possible to reduce the
number of words and syllables the vocal apparatus must produce.
Otherwise, one will fall prey not only to errors of language and meaning
but also to errors of articulation or enunciation, for example confusing
two similarly pronounced words, such as 'statesmen' and 'statements'.

When the high speed of delivery makes it necessary for an interpreter to resort to short cuts or to 'edit' the speech in order to get across
the essential elements of the message, certain non-essential items can be
deleted, abridged or treated by short references to what has already been
said at full length. The most obvious candidates for 'compression' are
the redundant and the obvious. If a speaker repeats the same point several times in the same passage of his speech, the redundant repetitions
can be deleted or abridged once the point has been made clear. (However,
a **final** repetition at the conclusion of the speech should not be deleted,
since it is meant to 'round out' or 'wrap up' the speech.) Redundant

adjectives can also sometimes be compressed with no loss of meaning, for example 'justo y equitativo' = just. Similarly, an item in a statement which is a matter of common knowledge or which the interpreter knows is already familiar to the audience may sometimes be sacrificed when the speaker's speed is such that 'something has to go' and there are other ideas in the statement which are more important or relevant.

Second, resorting to abbreviations or acronyms can reduce the number of syllables one has to pronounce at high speed. For example, 'The Organization for Economic Co-operation and Development' can be reduced to 'OECD' (four syllables instead of 20), once the organization has been identified in the speech. In a speech to physicians about the work of General Practitioners, it would be acceptable, once that theme has been made clear, to reduce subsequent references to 'doctors' (two syllables instead of seven). Or, in a presentation to an audience of specialists in Obstetrics and Gynecology, once that nine-syllable theme has been mentioned, shortening subsequent references to 'Ob-Gyn' (two syllables) would be acceptable. One should make an effort to be familiar with common abbreviations that are widely recognized and save syllables, for example SUV (three syllables) for Sports Utility Vehicle (eight syllables).

Where French is concerned, it should be remembered that French tends to use more nouns than English (e.g. 'voyageurs à **destination** de Paris' = 'travelers to Paris') and that such recurring 'noms d'étoffement' which add nothing to the meaning in English should usually be deleted if they prevent you from keeping up with the speaker.

Elegant variations. 'Elegant variations' and over-abundant illustrations can also be dealt with briefly. When an idea has once been made clear, subsequent (and often wordier) renamings of that idea that are done purely for the sake of variety need not be translated literally, as the style may be sacrificed for the meaning if one or the other must go. For example, once a speaker's reference to 'los próceres fundadores de la República' has been translated, any subsequent repetitions of 'the founding fathers of the republic' could be dealt with as 'the founders' (three syllables instead of 14). Similarly, when a speaker, out of mere wordiness, gives a lengthy list of items that are purely illustrative of his main point, some of those items can be safely deleted without distorting his meaning. For example, the phrase 'farm livestock, such as cows, sheep, goats, pigs, chickens and so forth . . .' could be safely boiled down to fewer items.

Anaphoric markers. Anaphoric markers (expressions that point back to what has been said) are another concise way of avoiding repetition. The two most common anaphoric markers to keep in mind in English are (a) **that** and (b) **the foregoing**, for example: (a) 'Depletion of the ozone layer is permitting unusually high levels of ultraviolet light to overheat the atmosphere, melting the icecaps and raising the sea-level. **That** is why small-island states are calling this conference. **That** is why urgent measures are needed. **That** is what I would like to talk about today.' (The anaphoric marker **that** sums up the content of the entire previous sentence and could do so in several subsequent sentences.) (b) 'Failure of the import-substitution strategy to spark industrial growth is leading developing countries to lower barriers to foreign direct investment especially in infrastructure. But that alternative strategy could, over the longer term, lead to a problematic loss of control over national resources. **The foregoing** is at the core of the current debate in Mexico. **The foregoing** is also our main concern at this conference.' (The anaphoric marker **the foregoing** can sum up the contents of several previous sentences, and can be used to do so in several subsequent sentences.) Can you think of other words and expressions, in English or in your other languages, which can serve to sum up or recapitulate what has been said? Are the French words 'Ainsi, ...', 'Donc, ...' and 'Or, ...' anaphoric markers? Are the Spanish expressions 'Ahora bien, ...', 'Así pues, ...' and 'Por ello, ...' anaphoric markers? These and others are often translatable into English by the word **Accordingly, ...**. How many others can you think of, in each of your working languages?

Personification. Finally, when interpreting into English, personification of documents or gatherings is another helpful device to save precious syllables and seconds. For example, once the speaker has made it clear that he or she is quoting from or referring to the International Covenant on Civil and Political Rights, wordy phrases such as 'Il est prévu dans le Pacte sur les Droits Civils et Politiques que ...' can be shortened to 'The Covenant provides that ...'; 'Le rapport fait figurer dans son annexe ...' can be shortened to 'The report annexes ...'. Obviously, it is not the document itself that 'provides' or 'annexes', but this is a natural and often-used form of personification in everyday spoken English (e.g. 'today's paper said that ...', 'the record shows that ...' etc.) which rarely causes any confusion. (Personification can also be used with inanimate objects and with meetings or organizations, e.g. 'The hospital triage desk stopped each arriving stretcher to check the patient's identity'; 'The chamber of commerce cleaned the streets during the city's budget crisis.') Note that another form of personification, 'changing the subject', is also a useful device for interpreting into English the abstract passive constructions that are so often used in French and Spanish. For example, 'Queda prohibido en las leyes de mi pais, Mexico, enajenar propiedades conteniendo yacimientos de hidrocarburos sin efectuar previamente las solicitudes del caso ante la autoridad competente' can be more easily and quickly interpreted if the passive construction is turned into an active construction, and one way of doing this is to change the subject (without changing the meaning): 'We in Mexico prohibit assignment of lands containing hydrocarbon deposits without first obtaining the required authorizations.'

(a) In each of the following sentences you will find a phrase in brackets containing two highlighted words. Without changing the meaning of the sentences, translate them into English by eliminating one of those two words.

> *Example*: A la fin de l'élection, (le **décompte** des **voix**) se fera en séance publique. = At the end of the election, the tally will take place at a public meeting.

- ○ (El último **año transcurrido**) ha sido crucial para el futuro del Oriente Medio.
- ○ (La **celebración** de las **elecciones**) palestinas deberá conducir al establecimiento de un gobierno democrático.
- ○ La Unión Europea quisiera rendir tributo a (los **esfuerzos emprendidos**) por las partes.
- ○ El Presidente del Consejo de la Unión (**realizó** una **gira**) por la región.
- ○ Acogimos con satisfacción (la **reanudación de** negociaciones) entre Israel y Siria.
- ○ Para que el proceso de paz (**se salde** con **éxito**), es imprescindible que la negociación política esté acompañada de progreso económico.
- ○ Le programme doit être réalisé (dans un **délai** d'une **année**).
- ○ Tout (**projet envisagé**) sera discuté en détail.
- ○ Le monde reconnaît les (**sacrifices consentis**) par ces soldats courageux.
- ○ Le groupe de travail se fera un devoir (d'**effectuer** immédiatement le **démarrage**) de ce programme d'études.
- ○ Tôt ou tard, ce processus (**aboutira** à une **conclusion heureuse**).
- ○ Nous vous prions, Monsieur le Président, de faire connaître à l'assemblée la (**conclusion** à laquelle nous sommes **arrivés**).

(b) Translate the following sentences into English. Where a document is mentioned, attribute the statement to the document itself, for example 'The Declaration says ...'.

- Il est prévu dans la constitution de mon pays que l'égalité entre les sexes doit être respectée dans la fonction publique.
- Dans la déclaration que nous avons adoptée l'an dernier, nous avons annoncé le début de la décennie de l'enfance.
- Les peines prévues au code pénal pour ce genre de délit ne sont pas très sévères.
- Queda constancia en las actas de la conferencia que no hubo acuerdo alguno sobre esta cuestión.
- Se ha previsto en la ley laboral que todo trabajador industrial tendrá por lo menos un día de descanso semanal.
- En los libros de historia se ha dicho mil veces que los actos de agresión siempre se castigan.

Parenthetical phrases. Like general adverbial clauses (see Chapter 5), parenthetical phrases or clauses can usually be moved to another position in the sentence and can often stand on their own. It is therefore important for an interpreter to be alert to them, since the ability to move part of a sentence to a later position in the sentence helps the interpreter to cope with complexity and speed. In the following example, notice that there are two ways to simplify the syntax of the sentence: first, by deleting a superfluous noun; second, by rephrasing and/or moving the parenthetical phrase in bold type.

We welcome this conference, **the convening of which has long been called for by developing countries**, as a sign of hope for the future.

- *Drop superfluous noun*: We welcome this conference, which has long been called for by developing countries, as a sign of hope for the future.
- *Reword parenthetical phrase*: We welcome this conference (the developing countries have long called for it) as a sign of hope for the future. / We welcome this conference as a sign of hope for the future. The developing countries have long called for it.

(c) Reformulate the following sentences using this approach:

- We cannot tell our farmers, whose hard work on their crops has been destroyed by the drought, that the irrigation project must now be canceled.
- The operation, whose modest beginnings did not foreshadow such success, has achieved all of its goals in record time.

- o   Les quelques soldats restants, qui croyaient les conflits de la crise surmontés, furent surpris de voir les forces opposantes ouvrir le feu encore une fois.

- o   L'économie nationale, dont les vicissitudes avaient longuement inquiété la Banque Mondiale, a commencé à donner quelques signes de vie.

- o   La especie marina estudiada, que parecía estar en mayor peligro de desaparecer, ha recuperado paulatinamente y repoblado las aguas costeras.

- o   Al llegar a la montaña, desde cuya cumbre se pueden ver todos los campos de nuestros agricultores, el equipo debe evaluar las perspectivas de expansión de este cultivo.

(d)   Using the same approach, translate the sentences into another working language.

4 Word Order/Clusters

It is important to avoid automatically following the word order and structure of the source language when translating and interpreting. The words of the source language must be recognized and the sentences must be understood. But the words are only the trees, and it is more important to see the forest. The 'meaningful structures' with which translators and interpreters deal are neither words nor sentences. They are *units of meaning*, which may comprise a number of words, or part of a sentence, or more than one sentence at a time (see Strang, 1968: 73).

Notice, for example, that the units of meaning in the following text, marked off with brackets, do not correspond to single words or to whole sentences:

> [Once upon a time] [there was] [a lovely little girl] [by the name of] [Little Red Riding Hood]. [One fine day] [she decided] [to go and visit] [her poor, dear old grandmother], [who lay sick in bed]. [Taking a basket] [filled with flowers and fruit] [under her arm], [Little Red Riding Hood] [set out happily] [through the forest]. [Little did she know] [that] [deep in those dark woods] [lurked] [the Big Bad Wolf]!

It is important quickly to identify units of meaning by scanning a speech as you hear it for phrases or clusters of words that can be translated into corresponding clusters of words in the target language.

The way words are organized into clusters in the source language will not necessarily correspond to the way they should be organized in the target language. But the *meaning* will correspond.

Two kinds of clusters are especially important:

- noun + adjective clusters
- verb + object clusters

Noun + adjective clusters must be dealt with as units because adjectives in different languages fall into different sequences in a noun phrase. For example, in English, the adjective of size must come before the adjective of color ('big black dog', not 'black big dog'), whereas in French the adjective of size comes before the noun and the adjective of color comes afterwards ('grand chien noir', not 'grand noir chien'). Moreover, in English, adjectives of age generally precede adjectives of color ('old blue car', not 'blue old car'), adjectives of size precede adjectives of age ('big old house', not 'old big house'), and all of the foregoing precede an adjective of nationality ('old blue French car', not 'French old blue car'). As a result of the complex rules governing adjective sequence in different languages, a phrase like 'la grande conférence Brésilienne sur l'environnement mondial de 1992' becomes 'the big 1992 Brazilian global environment conference'. Phrases containing several adjectives will become unmanageable for a simultaneous interpreter unless they are mentally processed as a unit.

Verb + object clusters should be dealt with as units because, as a practical matter of usage, some verbs will not work with some objects and vice versa. For example, in French the verb that usually goes with 'plainte' is 'enregistrer' or 'porter' and the verb that usually goes with 'progrès' is 'enregistrer'; but in English you do not 'register' or 'carry' a complaint – you 'make' or 'file' or 'lodge' a complaint; and you do not 'register' progress – you 'make' progress. In other words, these verb + object combinations have become crystallized by usage into clusters: 'porter plainte' = 'file a complaint'; 'enregistrer des progrès' = 'to make progress'.

Treating clusters as single units of meaning will also help you to identify those cases where you can compress wordiness by translating several words with one, which is especially useful in interpreting a fast speech, for example: **'aboutir à une conclusion heureuse'** = **'to succeed'**; 'para **facilitar la comprensión** de nuestra propuesta . . .' = 'to **clarify** our proposal . . .'. A good way to identify these cases is to 'listen for definitions' and then use the word corresponding to the definition you have just heard. For example, if you hear a speaker say 'Nous traversons **une période de grande prospérité** . . .' you can say 'We are experiencing a **boom** . . .'. To develop this skill, it is helpful to browse dictionaries and do crossword puzzles.

Exercises

(1) Form the habit of looking for word clusters whenever you read, and learn to 'scan' the text for them when you interpret. You will find that, very often, if you can think of the right verb in the target language, it

will remind you of the word you are searching for to translate the object. And, if you can think of the right word for the object, it will remind you of the word you need to translate the verb. Similarly, calling the right adjective to mind will often remind you of the noun you need, and vice versa.

(2)   Study the examples of word clusters given in Chapter 7 (pp. 64–110).

In a newspaper or magazine article of your own choosing, find and underline examples of verb + object clusters and of noun + adjective clusters.

In a newspaper or magazine article of your own choosing, find and underline examples of other kinds of word clusters that constitute units of meaning, such as idiomatic expressions, proverbs, clichés, figures of speech, stock phrases, phrasal verbs, prepositional verbs, etc. Repeat this exercise in each of your languages.

(3)   (a) Connect the verb with the appropriate object:

exert	tribute
set	efforts
frame	goals
pay	proposals
remit	an apology
proffer	a will
draft	an injury
sustain	funds
entertain	a statement
overrule	entry
retract	a motion
gain	an objection
endorse	a truce
declare	an agreement
lift	a proposal
conclude	sanctions
administer	an embargo
rectify	a supposition
impose	an oath
corroborate	an error

(b)   Connect the noun with the most suitable adjective:

wild	attack
savage	competition
unbridled	wilderness
untamed	animal
steadfast	faction
radical	position
extreme	stand
uncompromising	resolve
falling	memory
declining	rocks
fading	hold
tenuous	economy
grim	predicament
inevitable	plight
desperate	prospect
hopeless	fate
troublesome	habit
relentless	feature
worrisome	harassment
irksome	contingency

(4)   Rewrite the following sentences in English, treating the phrase in bold type as a single unit of meaning and finding a more concise expression for that unit of meaning. Then translate the sentences in the same manner.

> *Example*: Ghana has shown **the will and readiness to come to the help of** nations in distress. = Ghana has shown **solidarity** toward nations in distress. = Le Ghana a fait preuve de **solidarité** envers des pays en détresse. = Ghana a mostrado **solidaridad** hacia países asediados de problemas.

- Thanks to the end of the cold war, the political landscape in Europe has changed and **has impacted positively, if only with partial success**, on Cambodia, Mozambique and the Middle East.

- One must recognize that no progress would have been possible without **the exemplary statesmanship of the leaders involved** in finding solutions.
- Somalia and Liberia **are coming close to being written off**, as Afghanistan has been.
- Small states like Ghana **are being called upon to bear the burden** of securing a peaceful world.
- Ghana is directly face to face with **the ambitions, rivalries, prejudices, misconceptions and lack of common purpose** even within ECOWAS and with the misrepresentations that have **made the solution of the problem elusive**.
- Nations are unwilling to get involved in conflicts **far from their shores and in respect of which their national interests are not manifest to their electorates**.
- Security in this final decade of the 20th century … must involve people – how they live and how they **exercise their choices**.
- There is another **bright spot giving all of us hope for a more peaceful world**.

(5) Translate the following sentences, treating the verb + object cluster as a unit and finding an equivalent idiomatic unit of meaning in the target language.

> *Example*: Este cuadro idílico había **sufrido una alteración**. = That idyllic picture had **undergone a change**. = Ce tableau idyllique avait **subi une modification**.

> Los **peligros por que habían pasado** impelieron a los romanos a construir templos. / La educación de la mente quedaba **confiada a la familia**. / Esta extraña costumbre **generó una serie de confusiones**. / Se les enseñaba que en el hogar **la llama no debe extinguirse** nunca. / No se deben **proferir improperios** en este foro solemne. / Las tribus gálicas **opusieron resistencia** a Roma. / Cuando **soplan** esas **ventoleras**, no hay manera de pararlas.

> L'étudiant en traduction juridique doit **faire preuve d'un effort** soutenu. / Au début de l'année nous **mettons en recouvrement** les sommes dues à l'organisation. / Les anciens habitants du village **revendiquent la propriété** des logements. / Elle s'est **constituée partie civile** lors du procès. / Le tribunal a décidé de **renvoyer l'affaire** devant la cour de cassation.

> The recession **raises many obstacles** to enacting remedial legislation. / The force's mandate is to **bar arms** from this zone. /

Resentment among local residents has been **festering** for years. / A **chorus** of protests has been **swelling** from the refugees. / We must **interpose an objection** at an early stage in the proceedings. / It is too early to **draw conclusions**. / The central bank is trying to **quell a surge** of speculation against the currency.

(6) Translate the following sentences, treating the adjective + noun cluster as a unit and finding an equivalent idiomatic unit of meaning in the target language.

Example: The troops advanced at **breakneck speed**. = Las fuerzas avanzaron **a rapidez vertiginosa**. = Les forces ont avancé **à pas de géant**.

Los **cruentos combates** duraron años. / Circulaban **insistentes rumores**. / La empresa lo consideraba **un matón a sueldo**. / Nuestros países mantienen **estrechas relaciones** de amistad. / La operación fue un **ejemplo típico** de ineficiencia. / Hacemos **tesoneros esfuerzos** para lograr un acuerdo. / Apoyamos las **políticas para la igualdad de oportunidades** concebidas para las **minorías en desventaja**. / Les denunció con **encendidas palabras**. / Aníbal eludió una **batalla campal** con los Romanos. / Se gastaron **sumas ingentes**.

La police a décelé les **comptes clandestins** des malfaiteurs. / Le portrait présente un **sourire indéchiffrable**. / Il regrette son **rendez-vous manqué** avec son homologue. / Ils sont allés voir le **somptueux feuillage** d'automne. / L'enfant avait un **rire contagieux**. / Le conflit s'est transformé en **foire d'empoigne**.

The typhoon has been a **harrowing experience**. / The new equipment has higher **performance requirements** than the old. / We must be ready for any **untoward consequences** that may ensue. / They are organizing a **disaster assistance response team** for the mission. / The whole presentation was nothing more than **a dog and pony show**. / The firm's **capital adequacy** has been assessed. / Reporters forced to divulge their sources are demanding a **shield law**. / The specialized agencies are focusing efforts on **capacity building**. / The organization does not enjoy **absolute immunity**. / The **anti-graft magistrates** investigating the case need police protection.

(7) One of the most difficult features of English to interpret into other languages is a noun phrase with several adjectives. Translate the following noun + adjective clusters into your other languages:

multinational peacekeeping contingent / forward-looking economic recovery plan / open-ended inter-sessional inter-agency task force /

ad hoc multinational human rights monitoring team / mobile battery-powered life-support equipment / self-contained underwater breathing apparatus / trouble-free orbiting nuclear power source / multi-sectoral intra-country technical consulting services / high-altitude fixed-wing unmanned observation aircraft / incurable sexually-transmitted viral infection / people-centered grass-roots capacity-building initiatives / insecticide-resistant mutating crop-destroying insect pest / non-military remote-sensing geostationary satellite / high-profile post-conflict election monitoring program / integrated poverty-eradication program guidelines / high-visibility interdisciplinary research program / long-term structural adjustment program / exchange rate-sensitive regional mutual funds / military bacteriological warfare experiments / slow-growth low-inflation full-employment economy / part-time minimum-wage assembly-line jobs / conventional water-cooled enriched-uranium nuclear plant / long-range nuclear-powered missile-carrying submarine / multilingual wireless simultaneous interpretation / built-in automatic remote-control activation circuit / transparent multilateral decision-making machinery / state-subsidized family-owned acre banana plantation / reconditioned 50-cc 6-cylinder automobile engine / multi-story steel-frame earthquake-resistant building / out-of-control self-destructive consumer civilization / privatized deregulated non-profit mass transit system / self-activated retro-fitted jet aircraft canopy / self-motivating savvy dynamic executive officer / uneconomical remotely located low-grade iron ore deposits / highly imaginative high-flying advertising ideas-man / low-sodium high-fiber weight-loss diet / strict repeat-offender felony sentencing guidelines / safety-conscious built-in redundancy systems/ mass-produced modular housing unit design specifications / widespread chronic glandular dysfunction / intractable ongoing partisan policy dispute / unilaterally enacted non-tariff trade barriers / consensus-based multilateral environmental standards / bicameral popularly elected representative assembly / internationally recognized civil and political rights / voluntary effluent and emission industry standards / recurrent large-scale human rights violations / grass-roots private sector activity / double bottom-line considerations / universally accessible web-based global information clearinghouse / remotely operated seabed core-sampling vehicle

5   General Adverbial Clauses

A general adverbial clause modifies the main verb in the sentence. It is often used to set the scene for the rest of the sentence. The following two examples are taken from a speech made by the representative of Belarus at the 48th session of the UN General Assembly. First is a translation following the original phrasing or structure, then the official English translation as it appeared in the UN Official Records after being interpreted and edited.

Example 1

Original structure: Let us take a look at this experience and potential in those areas which, **as is widely recognized and attested to even by this current debate**, have become very important for preserving world peace and security.

Official English version: Let us take a look at this experience and potential in those areas which have become very important for preserving global peace and security, **as is widely recognized and attested to even by this current debate**.

Example 2

Original structure: Taking an authoritative position on these issues, Belarus intends to present **during this session** of the General Assembly, **on behalf of and on the instructions of** the states of Commonwealth of Independent States, a joint declaration of the CIS on issues of the non-proliferation of weapons of mass destruction and their delivery systems.

Official English version: Taking an authoritative position on these issues, Belarus, **on behalf of and on the instructions of** the states of the Commonwealth of Independent States, intends **during this session** to present a joint declaration by the CIS on issues of the non-proliferation of weapons of mass destruction and their delivery systems.

These two passages illustrate a feature which is very important to translators and invaluable to interpreters: the fact that a general adverbial clause modifying the main verb (also known to some grammarians an 'absolute phrase' because it can stand alone) can be put in any one of several different positions (regardless of where it appears in the original language) without doing violence to the meaning. In Example 1 the basic subject–complement structure of the sentence is 'areas are becoming', and in English the general adverbial clause (marked in bold type) could go before the verb, or after the verb, or even at the end of the sentence, as has been done in the official version. In Example 2, the basic subject–complement structure of the sentence is 'Belarus intends to present a declaration', and the two general adverbial clauses (marked in bold type) could also go in several different positions, or could be combined together ('Belarus intends, during this session, on behalf of and on the instructions of . . .'), or could even be combined and inserted at the end in a separate sentence ('We shall do so during this session, on behalf of and on the instructions of . . .'). A short adverbial clause can also be squeezed in between two parts of a composite verb, as has been done with 'during this session' in Example 2 above (between the auxiliary 'intends' and 'to present').

Notice that this feature gives one much greater leeway in interpreting than if one were forced to follow the original sequence of phrases. If the adverbial clause is short, one can slip it in before or after the verb ('We intend, **at this session**, to declare . . .' or 'We intend to declare **at this session** . . .') or place it before the subject ('**At this session** we intend to declare . . .'). If it is so long that leaving it in the middle tends to disrupt the sentence (as in Example 1 above), one can save it for the end of the sentence. Or, if speed is a problem, one can save it, making an independent sentence out of the adverbial clause and slipping it in during the speaker's pause between sentences ('We shall do so at this session.').

Exercises

(1) In the sentences given below: identify the basic subject–complement structure of the sentence; identify the general adverbial clauses that modify the main verb; then translate the sentences into English in as many different ways as you can without altering the basic meaning:
   • Teniendo en cuenta todos los antecedentes, debemos proceder con suma cautela en una materia tan delicada.

- Dada la urgencia del problema, mi país no ha escatimado ningún esfuerzo para resolverlo dentro de un plazo razonable.
- El mundo, al entrar en esta época nueva, se ha dado cuenta que no logrará la paz, a menos de resolver los problemas acuciantes del subdesarrollo.
- Gardant à l'esprit tous ces évènements, nous devons avancer avec une grande circonspection dans une matière aussi délicate.
- Etant donné l'urgence de ce problème, mon pays n'a épargné aucun effort pour le résoudre dans un délai raisonnable.
- Le monde, à l'aube de ce nouvel âge, s'est rendu compte qu'il n'atteindra pas la paix, à moins de résoudre les problèmes douloureux du sous-développement.

(2) In the following excerpts from speeches, identify any clauses that can stand on their own. Then translate each passage in as many different ways as you can, making separate sentences out of the independent clauses or placing them in different positions in the sentence.

> La perspectiva de multiplicación de tribunales ad hoc, con los consiguientes problemas que ello puede aparejar en cuanto a certeza jurídica, estabilidad, falta de uniformidad en el derecho aplicable, distinta jurisprudencia, e incremento de costos, sumado a la necesidad de dar una adecuada respuesta a problemas que crean situaciones de particular tensión internacional, despertaron la reacción de la opinión pública, otorgando al tema que hoy nos ocupa, renovada vigencia. (Statement by representative of Uruguay)

> Since it will to some extent involve a renunciation of sovereign rights, every state must of necessity proceed with caution and circumspection, subjecting its far-reaching provisions to an exacting scrutiny before jettisoning to some extent existing arrangements and procedures as to interstate co-operation and mutual assistance in this field and venturing on uncharted seas. (Statement by representative of Sri Lanka)

> D'ailleurs, en nous ayant fait l'honneur de sa présence à la Cinquième Conférence des Chefs d'Etat et de gouvernement des pays ayant le français en partage, qui se tenait en octobre 1993 à Maurice, Monsieur le Secrétaire Général nous avait offert l'occasion de préciser nos convergences et de confirmer le plein appui de la communauté francophone à ses démarches. (Statement by the President of the Conseil Permanent de la Francophonie)

(3) Notice where the general adverbial clause (in bold) appears in the following excerpt and how it has been treated in each language:

> **As one of the implementing agencies of the Montreal Protocol on Substances that deplete the Ozone Layer**, UNEP assists countries to prepare Country Programmes which lay the groundwork for the phase-out of ozone depleting substances. (UNEP, 1993)
>
> **Le PNUE est l'une des agences chargées de la mise en oeuvre du Protocole de Montréal relatif aux substances menaçant la couche d'ozone**. A ce titre, il assiste les pays dans la préparation de programmes nationaux visant l'élimination progressive de ces substances. (UNEP, 1993)
>
> **La PNUMA, una de las agencias impulsoras del Protocolo de Montreal sobre sustancias que dañan la capa de ozono**, asiste a los países en la preparación de planes nacionales que sienten las bases para la eliminación gradual de dichas sustancias. (UNEP, 1993)

(a) Following the structure of the English version, rewrite the French and Spanish versions.

(b) Following the structure of the French version, rewrite the English and Spanish versions.

(c) Following the structure of the Spanish version, rewrite the English and French versions.

(4) Many general adverbial constructions in English begin with the words 'as' and 'in', for example:

> As is well known, ... / As we take up ... / As this committee is well aware ... / As our mandate requires, ... / As the body charged with the task of ... / As we come to the end of our deliberations ... / In addressing the problem of ... / In the context of ... / In taking the floor here for the first time ... / In this landmark year of ... / In setting about the task of ...
>
> Make a list of as many English adverbial constructions as you can think of which begin with the words 'as' or 'in', then write illustrative sentences with each construction and translate the sentences into your other languages in as many different ways as you can.

6 Untranslatability

There is a grain of truth to the proverb 'Traduttore, traditore'. No matter how good the translation, something always seems to be lost. It is that 'untranslatable' residue of meaning that cannot be brought out in the target language which leads some linguists to proclaim that in a theoretical sense translation is 'impossible'. However, it will help the translator or interpreter to recall that 'untranslatability' is chiefly due to the inherent features of cultures and languages, not to the individual abilities of the translator or the limitations of the craft.

The problem of 'untranslatability' arises from the fact that different cultures divide up the universe in different ways, and that their languages therefore contain ideas, words and expressions to describe those different concepts and culture-specific features. To cite some familiar examples, the languages of desert peoples have many words for different aspects of a feature of the physical world that English speakers simply call 'sand', the Inuit language has many words for 'ice', French has many words to describe the qualities of wine (e.g. 'gouleyant' and 'charpenté'), which cannot be very satisfactorily translated into English, etc.

However, linguists have shown (e.g. with experiments on color perception) that the vocabulary of our native language only determines what we can *say* about the world, not whether we can *perceive* it. If the word 'Ouch!' did not exist, an English speaker would still feel pain when hitting a thumb with a hammer, but the English translator would have one less English word available to translate 'Zut!' Consequently, specific realities singled out by the source language should not be treated as if they were hopelessly unrecognizable to speakers of the target language simply because speakers of the target language 'don't have a word for it'. Rather, the interpreter should try to devise some way of getting the idea across.

In some cases, the problem of 'untranslatability' really is insurmountable, and the translator, after scouring through all the dictionaries on the shelf, is finally reduced to leaving the word in the original language and inserting an explanatory footnote or paraphrase, while the interpreter is reduced to paraphrasing, describing, keeping the untranslatable world in the original or skipping the word.

But one must not confuse difficulty with untranslatability. There are many ways to translate words and expressions that do not travel well from one language to another, and quite often 'untranslatability' is a misnomer, because an exact or complete translation is not necessary, and an approximate equivalent may be all that is needed in a given context.

Dealing with the problem of 'untranslatable' utterances requires one to bear in mind that the same idea may find expression in different ways from one culture to another. It involves asking questions like the following. What am I translating? A word? An idea? The name of a concrete object or of an abstraction? The title of a person? The name of a cultural institution or artifact? A technical term? A specialized use of an ordinary word? An archaic word? An idiomatic expression? The expression of an emotion? An image? A figure of speech? A newly coined term? Should I look for a different part of speech (e.g. a noun rather than an adjective)? Is there anything in my culture which occupies roughly the same place or which plays roughly the same role? Is there anything in my culture that is thought of or talked about in a comparable way? Is the target audience expecting a complete translation? Does the context or the sub-text make clear the untranslatable implications?

Sometimes an apparent case of 'untranslatability' can be solved by finding the equivalent register, or level of language. For example, the speeches of Winston Churchill might provide a good model to help you translate a speech by Charles de Gaulle; or, at the other end of the spectrum, American urban 'rap' or old Chicago gangster-slang might provide an equivalent register with which to translate a French screenplay containing Marseilles 'argot du milieu'.

Because meaning is largely contextual, the context in which a word appears may at first make the word seem 'untranslatable'. But this is often a problem of 'not seeing the forest for the trees'. The French word **corde** may variously mean 'cord' or 'string' or 'rope', but if you are translating the French expression 'Il pleut des cordes', you need not wonder which to choose, because what you are actually translating is a French colloquial idiom conveying the idea of very heavy rainfall, and the best translation would be the English or Spanish idiom commonly used in that situation: 'It's raining cats and dogs' / 'Llueve a cántaros'. In the Spanish expression **régimen carcelario** the adjective may at first seem untranslatable because English does not have a special adjectival form corresponding to the noun 'prison' or 'jail', but if you focus on the sense of the whole phrase rather than the word, you can immediately see that the best English equivalent is 'police state'.

Similarly, equivalents can often be found for seemingly 'untranslatable' recent coinages or neologisms if one pauses to consider the social context in which they are used. If a French speaker tried to translate the contemporary American coinage 'yuppie' by searching for a one-word equivalent in French, he probably would never find one. But if one asks, 'What kind of person is a "yuppie" in America, and what do we call people like that in France when we want to poke fun at them?', one will probably hit upon the ironic expressions 'jeune cadre dynamique' or possibly 'BCBG', both of which are close enough to the meaning of 'yuppie': a young, ambitious, stylish social-climber.

If we look in dictionaries and thesauruses for a one-word English equivalent of the contemporary Japanese word karoshi ('death from overwork'), we will probably not find one. But if we ask ourselves, 'What's the phrase we most often use in talking about overworked executives running themselves into the ground?', we will probably hit upon the term 'executive stress', which is weaker than karoshi but would probably be an adequate translation in most contexts.

In tackling an 'untranslatable' word or expression, consider using other parts of speech, or figures of speech. In an entertaining book about 'untranslatable' words, *They Have a Word for It*, Howard Rheingold (1988) includes the French word dirigiste. True, the word itself is not easily translatable by any single English word. Its meaning is so specific that even English-speaking economists make no attempt to translate it and have in fact adopted it as if it were an English word. Thus, a recent World Bank study on Latin America by an American economist includes the following sentence: 'A particularly important issue is . . . whether the reforms are likely to be durable or whether, on the contrary, they are likely to be reversed, plunging Latin America back into *dirigisme*, populism, and inequality.' Here, the French word dirigisme is apparently being used, by an English-speaking specialist, because there is no English word that conveys all of the same nuances. We might therefore be tempted to conclude that the word dirigisme is 'untranslatable'. But a translation or interpretation does not have to use the same parts of speech as the original. If we ask ourselves what English words are usually used in the context of discussions about government regulation of business, we find at least one possible equivalent noun phrase, 'command economy', as well as two adjectives, 'prescriptive' or 'directive', which are fairly close in meaning. So a phrase like 'une économie dirigiste' could be translated as 'a command economy' (and 'une réglementation écologique trop dirigiste' could be translated as 'an overly prescriptive set of environmental regulations'). In some cases, 'dirigiste' can probably be translated as 'regulatory' if an intensifier is added, for example 'un code de conduite dirigiste' = 'an aggressively regulatory code of conduct'. Thus, the word itself may seem 'untranslatable', but the idea is not. To help create the necessary associations in your mind to enable you to find such solutions, an exercise that the author has found helpful is to form the habit of writing out 'strings' of related words and ideas (see pp. 136–150). An interpreter should try always to have more than one way to express any given idea.

Exercises

(1) (a) How many different ways can you think of to translate the following French expressions?

esprit de l'escalier / idée force / bricoleur / faire valoir / dérapage / dépassement / bavure / la dérive / fuite en avant / le rayonnement de la France / des remous dans les relations internationales / faire du forcing / respecter l'alternance / peser les enjeux / chez l'habitant / être solidaire de / la prégnance / amalgame / avec rigueur / cheville ouvrière / chantier / levée de boucliers / fin de non-recevoir / acheminement / faire le bilan de / lucide / sursaut / médiatique / retenir / éventuel

(b) How many different ways can you think of to translate the following Spanish expressions?

cacique / cacicazgo / la convivencia / confianza / garbozo / vocación pacifica / la concertación / estar acosado por / estrepitosamente / armamentismo / fuero / foral / figura jurídica

(c) Form a sentence with each expression above and then try to translate it by using different parts of speech, or figures of speech. For example, the French noun 'amalgame' is generally used to mean a deliberate mixing of unlike things, so that the expression 'faire l'amalgame' means to create deliberate confusion by mixing up things that should be treated differently. If a corresponding noun in common use in English does not come to mind, could one use the English verb 'to commingle', which means to mix together unlike things? Could one use the expression 'to mix apples and oranges'? Could 'patchwork' or 'hodgepodge' be used if the speaker's register is colloquial enough?

(d) Form a sentence with each expression above and then try to translate it by a paraphrase. For example, the French word 'alternance' is often used in the French press in reference to the idea that different political parties should have equal access to power and, in a sense, 'take turns' governing the country. There being no common noun in English that fully sums up that idea (the closest is perhaps 'pluralism'), could one translate it by the paraphrase 'alternation of political office'?

(2) Make a list of the most 'untranslatable' words or expressions you have heard or read, and try to translate them with the approach outlined above. Bring copies of the list to class with you for discussion. Exchange these 'problem lists' with other students and see whether a fresh perspective on the problem by someone else can create solutions. Always consider the possibility that an 'untranslatable' word may simply be a word which you have not heard before. Try asking a native speaker of the language or a specialist in the field to which the word pertains. For example, the author was once stumped by the words **gouleyant** and **charpenté** in translating advertising copy for French wines. After asking several Frenchmen and a wine expert, it became clear that these words were not 'untranslatable'; they correspond closely enough to **mouthwatering** and **full-bodied**.

(3) Read the following excerpt from an article about the Sami language of Finland. Are any of the various Sami words for 'snow' translatable into English, Spanish, French or your other working language(s)?

> *The Lyricism of Same*
> To give you an idea of how beautiful and expressive Same can be, here's an abbreviated list of some Lule-Sami words for snow:
>
> Muotta – snow in general
> Slievar – new snow, dry, soft and powdery, stirred by the wind
> Sakkih – new snow with cold weather, creating tough skiing conditions
> Nuvar – powder snow on top of previously trampled paths
> Siebbor – soft, fluffy snow in which skis sink deep, resulting in difficult skiing with occasional icing underneath and snow accumulations on top of the skis
> Skarta – snow layers that were frozen to moss and lichen in the fall, resulting in inferior grazing conditions for reindeer
> Suorve – snow that clings to objects, clothing and trees, creating difficult conditions and impeding movement
> Galav – deep, soft snow to wade through
> Hablek – snow falling in very large flakes
> Cieggat – slush or snow mush that skis sink down in. (Göran Nordell, *Stockholm News* (excerpt))

(a) Like the Sami of Finland, the Inupiats of Alaska have a highly developed 'winter vocabulary': more than 30 words for snow and more than 70 words for ice. Could you find equivalents for some of these words by talking to skiers or meteorologists who are accustomed to describing snow conditions? For example, do any of the following English words correspond nearly enough to any of the Sami words for 'snow'?

>sleet / slush / hardpack / powder / dusting / blizzard / avalanche / flurry.

(b) Are there any cultural characteristics of your country or natural features of your land or climate that are so unique as to be 'untranslatable' into other languages? Could they be translated by analogy? By paraphrase? By description?

(c) Are you likely to find a single-word equivalent of the English word 'blizzard' in the standard vocabulary of a Spanish-speaking tropical country? Are you likely to find a single-word equivalent of the word 'tsunami' in the standard vocabulary of a land-locked country? If not, you immediately know that you will have to treat those 'untranslatable' words by way of an explanatory or descriptive paraphrase. What would be the shortest possible paraphrase of 'blizzard' and 'tsunami' in each of the languages you know?

(4) Read the article on bullfighting in Chapter 15 (pp. 254–257), and notice how the untranslatable Spanish bullfighting terms in bold type (tremendista, desplante, alternativa, tentaderos) have been introduced to the English reader with the addition of explanatory phrases. Notice also that some Spanish bullfighting terms (torero, matador), precisely because they are too culture-specific to be translatable, have become acceptable English words that need no longer be translated or explained.

Although some rough English equivalents for such terms might be found or coined (e.g. 'tremendista' = 'daredevil' / 'desplante' = 'death-defying feat'), it seemed more respectful of Spanish cultural conventions to retain the Spanish term with an explanatory English paraphrase. Do you agree?

(5) The following excerpt from a Le Monde article on economics contains three difficult terms. The French word 'libéralisme' as it is used here refers to the economic theory of free markets, deregulation and privatization that was prevalent in the 1980s and 1990s. The English word 'liberalism' conveys that same meaning to both British and American economists; however, to most ordinary Americans it merely means the opposite of 'conservatism' and relates more to social issues (e.g. civil rights, reproductive rights, law enforcement) than to economic issues.

The French word 'dirigisme', used here as a qualifier, apparently refers to a form of free-market economics which admits some degree of government intervention in the economy.

The French word 'solidarité' is used here not in the usual sense of fellowship with one's fellow man, but in the institutional sense of social security and welfare programs.

Paradoxes et records
*Libéral-**dirigisme*** Le **libéralisme** tempéré de M. Balladur l'a ainsi amené à trop ronger l'image d'économie mixte que M. Mitterrand avait voulu donner à la France, en amorçant la privatisation de vingt et une entreprises publiques, et en commençant à faire valser en douceur quelques présidents de sociétés nationales, tout en rétablissant l'Etat dans son rôle, défini . . . comme 'le garant de l'ordre social de la **solidarité**'. (Noblecourt, 1993 (excerpt))

(a) How would you translate or interpret this passage to an audience of English-speaking economists?
(b) How would you translate or interpret this passage to an audience of American non-economists?
(c) How would you translate or interpret this passage for English-speaking people from various parts of the world?
(d) Would '**libéral-dirigisme**', as used above, be equivalent to '**liberalismo social**', the term used in Mexico to describe a free-market system with a social safety net? Would '**liberalismo social**' be an appropriate translation into Spanish of '**libéral-dirigisme**'?
(e) Does the French word **libéralisme**, as used above, differ from the English word **liberalism** and the Spanish word **liberal** as used in the two excerpts below? What does each word refer to?

> The eclipse of **liberalism** may have other causes in other places, but in New York City it is directly correlated with rising crime rates and the perception, encouraged by the city's tabloid media, that order is about to give way to anarchy. (Conason, 1995: 779)

> Para los clásicos no existía dilema: el orden **liberal** en la economía y en la política era uno y el mismo. El dilema se presenta para los **liberales** mexicanos precisamente porque esa identidad no existe. (Rubio, 1992: 70)

(f) When a prominent European Union official recently argued against '**le libéralisme sauvage**' to a non-specialist American audience, using the English word 'liberalism', she was saying the opposite of what she meant to say. Which of the following possible alternatives would be closest in meaning to '**le libéralisme sauvage**'?

- free-market economics
- hard-line free-market economics
- extremist supply-side economics
- deregulated free-market economics
- robber-baron capitalism
- free-market forces
- cut-throat capitalism
- laissez-faire capitalism

Notice that all of the above alternatives imply a value judgment, positive or negative. That being the case, the interpreter should choose the alternative which conveys the same value judgment intended by the speaker. Which would you choose in the above case? Which would you choose in the following case, in which the French Prime Minister objects to competition between two small-business credit institutions as counterproductive?

> Pour corriger le manque de fonds propres des PME, le premier ministre a décidé l'augmentation des possibilités d'intervention de la société à capital risque Sofaris, ainsi que son rapprochement avec le CEPME (Crédit d'équipement aux PME), qui 'cessera de s'épuiser dans une concurrence stérile qui a été voulue au nom d'un **libéralisme trop doctrinaire**'. (*Le Monde*, 1995c)

(6) In a committee debating development issues, an English-speaking representative proposed an amendment which called for using the word 'resourcefulness' in reference to countries' efforts to make the best use of their resources in pursuing economic development. In that context, it proved difficult for the French interpreter to translate the words 'promoting resourcefulness', and the Spanish interpreter managed to do so only by means of a paraphrase. A current French equivalent of 'resourceful' (in reference to a person) is 'débrouillard', but it is too colloquial to use in drafting a formal document. The expression 'avoir de la ressource' is apparently too rarely used. How would you translate 'resourcefulness' in Spanish or French by means of a paraphrase? Is the problem due to the fact that the concept itself is somewhat unfamiliar to the French or Spanish languages?

(7) A special form of 'untranslatability' relates to the *emotional tone* of the speaker. Sometimes certain emotional tones, such as extreme anger or irony, can be difficult to translate or interpret, not because of the limitations of the target language but because the interpreter has trouble identifying with or matching the speaker's mood or tone. But sometimes

even the fullest sympathy with the speaker does not seem to help and the target language seems inadequate to the task. This feature emerges most clearly in the context of opera, and it is of interest to interpreters to consider why this is so. It is thought by many people well versed in music that certain languages, such as Italian, have unique lyrical qualities which cannot be fully translated. Thus, Italian opera is rarely translated, and the burden falls to the non-Italian-speaking audience to make sense of the action by reading the libretto.

> During most of opera history, two alternative principles have ruled in linguistic matters: either an opera was sung in the language of the audience, or it was sung in the language of the singers. In the greater number of cases, the two principles were not even in conflict; singers and audiences shared a common language, and many singers who performed in other than their native language restricted themselves to a single one they had learned fluently. Perhaps most tellingly, polyglot performances were found perfectly acceptable to accommodate visiting stars: German listeners preferred to hear Caruso, for example, sing eloquently in Italian rather than by rote in a language he didn't speak or understand. Not until well into the twentieth century did the principle of original language become the overriding one, and even now it is the rule primarily in the Anglo-Saxon countries and in a few large theaters elsewhere that employ an international range of stars. When observed in smaller houses and even frequently in the big ones, the original-language principle often yields a result that in the past would have been found absurd, especially by most of the great composers: opera sung by people in a language they don't really speak, before audiences who don't understand it. (Hamilton, 1988 (excerpt))

Why do people listen to lengthy lyrical works in languages they do not understand? Is it for the same reason that American audiences once raved over Carmen Miranda even when they did not understand a single word of the Portuguese songs she sang? (Her impresario observed that 'She could just as well have been singing in Japanese.') Do certain languages have certain inherent musical or emotional qualities that inevitably get completely lost in translation? Or is there simply a lack of *good* translations of such works? If it is the former, then there may be instances in which 'the best translation is no translation', or 'a minimal translation'.

7 Figures of Speech

Words are often used to form units of meaning in ways that convey more than is dictated by the rules of grammar. Such combinations or clusters of words are used deliberately because they are 'more than the sum of their parts' and thus serve as a kind of shorthand, which makes them especially useful to interpreters. Translators and interpreters must be alert to figurative language and remember that a figure of speech in one language can often by rendered by a different figure of speech in another language, for example a metaphor by a proverb, or by non-figurative language.

The most common pitfall to be avoided is not recognizing figurative or idiomatic language and translating it literally. For example, an English interpreter unfamiliar with the French idiom 'jouer les empêcheurs de danser en rond' (to be a spoilsport) translated it as 'going around in circles'. Failure to recognize the meaning of a figure of speech, or failure to accept and convey the meaning thereby intended by the speaker, can result in embarrassment for an interpreter. For example, in the following situation, a Russian interpreter apparently failed, or refused, to understand and render the meaning of the common English proverb 'Don't throw out the baby with the bathwater':

> Rudenko was accompanied by his deputy, Colonel Yuri Pokrovsky, ... and a young lady interpreter, who introduced herself as Miss Dmitrieva. ... Miss Dmitrieva's interpreting was beginning to improve somewhat, but her lapses were often comical and there was a good deal of mirth, which she took with great good humor. However, she was the soul of propriety, and when someone at the table used the expression 'to throw the baby out with the bath water', she blushed to the roots of her hair and declared severely, 'I weel not translate that; it eez not *nice*.' Hazard explained the figure of speech in Russian to Colonel Pokrovsky's satisfaction, but the lady still seemed troubled by this vision of a naked baby tumbling out of a tub. (Taylor, 1992: 100–102)

Exercises

(1) If Miss Dmitrieva did recognize the proverb (which also exists in Russian), was she entitled to censor the speakers for whom she was working because she found the expression distasteful? If the English speaker had conveyed his meaning by means of the expression 'Do not cut off your nose to spite your face', would Miss Dmitrieva still have refused to interpret him because it was 'not nice'? Does a too-fastidious interpreter behave rather like a dictionary that omits 'rude' words? If Miss Dmitrieva could not overcome her aversion to what she thought was impolite language, could she not have simply rendered the meaning of the proverb literally, that is 'don't go so far that your action is self-defeating' or 'don't overdo it'? If she could not bring herself to utter the words 'throw out the baby' even when the objectionable expression was purely figurative, how do you suppose she would have coped, as an interpreter, with a speech in which the image was not figurative at all, as in the following remarks by Hillary Rodham Clinton?

> The voices of this conference and of the women at Hairou must be heard loud and clear. It is a violation of *human* rights when babies are denied food, or drowned, or suffocated, or their spines broken, simply because they are born girls. It is a violation of *human* rights when women and girls are sold into the slavery or prostitution. It is a violation of *human* rights when women are doused with gasoline, set on fire and burned to death because their marriage dowries are deemed too small. (Hillary Rodham Clinton, Address to the United Nations Fourth World Conference on Women, Beijing, China, 5 September 1995)

(2) Read the following classification of the main figures of speech often used by writers and speakers, and make a list of some examples of each figure of speech in each language you know:
  * *idiom*: an expression in the usage of a language that is peculiar to itself either grammatically (as 'no it wasn't me') or in having a meaning that cannot be deduced from the combined meanings of its elements, for example: 'Monday week' for 'the Monday a week from next Monday'.
  * *simile*: a figure of speech comparing two things, often introduced by 'as' or 'like', for example: 'Bureaucracies, **like plants**, need pruning from time to time, lest they become all branches and no blossoms' (statement by US ambassador).

- *parody*: a mocking or humorous imitation of another person's speech or manner of speaking.
- *paronomasia*: a pun, a play on words, usually formed by juxtaposition of two words with similar sound or spelling but different meaning (see Chapter 15, pp. 250–253).
- *parrhesia*: deliberate use of coarse or offensive language to 'shock' (see Chapter 15, pp. 250–252).
- *euphemism*: deliberate use of a weaker expression to avoid giving offense, or to place an idea in a more positive light, for example: 'daytime drama' instead of 'soap opera'.
- *hyperbole*: extravagant exaggeration used as a figure of speech.
- *epigram*: a terse, sage or witty, often paradoxical saying, for example: 'Democracy is the worst form of government, except all other forms that have been tried from time to time' (Winston Churchill). / 'The United States and England are the only two nations separated by a common language' (George Bernard Shaw).
- *bromide*: an epigram that has become trite or stale from over-use.
- *proverb*: a brief popular epigram or maxim; an adage (in Spanish: un refrán), for example: 'Don't count your chickens before they're hatched'.

    Many common proverbs exist in several languages in similar versions. Some use the same image to convey a given idea, for example: 'Absent le chat, les souris dansent.' = 'When the cat's away, the mice will play.'

    Others may convey a given idea through different images, for example: 'Don't put the cart before the horse.' = 'No hay que comenzar la casa por el tejado.' / 'We're not yet out of the woods.' = 'Nous ne sommes pas sortis de l'auberge.' / 'tourner autour du pot' = 'to beat around the bush'.

- *aphorism*: a concise statement of a principle, an adage, for example: 'A buen entendedor, pocas palabras.' = 'A word to the wise.'
- *apothegm*: a short, pithy saying, for example: 'If you must lie, be brief.'
- *motto, slogan, byword*: a concise saying, usually used as a guide for conduct or as a rallying cry for a movement (in Spanish: lema), for example: 'In God we trust.' / 'Ban the bomb!' / 'Je me souviens' (motto of Québec).
- *maxim*: a general truth, fundamental principle or rule of conduct, for example: Sic utere tuo ut alienum non laedas. = 'Use your own property in such a manner as not to damage that of another.'

    NB: Certain maxims (e.g. the 'maxims of equity') are applied by courts as rules of law, not just as moral precepts. Some maxims are used to codify, expound or express key ideas in specific fields, for example, the political maxim 'No taxation without representation.'

- *metaphor*: figure of speech in which a word or phrase literally denoting one kind of object or idea is used in place of another to suggest a likeness between them, for example: 'The ship plows the sea.' / 'Thine eyes are those doves' (medieval motet). (For further examples of the evocative power of metaphors, see the article 'Alien Expressions' in Chapter 9, p. 159–160.)

- *extended metaphor*: a metaphor which the speaker elaborates upon in order to convey further aspects of his main idea, for example: 'The *Independent* ... compares Mr. Rao to a crocodile, lying so still that everybody thinks he is a harmless log. It says now he has finally pounced, snapping at his adversaries ...' (*British Media Review*, British Information Services, 18 January 1996).

  NB: An extended metaphor can pose serious problems for an interpreter who translates the initial metaphor by a different image in the target language. For this reason, it is often better to follow the speaker literally when possible.

- *mixed metaphor*: the addition to a metaphor of another element which is incongruous or renders the metaphor absurd through an unfortunate choice of words or images, for example: 'A virgin forest is a place where the hand of man has never set foot.' / 'That cock and bull story is a red herring.'

  NB: Not *all* mixed metaphors are bad. Two different images may also be gracefully and harmoniously combined, for example: 'On these winds of change, the imagination of our young people has taken flight.' And an awkward mixed metaphor in the source language can be translated gracefully into the target language, for example: 'We have here a triangle of clusters.' = 'Nous avons trois groupes de questions.'

  Also, note that two metaphors placed close together do not necessarily constitute a mixed metaphor, for example: 'The apparent *linchpin and crown jewel* of the Republican House majority's "contract with America" is a proposed constitutional amendment to require balanced budgets by Congress by the year 2002 ...' (linchpin = the feature holding the proposal together / crown jewel = the most attractive feature). Such a construction is stylistically awkward, but the distinct meanings of the two metaphors need to be brought out in translation or interpretation even at the expense of style.

- *allegory*: the expression by means of symbolic fictional figures and actions of truths or generalizations about human conduct or experience, for example: the story of the tortoise and the hare.
- *fable*: a fictitious narrative, often intended to teach a useful truth, especially one in which animals act and speak as humans.
- *parable*: a usually short fictional story that illustrates a moral concept or religious principle. The following example is translated from German:

> And now for the Disarmament Conference. Ought one to laugh, weep, or hope when one thinks of it? Imagine a city inhabited by fiery-tempered, dishonest and quarrelsome citizens. The constant danger to life there is felt as a serious handicap which makes all healthy development impossible. The magistrate desires to remedy this abominable state of affairs, although all his counsellors and the rest of the citizens insist on continuing to carry a dagger in their girdles. After years of preparation the magistrate determines to compromise and raises the question, how long and how sharp the dagger is to be which anyone may carry in his belt when he goes out. As long as the cunning citizens do not suppress knifing by legislation, the courts, and the police, things go on in the old way, of course. A definition of the length and sharpness of the permitted dagger will help only the strongest and most turbulent and leave the weaker at their mercy. You will all understand the meaning of this parable. (Einstein, 1949: 57–58)

- *antonomasia*: figure of speech in which a name is replaced by another, or by a paraphrase, for example: un Mécène (a patron of the arts) / un Aristarque (a critic).
- *synecdoche*: a figure of speech in which a part is used for the whole (as in '50 sail' for 50 ships), or the whole for a part (as in 'the smiling year' for spring), the species for the genus (as in 'a cut-throat' for an assassin), the genus for the species (as in 'a creature' for a man), or the name of the material for the thing made of it (as in 'asphalt' for road).
- *metonymy*: use of the name of one thing for that of another of which it is an attribute or with which it is associated, for example: 'lands of the crown' to mean royal lands.
- *apostrophe*: an incidental remark addressed to an imaginary person or to a personified inanimate object, for example: 'Oh, cruel fate!' / 'Lead kindly, light!'
- *oxymoron*: a contradiction in terms, for example: 'negative growth' / 'Make haste slowly.'

(3) A Russian speaker quoted what he said was 'an old Russian saying' which, translated literally, went: 'Don't vaccinate telephone poles against typhoid.' How old could this proverb be? If no equivalent English proverb comes to mind, could you translate it as 'Don't go overboard with needless precautions'?

(4) (a) A Mexican speaker referred to a public figure in his country as 'un verdadero Juárez'. Since Juárez was a contemporary and admirer of Lincoln and, like Lincoln, a leader of his country in time of crisis, could this allusion be appropriately rendered into English as 'a veritable Lincoln' to an audience that would not recognize Juárez?

(b) In the following quotation, are the names transposable in translation or are both names better left alone?

> Notre véritable Homère, qui le croirait, c'est La Fontaine! (Sainte-Beuve)

(5) A French speaker at an international meeting referred to a seemingly far-fetched proposal as 'gagaesque'. This is a pun combining 'Dadaesque' (alluding to an absurdist art movement) and 'gaga' (slang for 'crazy', i.e. 'nuts'). Since such puns are usually untranslatable, would it be an adequate English translation to refer to the proposal as 'surrealistic'? In a more colloquial vein, would 'off the wall' be a good equivalent?

(6) (a) A Cuban speaker used the expression 'echar anzuelos a alguien' in the sense of 'to catch someone unawares'. If no equivalent English metaphor with 'hooks' comes to mind, would the expression 'to trip someone up' be an adequate English translation?

(b) A Costa Rican speaker used the following image: 'Por el peso y el valor intrínseco de su temática y por el alcance de su contenido sustantivo y programático, la Declaración y el Programa de Acción se han ido perfilando y consolidando *como una especie de paraguas envolvente y articulador* de un proceso de fundamentales definiciones ...'. Could this idea be rendered by the metaphor of an 'umbrella', an 'envelope' or a 'package'? Even if it could, does the expression of this idea require the use of so elaborate a metaphor, or of any metaphor at all? Would the use of a metaphor in translation clarify or complicate this idea?

(c) An Argentine speaker used the expression 'una sesión a la francesa' and then went on to explain that, in his country, this expression refers to an informal meeting where people get together to exchange

ideas freely before the formal meeting where they will be expected
to state a formal position. Would 'brainstorming session' be a suitable English equivalent? Could this expression, or the English
expression 'to take French leave', be translated literally into French?
What do they have in common with the French expression 'filer à
l'anglaise'?

The same Argentine speaker, referring to occasions when a dramatic proposal or piece of news is suddenly made known, used the
expression 'un bombazo'. Would the following be suitable equivalents? English: 'letting loose a bombshell'; French: 'jeter un pavé'.

(d) In a drafting group, several divergent opinions have been expressed
regarding the proper meaning of a key word in a document. Finding
some of these interpretations far-fetched, a Cuban speaker says, 'No
hay que *buscarle la quinta pata a la mesa.*' What does he mean? How
would you say it in French, English or other working languages?

(7) When an English speaker says 'we are *yoked* to our partners in this venture . . .', is this a simile or a metaphor?

Of the two following figures of speech used by Elsa Triolet, which
is the simile and which is the metaphor? Which is more apt or plausible?
Which would sound more plausible in translation?

L'ébullition en lui, le Vésuve de sa tête, finirait bien par se calmer,
cesserait de cracher le feu, la lave.

Elle était vive et à son affaire, les travaux domestiques devaient lui
être naturels comme à une poule de picorer et de pondre. D'ailleurs,
elle ressemblait un peu à une poule, lourde sur ses jambes grêles, le
nez pointu et l'oeil rond. (Triolet, 1959: 11–16)

A metaphor, by omitting the comparative word 'like', implies a stronger comparison than a simile. But if the image used for the comparison
is not itself apt, accurate or elegant, the metaphor can sound awkward,
absurd or extravagant in English. It will sound even more absurd if the
comparison is extended, as is the case with both comparisons above.
When this occurs in a speech, the English interpreter should consider
inserting the word 'like' and turning the metaphor into a simile.

(8) (a) On 5 March 1995 a newspaper reported that President Carlos
Salinas of Mexico had said that he was being criticized 'without
misery'. What President Salinas probably said was that he was
being criticized *sin misericordia*, that is 'without mercy'. Was the
reporter misled by an apparent cognate? Would 'harshly', 'unfairly',
'mercilessly' or 'ruthlessly' be suitable English equivalents for this

expression? What would a good equivalent be in French or in your other working languages?

(b) A prominent French official speaking English warned his audience that, if they pursued a certain unwise course of action, they would be 'shooting at their feet'. What was the expression he intended to use? What would a good equivalent be in Spanish or in your other working languages?

(c) The same speaker mentioned that he had encountered a certain economic problem 'in 36 countries', but added that he used the number 36 only because of a 'convention of language in his country'. What was the expression he had in mind, and what would be the proper way of putting it in English? Would 'in any number of countries' be suitable? What would a good equivalent be in Spanish or in your other working languages?

(9) Does the allegory of 'the tortoise and the hare' convey approximately the same meaning as the proverb 'Haste makes waste'? Does it convey approximately the same meaning as the French proverb (from La Fontaine) 'Patience et longueur de temps font plus que force ni que rage'?

(10) Translate the following extended metaphor into Spanish, French or other working languages:

> Mr Chairman, we are in an untenable position. We are, so to speak, up a creek without a paddle. We once had a paddle, which was the Agreement we all signed. We felt confident that we could paddle our own canoe. But, little by little, as we proceeded down the creek, the waters became more and more turbulent and we encountered ever greater problems. Some of us began to loosen our grip on the paddle. Now, we find our canoe about to sink into the rapids. The current grows ever more swift. And the mouth of the creek is still nowhere in sight. And, who knows, this creek may well be but a small tributary to the great, surging river that lies ahead. What will we do when we come to that raging torrent? We must quickly exchange our frail canoe for a sturdy row-boat with stout oars before we get there. And then we must all row together, for we are all in the same boat. Otherwise, it will be every man for himself, and sink or swim!

(11) Translate the following extended metaphor into English, French or other working languages:

> Señor Presidente, se trata aquí de predicar con el ejemplo. Nuestra organización no puede imponer a otras un catecismo de austeridad contra el cual nosotros mismos seguimos pecando. El buen predicador

no se conforma con difundir el evangelio, sino que demuestra a los feligreses lo que es la buena conducta. No nos comportemos como aquellos párrocos supuestamente piadosos que hacen desaparecer la colecta del Domingo en un santiamén.

(12) Translate the following extended metaphor into English, Spanish or other working languages:

Monsieur le Président, nos interlocuteurs dans cette négociation font penser au chasseur qui vend la peau de l'ours avant de l'avoir tué. Ils voudraient nous faire croire, sans aucune vérification, qu'ils ont déjà enregistré un énorme progrès vers le désarmement complet. C'est donc là une belle fourrure qu'ils voudraient nous vendre. Mais, l'ours est-il mort? Ou bien, a-t-il simplement changé de peau? Pour ma part, je l'entends grogner encore quelque part dans la forêt, et je me sens fort mal dans ma peau. Je me demande si je dois payer ce brave chasseur en argent comptant tant que cette bête dangereuse rôde dans les parages!

(13) (a) Restate the three extended metaphors above, expressing the ideas by means of images or figures of speech *different* from those used by the speaker.

(b) Restate the three extended metaphors above in simple, non-figurative language.

(c) How do these three extended metaphors differ from the parable by Einstein given in (2) above (pp. 68–69)?

(d) Read the article on xenophobic metaphors, 'Alien Expressions' in Chapter 9 (p. 159–160). Are any of the metaphors given in that article examples of extended metaphors?

(14) (a) Translate the following extended football metaphor into Spanish, French or other working languages, using an extended metaphor from soccer or another sport:

The nature of an activist President in any case, in Sam Lubell's phrase, was *to run with the ball until he was tackled*. As conditions abroad and at home nourished the imperial presidency, *tacklers* had to be more than usually *sturdy and intrepid*. (Schlesinger, 1973: 409)

(b) Explain the following terms and, for each one, try to think of comparable terms with roughly the same meaning from another sport or game:

goal / technical knockout / checkmate / stalemate / home run / foul / pass / field goal / bull's eye.

(c)   Translate the following extended metaphor or parable into Spanish, French or other working languages, using either the original metaphor or an equivalent story or other figure of speech:

> How to make external checks effective? Congress could *tie* the *Presidency down by a thousand small legal strings,* but, *like Gulliver and the Lilliputians,* the President could always *break loose.* (Schlesinger, 1973: 409–410)

(d)   Translate the following simile into Spanish, French or other working languages using first the original simile and then an equivalent simile (or other figure of speech) in each language:

> 'An idea in politics is *like a Christmas fruitcake,*' James Carville, the Democrat strategist said, recycling a simile he himself has used in the past. 'There's only one, and everyone just passes it around.' (*The New York Times,* 1996c, section 4: 5)

(15) When a speaker warns you in advance that he or she is about to utter a proverb by using words like, 'We have a saying ...' or 'As we say in my country ...', you may find it useful to preface your interpretation of the proverb with the words 'We have a saying *to the effect that* ...'. This will enable you to do either of two things gracefully: (i) give a suitable equivalent if you can think of one fast enough, or (ii) give an approximate translation of the original proverb, for example: 'Comme l'on dit chez moi, "Vingt fois sur le métier remettez votre ouvrage".' = (i) 'There is a saying in my country to the effect that "Practice makes perfect"', or (ii) 'There is a saying in my country to the effect that you must go back to your work time and again until you get it right'. Obviously, the former is the better translation, but the latter is adequate, and either will work with the prefatory words 'to the effect that'. Try this technique with some of the proverbs listed in (17)–(19) below.

(16) In many cases the point a speaker is trying to convey by a proverb or maxim is a simple and obvious one that is clear from the context. Speakers will sometimes use a complex or obscure proverb or figure of speech *merely for effect*, although the substantive point they are making is straightforward and can be stated simply in any number of ways.

   When this happens, there is nothing wrong with stating the 'moral of the story' in simple terms if you cannot think of an equivalent proverb or other figure of speech in the few seconds available to you when interpreting. Accuracy is more important than affectation. If you cannot think of 'Time and tide wait for no man' or 'There's no time like the present' or 'Never put off till tomorrow what you can do today', just say

'Let's not delay'. Similarly, while the expression 'to shoot from the hip' may not have an equally colorful equivalent in current French, it simply means 'réagir instinctivement' and can be so translated. While it may be more polished to render a proverb by a proverb, it is unprofessional to become tongue-tied over a simple idea. For figures of speech, as for all other forms of speech, the interpreter's job is to get the gist of the meaning across to the audience within the time limits dictated by the speaker's speed.

For example, in the following hypothetical statements, guess the meaning of the (non-existent) 'proverb' and translate the idea:

> My country has invested heavily in this soil conservation scheme every year for many years. Yet, no matter how much we invest, it still has not worked, and erosion continues. We feel like the proverbial turtle who built his nest from sand! It is time to declare the project a failure.

> We have been waiting for years for the major polluter countries to join the Environmental Convention, postponing action in the vain hope that their membership would make our task easier. But none has yet joined! As the proverb in my country says, 'The shepherd lost his flock while waiting for the stray sheep.' We must take action without further delay!

(17) Proverbs can sometimes be translated literally, but often their meaning is not readily apparent from a literal translation, for example the Chinese proverb 'Even the best needles are not sharp at both ends'.

Moreover, the same image or word may be used in different languages to convey very different ideas, and this has considerable potential for confusion. For example, the common English idiom using the word 'elbow', 'to bend the elbow', refers to misbehavior (getting drunk), but the Chinese proverb 'The elbow bends inward' is a moral precept meaning 'It is natural to think first of one's own family' (Yutang, 1960: 481). Thus, a literal translation of such a proverb could be both incomprehensible and incongruous.

If a literal translation sounds incongruous or meaningless in the target language, one should try to grasp the underlying idea from the context in order to translate or interpret a proverb.

(a) Focusing on the underlying idea, translate the following English proverbs into Spanish, French or your other working languages:

> Do unto others as you would have them do unto you. / Absence makes the heart grow fonder. / Out of sight, out of mind. / Actions

speak louder than words. / You can't teach an old dog new tricks. / A leopard never changes its spots. / When angry, count ten. / The grass is always greener on the other side of the fence. / Hitch your wagon to a star. / A rising tide lifts all boats. / Birds of a feather flock together. / Beauty is only skin deep. / Once bitten, twice shy. / Never cross a bridge until you come to it. / Business is business. / He who pays the piper calls the tune. / Half a loaf is better than none. / Be grateful for small blessings. / Don't put all your eggs in one basket. / Never hit a man below the belt. / Beggars can't be choosers. / A fool and his money are soon parted. / Charity begins at home. / Never change horses in mid-stream. / If you can't lick 'em, join 'em. / If it ain't broke, don't fix it. / It's no use crying over spilt milk. / What's good for the goose is good for the gander. / Don't kill the goose that lays the golden eggs. / One who acts as his own lawyer has a fool for a client. / People in glass houses shouldn't throw stones. / Discretion is the better part of valor. / All's fair in love and war. / All things come to he who waits. / A penny saved is a penny earned. / A bad penny always turns up sooner or later. / Better the devil you know than the devil you don't know. / To err is human, to forgive is divine. / One man's meat is another man's poison. / Two wrongs don't make a right. / Where there's smoke, there's fire. / Still waters run deep. / When the cat's away, the mice will play. / A rolling stone gathers no moss. / Leave well enough alone. / Let sleeping dogs lie. / Two heads are better than one. / Where there's a will there's a way. / A little knowledge is a dangerous thing. / Any port in a storm. / A friend in need is a friend indeed. / Power corrupts. / The best things in life are free. / Nothing succeeds like success. / It is better to give than to receive. / Talk is cheap. / Don't look a gift horse in the mouth. / Opportunity knocks but once. / Every cloud has a silver lining. / The night is always darkest before the dawn. / When it rains, it pours. / Physician, heal thyself. / You can't teach your grandmother to suck eggs. / Tit for tat. / One good turn deserves another. / No man is an island. / The road to hell is paved with good intentions. / A rose by any other name would smell as sweet. / What's in a name? / The race is to the swift. / Rome wasn't built in a day. / The devil take the hindmost. / The devil is in the details. / What you don't know won't hurt you. / Misery loves company. / As you sow, so shall you reap. / Never put off until tomorrow what you can do today. / It's an ill wind that blows no good. / There's many a slip twixt the cup and the lip. /

Ignorance is bliss. / Lightning never strikes twice in the same place. / Sticks and stones can break your bones but words can never hurt you. / If the shoe fits, wear it. / Don't mix apples and pears. / Waste not, want not. / Less is more. / A watched pot never boils. / Success has many fathers; failure is an orphan. / Build a better mousetrap, and the world will beat a path to your door. / Don't wash your dirty linen in public. / Great oaks from little acorns grow. / The proof of the pudding is in the eating. / Loose lips sink ships. / You can lead a horse to water but you can't make him drink. / The chickens have come home to roost. / Time flies. / Silence is golden. / Silence is consent. / Gather rosebuds while ye may. / Don't rock the boat. / Make hay while the sun shines. / Strike while the iron's hot. / Fine words will butter no parsnips. / A stitch in time saves nine. / Justice delayed is justice denied. / The opera ain't over till the fat lady sings. / Fools rush in where angels fear to tread. / The best things in life are free. / Man does not live by bread alone. / Money isn't everything. / Easy come, easy go. / Here today, gone tomorrow. / Look before you leap. / Something is rotten in the state of Denmark. / You can't make a silk purse out of a sow's ear. / A journey of a thousand miles starts with a single step. / Practice makes perfect. / Virtue is its own reward. / An ounce of prevention is worth a pound of cure. / Nothing ventured, nothing gained. / A picture is worth a thousand words. / Spare the rod and spoil the child. / Children should be seen and not heard. / All the world loves a lover. / A man is judged by the company he keeps. / Paddle your own canoe. / There's a rotten apple in every barrel. / Don't bite the hand that feeds you. / The child is father to the man. / Youth comes but once. / Let the punishment fit the crime. / The squeaky wheel gets the grease. / Laughter is the best medicine. / There is nothing new under the sun. / It is better to light a candle than to curse the darkness. / No news is good news. / You can't fight City Hall. / Two things in life are certain: death and taxes. / Hell hath no fury like a woman scorned. / No man is a prophet in his own land. / New times, new mores. / Breeding will out. / No pain, no gain. / The spirit is willing but the flesh is weak. / A man has as many masters as he has vices. / An apple a day keeps the doctor away. / The early bird gets the worm. / Good fences make good neighbors. / Opposites attract. / You can't put the genie back in the bottle. / Nothing is more powerful than an idea whose time has come. / An apple never falls far from the tree.

(b) Focusing on the underlying idea, translate the following Spanish proverbs into English, French or other working languages:

De tal palo, tal astilla. / Cría cuervos, y te sacarán los ojos. / Dime con quien vas, y te diré quien eres. / Caminante, no hay camino; se hace el camino al andar. / Más sabe el diablo por viejo que por diablo. / Preguntando se llega a Roma. / Cada uno es hijo de sus obras. / Poderoso caballero es Don Dinero. / Cada uno sabe donde le aprieta el zapato. / El pez por la boca muere. / En boca cerrada no entran moscas. / A buen entendedor, pocas palabras. / No hay mal que por bien no venga. / Tres cosas hay en la vida: salud, dinero y amor. / En la tierra de los ciegos, el tuerto es rey. / Perro que ladra no muerde. / Si se alivia, fué la Virgen, si se muere, fué el doctór. / Cada cabeza es un mundo. / Candil de la calle y oscuridad de su casa. / Allá van leyes do quieren reyes. / Cuando a Roma fueres, haz como vieres. / Bueno está lo bueno. / Cuando las barbas de tu vecino véas pelar, pon las tuyas a remojar. / Un clavo saca otro clavo. / Entre bomberos, no se pisan las mangueras. / Crea fama, y acuéstate a dormir. / El que es buen gallo, en cualquier muladar canta. / El que a buen palo se arrima, buena sombra le cobija. / También el arte es don celeste. / Indio comido, indio ido. / Siembra si pretendes cosechar. / Más vale prevenir que castigar. / Nunca digas 'De esta agua no tomaré'. / Aunque la mona se vista de seda, mona se queda. / Del dicho al hecho hay mucho trecho. / Cada cardumen tiene su pescador. (Uruguay) / Al que madruga, Dios lo ayuda. / No se le puede sacar peras al olmo.

(c) Focusing on the underlying idea, translate the following French proverbs into English, Spanish or other working languages:

L'habit ne fait pas le moine. / La nuit porte conseil. / Chacun à son goût. / Le mieux est l'ennemi du bien. / La revanche est un plat qui se mange à froid. / Aide-toi, et le ciel d'aidera. / Il faut donner le temps au temps. / Les absents ont toujours tort. / Absent le chat, les souris dansent. / On ne fait pas une omelette sans casser des oeufs. / Il n'est jamais trop tard pour bien faire. / L'appétit vient en mange-ant. / Les extrêmes se retrouvent. / Mieux vaut tard que jamais. / A beau jeu, beau retour. / A bon chat, bon rat. / A bon vin point d'enseigne. / A bon cheval point d'éperon. / A chacun son fardeau pèse. / Chat échaudé craint l'eau froide. / Il vaut mieux entendre ça qu'être sourd. / Patience et longueur de temps font plus que force ni que rage. / Du sublime au ridicule il n'y a qu'un pas. / Il ne faut pas mélanger les torchons et les serviettes. / Qui trop embrasse mal étreint. / Une fois n'est pas coutume. / Mieux vaut plier que rompre. / Les bons comptes font les bons amis. / Il faut donner le temps au temps.

(18) Which Spanish proverb above corresponds to 'Money talks'? Which English proverb above corresponds to 'Dime con quien vas, y te diré quien eres'? Which French proverb above corresponds to 'Don't judge a book by its cover'? Which English proverb above is closest in meaning to 'Le mieux est l'ennemi du bien'? Match as many proverbs as possible in the above lists with an approximate equivalent in another language.

(19) Would the German proverb 'An old bear is slow in learning to dance' convey approximately the same meaning as 'You can't teach an old dog new tricks'? Could the German proverb 'A lovelorn cook oversalts the porridge' be paraphrased to translate 'Too many cooks spoil the broth', or vice-versa? Is the basic idea of the German proverb 'Eile mit Weile' ('The more hurry, the less speed') the same as the English proverb 'Haste makes waste'? Could the German proverb 'The sparrow in my hand is better than the dove on the roof' be translated by the English proverb 'A bird in the hand is worth two in the bush'? Is it equivalent to the Italian proverb 'Better have an egg today than a hen tomorrow'? Can you guess the meaning of the German proverb 'To jump over your shadow'? Does the German proverb 'Man soll nicht den Tag vor dem Abend loben' ('Don't praise the day before evening') have the same meaning as the English proverb 'Don't count your chickens before they're hatched' and the French proverb 'Il ne faut pas vendre la peau de l'ours avant de l'avoir tué'?

Could the Italian proverb 'He who commences many things finishes but few' be paraphrased to translate the English proverb 'A jack-of-all-trades is master of none' or the French proverb 'Qui trop embrasse mal étreint'? Could the central idea in these proverbs also be rendered in English by the expressions 'Don't overextend yourself' or 'Don't spread yourself out too thin'? Does the Latin maxim 'Non omnia possumus omnies' convey the same idea? Could one also take the opposite cliché of 'a man for all seasons' and express the same idea by negating it?

Would the Chinese proverb 'No cure, no pay' convey approximately the same meaning as the Spanish proverb 'Músico pagado, mala canción'? Could the Chinese proverb 'One foot cannot stand on two boats' be used to translate 'No man can serve two masters'?

Would the Arabic proverb 'How degrading is folly in old age!' convey approximately the same meaning as 'There's no fool like an old fool'?

Could the Arabic proverb 'Revenge produces sorrow; pardon gladness' be used to translate 'To err is human, to forgive divine'?

Would the Russian proverb 'Necessity teaches the bear to dance' convey approximately the same meaning as 'Necessity is the mother of invention'? Would the Russian proverb 'There are no barriers to a rich man' convey the same meaning as the Spanish proverb 'Poderoso caballero es Don Dinero'? Does the Russian proverb 'Tomorrow is time enough for revenge' convey the same meaning as the French proverb 'La revanche est un plat qui se mange à froid'? Can the Russian proverb 'Only the grave can straighten out a hunchback' be translated by 'A leopard can't change his spots'?

Try to work out the meaning of the following West Indian proverbs, and think of equivalents in Spanish, French or your other working languages:

Jamaica: 'The cow never knows the use of its tail until it loses it.' / 'Do not put your hand into fire for anyone.' / 'Today does not kill tomorrow.' / 'Cats and dogs do not have the same luck.' / 'Too many rats never dug a good hole.' / 'A good friend is better than money in the pocket.' / 'What you don't know is older than you.' / 'Every day bucket go to well, one day it come home empty.' / 'One-one coco, full basket.' / 'The new broom sweeps clean, but the old one knows the corners.' / 'You're in the right church, but in the wrong pew.' / 'Lie down with dog, get up with fleas.' / 'If it no itch, no scratch.' / 'If you see old woman run, don't ask why, run too.'

Barbados: 'An empty bag can't stand up.' / 'Tree does wet you twice.'

Does the Malay proverb 'Just because the river is quiet, don't think the crocodiles have left' express the same idea (unseen danger) as 'Something is rotten in the state of Denmark'? Does it differ from 'to smell a rat', from 'There's something fishy', and from 'Il y a anguille sous roche'? Does the Swahili proverb 'Don't curse the crocodile before you have crossed the river' express the same idea as 'Don't count your chickens before they're hatched' (i.e. don't take success for granted prematurely) or is it closer in meaning to 'Don't tempt fate'? Is it likely that the expression 'to shed crocodile tears' could be translated literally into most other languages and be understood? Does it depend on the listener's actual familiarity with the habits of crocodiles? In the following sentence, describing the route which the author followed home from school, can one translate literally the expression 'lagarto lagarto'?

Tomaba por (las calles) Sierra, Jackson, Bulevar España ... hasta la penitenciaria, que era *(lagarto lagarto)* mi destino final. (Benedetti, 1992: 81)

Try to think of an equivalent in Spanish, French or other working languages for the following Egyptian proverbs: 'Feed the mouth, and the eye will be shy' (proverb said when you need a favor or service from someone – you 'feed' him/her to get what is needed; also used to mean 'paying somebody to keep quiet'). / 'Turn the jar on its mouth; The girl will take after her mother.' (The first line about the jar is there only for the sake of the rhyme. This proverb is used to refer to wanton girls.)

Could the Egyptian proverb 'We give him a glimmer of hope, and he takes full advantage' be translated by the English proverb 'Give them an inch and they'll take a mile'? Could the Egyptian proverb 'He who resembles his father gives up none of his rights' be translated by a paraphrase of the English proverb 'Like father, like son'?

Could the Latin proverb 'Carpe diem' ('Seize the day') be translated into English by the proverbs 'Gather rosebuds while ye may' or 'Strike while the iron is hot' or 'Make hay while the sun shines'? How do these differ from the saying 'Live for today, for you know not what tomorrow may bring'?

In a radio interview broadcast on 1 January 1996, the Dalai Lama's interpreter explained that one of the more difficult precepts of Tibetan Buddhism to put into English was the concept of *karma*, that is the idea that one must eventually atone for one's past actions. The American interviewer immediately suggested the American proverb 'What goes around comes around.' Another more colloquial version of the same idea is 'The chickens will come home to roost'. Would these two proverbs, in the proper context, be adequate to express the concept of *karma*? When would they *not* be appropriate, due to differences in level of language? Can you translate this concept into other languages you know by means of a proverb or other figure of speech?

Could the humorous Latin-American colloquial expression 'Para qué tanto brinco estando tan parejo el suelo?' be translated by the humorous American colloquial expressions 'If it ain't broke, don't fix it' or 'a tempest in a teapot' or 'Why all the fuss'? Can you think of (or invent) an equivalent in French or other languages?

Could the French colloquial proverb 'Quand on veut noyer son chien, on l'accuse de rage' be translated by the English colloquial proverb 'Give a dog a bad name and hang it'? Can you think of an equivalent in Spanish or in other languages?

Can the French stereotype 'médecin malgré lui' be used to encapsulate the same idea as the English proverb 'Necessity is the mother of invention'?

Could the French-African proverb 'Les cailloux qui vont dans la brousse tuent les oiseaux' (meaning that the more well-directed efforts are the ones that will pay off) be translated by paraphrasing the English expression 'to kill two birds with one stone'? Can the French-African expression 'danser tout seul' be translated by the English proverb 'It takes two to tango'? Could the Nigerian expression 'The snake has been scorched but not killed' be translated into Spanish by paraphrasing the Argentine expression 'matar la víbora ahora mismo' (which usually means 'to nip in the bud')?

Does the Indonesian expression 'getting all the shrimp under the stone' mean the same thing as 'to leave no stone unturned'?

Can you guess the meaning of the Bolivian expression 'It's the eye of the owner that fattens the cattle'?

There often exist proverbs stating directly opposite 'truths', for example 'Absence makes the heart grow fonder' and 'Out of sight, out of mind'. When you encounter such a pair of opposites, consider whether it would be possible to use one of them with a negative to express the opposite idea, for example 'Absence does not make the heart grow fonder'. This could prove useful if you forget one but happen to remember the other.

(20) Translate the parable by Albert Einstein in (2) above (p. 68) into Spanish, French or your other working languages. Can you think of (or invent) a proverb or other expression which concisely sums up the meaning of that parable?

(21) Browse the following potpourri of images, stock phrases, idioms, symbols, names, clichés and stereotypes. (a) Look up any with which you are not familiar; (b) write out the shortest possible explanation, definition or paraphrase of each one; (c) translate them into your other languages; (d) use them in illustrative sentences; (e) make lists of those which can be transposed into another language, those whose meaning is clear in literal translation, and those which seem to be 'untranslatable'; and (f) continue the lists by adding more items of each type when you hear them or as they occur to you.

to snowball / to be snowed under / to stonewall / to boomerang / to backfire / white collar / blue collar / a rude awakening / a litmus-test issue / to stump / the power behind the throne / to nip in the bud / pound of flesh / to wield the scepter / mending fences / to be on the mend / to beat around the bush / free ride / free lunch / the cream of the crop / a rotten apple / the die is cast / parting of the ways / to clear the decks / parting of the waters / to iron out differences / to split the difference / to come to blows / take-off point / to crack the whip / soft landing / the sky's the limit / time bomb / golden handshake / to play ball / to drop the ball / to start the ball rolling / golden parachute / fool's errand / wild goose chase / tidal wave / milestone / milepost / yardstick / benchmark / to move the goal post / dragon's teeth / law of the jungle / the lesser of two evils / carrot and stick / the ball is in your court / stacked deck / loaded dice / to turn on a dime / knight in shining armor / back-seat driver / Monday morning quarterback / armchair philosopher / gatekeeper / ivory tower / the smell of the lamp / Judas priest / nemesis / maverick / figurehead / lifeblood / the emperor's new clothes / banner day / black sheep / Gordian knot / to wear the pants / Cyclops / Grand Inquisitor / good Samaritan / Achilles' heel / chink in the armor / by hook or by crook / featherbedding / between a rock and a hard place / firebrand / reed in the wind / on an even keel / to take the wind out of someone's sails / taking coals to Newcastle / through the back door / to re-invent the wheel / old wine in new bottles / a Martinet / knife in the back / take the bull by the horns / to hit the bull's eye / to hit the nail on the head / herd instinct / the salt of the earth / to take French leave / bears and bulls / cannon-fodder / out in the cold / green thumb / rank and file / the four horsemen of the Apocalypse / stampede / right as rain / everything in the garden is lovely / Pyrrhic victory / Citizen Kane / rocket scientist / mother's milk / to wear one's heart on one's sleeve / blank check / the glass is half empty / swan song / Waterloo / Sublime Porte / Watergate / Spartacus / gadfly / poison pill / burning bush / sitting duck / Tower of Babel / millstone around one's neck / albatross / white elephant / red herring / cornerstone / keystone / linchpin / kingpin / juggernaut / sugar-coated / rotten apple / the Great Helmsman / Lion of Judah / to beat swords into plowshares / handle with kid gloves / to Balkanize / snake in the grass / flash in the pan / shot in the dark / ship in the night / face in the crowd / from the cradle to the grave / the milk of human kindness / red-blooded / to sit on the fence / to sweep off one's feet / dark horse / workhorse / straight from the horse's mouth / Tammany Hall / gerrymander / the upper crust / to buy a pig in a poke / a hard row to hoe / crocodile tears / barking up the wrong tree / turn the knife in the wound / from pillar to post / to call a spade a spade / Delphic oracle / penny wise and pound foolish / the whole kit and caboodle / a whale of a time / whopper / burn the midnight oil / a Lothario /

Moloch / Leviathan / dog days / naysayer / doomsayer / soothsayer / play hooky / in one fell swoop / last straw / the straw that broke the camel's back / glitch / bug / to make hay while the sun shines / long in the tooth / spoilsport / gadfly / to give lip service to / fire and sword / not my cup of tea / two-edged sword / as plain as a pikestaff / to pull the wool over someone's eyes / sour grapes / to have the bit between one's teeth / sword of Damocles / jewel in the crown / to throw in the towel / king's ransom / hard knocks / surfing the net / hacker / to fly by the seat of the pants / a horse of a different color / another kettle of fish / get into the act / the game is not worth the candle / to give a wide berth to / a Lucrezia Borgia / a Mata Hari / to take the wind out of someone's sails / to get down to business / to get down to brass tacks / shoulder to the wheel / to play along with / yeoman's labor / sea change / cheek by jowl with / hand in glove with / to turn the other cheek / What cheek! / one-size-fits-all / to blow your own horn / whistling past the graveyard / at one stroke / Pandora's box / can of worms / hornet's nest / nest of vipers / slippery slope / hand on heart / warts and all / the good, the bad, and the ugly / a Quisling / a Malthusian / survival of the fittest / pushing up daisies / Punch and Judy show / a King Canute / behind the curve / to be in the loop / to be in the doghouse / straws in the wind / top man on the totem pole / cold comfort / to pull a rabbit out of a hat / Lead kindly, light! / to go one better / one-upmanship / brinkmanship / to leave someone open-mouthed / the lion and the lamb / to cross the Rubicon / smoking gun / the dog that did not bark / unbeknownst to / Lebensraum / elbowroom / leeway / the bottom line / from scratch / back to square one / fighting words / to be under someone's thumb / horse-trading / log-rolling / backscratching / to come out in the wash / to face the music / carved in stone / graven in stone / to own up to / to take a leaf from someone's book / to take someone to the cleaners / to give someone a dressing down / pennies from heaven / a penny for your thoughts / ballpark figure / to cut someone slack / vicious circle / the chicken or the egg / sacred cow / virtuous circle / humbug / skeletons in the closet / with the wolf at the door / wolf in sheep's clothing / to cry wolf / women and children first / not to give a fig about / a Messalina / sounding-board / tinderbox / powder-keg / red flag / hand-wringing / to make a difference / a can-do attitude / to be gung-ho about / Daniel in the lions' den / avatar / crystal ball / Icarus / forbidden fruit / jury-rigged / die-hard / dyed-in-the-wool / hardcore / once-and-for-all / the calm before the storm / in the eye of the storm / a level playing field / to leave no stone unturned / a crying shame / to bend over backwards / to run out of steam / under the gun / home free / deadbeat / garden-variety / shadow chancellor / payback / bailout / payoff / to pan out / just this once / to be in clover / domino effect / the domino theory / devil's choice / Hobson's choice / happy as a clam / in due course / squaring the circle / more than meets the eye / skeleton staff / bargaining chip / foot-dragging / in the bag / with a straight face / till you're blue in the face / to go to bat for someone / to have a place in the sun / stalking horse / Trojan horse / warhorse / hobby-horse / to get on one's high horse / scatter-shot / to play musical chairs / to throw the book at someone / bugbear / bogeyman / to bring someone to book / snail's pace / with all deliberate speed / to make haste slowly / my brother's keeper / to badmouth someone / as bent as a left-handed corkscrew (UK) / to upset the applecart / topsy-turvy / to pave the way for / to take up the slack / a ghost at the feast / lashed to the wheel / to lay to rest / holy writ / gospel truth / chapter and verse / on sufferance / to step on someone's toes / in step with the times / to step out of line / one step at a time / stepping-stone / the crunch / hectoring / to weigh in on the side of / to hit below the belt / star wars / wildcat / pie in the sky / user-friendly / networking / to take on board / to come on stream / to play hardball / to play dirty pool / plain vanilla / trickle down / guru / sherpa / czar / to be a thorn in the side of / quantum leap / entropy / a Wunderkind / enfant terrible / Young Turk / to sound the clarion call / to make something stick / up and running / to come with the territory / without batting an eyelash / strong suit / trump card / feeding-frenzy / logjam / gridlock / to be hoist by one's own petard / cock o' the walk / to rule the roost / a drop in the bucket / too little and too late / ways and means / to see how the other half lives / to live on the wrong side of the tracks / the lost generation / the wasted decade / the power elite / the upper crust / the lonely crowd / a song and dance / to go on one's merry way / quiet diplomacy / paradigm shift / silent majority / cloak and dagger / to fly off the handle / sackcloth and ashes / ugly duckling / poor relation / wallflower / backhanded compliment / truth to tell / holy grail / Armageddon / like a bolt from the blue / as if there were no tomorrow / sugar-coating / to sweeten the pot / a spoonful of sugar / to lay something at someone's doorstep / strange bedfellows / to receive something on a silver platter / without breaking stride / to pull one's weight / to throw one's weight around / to make no bones about something / to march to the sound of a different drummer / to call the tune / a minority of one / unwanted consequence / heads will roll / the man of the hour / a man for all seasons / the widow's mite / in a saw-tooth pattern / with a fine-tooth comb /

Proteus / cornucopia / to be dragged into something kicking and screaming / to be put on the spot / to be in the limelight / to keep a low profile / to keep under wraps / to cry all the way to the bank / before the ink was dry / to remain a dead letter / old wives' tales / to be jinxed / a new lease on life / fair-weather friend / the jury is still out / to cramp one's style / straitjacket / smoke and mirrors / the big lie / iron determination / at the crossroads / to go the whole hog / you bet your boots / of the first water / to go with the flow / to be out of one's depth / checks and balances / to pull out all the stops / to seek someone's indulgence / an ace in the hole / a loose cannon / warp and woof / seamless web / to call the shots / to toe the line / to be left high and dry / red tape / to face the fire / to face the music / to cast about for / to know where one stands / to know what one is up against / hairsplitting / a textbook case / to pull the rug out from under / to sweep under the rug / right and left / at low ebb / to touch base / clearinghouse / to have other fish to fry / fire and brimstone / to put a spring in one's step / neither use nor ornament / to add insult to injury / to contain the damage / to cut one's losses / to ride out the storm / to throw good money after bad / to run the gauntlet / whistling in the wind / preaching to the converted / ball and chain / to hang out one's shingle / to plead poverty / to bear the banner of / the movers and shakers / shell game / to withdraw into one's shell / to get one's dander up / the chicken and the egg / trial balloon; feeler; probe / to tell someone to go hang / a significant other / ripple effect / multiplier effect / to percolate / to resonate / to put the squeeze on someone / pincer movement / frontal assault / the salami tactic / grade creep (US) / to be born with a silver spoon in one's mouth / to turn over a new page; to begin a new chapter; to see the error of one's ways / to turn the tables on someone / tunnel vision; one-track mind; blinkered view; crabbed interpretation / beggar-thy-neighbor policy / stealing from Peter to give to Paul / slash-and-burn tactics / no-holds-barred contest / taproot / to tap into / the good egg in the basket / kangaroo court / drumhead tribunal / star chamber / beyond the pale / the gift of gab / to gain ascendancy / a meal ticket / bell, book, and candle / lock, stock, and barrel / a killjoy; a spoilsport; a wowser (Australia) / spot-on (UK) / to catch someone dead to rights; to catch someone red-handed / social safety net / a win-win situation / a no-win situation / a zero-sum game / according to Hoyle / to keep one's head above water / to fly off the handle / to be on the wagon / to roll up one's sleeves / to stand someone up / to play into someone's hands / to be a glutton for punishment / with an iron hand / to mushroom / to weed out / to spread like wildfire / like a child in a candy store / like an elephant in a china shop / like a fish out of water / a spent force / the unkindest cut / to roll with the punches / to believe in horse feathers / to buy the Brooklyn bridge (US) / to earn one's wings, stripes / to hit the ceiling / to hit the road / the moment of truth / judgment day / the sleep of the just / neither fish nor fowl / We're not out of the woods. / This is the kicker. (Caribbean) / not to see the forest for the trees / leapfrogging / piggyback / to split the difference / to treat with kid gloves / Hecuba / to build up a head of steam / the pot calling the kettle black / fire brigade / double standard / This is a stretch. / the ins and outs of something / point blank / to do an end-run around (US) / wishful thinking / to make a dead letter of something / goody two-shoes / unbeknownst to / in the here and now / It's a non-starter. / to zero in on / to fish in troubled waters / to throw oil on the fire / to hold one's fire / to throw down the gauntlet / sunset clause / top-down approach / bottom-up approach / to rise to the challenge / to be on the ball / to blind someone with science / to cross a bridge when you come to it / to put on auto-pilot / to put on the back burner / banana republic / by a twist of fate / to be at daggers drawn / to be at loggerheads / if looks could kill / to fall through the cracks / to flesh out / to be asleep at the switch / to be out to lunch / growing fast as daffodils / to damn with faint praise / to be the poor relation / to have the noose around one's neck / to leave someone twisting in the wind / to kill two birds with one stone / to bury the hatchet / to go for the jugular / going to Saint Ives / to go where angels fear to tread / close, but no cigar / not to put too fine a point on it / to raise a hue and cry / to read someone the riot act / to mince words / to get off dead center (US) / letting the fox guard the chicken-coop / to jump the gun / to cast a pall over / square peg in a round hole / to bite the bullet / a full head of steam / the tail wagging the dog / donkey trading / horse trading / higgledy-piggledy / ready-to-wear / to clam up / water under the bridge / yester-day's papers / grin and bear it / business as usual / swept into the dustbin / to work like a Trojan / hold the reins / to fit like a glove / Neptune / Davy Jones' locker / Goliath / to push the envelope

l'esprit de l'escalier / la salle des pas perdus / des économies de bouts de chandelle / dormir comme un loir / faire long feu / avoir la vie dure / entre deux chaises / survoler la question / le téléphone Arabe / Parnasse / un Jacobin / les Lumières / Pléiade / Janséniste / Bovarysme / Tartuffe / Baron Samedi (Haiti) / malade imaginaire / précieuses ridicules / cri du cœur / en son âme et conscience / ne pas savoir à quel saint se vouer / avocat du diable / médecin malgré lui / garde-fou / à cœur ouvert /

remettre aux calendes grecques / à pas de géant / beau monde / le tout-Paris / la crème de la crème / cordon sanitaire / Marie-Antoinette / revenons à nos moutons / au diable-vauvert / mettre les pieds dans le plat / jeter un pavé dans la mare / appeler un chat un chat / esprit gaulois / esprit cartésien / tout le bastringue / un Auvergnat / Tartempion / Cassandre / Vichy / de premier chef / l'école buissonnière / mouche du coche / jouer les empêcheurs de danser en rond / un Crésus / une sainte-nitouche / une pactole / rabat-joie / faire la part égale à / faire les frais de / prendre le contre-pied de / de rigueur / jeter l'éponge / fuite en avant / entre le marteau et l'enclume / comme sur des roulettes / Untel / un richard / il en va de / la puce / au pif / sans foi ni loi / à petit feu / jeter sa gourme / en sourdine / cheville ouvrière / en filigrane / prêcher pour sa paroisse / avoir l'art du rebond / panier de crabes / Roi Soleil / la loi du talion / chercher midi à quatorze heures / brûler les étapes / en découdre / à la belle étoile / finir en queue de poisson / effet de manche / à l'insu de / bouc émissaire / Bonté divine! / inventer la poudre; inventer le fil à couper le beurre / cul de sac / sauve qui peut / tomber à pic / tomber comme un cheveu sur la soupe / se mettre à table / bras séculier / tête de Turc / enfoncer une porte ouverte / couper des cheveux en quatre / Quel culot! / tourner le couteau dans la plaie / enfoncer le clou / fourre-tout / en faire des choux gras / en bras de chemise / poser un lapin à quelqu'un / mettre quelqu'un en boule / effet d'entraînement / hypothéquer quelque chose / dédouaner quelqu'un; sortir quelqu'un d'affaire / deux poids, deux mesures / mesurer ses mots / avoir des états d'âme / crever l'abcès / chien de faïence / mener à bon port / se voiler la face / tailler les croupières à quelqu'un / serrer les coudes / les coudées franches/ dépasser sa pensée / faire du forcing / la langue de bois / être dans les pommes / enfant terrible / coup de théâtre / un autre son de cloche / chiffres à l'appui / effet pervers / au fur et à mesure /donner carte blanche à quelqu'un / à compte-goutte / un baroud d'honneur / un atout / rester en rade / rester en carafe / battre à plate couture / excès de zèle / pointillisme / cas d'école / un constat d'échec / se rendre à l'évidence / à tort et à travers / à droite et à gauche / ici et là / avoir d'autres chats à fouetter / à la guerre comme à la guerre / commettre une bavure / avoir des atomes crochues avec / mesurer quelque chose à l'aune de / mesurer les autres à son aune / donnant-donnant / violon d'Ingres / à huis clos / prophète de malheur / se montrer bon prophète / bête noire / la poule et l'œuf / faire le jeu de quelqu'un / monter sur ses grands chevaux / faire tache d'huile / faire tache / une autre paire de manches / retrousser ses manches / ni chair ni poisson / avoir la bosse de / Nous ne sommes pas sortis de l'auberge. / un touche-à-tout / loucher sur / les tenants et aboutissants de quelque chose / de but en blanc / baigner dans l'huile / poisson d'avril / un capharnaüm / opposer une fin de non-recevoir à quelque chose / susciter une levée de boucliers / donner blanc-seing / entrer dans le vif du sujet / en marge de / battre en brèche / autant que faire se peut / tourner autour du pot / rendre gré à quelqu'un / être acculé / montrer patte blanche / vider son sac / éclairer la lanterne de quelqu'un / faire d'une pierre deux coups / comme dans un fauteuil / de haute lutte / à la bonne franquette / faire entrer le loup dans la bergerie / faire le dos rond / faire le gros dos / de haut vol / avaler une couleuvre / faire les trois-huits / balayer devant sa porte / n'y voir que du feu / sens dessus-dessous / gagner haut-la-main / de deux choses l'une / voler la vedette à quelqu'un / stratégie de l'arrosoir / Chassez le naturel et il revient au galop. / couper l'herbe sous les pieds à quelqu'un

por las buenas o por las malas / vayamos a nuestro asunto / en el seno de / mantener su criterio / darse de baja / hacer las salvedades del caso / intentona / balconazo / pronunciamiento / cacique / cacicazgo / más cuanto más / Don Juan / El Cid / Bolívar / salir el tiro por la culata / Fulano de Tal / mirar con otras gafas / tragar saliva / jarabe de pico / darse por vencido / vivito y coleando / quedar en el tintero / dar a Dios lo que es de Dios y a César lo que es de César / donde Dios pasó de largo / a Dios rogando y con el mazo dando / encajar la afrenta / arremangarse la camisa / andar sobre ruedas / aguantar a la inglesa / con el agua al cuello / salir de apuros / ricachón / monte de piedad / harina de otro costal / de gran fuste / Sancho Panza / a prueba de bomba / entrar en liza / a duras penas / en fin de cuentas / ir por buen camino / manos a la obra / mojar el pan en / hacerlas de todos los colores / mirarse de reojo / de mala gana / la flor y nata / ni pizca / entregarse en cuerpo y alma a algo / de un embate / ni chicha ni limonada / no pararse en pelillos / quedar pasmado / no tener pelillos en la lengua / buscarle tres pies al gato / entre bastidores / ni siquiera pestañear / quemar las etapas / chivo expiatorio / brillar por su ausencia / arrimar los hombros / sin velos ni cortinas / atando cabos / aumentar la dosis / irse al traste / echar toda la carne a la parrilla (Argentina) / a sabiendas de / dar el visto bueno / tener fuste de / proferir improperios / de improviso / de su calaña / fuera de quicio / ser puntal de / tener la manga ancha / vivir como un polluelo en la estopa / estar anonadado por / abalanzarse contra / lanzar un vítor a / inferir ofensas / apegarse a la antigua usanza / estar atareado / chismorreos / desplegar un cometido / desenredar la madeja / con pocos cuartos / sostener el alma con los dientes / estar bajo la zapatilla de alguien / ser un cero a la izquierda / no importarle algo a uno un ardite, un comino, un bledo /

callejón sin salida / sálvese quien pueda / tomar ojeriza a / poner coto
a algo / un atisbo de / calentarle algo los cascos a uno / hacer aspavien-
tos / cabeza de Turco / no entender ni jota / no pararse en barras /
coger de revés a / frotarse las manos / rebajar la tara de algo / sacar de
quicio a alguien / Que concha! / de poca monta / morderse los puños
/ dar soga a alguien / quedarse como perico en la estaca / moneda de
cambio / al margen de / un Torquemada / de marras / tirar por la borda
/ a desagua / batir millas a la redonda / por puro sabido se olvida /
según su leal saber y entender / pegar el grito en el cielo / asestar un
golpe bajo a alguien / entrar de golpe y porrazo / de frente / no venir
al caso / sin trapujos / echar algo en el saco roto (olvidar) / puras papas
/ llevarle la corriente a alguien / echarle con el rayo a alguien / por
debajo del tapete / más de la cuenta / una vaina / poner en cintura /
tener reparos en / caballito de batalla / predicar en el desierto / lo antes
posible / acto seguido; al tiro (Chile); cuanto antes / poner la otra
mejilla / llover a cántaros / hacer buenas migas con alguien / tener
palito para algo (Colombia) / un paracaidista (squatter) / mala yerba /
a regañadientes / estar en la cartelera / en un tono bajo / talón de
Aquiles / caer en terreno abonado / hacer el parto de los montes / tratar
con guantes de seda / terminar algo con broche de oro / ver la paja en
el ojo del vecino y no la viga en el ojo propio / hacer tabla rasa de algo
/ a sabiendas / a costas de / atar la soga a su cuello / dimes y diretes /
matar la víbora ahora mismo (Argentina) / abonar el terreno / tapar el
sol con un dedo / bajar la guardia / como anillo al dedo / noticias tras-
nochadas / llamarse al engaño / sobran los ejemplos / dormir en sus
laureles / de un tajo / monstruo sagrado / llevar registro de / Los victo-
riosos escriben la historia.

(22) (a) Compare the three lists above and see how many items you can
find which correspond fairly closely to each other in meaning, for
example: 'to call a spade a spade' = 'appeler un chat un chat' / 'Let's
get down to business.' = 'Manos a la obra.'

(b) How many of the expressions listed above are based on some form
of comparison (simile or metaphor)? How many are based on some
form of contrast or opposition between two things?

(c) Classify the expressions listed above according to the categories of
figures of speech given in (2) above (pp. 65–68). Are there any
which do not fit into any of those categories?

(d) Classify the expressions listed above according to level of language,
that is formal, colloquial or slang. Are there any 'borderline cases'? In
English, some slang expressions are sometimes heard, tongue-in-cheek,
even in formal speech (e.g. 'If it ain't broke, don't fix it.') because they

convey an idea very precisely. Are there any such expressions in Spanish or French or in your other working languages?

(23) (a) Give the referent of each of the following cases of antonomasia: l'Hexagone / outre-Rhin / outre-Atlantique / outre-manche / le Roi Soleil

el país Galo / el benemérito de las Américas / el libertadór / el cono sur / los reyes católicos / el manco de Lepanto

south of the Rio Grande / the knight of the sorrowful countenance / the windy city / the ship of the desert / the middle kingdom / the stars and stripes / the city of light / the emerald isle / the mad monk / the evil one / the great emancipator / the roof of the world / the new world / old-world / the grand old party / old hickory / the city of the seven hills / the iron chancellor / the Chicago boys / the lion of Judah / the dismal science / tinsel-town / the empire state / the great helmsman / the Sublime Porte / the admiral of the ocean sea / old ironsides / the mother of parliaments / the arsenal of democracy / the father of the atomic bomb / down under

(b) Are any of the above cases of antonomasia also examples of hyperbole? Are any of them examples of clichés or stereotypes?

(c) Identify or describe the kind of person referred to by the following cases of antonomasia:

a maven / a fan / a spook / a pundit / a spin doctor / a Sherpa / an ad-man / a cover-girl / a pin-up / a dirt lawyer / a mogul / a stringer / an egghead / a computer nerd / a king-maker / a strongman / a gumshoe / a sleuth / a shrink / a curmudgeon / a ghost writer / a point man / a facilitator / a straw man / a hoofer / a bookworm / a bean counter / a policy wonk / an apparatchik / a hack / a hacker / a ham / a paper-shuffler / a gopher / a hatchet-man / a whistle-blower / a highbrow / an angel of mercy

une midinette / un rond-de-cuir / un chef-de-file

un malinchero / un cacique / un hincha

(d) How do the following differ in their connotations?

spy / agent / spook / intelligence operative / member of the intelligence community

expert / egghead / academic / scholar / specialist / pundit

paper-shuffler / bureaucrat / official / civil servant / staffer / staff member

(24) (a) Match the expression in one column with the corresponding one in the other:

when the penny dropped	il pleut des cordes
to take a short cut	se déchaîner
it's raining cats and dogs	manquer le train
to miss the bus	tiré par les cheveux
off the wall	lorsque la lumière jaillit
to let rip	prendre à travers les champs

(b) Match the Chinese proverbs with the corresponding English ones:

Chinese	English
Playing classical music before a cow	Crocodile tears
Leave a chicken in the care of a wildcat	Birds of a feather flock together
Foxes of the same hole	You get what you pay for
A rabbit crying at a fox's funeral	Casting pearls to swine
Three cents money, three cents goods	Asking the fox to guard the chickens

Source: Yutang (1960: 479–485).

(c) Using words from column (i), express the ideas in column (ii):

(i)	(ii)
lemon	He is in a hopeless predicament.
apple	Pavarotti sang in flawless tones.
pear	Paul is a good provider.
egg	He confessed everything.
bacon	Mary is her father's favorite child.
pickle	This is Hollywood's worst film ever.
peanuts	That used car is a piece of junk.
cherries	John is a good, kind-hearted fellow.
orange	I bought this for next to nothing.
beans	Life is full of pleasures.
salami	You can't compare unlike things.
	Make your demands one at a time.
ostrich	He was completely delighted.
duck	She constantly annoys everyone.
crab	He is feigning grief.
hound	They were forced to admit their mistakes.
alligator	He refuses to face the facts.
rabbit	My computer has a desktop cursor command.
crow	He stunned us with his last-minute solution.
clam	He was driven out of office by his enemies.
mouse	This exposed building is an easy target.

(i)	(ii)
canard	What they did was mean.
chouette	She is obsessed with that idea.
vache	The apartment is nice.
cheval	It's only a rumor.

(i)	(ii)
wolf	The foreign minister is a militarist.
lion	The professor is a pacifist.
dove	He is a fierce individualist.
hawk	They got the largest share.

(i)	(ii)
beurre	There's a glitch.
poire	What is the bone of contention here?
pépin	He wants to have his cake and eat it too.
pomme	I am minding my own business.
oignons	Let's meet each other half way.

(i)	(ii)
chasm	an overwhelming electoral majority
peak	a morally unassailable position
summit	an unbridgeable difference of views
landslide	a meeting of high officials
high ground	a climax in the course of events

(d) From the above examples, can you discern any pattern in the way metaphoric idiomatic expressions are formed and how they can be translated?

For example, would it be true to say that metaphors based on common, everyday objects (e.g. 'the *glass* is half empty, not half full') can usually be translated literally? (In this connection, remember, when you are working as part of a multi-language team involving relay, that your sophisticated rendition of a metaphor or proverb into your target language may be quite accurate but still unmanageable to a fellow interpreter taking relay from you in another booth, so that a more literal translation, if it carries the gist of the meaning, may be preferable.)

Notice, for example, that the following reference to a 'local' symbol, because it happens to refer to a common object known to all cultures (a table), can probably be translated literally into any language and be properly understood:

> It is part of his job, [President Aristide] acknowledged, 'to support all the candidates in terms of being neutral'. But, he added, 'Lavalas is Lavalas, so I am around the table', *a reference to the party's symbol of four people seated at a table.* (New York Times, 1995c: A3)

By contrast, consider the following passage containing references to three 'local' Italian symbols. Only two of the three would be fully understood in other languages if translated literally:

> L'**olivier** (*Ulivo*) est une coalition de centre-gauche dirigée par Romano Prodi. Le **chêne** est l'emblème du PDS. Les **buissons** (*cespugli*) sont des mini-partis, souvent sans représentation parlementaire, gravitant autour du centre-gauche (Alliance démocratique, libéraux, etc.). (*Courrier International*, 1995)

The oak tree would convey approximately the same symbolic meaning in other languages (strength, solidity, etc.), and the ironic label 'shrubs' applied to Italy's splintered 'mini-parties' would also carry the same meaning in other languages. But the symbolic meaning of the 'olive-tree' in Italian political discourse probably cannot be fully translated.

Similarly, note the complex symbolic value of the word *carroccio* in the following passage. All of its implications can probably not be captured by any single word in translation; thus, a definitional phrase becomes necessary:

> Bossi is passionate about the first Lombard League – so much so that his followers gave him an oversize oil painting in which he is portrayed as the central figure, in crusader garb, brandishing a sword at the battle of Legnano, the historic defeat of Barbarossa. At that battle, in May of 1176, twelve thousand soldiers of the League halted the march of the Germanic emperor and his four thousand men, who were advancing from Como toward Pavia. Such was the rout that the *carroccio* (a tall battle-chariot flying imperial or local colors which served as the rallying-point for the scattered forces arrayed in battles between city-states) rolled right through the lines of the elite troops and trumpeters surrounding it. Today, the League sees itself as the *carroccio* of Padania in its campaign for independence. (Egurbide, 1996; trans. James Nolan)

Would the symbol used by the Reverend Jesse Jackson's political movement in the United States, the *rainbow*, be translatable into other languages? Would it convey the same idea, that of an all-inclusive diverse coalition?

What are the implications of the symbol used in the following statement (made in reference to the prospect of nuclear proliferation)? Are those implications brought out by a literal translation of the symbol into other languages? If so, why?

A *dark sun* has appeared over the skies of Southern Asia. (Statement by representative of Pakistan)

(e)   The following is a selection of 'universal lexical concepts', that is ideas which linguists have found to exist in virtually all known natural languages. Make a list of as many expressions as possible which use these concepts in each language you know, and then see whether they can be meaningfully translated into the other languages you know:

woman / man / person / fish / bird / dog / tree / seed / leaf / root / bark / skin / flesh / blood / bone / egg / horn / tail / leather / hair / head / ear / eye / nose / mouth / tooth / tongue / claw / foot / knee / hand / belly / neck / breasts / heart / liver / night / name / sun / moon / star / water / rain / stone / sand / earth / cloud / smoke / fire / ash / burn / path / mountain

drink / eat / bite / see / hear / know / sleep / die / kill / swim / fly / walk / come / lie / sit / stand / give / say

all / many / big / long / small / hot / cold / full / new / good / round / dry / red / green / yellow / white / black

(f)   What human qualities or characteristics are usually attributed to the following animals?

fox / wolf / snake / lizard / turtle / hare / dove / lion / lamb / sheep / hawk / monkey / crocodile / worm / ant / bee / beaver / elephant / cow / mule / donkey / eagle / horse / scorpion / dog / pig / shark / weasel / ostrich / eagle

(g)   Explain, illustrate and translate the following:

strong as an ox / busy as a bee / blind as a bat / free as a bird / stubborn as a mule / a mole / sly as a fox / like a bat out of hell / to smell a rat / something fishy / harebrained / to make a monkey of someone / a sitting duck / for the birds

sordo como una tapia / matar la víbora / ser burro

dormir comme un loir / comme une mère-poule / un chat-fourré / anguille sous roche / avaler des couleuvres / avoir une araignée au plafond / faire tourner quelqu'un en bourrique

(h) Why do so many countries portray the eagle on their national crest or emblem?

(i) Explain, illustrate and translate the following:

once in a blue moon / a blue dog Democrat / till you're blue in the face / black humor / purple passion / a greenhorn / to have a green thumb / not one red cent / to be yellow / a gray eminence / to wear black robes / black box / lily-white / blue-eyed boy / a blue-ribbon commission / cordon-bleu / green party / to make it into the black numbers / to be in the red

une arme blanche / être gris / espaces verts

un chiste verde / poner a uno verde / leyenda negra

(j) What does this exercise tell you about the value of using metaphors in simultaneous interpretation, when concision is at a premium during a fast-paced speech?

(25) The following passage has been translated twice, first from Japanese to French, then from French to English:

In the world of the stock exchange there is a saying that has long been popular: 'Behind the beaten path there is another that leads to the mountain of flowers.' It means that, to succeed in business, you should do the opposite of what others are doing. (Swimming against the current, *Asahi Shimbun* (Tokyo) (excerpt))

(a) Do you think it probable that the *flavor* of the original Japanese saying has been preserved through both translations? If so, why?

(b) In this particular case, is it more appropriate to translate the proverb literally, as has been done above, or to attempt to transpose the idea into an equivalent saying in the target language?

(c) If this were a speech rather than an article, would the interpretation of the proverb be particularly difficult, since the speaker himself goes on to explain in plain words precisely what it means?

(d) Could the image of 'the pot of gold at the end of the rainbow' be used to transpose the Japanese image of 'the mountain of flowers'?

If so, how would the rest of the statement be phrased? (see Chapter 12: Transposition, pp. 205–210.)

(e)   Since the thrust of the Japanese saying is that businessmen should be bold enough not to follow the crowd, could the proverb 'Nothing ventured, nothing gained' be paraphrased to translate the above passage?

(f)   Could the American stock-exchange image of 'bulls and bears' be called into service to translate this Japanese saying, or would it do violence to the flavor of the original?

(26) In the following statement, notice that the idea underlying the simile could be expressed in a variety of ways besides the figure of speech chosen by the speaker:

> pour conduire toutes ces actions, l'ONU a besoin de moyens financiers. Nous devons les lui donner à travers les contributions des Etats; car sans elles notre Organisation serait comme *'une voiture sans carburant'*. (Statement by the President of Gabon)

The speaker is simply saying that, without money, the UN cannot perform its functions. One could put this in various ways, for example 'a car without fuel' or 'a locomotive without steam' or 'a ship without sails', etc. Translate the statement into English, Spanish or another language in as many different ways as you can. Then repeat the exercise, into French, Spanish or another language with the following excerpts from another speech:

> And, as we build an international capacity to keep peace, let us join in dismantling the national capacity to wage war. This will require new strength and new roles for the United Nations. For disarmament without **checks** is but a **shadow** – and a community without law is but a **shell**. ... Today, every inhabitant of this planet must contemplate the day when this planet may be no longer habitable. Every man, woman and child lives under a nuclear **sword of Damocles**, hanging by **the slenderest of threads**, capable of being **cut** at any moment by accident or miscalculation or by madness. The weapons of war must be abolished before they abolish us. ... And unless man can match his **strides** in weapons and technology with equal **strides** in social and political development, our great strength, **like that of the dinosaur**, will become incapable of proper control – and, like the **dinosaur**, will vanish from the earth. ... In that search we cannot expect any final triumph – for new problems will always arise. We cannot expect that all nations will adopt like systems – for **conformity is the jailer of freedom and**

the enemy of growth. Nor can we expect to reach our goal by contrivance, by fiat or even by the wishes of all. (Statement by President John F. Kennedy to the United Nations General Assembly, 25 September 1963 (excerpts))

(27) (a) Translate the following passage into French, Spanish or other working languages. Translate the proverb first literally and then, if possible, by an equivalent proverb or other figure of speech:

> voices can be heard today expressing pessimism about the future of our organization. We prefer the opinion that this organization is proving its continuing viability through its actions. Let me refer to a **Slovak proverb, 'If you do nothing you cannot make a mistake'**. In this respect the willingness ... of the United Nations to take and further accept the burden of great responsibility deserves our highest appreciation. (Statement by the President of the Slovak Republic)

(b) Translate the following passage into English, Spanish or other working languages. Translate the proverb first literally and then, if possible, by an equivalent proverb or other figure of speech:

> Si seule une minorité de bureaucrates profite réellement du pillage de l'Etat, il n'empêche que le processus de redistribution touche à de nombreux effectifs. **'Si tu ne voles pas l'Etat, tu voles ta famille'** confirme **un proverbe tchèque**, qui pourrait tenir lieu de devise à bien d'autres pays de la planète. (Tolotti, 1955)

(c) Could the Czech proverb above be translated by means of a paraphrase of the expression 'robbing Peter to give to Paul'?

(d) Translate the following passage into English, French or other working languages. Translate the parable first literally and then by means of an equivalent parable, proverb or other figure of speech:

> El Senado, **con el agua al cuello**, mandó embajada tras embajada a los plebeyos para inducirles a regresar a la ciudad y a colaborar en la defensa común. Y Menenio Agripa, para convencerles, les contó **la historia de aquel hombre cuyos miembros, para fastidiar al estomago, se habían negado a procurarle comida: con lo que, habiéndose quedado sin alimento, acabaron por morir ellos también, como el órgano del cual querían vengarse**. (Montanelli, 1959; trans. Pruna, 1969: 45)

(e) Translate the following passages into Spanish, French or other working languages, using equivalent figurative language:

> The Amman Summit, in accordance with the Casablanca Declaration, also **mapped** out **key** institutional arrangements to **underpin** the peace process.

> Even more than the 'distinct society' provision, the Chrétien veto formula has **roiled waters** in western Canada ... A popular talk-show radio host in Vancouver likened the provincial anger to **a slow burn in a peat bog** that 'will become an ever-increasing resentment against both Quebec and the Federal Government'. He added, 'It will eventually **burst into the flames** of a far western separation'. (*The New York Times*, 1995c: A3)

(28) (a) Using concrete images and objects from everyday life, make up proverbs that convey the following lessons:

> Children are often wiser than their elders. / Politicians will promise everything to everyone merely to get votes. / Countries that invent new weapons are inviting trouble. / Making money too easily spoils one's character. / Leadership is acquired through experience. / Statistics can be used to prove anything. / Humor makes life bearable. / In war there are no winners or losers. / It takes courage to compromise.

(b) It has been suggested that Julius Caesar was assassinated partly because he was too generous and unsuspecting toward his enemies. He could not have failed to know that plots were being hatched around him but he doubted that his enemies were brave enough to take action. State the lesson of this story in the form of a proverb or maxim. Then read the fable 'Les Loups et les Brebis' (La Fontaine, 1962: 95–96). Does it convey the same message?

(29) (a) The following maxims have been translated from French into Spanish. Explain their meaning, and try to reconstruct the original French from the Spanish translation. Then, relying on the Spanish and French versions, translate the meaning into an English maxim or other figure of speech:

> 'Todo el mundo habla mal de su memoria y nadie de su entendimiento.' / 'El rehusar la loanza es deseo de ser dos veces loado.' / 'Muchos se enamorarían si no hubieran oído hablar nunca del

amor.' / 'Loar a los príncipes de las virtudes que no tienen es injuriarlos impunemente.' / 'A veces basta ser ignorante para no ser engañado por un hombre hábil.' / 'Remedios hay para curar la locura, pero no los hay para curar un espíritu rebelde.' (La Rochefoucauld, in Azorín, 1958: 53–56)
'No existe otra manera de conocer sino por discusión' / 'Conocer por sentimiento es la mas alta manera de conocer.' / 'No hay siglo ni pueblo que no hayan establecido virtudes y vicios imaginarios.' (Vauvenargues, in Azorín, 1958)

(b) How does La Rochefoucauld's maxim 'L'esprit est toujours la dupe du Coeur' ('The mind is always deceived by the heart') differ from the saying 'Le Coeur a des raisons que la raison ne connaît pas' ('The heart has reasons that reason does not know')?

(30) The following sentences have been well translated from idiomatic Italian into idiomatic Spanish. Translate them into equally **idiomatic** English, French or other working languages, taking special care with the idioms in bold type:

'Fue una lucha prolongada y **sin exclusión de golpes**, pero al vencido **no le dejaron ni ojos para llorar**.' (Montanelli, 1959; trans. Pruna, 1969: 16) / '... la República romana reemprendió **el camino de la guerra** a **mitad** del cual se habían detenido sus antiguos reyes. ...' (ibid., p. 41) / 'Tal vez Tarquino **alargó tanto la mano** para hacer olvidar el modo con que **subió al trono sobre el cadáver de** un rey generoso y popular.' (ibid., p. 34) / 'De aquella masa, sólo la inscrita ya en los "comicios curados" **tenía voz en capítulo** y podía votar.' (ibid., p. 32) / 'La división racial continuó lo menos cien años, durante los cuales latinos y sabinos, fusionados ya en el tipo romano, **debieron tragar mucha saliva**.' (ibid., p. 22) / 'No había funcionado **la cochura**, es decir, la fusión entre las razas y las clases que constituían su pueblo.' (ibid., p. 40) / 'Esta gran victoria y el ejemplar castigo **que la rubicó** llenaron de orgullo a los romanos.' (ibid., p. 46) / 'Como de costumbre, Roma **encajó la afrenta**, pero no pidió paz.' (ibid., p. 51) / 'Era, en suma, como se diría hoy, **un tipo que buscaba maraña**.' (ibid., p. 52)

(31) Translate the following into idiomatic English, Spanish or other working languages:

Bill Clinton rencontre ... des difficultés à convaincre le Congrès d'approuver l'envoi de quelque 20,000 soldats américains en Bosnie. Or l'un des moyens dont il dispose est de pouvoir affirmer que l'opération sera entièrement **pilotée** par l'OTAN, l'ONU, **bête noire** des républicains, étant **tenue à l'écart**. (*Le Monde*, 1995a)

(32) (a) Translate the proverbs and idiomatic expressions below into their underlying idea and then into French, Spanish or your other working languages by expressing the idea without using the image of 'fire'.

> *Example*: 'Where there's smoke there's fire.'
> *Underlying idea*: two natural phenomena so closely associated that the presence of one is a sure sign of the other.
> *Translation*: 'Donde hay lluvia, hay nubes.'

> to tend the fires / to keep the home fires burning / to have more than one iron in the fire / to jump from the frying-pan into the fire / to play with fire / the fad spread like a house on fire / to throw oil on the fire / to pull someone's chestnuts out of the fire / to fight fire with fire / to throw the fat into the fire / with fire and sword / to build a fire under someone / to put one's hand in the fire for someone

(b) Which of the explanatory paraphrases below do you think best sums up the meaning of the old Native American proverb 'White men build big fires and sit far back; Indians build small fires and sit close up'?

- White men are less resistant to cold weather.
- White men can afford more firewood.
- White men are more wasteful than Indians because they lack respect for nature.
- Indians are afraid of big fires.
- White men don't like to sit close together.

If an unfamiliar proverb is likely to be misunderstood by the listeners, should an explanatory paraphrase be preferred by the interpreter?

(c) Translate the expressions below by expressing the underlying idea without using the 'foot' image:

> to sweep someone of his feet / to drag one's feet / to shoot oneself in the foot / to stand on one's own two feet / to put your foot in it / to kick up one's feet / to have one foot in the grave / to have both feet on the ground / to have one foot in the door / to put one's best foot forward / to think on one's feet / to foot the bill / from head to foot / to jump in with both feet

mettre les pieds dans le plat / à pied levé / faire des pieds et des mains / vivre sur un grand pied / sur un pied d'égalité / de pied ferme / mettre quelqu'un au pied du mur

dar pie a / meter la pata / al pie de la hora / echar el pie atras a

(d) How many idioms can you think of, in any language, which use the following words pertaining to the human body?

skin / hand / arm / leg / face / neck / back / finger / thumb / eye / ear / head / stomach / shoulder / nose / cheek / knee / knuckle / hair / brow / wrinkle / chin / beard / tooth / tongue

(e) Explain, illustrate, and translate the following:

to put one's finger to the wind / to do an about-face / in one ear and out the other / to take it on the chin / to cost an arm and a leg / within earshot / back-breaking / to be on someone's back / to slip through one's fingers / to turn one's back on / to have a chip on one's shoulder / not to lift a finger / the long arm of the law / to wear your heart on your sleeve / to keep an ear to the ground / to keep someone's nose to the grindstone / to thumb one's nose at / as plain as the nose on one's face / to fly in the face of / high-handed / to lay hands on someone / to lay a hand on someone / a laying-on of hands / all hands on deck / to give someone a hand / a show of hands / to have something at hand / to have a hand in something / to be in someone's hands / to hold out one's hand to someone / I've got to hand it to you. / to unhand someone / to do something with both hands tied behind one's back / to keep on hand / to raise one's hand in anger / to be handy / to do something handily / to go hand in hand with / to throw up one's hands / to click one's tongue / the evil eye / by a hair's breadth / to make one's hair stand on end / to bend over backwards for someone / to split hairs / to let one's hair down / to keep at arm's length / an arm's-length relationship / to go to one's head / It's a load off my shoulders. / to raise eyebrows / to stand the truth on its head / to shake a leg / to touch one's forelock / the shoe is on the other foot / straight from the shoulder / to shoot from the hip / to make the cut / to make the grade / to go for the jugular / to see eye to eye with someone / to be on equal footing / to think on one's feet / to elbow out / to scratch someone's back / to stick out one's neck for someone / to give someone a leg-up / to lay something at someone's feet / Don't bite the hand that feeds you. / to keep an eye out for

faire une tête-à-queue / faux-nez / coûter les yeux de la tête / faire le gros dos / en avoir plein le dos / avoir bon dos / se mettre tout le monde à dos / se mettre le doigt dans l'œil / avoir froid aux yeux / tiré par les cheveux / monter à la tête / dormir sur ses deux oreilles / se casser la tête / se casser le nez / se casser les dents sur / se casser la figure / travailler d'arrache-pied / avoir les coudées franches

a dos dedos de / alzar el dedo / irse de los dedos / tener en la punta de los dedos / poner el dedo en la llaga / sacar pecho / una tomada de pelo / con pelos y señales / dejar a alguien boquiabierta / jugarse el pellejo / subírsele a uno los humos a la cabeza

(f)   Translate the expressions below by expressing the underlying idea without using the word 'tooth':

to be long in the tooth / to cut one's teeth on / to sow dragon's teeth / to get one's teeth into / by the skin of one's teeth / in the teeth of / armed to the teeth

de dientes afuera / más cerca están mis dientes que mis parientes / enseñar los dientes / hablar entre los dientes / hincar el diente en / pelar el diente / tener buen diente

ne pas desserrer les dents / cela fait grincer les dents / montrer les dents / avoir une dent contre quelqu'un / avoir la dent dure / avoir les dents longues / être sur les dents

(g)   Translate the following by expressing the underlying idea without using the word 'cat':

There's more than one way to skin a cat. / He has more lives than a cat. / He was as nervous as a cat on a hot tin roof. / When the cat's away the mice will play. / She had a Cheshire-cat smile. / Curiosity killed the cat. / Like a cat, he always lands on his feet. / You're the cat's pajamas. / He came in looking like the cat who got the cream. / Has the cat got your tongue? / Don't let the cat out of the bag.

No hay que buscarle tres pies al gato. / correr como gato por ascuas / vender gato por liebre / buscar el gato en el garbanzal / De noche todos los gatos son pardos. / Se pelearon como gatos callejeros. / echarle a uno el gato a la barba / El gato maullador, nunca buen cazador. / llevar el gato al agua / Hasta los gatos quieren zapatos!

Chat échaudé craint l'eau froide. / Il faut appeler un chat un chat. / avoir un chat dans la gorge / A bon chat, bon rat. / Il n'y a pas un chat ici. / acheter chat en poche / Ne réveillez pas le chat qui dort.

(h) How many idioms can you think of, in any language, which use the following words pertaining to food and the table?

harvest / meat / fruit / cup / dish / glass / spoon / skewer / salt / wine / bread / spice / cake / feast / tea / cook / kitchen / grill / butter / sauce / soup / milk / honey / stew / pudding / pie / apple

(i) Explain, illustrate and translate the following:

to have one's cake and eat it too / grapes of wrath / to scatter banana peels / pie in the sky / to be sandwiched between / to be in the soup / to stew / from soup to nuts / cherry-picking

couper la poire en deux / comme un cheveu sur la soupe / chercher des noix / On ne fait pas d'omelette sans casser des œufs. / Ils essaient d'écrémer les postes les plus avantageux.

(j) Translate the following by expressing the underlying idea in a sentence without using the word 'devil':

Better the devil you know than the devil you don't. / We've agreed on the principles, but the devil is in the details. / We must do the right thing, to beat the devil. / Our environmental laws have gone to the devil. / She's as happy-go-lucky and devil-may-care as they come. / Keep busy; idle hands are the devil's play. / We're between the devil and the deep blue sea. / The kids spent their holiday raising the devil. / There is a campaign by the press to demonize our president. / It's the old 'the devil made me do it' attitude. / I was only playing devil's advocate.

Mi abuelo dice que más sabe el diablo por viejo que por diablo. / Corrige tu conducta; no le des quehacer al diablo. / Toda esa gente se ha dado a los diablos. / De repente, tiró el diablo de la manta. / Vaya el diablo por ruin! / El diablo harto de carne se metió a fraile.

Ils font le diable à quatre. / Ces pauvres gens tirent le diable par la queue. / Laissez-moi faire l'avocat du diable. / L'enfant s'agitait comme un diable dans un bénitier. / Ils habitent au diable vauvert.

(k) Which of the French 'devil' idioms above corresponds to the English idiom 'like a cat on a hot tin roof'? Which of the English 'devil' idioms above corresponds to the Spanish idiom 'irse al traste'?

Which of the Spanish 'devil' idioms above corresponds closely to the English idiom 'to pull a rabbit out of a hat'? Which English 'devil' idiom above corresponds closely to the Spanish idiom 'estar entre la espada y la pared'?

(l) Translate the following without using words relating to 'string', 'cord' or 'rope':

Those hollow promises are meant just to string us along. / In the nuclear era, we live under a sword of Damocles hanging by the slenderest of threads. / We are tied down by a thousand legal strings like Gulliver in Lilliput. / For non-oil-producing developing states, the energy crisis is a Gordian knot. / We're at the end of our rope. / His ideas sound a bit ropey. / Be careful; there's a loophole in this agreement. / If you accept that offer, you're putting your head in the noose. / It's money for old rope.

El profesor comenzó a apretar la cuerda. / La opera no es de mi cuerda. / Eres muy estricto; afloja la cuerda. / Andas en la cuerda floja; decídete una vez por todas! / Tal vez tengas razón, pero no somos de tu cuerda. / La oposición actuó por debajo de la cuerda. / Aquí no hay privilegios; tiramos de la cuerda para todos.

C'est un argument cousu de fil blanc. / Il faut avoir plus d'une corde à son arc. / Le président évolue sur une corde raide. / Prends ton parapluie; il pleut des cordes. / Les informaticiens croient avoir inventé le fil à couper le beurre. / Je n'ai pas pu suivre le fil de cet argument.

(m) Translate the following without using the word 'horse':

To everyone's surprise, the party convention produced a dark horse candidate for the presidency. / The candidate appearing on the bill-boards is merely a stalking horse; the party secretary general will wield power if they win the election. / She will go out with you, but she says that marrying you would be a horse of a different color. / French chefs say that Americans who eat the salad first are putting the cart before the horse. / The boy did not mean to hurt anyone; he was just horsing around. / Wild horses could not drag me to that dull reception. / NASA plans to use the space shuttle as a work-horse for building an orbital station. / He got on his high horse and gave us a long sermon about double standards. / If you don't believe me, ask the director and get it straight from the horse's mouth. / He's still lampooning his rival even after winning the election; he's flogging a dead horse. / Don't ask why they gave you the scholarship; never look a gift horse in the mouth. / The entry of that faction into the group is a Trojan horse.

La situation dans ce pays ravagé exige un remède de cheval. / La délégation américaine est à cheval sur la question de la réforme administrative.

La productividad se ha vuelto el caballito de batalla de los economistas neo-liberales.

(n)   Write new illustrative sentences with each of the expressions in (m) above. Then translate each sentence, using an idiomatic expression with equivalent meaning if one exists.

(33) (a)   At an international meeting, an American speaker objected to a perceived redundancy by describing it as 'a belt-and-suspenders style of thinking'. Another common way of making this point in English is to describe something as 'overkill'. How would you say this figuratively in Spanish, French or other working languages?
At a budgetary meeting, a participant expressed suspicion about a funding request because it was so elaborately justified. He used the French expression 'Celui qui s'excuse s'accuse'. Could the word 'overkill' also be used to render this idea?

(b)   At an international meeting, an American speaker referred to a very general policy prescription as 'a one-size-fits-all policy'. How would you say this figuratively in Spanish, French or other working languages?

(c)   At an international meeting, a British speaker advocating reduced funding ironically said that a given program would not be implemented unless it could find 'a fairy godmother'. How would you say this in Spanish, French or other working languages?

(d)   At an international meeting, an American representative objecting to bureaucratic hypertrophy described a proposed program as having potential for 'mammoth' growth. How would you say this in Spanish, French or your other working languages? Could the word 'mammoth' sometimes be used to translate 'faraónico' or 'pharaonique', in the sense of 'proyectos faraónicos' / 'projets pharaoniques'? Would 'gargantuan' be another equivalent? Can you think of others?

(e)   At an international meeting, a Mexican representative objecting to excessive resource reductions warned that austerity could be pushed to counterproductive extremes by saying, 'Sí, ahorremos forraje, pero tengamos cuidado que el caballo no se muera de hambre!' Can this image, based on a familiar animal, be translated literally? How many other ways can you think of to make this point in English, French or your other working languages?

(f)   At an international meeting, an Argentine speaker expressed his satisfaction at being fully informed about a peace agreement by using a mixed metaphor combined with a folk proverb: 'Antes, recibíamos solamente **píldoras** de información. Ahora, como se dice en mi país, se nos ha puesto **toda la carne en la parrilla**!'

The English interpreter translated the first part of the mixed metaphor as 'We used to receive only pills of information ...' but was then thrown off by the sudden switch in the mixed metaphor from the medical to the culinary domain and translated the second part as 'Now, as they say in my country, we have put all the meat on the fire'. However, to make sure that the point was clear, the English interpreter added 'we now have a great deal on the table' and 'we now have plenty on our plate' at subsequent points in the Argentine speaker's statement where he repeated his image. The point was understood, and the meeting went on.

However, the Argentine speaker was not satisfied with this rendition and, at the end of the meeting, repeated his proverb and corrected the English interpreter. The second time, the interpreter rendered the proverb as 'putting all the meat on the grill'.

The Argentine representative was still not satisfied and insisted that the correct English translation was 'To put all the meat on the barbecue'.

The English interpreter had avoided the word 'barbecue' for two reasons. First, it is a peculiarly American usage which might have been difficult to translate by the interpreters relaying from English, whereas 'fire' or 'grill' are more concrete and cross-cultural, and hence more easily transposable into the figurative repertory of other languages. Second, in American speech registers, 'barbecue' has a vernacular and festive resonance, much like the word 'carnival', which seemed to clash with the serious and solemn tone of a meeting marking the end of a long war. (The Argentine speaker may have been unaware of this because the Spanish word 'barbacoa', from which the American 'barbecue' derives, has a neutral resonance.)

•   What should an interpreter do when the speaker insists on his own translation of a proverb or figure of speech peculiar to his culture?

- If the speaker is unaware that his or her preferred translation is stylistically awkward, should the interpreter make any effort to correct the speaker?
- In the above example, there was no doubt that the speaker had clearly gotten his point across. Consequently, the correction of the interpreter at the end of the meeting was gratuitous. How should an interpreter respond to such 'corrections'?
- Can you think of a better translation of the Argentine proverb?

(g) In a televised interview, US General Norman Schwartzkopf said that, if the United States had remained in Iraq after the Gulf War, it would have been in the position of 'a dinosaur in a tar pit'. Translate this idea into Spanish, French or your other working languages using different images.

(h) At an international meeting on the financial problems of the UN, a New Zealand representative objected to a proposal for creating incentives to get countries to clear their UN arrears by saying: 'There can be no cookies for those who are raiding the cookie jar'. How might you say this in Spanish, French or your other working languages?

(34) (a) What is the meaning of 'fuite en avant' in the two passages below? Of the following possible English equivalents, choose the one that would work best in each case:

> evasion / plunging ahead / open the floodgates / escapism / obstinacy / denial / to be in denial / to persist in error / self-delusion / wishful thinking

> A l'Est, la libéralisation économique et politique a provoqué une véritable **fuite en avant**. 'Il n'y a plus d'éthique de la nomen-klatura administrative,' constate Marie Mendras, spécialiste de la Russie. (Tolotti, 1995)

> On comprend mieux, sans les excuser, les folies financières d'un Crédit lyonnais cherchant à maintenir son rang international par une **fuite en avant** qui s'est révélée suicidaire. (Simonnot, 1995)

(b) Is the French expression 'fuite en avant' roughly equivalent to the Spanish verb 'despeñarse'? Is it roughly synonymous with the French 's'obstiner'? At another level of language, can it mean the same thing as the English expression 'to be pigheaded'?

(35) Paraphrase the clichés listed below so that their conventional meaning is reversed, for example: 'It's a nice place to visit, but I wouldn't want to live there' > 'It's a nice place to live, but I wouldn't want to visit there.' Consider what your paraphrase means and whether it would be recognized as a paraphrase of the original cliché.

They snatched victory from the jaws of defeat. / The rich get richer and the poor get poorer. / It is better to give than to receive. / Hell hath no fury like a woman scorned. / East is East and West is West. / The bigger they are, the harder they fall. / Where there's a will there's a way. / Slowly, slowly catchy monkey. / Too many cooks spoil the broth. / You can't have your cake and eat it too. / He who ignores history is condemned to repeat it. / He who pays the piper calls the tune. / Good fences make good neighbors. / All dressed up and nowhere to go.

Les bons comptes font les bons amis. / Les absents ont toujours tort.

A buen entendedor, pocas palabras.

(36) Explain the meaning of the following numerical expressions. Form illustrative sentences with each, then translate the sentences into your other working languages:

foursquare / fourscore / three square meals / within the four corners of / at the eleventh hour / to give someone the third degree / to take the fifth / to be in seventh heaven / the seven seas / the seventh art / a baker's dozen / Two's company, three's a crowd. / The third time's the charm. / the third world / the third way / the fourth world / the big four / the twelve / the permanent five / the seventy-seven / to be behind the eight-ball / to cry to the four winds / the fourth estate / third party / third state / third-rate / second-class / to play second fiddle / the third age / It takes two to tango. / the whole nine yards / fifth column / double-dealing / to be two-faced / two-timing / to listen to one's second mind / to second a motion / to have second thoughts / to catch one's second breath / the hundred names / the seven wonders of the world / the seven deadly sins / to be at sixes and sevens / from the four corners of the earth / the four horsemen of the Apocalypse / the three tigers / double dipping

faire les cent pas / se mettre en quatre pour quelqu'un / ne pas y aller par quatre chemins / Il n'y a pas trente-six solutions. / un de ces quatre matins / trois-étoiles / le troisième age / avoir la quarantaine

/ des dizaines / en moins de deux / à deux pas / avoir plus d'une corde à son arc

buscarle la quinta pata al gato / diezmar / cada dos por tres / en un dos por tres / entre dos aguas / un cero a la izquierda

(37) *Analogy.* An argument by analogy is an argument that presents 'the big picture'. Analogy is often used as a compelling way of conveying the broad sweep of situations that speakers consider important. It differs from the metaphors that may intersperse a speech in the same way as a large canvas occupying a whole wall at an exhibition differs from a series of small canvases hung along a corridor. Metaphors are impressionistic; analogies are panoramic.

Identifying an analogy is important to interpreters because, while metaphors can be considered in the same category as various other figures of speech, an analogy has to be rendered as a unified whole, including all the details.

Below are two analogies that were used by influential speakers at the beginning and at the end of World War I. One was intended to convince people to go to war, while the other was intended to convince people that wars could be prevented. The first formed the conclusion of a speech by Lloyd George in London on 19 September 1914, and the second formed the conclusion of a speech by Woodrow Wilson at Pueblo, Colorado on 25 September 1919:

> May I tell you in a simple parable what I think this war is doing for us? I know a valley in North Wales, between the mountains and the sea. It is a beautiful valley, snug, comfortable, sheltered by the mountains from all the bitter blasts. But it is very enervating, and I remember how the boys were in the habit of climbing the hill above the village to have a glimpse of the great mountains in the distance, and to be stimulated and freshened by the breezes which came from the hilltops, and by the great spectacle of their grandeur. We have been living in a sheltered valley for generations. We have been too comfortable and too indulgent, many, perhaps, too selfish, and the stern hand of fate has scourged us to an elevation where we can see the great everlasting things that matter for a nation – the peaks we had forgotten, of Honor, Duty, Patriotism, and, clad in glittering white, the great pinnacle of sacrifice pointing like a rugged finger to Heaven.

> You will say, 'Is the League [of Nations] an absolute guarantee against war?' No; I do not know any absolute guarantee against the

errors of human judgment or the violence of human passion, but I tell you this: with a cooling space of nine months for human passion, not much of it will keep hot. I had a couple of friends who were in the habit of losing their tempers, and when they lost their tempers they were in the habit of using very unparliamentary language. Some of their friends induced them to make a promise that they never would swear inside the town limits. When the impulse next came upon them, they took a streetcar to go out of town, or to swear, and by the time they got out of town they did not want to swear. They came back convinced that they were just what they were, a couple of unspeakable fools, and the habit of getting angry and of swearing suffered great inroads upon it by that experience. Now, illustrating the great by the small, that is true of the passions of men, however you combine them. Give them space to cool off.

(a)   Which of the above speakers tells his story more vividly, Lloyd George or Woodrow Wilson?

(b)   Which speaker faces the more difficult challenge, Lloyd George urging his fellow citizens that they must sacrifice in order to win a war that is inevitable, or Woodrow Wilson urging his fellow citizens that, if they sacrifice now, future wars are not inevitable? Since the latter argument probably seemed to fly in the face of the received wisdom of the times, was Wilson's homely analogy sufficiently compelling? Can you think of a better analogy to make the same point?

(c)   Translate the above passages into French, Spanish or your other working languages, taking care to preserve the narrative unity of each story as well as the details.

8 Argumentation

Argumentation relies primarily on logic and/or emotion, in varying doses. An interpreter must be alert to both and remember that they are not mutually exclusive and that neither is better per se. A logically sound argument can be embellished or made more compelling by a poetic choice of words, or a moral argument can be stated in such powerful terms that it overwhelms all logical objections. If a speaker's logic is faulty, the interpreter's voice must not betray the absurdity. And if the speaker waxes lyrical to a degree that the interpreter finds ridiculous, the interpreter's voice must not betray his skepticism. This requires interpreters to be aware of patterns in speech (see Annex III) and to develop some appreciation of both logical and emotive rhetoric.

Exercises

(1) Imagine that you are delivering a speech to an association in order to advocate a change in a law which you consider foolish. What arguments would you use? In what order? From the simplest to the most complex, or vice versa? What evidence could you offer in support of your proposal? Would you state your proposal at the outset or conclude with it? Would you spell it out plainly, or only hint at it and let the audience reach its own conclusions? How would you refute any counter-arguments you might anticipate?

(2) Read the excerpt below from Abraham Lincoln's 'Address at Cooper Institute', a presidential campaign speech delivered in 1860 and subsequently reprinted in many newspapers. This speech illustrates the use of cold logic in the midst of a passionate debate. It also provides a good example of skillful political polemics and, at the same time, a good lesson in constitutional legal argument, or argument from authority. In a speech of this kind, it is precision, not hyperbole, that counts. Such statements demand great attention to detail on the part of an

interpreter, who must carefully follow every step in the speaker's train of thought.

It is important for an interpreter to bear in mind that, in a speech of this kind, a speaker may have to present in detail positions with which he or she is known to disagree. Unlike the situation where the speaker *inadvertently* says the opposite of what he means (in which case the interpreter may correct the speaker's slip of the tongue), the speaker making this type of argument is *deliberately* making a full statement of his opponent's case before proceeding to refute it.

Notice that the speech does not simply set up Lincoln's theory against those who argue the opposite theory. Rather, as the good lawyer that he was, Lincoln accepts their premises, meets them on their own ground and goes on to prove that they are wrong *by their own standards*. The bulk of the speech is devoted to showing that, even if 'founding father knew best', he, or they, did not intend that pernicious institutions like slavery should forever remain a part of the American political landscape. Remember that, at the time of this speech, slavery still existed throughout the American South and threatened to spread. Consequently, there was nothing academic or theoretical about Lincoln's argument and indeed, in his day, he ran the risk of seeming eccentric by suggesting that something which had 'always existed' should cease to exist. It was crucial, therefore, that his arguments be flawlessly logical and cogent, as they are.

> Mr. President and fellow citizens of New York: The facts with which I shall deal this evening are mainly old and familiar; nor is there anything new in the general use I shall make of them. ... In his speech last autumn at Columbus, Ohio ... Senator Douglas said: 'Our fathers, when they framed the Government under which we now live, understood this question just as well, and even better, than we do now'. I fully indorse this, and I adopt it as a text for this discourse. ... It simply leaves the inquiry: 'What was the understanding those fathers had of the question mentioned?' What is the frame of government under which we live?
>
> The answer must be 'The Constitution of the United States'. That Constitution consists of the original, framed in 1787 ... and twelve subsequently framed amendments. ... Who were our fathers that framed the Constitution? I suppose the 'thirty-nine' who signed the original instrument. ...
>
> What is the question which, according to the text, those fathers understood 'just as well, and even better than we do now'? It is

this: Does the proper division of local from federal authority, or anything in the Constitution, forbid our *Federal Government* to control as to slavery *in our federal territories?* Upon this, Senator Douglas holds the affirmative, and Republicans the negative. ...

Let us now inquire whether the 'thirty-nine', or any of them, ever acted upon this question; and if they did, how they acted upon it – how they expressed that better understanding? In 1784, three years before the Constitution – the United States then owning the Northwestern Territory, and no other, the Congress of the Confederation had before them the question of prohibiting slavery in that Territory; and four of the 'thirty nine' who afterward framed the Constitution, were in that Congress, and voted on that question. Of these, Roger Sherman, Thomas Mifflin, and Hugh Williamson voted for the prohibition, thus showing that, in their understanding, no line dividing local from federal authority, nor anything else, properly forbade the Federal Government to control as to slavery in federal territory. The other of the four – James M'Henry – voted against the prohibition, showing that, for some cause, he thought it improper to vote for it.

In 1787, still before the Constitution, but while the Convention was in session framing it, and while the Northwestern Territory still was the only territory owned by the United States, the same question of prohibiting slavery in the territory again came before the Congress of the Confederation; and two more of the 'thirty-nine' who afterward signed the Constitution were in Congress and voted on the question. They were William Blount and William Few; and they both voted for the prohibition – thus showing that, in their understanding, no line dividing local from federal authority, nor anything else, properly forbids the Federal Government to control as to slavery in federal territory. This time the prohibition became a law, being part of ... the Ordinance of '87.

In 1789, by the first Congress which sat under the Constitution, an act was passed to enforce the Ordinance of '87, including the prohibition of slavery in the Northwestern Territory. The bill for this act was reported by one of the 'thirty-nine', Thomas Fitzsimmons, then a member of the House of Representatives from Pennsylvania. It went through all its stages without a word of opposition, and finally passed both branches without yeas and nays, which is equivalent to an unanimous passage. In this Congress there were sixteen of the thirty-nine fathers who framed the original Constitution. ...

This shows that, in their understanding, no line dividing local from federal authority, nor anything in the Constitution, properly forbade Congress to prohibit slavery in the federal territory; else both their fidelity to correct principle, and their oath to support the Constitution, would have constrained them to oppose the prohibition.

Again, George Washington, another of the 'thirty-nine', was then President of the United States, and, as such, approved and signed the bill; thus completing its validity as a law, and thus showing that, in his understanding, no line dividing local from federal authority, nor anything in the Constitution, forbade the Federal Government to control as to slavery in federal territory. (Lincoln, 1991c: 35 (excerpt))

(a) Summarize in as few words as possible the main argument by which Lincoln demonstrates that the framers of the US Constitution saw slavery as an evil to be contained until it could be abolished.

(b) Why does Lincoln repeat several times: '... thus showing that, in his [their] understanding, no line dividing local from federal authority, nor anything in the Constitution, forbade the Federal Government to control as to slavery in federal territory'? Could an interpreter, having once stated this point fully, abridge subsequent repetitions?

(c) Summarize in as few words as possible the argument by which Lincoln shows that it is lawful for Congress to legislate about slavery.

(d) Lincoln begins his speech by agreeing with Senator Douglas on a basic premise: that the US Constitution should be interpreted according to the intentions of the men who wrote it. Then he goes on to show that 23 of the 39 men who wrote it took legislative action implying that the federal government had the power to restrict slavery by law in federal territories. Thus, he begins from the same premise as Douglas, but reaches the opposite conclusion. What does this force his listeners to do?

(e) Which is more concrete, and therefore more comprehensible: Douglas's general opinion that reverence for one's forefathers requires respect for the status quo, or Lincoln's specific contention that the intentions of the framers must be judged according to what they actually said and did? If Lincoln had pitched his speech on the plane of high moral principle and emotional appeal, would it have been more effective or less effective?

(f)   Is every step in Lincoln's argument logically necessary to reach the conclusion? If this speech had been interpreted and the interpreter had incorrectly stated the premise, or the intervening steps, would the conclusion have sounded plausible?

(g)   Translate Lincoln's speech into Spanish, French or your other working languages, taking special care to preserve the clarity of his logic.

(3)   In a speech delivered at the Abyssinian Baptist Church in New York City on 22 October 1995, Cuban President Fidel Castro made the following argument: although everyone in the world opposed and denounced the old *apartheid* regime of South Africa, Cuba was the only country in the world which sent troops to fight against South Africa's intervention in Angola and Namibia, even though the South African Army was far more powerful and reportedly may even have had tactical nuclear weapons at its disposal. Today, Mr Castro said, 'everyone is happy' that *apartheid* has been defeated. But, as for Cuba's contribution, 'no one speaks about that', he added. Wryly, he concluded: 'Así se escribe las historia! Así se hace la política entre grandes potencias!'

(a)   Is this argument primarily intended to convey a general lesson about power politics and history, or is it primarily aimed at the trade embargo against Cuba?

(b)   Is the argument made more effective or less effective by the fact that it concludes with a general statement of principle (which could be put as 'Give credit where it's due.')?

(c)   Viewing this argument as illustrating a general truth about how history is written, and who gets the privilege of writing it, state 'the moral of the story' in the form of an aphorism, maxim, parable or proverb.

(4)   Consider the following argument made by a Latin-American representative:

> El tráfico ilícito o encubierto de armas constituye un elemento sumamente desestabilizador para muchos países. Una producción excesiva y descontrolada de armas también facilita su tráfico ilícito. Ante el argumento que no es posible controlar esta producción porque ello significaría un atentado contra los principios de la economía libre de mercado, es conveniente recordar que la inacción frente al tráfico ilícito conduciría a una intensificación sin precedentes del mismo, dada la remanencia de los problemas que enfrentamos en el escenario mundial, lleno de conflictos potenciales. En consecuencia, subsiste la obligación, de parte de los estados productores, de incorporar

o establecer controles mas eficientes en la transferencia de esta producción hacia otros países.

(a) Which of the following best summarizes the above argument?
- Nations should not produce too many weapons.
- Nations should not permit illegal weapons production.
- Nations should not permit illicit arms trafficking.
- Nations that overproduce weapons make illicit production and trafficking in arms easier and should therefore impose more effective controls to prevent illicit arms transfers.

(b) Does the speaker anticipate and refute the main counter-argument against his thesis?

(c) Would the argument have been strengthened if the speaker had given an example of how illicit arms transfers can destabilize countries, or some figures showing how large illicit trade in arms has grown?

(d) Translate the passage into English and then compare it with the following translation:

> Illicit or covert trafficking in weapons constitutes a highly destabilizing factor for many countries. Excessive and uncontrolled production of weapons also facilitates illicit trafficking. In response to the argument that it is not possible to control such production because it would mean an infringement of free-market economic principles, one should recall that inaction in the face of illicit trafficking would lead to an unprecedented expansion of such trafficking, given the persistence of the problems we face in the global arena, filled with potential conflicts. Accordingly, there is an obligation on the part of producer states to adopt or establish more effective controls on transfers of such production to other countries.

(e) Relying on the original Spanish and the English translation, translate the passage into French or other working languages.

(5) The following two arguments against the persistence of poverty appeared in statements by heads of state:

> The eradication of poverty continues to be the main challenge before the members of the organization. We must not rest until we have insured that he who is born poor is no longer condemned to die poor. (Statement by the President of El Salvador)

> Paradoxically, just as mankind has acquired the technology to reduce the distance between the Earth and other celestial bodies

in the universe, the gap between the rich and the poor has
alarmingly widened. (Statement by the President of Vietnam)

(a) Which of these two arguments relies more on emotion and which
appeals more to reason? Which one is stronger?

(b) Could the second argument be strengthened by going beyond stating a paradox and using the technique of *reductio ad absurdum*? Is it
the kind of argument that could be strengthened by statistics?

(c) Could the two arguments be combined? Try combining them into
one sentence.

(6) Unlike the incisive logic of Lincoln's speech (pp. 112–114), the following
excerpt from a speech by President Nelson Mandela of South Africa
relies almost entirely on emotional and moral rhetoric, yet is also very
compelling:

> When distinguished leaders came together half a century ago to con-
> sign to the past a war that had pitted humanity against itself, the
> ruins and the smoke from the dying fires were the monument for
> what should not have been. Fifty years after the formation of the
> United Nations, we meet to affirm our commitment with the found-
> ing idea and the common desire to better the life of all human
> beings. ... We come from Africa and South Africa on this historic
> occasion to pay tribute to that founding idea and to thank the United
> Nations for challenging, with us, a system that defined fellow humans
> as lesser beings. The youth at whom we have directed most of our
> awareness campaign on this golden jubilee should marvel at the nobil-
> ity of our intentions. They are also bound to wonder why it should
> be that poverty still prevails in the greater part of the globe, that wars
> continue to rage and that many people in positions of power and
> privilege pursue cold-hearted philosophies which terrifyingly pro-
> claim 'I am not your brother's keeper'. For no one in the north or the
> south can escape the cold fact that we are a single humanity.

(a) A rhetorical tactic which leaders often use is to 'shame' their listeners into taking action by asking 'What will history think of you?'
or 'What will your children think of you?' Which question is
President Mandela asking? Which is more powerful?

(b) Another rhetorical device so often used that it runs the risk of
sounding stale is the argument that 'We are all in the same boat'.
Does President Mandela's choice of words enable him to make this
point without sounding trite?

(c) Translate the above excerpt into Spanish, French or your other
working languages, taking special care with the poetic imagery of
the first sentence.

(7) Consider and compare the speeches by Abraham Lincoln (pp. 164–165) and Mikhail Gorbachev in Chapter 10 (pp. 168–169), from the standpoint of effective argumentation. Which technique do you find more powerful, the hortatory appeals used by Gorbachev or the 'train of horrors' technique used by Lincoln, relying chiefly on the power of negative example?

(8) A speaker may produce results somewhat contrary to those he intends by *overstating his case*. For this reason, it is very important for an interpreter to gauge correctly just how far the speaker is going with a delicate argument, and not to go the slightest bit farther. Consider the following example:

> Emotions ran high as [French President Jacques] Chirac took a stand completely contrary to that of his predecessor, François Mitterrand, who had always denied France's role in the tragedy and perpetuated the myth that the occupation Vichy government had been a mere interlude and totally illegitimate. ... The unfortunate thing is that the words the president used were laden with implications. Chirac mentioned 'collective blame'. He also declared that 'those dark hours are a permanent stain on our history', as if succeeding generations were doomed to bear that burden. With such statements, the president obviously went beyond his intentions, since he also spoke of the role of the French Resistance. ... In Germany, former President Richard von Weizsäcker had the wisdom to stress in May, 1985, that 'the guilt or innocence of an entire people is something that does not exist. Guilt, like innocence, is not collective but personal.' Drawing a distinction between responsibility, which is collective, and guilt, which is individual, enables future generations to face the past and pay the price without resentment. ... By failing to observe these nuances, Chirac lay himself open to the charge that he was seeking to placate a 'community'. The right-wing National Front lost no time in plunging into the fray. Mitterrand's position may have been weakened by his reputation for hypocrisy. But Chirac must take care lest he be accused of demagoguery. It would be unfortunate if a move that was meant to be generous served only to open up old wounds. (Slama, 1995 (excerpt); trans. James Nolan)

(a) Do you agree with the author of the above passage that President Chirac overstated his case by 'failing to observe' nuances between guilt and responsibility?

(b) If he had 'observed nuances', would his speech have been equally effective in light of its purpose (an apology)?

(c)   Does President Chirac 'lay himself open to the charge that he was seeking to placate a "community"'? Was the speech not specifically addressed to a community? Who was the 'target audience' of this speech?

(d)   If the effect of the speech was to immediately trigger a backlash from the right-wing National Front, could that have been avoided by 'observing nuances'?

(e)   This was obviously a speech written well in advance of delivery, in which every word was carefully chosen. Had you been assigned to interpret it, would you have asked for a copy of the speech to study in advance of its delivery?

(9)   After Rome successfully resisted the invasion of Hannibal, the women of Rome demonstrated and petitioned the Senate to repeal the austerity laws adopted during the emergency, which forbade them to wear jewelry and colorful dresses. It was the first time in Roman history that women had played any role outside the home. A conservative senator, Cato, spoke against them with the following arguments:

> Si cada uno de nosotros, señores, hubiese mantenido la autoridad y los derechos del marido en el interior de la propia casa, no hubiéramos llegado a este punto. Ahora henos aquí: la prepotencia femenina, tras haber anulado nuestra libertad de acción en familia, nos la está destruyendo también en el Foro. Recordad lo que nos costaba sujetar a las mujeres y frenar sus licencias cuando las leyes no permitían hacerlo. E imaginad lo que sucederá de ahora en adelante, si esas leyes son revocadas y las mujeres quedan puestas, hasta legalmente, en pie de igualdad con nosotros. Vosotros conocéis a las mujeres: hacedlas vuestras iguales e inmediatamente os las encontraréis convertidas en dueñas. Al final veremos esto: los hombres de todo el Mundo, que en todo el Mundo gobiernan a las mujeres, serán gobernados por los únicos hombres que se dejan gobernar por sus mujeres: los romanos. (Montanelli, 1959; trans. Pruna, 1969: 112–113)

Notice that, in this short speech, Cato uses 'every trick in the book'. He 'shames' the Roman male by suggesting that he is not man enough to keep women under control. He appeals to authority by saying that, if the laws were repealed, women would be placed on equal footing *even legally*! He appeals to morality by characterizing women as licentious. He ingratiates himself with his audience, speaking to them 'man to man' when he slyly says, 'you know what women are like'. He uses the 'train of horrors' or 'slippery slope' tactic by hinting darkly at the disastrous consequences that would ensue if women achieved equality.

He elicits sympathy and paints himself as the victim by saying that women have already destroyed men's freedom in the home. He appeals to self-interest by suggesting to the men that they would come to be dominated by women, but he portrays this selfish position as being civic-minded. He uses scare tactics by recalling 'you remember what it was like *before* we passed these laws'. He uses *reductio ad absurdum* humor by concluding that the Romans, who ruled the world, would be the only men in the world ruled by their own wives. And, last but not least, he frames the debate in his own terms, ignoring other issues.

(a) Identify the parts of Cato's speech which contain these different forms of argumentation. Are there any others?

(b) Write an equally concise speech using the same techniques of argumentation to refute Cato's position.

(c) Does Cato, at any point in his speech, address the central issue of whether emergency austerity laws adopted in wartime should be kept on the books during peacetime? Was his failure to address this key issue fatal to his other arguments? (The laws he favored were repealed.)

(d) Translate Cato's speech into English, French or your other working languages.

9 Diction/Register

In public fora, especially in the diplomatic arena, excesses of language are for the most part scrupulously avoided and interpreters must generally observe the conventions and forms of 'political correctness' dictated by the forum and the occasion, choosing moderation whenever in doubt. In international fora, even what amounts to a declaration of war will generally be framed in sober, carefully chosen words. However, strong language is not altogether absent, and words are often used which carry stern moral judgments. Words of moral disapproval or censure are especially common.

It is to some extent a matter of opinion among experienced interpreters how such language should be handled. Much depends on the occasion and the speaker's tone and intent. Sometimes intonation can be used to give a word the proper coloring.

Precise shades of meaning can be very important, especially in drafting groups. For example, the author once hesitated between saying 'grim prospects' or 'bleak prospects' to translate 'sombres perspectives' in a drafting group, chose the former, and found from the subsequent discussion that he had used too strong a word and had touched some raw nerves. The participants ultimately decided to put 'bleak prospects' into their document. But drafting groups may also be grateful to the interpreter for supplying the right word. For example, the author once used 'overtures to ...' in translating 'des tentatives de rapprochement dirigées à ...' and was later commended for supplying just the right word for the document in question.

Given the tendency of some speakers to blame the interpreter when they have gone too far or 'mis-spoken', many interpreters understandably take shelter in the 'better safe than sorry' approach. Others believe that verbal sparring has an important cathartic function, so that a speech which is calculated to give offense should not be expurgated or watered down. A cutting remark may be displeasing to utter and unpleasant for an assembly of diplomats in a conference room to hear, but it may also be the alternative to an act of violence in the streets or on a battlefield somewhere else ('The more they shout, the less they shoot.'). Consequently, common sense would suggest that there is a balance to be struck between diplomatic decorum and forceful debate.

Exercises

(1) In the following speech, a Latin-American ambassador refers to reprehensible actions of the Bosnian Serbs against UN peace-keeping personnel, such as abducting them and using them as 'human shields' against air strikes:

> Señor Presidente: El accionar de los líderes de los Bosnios Serbios contra los sitios seguros determinados por este Consejo en general, y contra la población civil de Sarajevo en particular, habían excedido todos los límites del derecho humanitario y transitado el inaceptable camino de la crueldad inusitada. Mi delegación comprende, entonces, que el accionar conjunto de las fuerzas de las Naciones Unidas y de la OTAN en curso se tornó desgraciadamente inevitable como recurso para procurar poner fin *al cerco de fuego que una y otra vez desangrara* a Sarajevo.
>
> El grado de crueldad a que nos referíamos incluyó, recordamos, las tan inéditas como *desgraciadas vejaciones* que se impusieran recientemente a los propios cascos azules ante el *estupor* de la comunidad internacional toda. La falta de respeto a las normas y límites dispuestos por este Consejo de Seguridad debe de una vez terminar. Todas las partes deben asumir sus respectivas obligaciones. En ese objetivo, Señor Presidente, estamos todos empeñados.
>
> Pese a ello, sin embargo, la esperanza de la paz parece haber renacido hoy en Ginebra. Ella debe todavía consolidarse, paso a paso, negociadamente. Y no será fácil. La lógica de la paz, edificada sobre una solución política, comienza sin embargo a vislumbrarse como posible. De allí nuestra ilusión de que solo transitando con espíritu amplio ese camino se llegará a una solución duradera.

(a) Find a suitable word to translate *vejaciones*.
(b) From the list of adjectives suggested below, choose the one that best translates *desgraciadas*:
    despicable / contemptible / repellent / repulsive / abhorrent / abominable / execrable / wretched / abject / shabby / odious / loathsome / nameless / rank / disreputable / disgraceful / shameful / unsavory

(c) Given the formal tone of the speech as a whole, which of these adjectives is of the most appropriate register? Which is the least appropriate?

(d) Rank the adjectives suggested above roughly according to their intensity, from the strongest to the weakest.

(e) Look up the suggested adjectives in a thesaurus and try to find other synonyms that carry approximately the same meaning and intensity. Do the same with the word you have chosen to translate *vejaciones*.

(f) Which of the following do you think best conveys the sense of *estupor* as used in the above speech?

amazed / overawed / astonished / shocked / stunned / surprised / taken aback / dismayed / baffled

(g) The phrase 'el *cerco de fuego* que una y otra vez *desangrara* a Sarajevo' is a mixed metaphor. A 'ring of fire' causes the victim to burn, not to bleed. But 'desangrar' is used here as a metaphor for the sufferings of war. Since mixed metaphors are best avoided in English, how is this phrase best translated? Which of the two elements of the mixed metaphor should be emphasized, and which should be de-emphasized and made to fit the other? Would 'a **circle of fire** that has time and again **besieged** Sarajevo' have the right intensity?

(2) As suggested by the above example, the interpreter must weigh the emotive resonance of a word and try to strike the right note, in keeping with the speaker's intention, without going too far. However, there is another pitfall to which interpreters must be alert. It is possible for an interpreter who is overly reluctant to use strong language in a diplomatic setting to disrupt the dignity of diplomatic discourse by turning a forceful statement into a ludicrous one through *incongruity of speech register*.

A good example of the kind of incongruity in register that can occur through mistranslation is offered by the linguist David Crystal:

> The story is told of one missionary, engaged in the conversion of an African tribe (which spoke a tone-language), who, having made a vernacular translation of a rousing English hymn, found that the English tune caused an apparently praiseworthy harangue against sinners to come out as a diatribe against fat people. The distinction between the meanings 'fat person' and 'sinful person' was carried by a difference of pitch height only. (Crystal, 1971: 185)

An equally striking example of incongruity of register is offered by Jean-Claude Gémar of the University of Montréal. In the French version of the film *Gone With the Wind*, when Scarlett O'Hara tearfully pleads with Rhett Butler not to leave her and he bluntly replies 'Frankly, my dear, I don't give a damn!', the French dubbing is 'Franchement, ma chère, c'est le cadet de mes soucis!' ('Frankly, my dear, that is the least of my concerns.'). Gémar is probably correct in explaining this incongruity by the French translator's stereotyped notion of how refined Southern gentlemen were supposed to speak; but, as he points out, the dramatic impact of the scene is spoiled for the French audience, since the watered-down line does not convey Rhett's anger and frustration (Gémar, 1990: 251).

Diplomats, like refined Southern gentlemen, are quite capable of saying 'That is the least of my concerns'. But they are also capable of saying 'I don't give a damn!' when the occasion arises. When a speaker intends to be blunt or abrasive, the interpreter is not helping the listeners by smoothing down the rough edges. Consider the following candid remarks by Hillary Rodham Clinton:

> It is a violation of *human* rights when individual women are raped in their own communities and when thousands of women are subjected to rape as a tactic or prize of war. It is a violation of *human* rights when a leading cause of death worldwide among women ages 14 to 44 is the violence they are subjected to in their own homes. It is a violation of *human* rights when young girls are brutalized by the painful and degrading practice of genital mutilation. It is a violation of *human* rights when women are denied the right to plan their own families, and that includes being forced to have abortions or being sterilized against their will. If there is one message that echoes forth from this conference, it is that human rights are women's rights. ... And women's rights are human rights. (Hillary Rodham Clinton, Address to the United Nations Fourth World Conference on Women, Beijing, China, 5 September 1995 (excerpt))

(3) Read the following passages and notice the use of the word 'valoriser' in French and 'valorizar' in Spanish:

> Car, Monsieur le Président, l'impact de la langue dépasse largement celui de la communication. Elle *valorise* également le patrimoine, l'expérience intellectuelle vécue. (Statement by representative of Benin)

> El internacionalismo de Naciones Unidas es interculturalismo. Ese carácter está directamente ligado con los fundamentos y los fines de Naciones Unidas y la palabra – oral y escrita – es el instrumento más

válido para *valorizar* cada cultura. (Statement by representative of Panama)

(a)   In what sense is the word being used?

(b)   Are the connotations positive or negative?

(c)   Is the dictionary meaning ('to develop', 'to actualize') adequate in this context?

(d)   Could it be translated with the English words 'enhance', 'give expression to', 'realize', 'fulfill' or 'shine through'?

(4)   In the following deliberately euphemistic statements, which of the alternative translations offered do you find more in keeping with the tone of the original?

Je crains fort, monsieur le président *qu'une erreur ne se soit introduite* dans le rapport que vous nous avez soumis ce matin.

- Mr Chairman, I'm afraid *there is an error* in the report you submitted to us this morning.
- Mr Chairman, I'm afraid *an error has crept into* the report you submitted to us this morning.

Les pays nantis soutiennent l'aide humanitaire *du bout des lèvres*.

- The affluent countries *pay lip service* to humanitarian aid.
- The affluent countries *genuflect* to humanitarian aid.

(5)   When the Spanish word 'hostigamiento' is used in reference to 'ethnic cleansing' in the former Yugoslavia, by which populations are driven from their homes, which of the following possible translations seems the closest English equivalent?

vexations / harassment / persecution

(6)   (a)   When the French word 'exactions' is used in the context of massive human rights violations, which of the following seems the closest English equivalent?

exactions / predations / abuses / outrages

(b)   When 'exactions' is used in the narrower sense of 'abuses of power', how should it be translated? Translate the following:

La déliquescence de l'Etat alimente la déliquescence de l'Etat. Ainsi, à Karachi, un poste de policier s'achète 20.000 roupies, une somme qui sera remboursée en quelques mois *à coup d'exactions*. (Tolotti, 1995)

(7)   Quite often in Spanish, and sometimes in French, superlative or absolute terms will be used in cases where English would use more restrained

language. Thus, committee chairmen are routinely congratulated in Spanish for 'su conducción *brillante*', which in English becomes simply 'your *able* handling', of the committee's deliberations.

Some commentators on language and style suggest that this is because English is more given to 'understatement', while Spanish and French are more given to 'overstatement'. A more likely explanation is that, in English, a frank criticism or a sincere compliment does not ring true in superlative form because the superlative is so often used ironically in English to imply its opposite. With this idea in mind, translate the following into English in a way that sounds equally intense without sounding melodramatic or insincere:

> la trayectoria *estelar* del Embajador Pérez / la elección *brillante* del presidente de la comisión / los esfuerzos *ingentes* de nuestro relator / el pueblo *mártir* de Bosnia / se cometieron toda suerte de *latrocinios y bribonadas* / nuestro presidente ha sido un *adalid* de su pueblo / la lucha *justiciera* / el pueblo *inerme* fue *sojuzgado* por la *cruenta represión* / actuar con *absoluta cordura* / preservar el *profundo arraigo tradicional* del pueblo / el vasto acervo cultural de nuestras culturas *milenarias* / la necesidad *impostergable* de erradicar la pobreza / mi gobierno recibió esta noticia con *júbilo* / debemos un apoyo *irrestricto* a estos principios / las *conquistas eternas* de la humanidad / los disturbios que *sacudieron* el país / los sectores *más sacrificados* de la población

> une *levée de boucliers* a suivi cet évènement / un diplomate *chevronné* / notre peuple *debout* saura *vaincre* son destin / les *affres* de la guerre *s'abattent* sur nous / on *s'acharne* sur les plus faibles / le *dévouement inébranlable* du secrétaire général / faire face à cette *incontournable nécéssité* / une stratégie *sinistre ourdie* par des forces *néfastes* / les *marchandages crapuleux* des syndicats de la drogue / 'La *démesure de l'abomination* commise' (Amalric, 1996).

(8)   Translate the following into formal French, Spanish or your other working languages:

- The visit was intended to *impress upon* the Serbs the *extent* of Washington's commitment.
- The United States is conducting a *final crescendo of diplomatic pressure*.
- No agreement is *in the bag* yet.
- There was no sign that a *crucial breakthrough on the territorial question was imminent*.
- Clearly it would be a *deal breaker* if we were not prepared to do anything for the Bosnians.

- The Administration's preference was to *'build down'* toward a rough military balance.
- Unless a lasting military balance *is contrived*, it will be difficult for NATO forces to leave after one year.
- The United States is assembling *nuts and bolts* for a Bosnia *move*.
- The *mundane but critically important* logistical side of the mission will determine at least the initial success of a NATO deployment in Bosnia.
- There is a *staggering amount of engineering data* for Bosnia.

(9) (a) Rank the following series of expressions roughly according to level of language, from the most formal or positive to the most colloquial or negative:

VIP / public figure / top man / boss / senior official / top brass / big gun / big shot / prominent person / dignitary / leader / celebrity

team / collaborators / colleagues / group / friends / pals / retinue / associates / inner circle / supporters / staff / clique

his peers / his disciples / his followers / of his stripe / of his ilk / and his like / his fellows / cohorts / henchmen / thugs / his apologists / hatchet-men / his associates

(b) From each of the above three series of expressions, single out the one expression which is most *neutral* in its connotations.

(c) Which of the expressions above best corresponds in meaning and level of language to the following expressions?
- ○ congénères / hommes de main / collègues
- ○ chef de file / gros bonnet / dirigeant
- ○ secuaces / matones / cúpula / coligados / ralea / turba / sicarios / sbirros / séquito / segundones
- ○ adalid / cacique / jefe / caudillo / mandatario / alto dignitario

(10) Observing nuances is especially important when translating references to rank or position. Translate the following into French, Spanish or your other working languages, paying special attention to the words in bold type:

> Jardines ... became the **centerpiece** of Hong Kong's economy ... and, in a sense, a metaphor for all that was colonial Britain. Now, with fewer than 600 days to go before China reassumes control over Hong Kong, the role of the company in the Opium War is **coming back to haunt** it. Instead of **swaggering** like the **consummate colonial occupier** it used to be, Jardine Matheson Holdings Ltd., while still a **giant** in business here, is having to **tiptoe like a**

supplicant. And it is not comfortable playing its new role. Jardines is no longer an integral part of the Government. And no longer is the company's **taipan**, the '**great boss**' of history … the **central personage** of Hong Kong society. … The company's **once magisterial** presence here has been **eclipsed** by **bigger** companies, controlled not by British families but by Hong Kong and other Chinese families. Its current **taipan** … is now **just another managing director**. (*New York Times*, 1995b: D1–6)

(11) (a) Rank the following statements according to level of language, from the most formal and solemn to the most informal and colloquial:
- ○ The war wiped out 5000 people.
- ○ The war claimed 5000 lives.
- ○ The war took a toll of 5000 lives.
- ○ The war killed 5000 people.
- ○ The fatalities in the war totaled 5000.
- ○ 5000 people died in the war.
- ○ In the wake of the war, 5000 people lay dead.
- ○ The war killed off 5000 people.
- ○ The war decimated 5000 people.

(b) Which of the statements above is most neutral in its connotations? Which is most dramatic?

(12) Rank the following expressions according to intensity, from the most emotively charged to the most neutral:
- to break free of
- to escape
- to cast off the bonds of
- to throw off the yoke of
- to break loose from
- to achieve release from
- to break the shackles of
- to liberate oneself from

(13) Rank the following series of words according to level of language, from the most formal to the most colloquial:
- rostrum / podium / stand / stage / dais
- ancestors / forerunners / forebears / founding fathers / framers
- room / hall / chamber / forum
- between a rock and a hard place / between the devil and the deep blue sea / between Scylla and Charybdis
- to doubt / to question / to gainsay / to challenge
- scheme / fraud / scam / swindle / travesty / charade / mockery

- situation / time / occasion / opportunity / juncture
- to herald / to prefigure / to foreshadow
- tocsin / wake-up call / alarm / alarum / warning sign / red light / heads-up
- commotion / turmoil / upheaval / chaos / anarchy / rioting / unrest / disorder
- nonsense / rubbish / gobbledygook / rot / humbug / baloney / poppycock / balderdash / bilge / twaddle
- to take leave of one's senses / to go crazy / to go mad / to have bats in one's belfry / to go berserk / to run amok / to go bananas / to go nuts / to lose it
- scapegoat / sacrificial lamb / patsy / goat / whipping boy / fall guy
- in the aftermath of / after / in the wake of / following
- para ello / a esos fines / a esos efectos
- derroche / pérdida / despilfarro
- sala / aposento / antro / aula / localidad / lugar / sitio / foro
- oficina / consultorio / despacho / bufete
- antepasados / próceres / padres / fundadores
- negligencia / desidia / inercia / parálisis
- derrumbe / colapso / desintegración
- en plus / en outre / de surcroît
- disparu / mort / défunt
- franchement / sans ambages / ouvertement / sans états d'âme

(14) The proverb 'He who hesitates is lost' applies with special force to the simultaneous interpreter. Because the interpreter's choice of words must be made in a few seconds, it is important to sharpen one's sense of nuances until it becomes automatic. Moreover, because memory is fallible, an interpreter should strive always to have two or three possible words at hand for any given idea. In this regard, it is important to recall that there are not only 'true synonyms', words which invariably have almost identical meanings (e.g. 'The committee was **inundated / deluged / flooded** with protests'), but also 'functional synonyms', that is words which will carry the same meaning *in context* although their dictionary meanings may differ slightly.

This requires practice in sensing the extent to which 'synonyms' are interchangeable. For each sentence given below, choose the most appropriate word to fill the blank from those suggested. Then, translate the completed sentences into each of your other languages.

(a)   overtly / patently / manifestly / tangibly / visibly / flagrantly

- The judge's opinion was _____ influenced by political considerations.
- The commissioners so _____ favored one party that the election had to be canceled for irregularity.
- Living standards here have been _____ affected by the drop in export earnings.
- The agreed commitments have been _____ violated by this notorious act of bad faith!
- After the crash the pilot was _____ shaken.
- The misdeeds alleged against us are _____ unfounded.

(b)   local / community-based / on the ground / in the field / grass-roots

- Practical know-how is best acquired _____, not at headquarters.
- With spokesmen so out of touch with people's problems, how can they call themselves a/an _____ movement?
- The _____ clinics proved more efficient than the ones planned by the central government.
- A/An _____ strategy is the best way to plan health care.
- The strategists in their ivory tower knew so little about the developments _____ that their plans went awry.

(c)   inflamed / inflammatory / inflammable / flaming / fulminating

- During martial law, extremist leaders were arrested for making _____ speeches in public places.
- In an instant, the bone-dry fields blazed into a/an _____ inferno.
- The crowd's resentment was _____ by this outrage, and they ran amok.
- The inter-ethnic talks were making headway, but this act of terrorism has produced a highly _____ situation.
- Radical leaders have been _____ against new austerity measures and are threatening to boycott the elections.

(d)   split up / broken up / fragmented / broken down / divided / riven / rent

- The federation was _____ into ungovernable rival cantons.
- With environmental movements _____ into several schools of thought, it was impossible to form a viable green party.
- Our society is _____ a generational conflict.
- A house _____ cannot stand.
- The division had to be _____ into logistical units and armored infantry units.

- The party is _____ by factionalism.
- The budget was _____ according to the purpose of each appropriation.

(e) stop / curb / halt / frustrate / thwart / prevent / stave off / hold at bay / avoid / avert / belie

- Every move towards peace negotiations was _____ by a new offensive on the battle-front.
- Only a vaccine can _____ the spread of Aids.
- Food shipments now will _____ starvation for another month.
- The international community must show the resolve to _____ the forces of hatred and xenophobia until education gradually teaches everyone to live together in peace.
- When you know no solution, you must _____ creating the problem in the first place.
- The mountains will _____ the advance of the enemy troops.
- This ill-conceived plan could _____ your best intentions.
- You cannot _____ population growth, you can only slow it down.
- These cutbacks in foreign aid _____ the rich countries' proclaimed commitment to humanitarian goals.
- Organizing team sports proved a good way to _____ teenage gang violence.
- We are making every effort to _____ a renewed outbreak of this viral infection.

(f) ominous / alarming / bleak / grim

- The 1980s were a _____ period for economic development.
- Amid _____ predictions of recession, stock market prices plunged.
- There are _____ signs that a new arms race is starting up.
- Widespread drought has created a/an _____ possibility of mass starvation throughout the continent.

(g) smoldering / festering / seething / boiling

- Resentment against corruption and abuse had been _____ for years before the crisis erupted.
- There is a mood of _____ anger among unemployed youth.
- The fires of discontent have been _____ and could burst into flame at any moment.
- Frustrations have reached the _____ point.

(h) activism / combativeness / militancy

- The lengthy strikes were attributed to the legendary _____ of France's labor unions.

- ○ Environmental NGOs have been showing a new _____ since the discovery of ozone depletion.
- ○ With the threat of an economic crisis looming, political apathy has been turning into citizen _____.

(i)   minutiae / details / particulars
- ○ The committee agreed on principles but has not yet discussed the _____ of the draft agreement.
- ○ The report was addressed to laymen and only the annex contained the technical _____ of measuring radioactive emissions.
- ○ The central bank insisted on being fully informed about all the _____ of the transaction before it took place.

(j)   infested by / infected by / rife with / rampant
- ○ Delegates were loath to embark on a negotiation they knew would be _____ intractable problems.
- ○ Much of the farmland in sub-Saharan Africa is _____ locusts during part of the year.
- ○ Hyperinflation was for some time _____ in South America.
- ○ The more sanguine members of the scientific community have not been _____ Dr Smith's pessimistic predictions on global warming.

(k)   reticence / trepidation / reluctance
- ○ Our _____ to broach the issue was prompted by our awareness of other groups' sensitivities.
- ○ Amid such passionate disagreement, it is with the greatest _____ that the Secretariat makes the following compromise proposal.
- ○ Given the financial burdens it imposes, we can understand developing countries' _____ to sign the convention.

(l)   befall / beset / besiege
- ○ Small island developing countries are _____ by economic pressures and environmental dilemmas.
- ○ The natural disasters that regularly _____ small island developing countries include typhoons and tidal waves.
- ○ A burdensome debt overhang and onerous terms of trade _____ the economies of small island developing states year in and year out.

(m)   duo / tandem / twofold / dual / duet / twin / double / twosome / couple / partnership / bilateral
- ○ Developed and developing countries can form a fruitful _____ by jointly conducting biological research.

- We are again threatened by that dreadful _____, inflation and stagnation.
- Canada and the United States held _____ trade negotiations.
- Drought and famine are the _____ evils stalking Africa.
- Most modern technologies are _____ use technologies.
- The agriculture and labor ministers proved to be an effective _____ on this fact-finding mission.
- Throughout the negotiations the foreign secretary and the prime minister performed as a _____.
- The disarmament commission has a _____ agenda: arms control and disarmament.
- Pavarotti and Carreras sang a _____.
- For interpreters, a fast speaker with a thick accent is a _____ headache.
- Like an old _____ they quarrel but always make up.

(n)   trio / troika / triptych / threefold / triple / trinity / threesome / triumvirate / treble / three-pronged

- Field commanders from England, Germany and France formed a working _____ for this peace-keeping mission.
- The neo-liberal economists are pursuing a _____ aim: liberalization, privatization and deregulation.
- When negligence is criminal, you can sue for _____ damages.
- The unholy _____ of poverty, hunger and disease is besetting much of the South.
- Lasting peace requires a _____ strategy: economic development, disarmament and peaceful dispute resolution.
- Translators, interpreters and précis-writers perform like a _____ during multinational conferences.
- The preamble, operative part and annexes of this convention form a _____.
- Debt, obsolete technology and poor market access are a _____ burden to the developing world.
- The chairman, secretary and rapporteur were an inseparable _____ throughout the conference.
- The United States, Europe and Japan are becoming an all-powerful _____ in some high-tech areas of international trade.

(o)   stop-gap / intermittent / sporadic / hit-or-miss / scatter-shot / haphazard / stop-and-go / by fits and starts / desultory

- Keeping the agency funded for a month at a time is at best a/an _____ solution.
- He has no sense of purpose; his work habits are _____.

- ○ Trade liberalization in the East is proceeding _____, only making real headway every two or three years.
- ○ Anti-desertification measures have had only _____ success.
- ○ This _____ approach of broadcasting a few publicity spots does not put the whole problem in focus.
- ○ Conferences on gender issues have so far been _____; they will henceforth be held at regular intervals.
- ○ Without a standardized test, judging the success of this curriculum worldwide is a/an _____ endeavor.
- ○ Being stuck in _____ traffic for hours was nerve-racking.
- ○ Despite the doctors' best efforts, success in fighting this disease had been _____ until the vaccine was invented.

(p) a raft of / a brace of / a host of / a bevy of / a spate of / a clutch of / a flurry of / a barrage of
- ○ In the last few years, there has been _____ natural disasters.
- ○ There was _____ elderly ladies chatting and knitting in the garden.
- ○ The president made _____ telephone calls to foreign leaders.
- ○ The foreign minister left amid _____ congratulatory speeches.
- ○ The ambassador was accosted by _____ excited reporters.
- ○ There is only _____ sullen dissidents who oppose this enlightened policy.
- ○ The company operated _____ small restaurants.
- ○ The conference was inundated with _____ new and complex proposals from special interest groups.

(q) laden / larded / laced / interspersed / peppered
- ○ It was a comedy _____ with a dash of high drama.
- ○ Nixon's decision to intervene in Cambodia was _____ with dire political consequences.
- ○ The speech was _____ with difficult puns and double-entendres.
- ○ The warm reception was _____ with occasional hostile demonstrations.
- ○ To the end, Mr Mitterrand maintained his habit of speaking in long sentences _____ with references reflecting his traditional education in Latin and Greek (*New York Times*, 1996b: A9).

(r) relic / residue / vestige / remnant
- ○ The mimeograph machine is a _____ from the pre-electronic days of printing.
- ○ Bonded labor is a _____ of the age of slavery.

- Mr Mandela has set out to rid his country of every last _____ of the apartheid system.
- Although the crash is over, there is a _____ of insecurity and panic in the markets.

(15) For each sentence given below, choose the most appropriate word, from those suggested, to translate the words in bold type. Then translate the complete sentence.

(a) colapso / derrumbe / desintegración / chute / effondrement / écroulement

- The official report on Barings said swift action by the bank's management could have averted its **collapse**.
- The **breakdown** of monetary stability is sending shudders through the commodity markets.
- The **break-up** of the union left several small sovereign states which were not economically viable.
- Some say the trusteeship system is no longer necessary since the **fall** of the colonial empires.
- This cynical decision represents the **downfall** of all our fondest hopes and aspirations for a better future.
- Consumer confidence has been **crumbling** since the devaluation.
- Pessimists say the market is headed for a **crash**.
- No one imagined the **collapse** of the new overpass during the earthquake.

(b) landmark / epochal / watershed / ground-breaking / record-breaking / monumental / breakthrough / quantum jump / tribute / leap / stride / historic

- La adopción del sufragio universal fue un **hito** en la historia de mi país.
- Le premier vol à la lune fut un **saut qualitatif** dans l'exploration de l'espace extraterrestre.
- La construcción de la autopista nacional será un **logro estupendo** de la ingeniería.
- La signature de ce traité constitue **un hommage** à la paix.
- La alfabetización del 90% de nuestro pueblo ha sido una **tarea asombrosa**.
- La convention sur le droit de la mer est l'un des **grands tournants** dans l'histoire du droit international.
- Los acuerdos de Río sobre el medio ambiente **quedarán inscritos para siempre en la historia**.
- Avec l'élimination des armes chimiques nous aurons **fait un grand pas en avant** vers le désarmement complet.

- ○ Los rayos X fueron una **invención fundamental** en la historia de la medicina.
- ○ Cet accord **marque un progrès sur lequel on ne reviendra plus jamais**.

(c) dismantle / disband / break up
- ○ La policía **desarticuló** una red de narcotraficantes.
- ○ La federación se **desintegró** en varias entidades.
- ○ Tras la guerra, se **desintegró** el ejercito enemigo.

(d) ensemble / suite / gamme / fourchette
- ○ The prosecutors presented a convincing **array** of evidence.
- ○ The defense presented a **series** of arguments.
- ○ The corporation makes a **range** of high-tech products.
- ○ Within the $30 to $50 **range** we offer synthetic blend shirts.
- ○ We've used the whole **spectrum** of antibiotics against this virus, but with no success.
- ○ The temperature **band** between 45 and 60 degrees Fahrenheit is the most comfortable.

(e) degree / extent / regard / caliber / in terms of
- ○ Le **niveau** d'infection en ville est devenu alarmant.
- ○ Le **niveau** d'intérêt montré par la jeunesse ne justifie pas le lancement de ce programme.
- ○ A ce **niveau**, notre réponse est positive.
- ○ Ce candidat n'a pas le **niveau** requis pour le poste.
- ○ Au **niveau** de la rentabilité, cette entreprise ne tiendra pas le coup.

(16) (a) For each series of words below, write a series of sentences to illustrate the distinctions between the words. Then translate the sentences.

(b) In each series of words below, identify those which can serve as synonyms for each other in most cases. Remember that two slightly different words can function as synonyms if they will mean the same thing *in context*.

(c) In each series of words below, identify any words which are comparatively neutral in their connotations. Then rank the remaining ones according to intensity.

(d) Where a word or words are given in brackets at the end of a series, select the word(s) which correspond best to the word(s) in brackets.
- ○ restoration / rebirth / renewal / renaissance / rejuvenation / revitalization / resurrection

- to eradicate / to eliminate / to quell / to stamp out / to curb / to check / to stem
- to detail / to assign / to post / to detach / to dispatch
- to expedite / to hasten / to accelerate / to step up
- moving / poignant / stirring
- dimension / branch / wing / aspect / area / department (volet)
- slot / niche / pigeonhole (créneau)
- to pare / to trim / to prune
- holistic / comprehensive / cross-cutting / across-the-board / interdisciplinary
- rump government / lame-duck government / transitional government
- celerity / speed / promptness / swiftness / dispatch
- staggering / mind-boggling / awesome / appalling
- to overhaul / to refurbish / to renovate / to streamline / to rehabilitate / to remediate
- cutting edge / top-of-the-line / world-class / high-tech
- panacea / cure-all / silver bullet / magic potion
- mournful / doleful / woeful / baneful
- seminal / germinal / fountainhead (pregnance)
- indulgent / obliging / deferential / lenient / solicitous / oversolicitous
- array / assortment / range / set / battery / miscellany / tier
- minutiae / details / particulars (pormenores)
- skein / net / tangle / web / morass / bog
- inextricable / insoluble / dead-end (sans issue)
- international / transnational / trans-boundary / cross-border
- breeding-ground / hotbed / nest / soil (foyer / caldo de cultivo)
- trials / ordeals / tribulations / vicissitudes / labors / woes / ills (déboires)
- germane / relevant / pertinent / apposite / material
- horrors / sufferings / ordeals (affres)
- tyrant / dictator / strongman
- to deport / to expel / to extradite / to exile / to ban / to banish
- fledgling / nascent / emerging / incipient / infant / budding / embryonic / dawning / potential / in-the-making
- defensible / plausible / arguable / respectable
- well organized / well thought out / consistent / cogent / coherent (cohérent)
- logical / rational / natural (logique)

- hidebound / hard-core / unreconstructed / unrepentant / staunch
- zealot / fanatic / extremist / fundamentalist
- activist / militant / advocate / proponent / supporter
- population / populace / mass / people / inhabitants / dwellers
- portent / omen / harbinger / herald / forerunner
- sign / symptom / bellwether
- benchmark / yardstick / baseline / landmark (repère)
- blithely / coolly / insouciantly / gaily / with gay abandon / without compunction / not to balk at
- churlish / snide / moody / sullen / brooding
- leadership / charmed circle / inner circle / exclusive club / in-crowd / those in the know / in the loop (cúpula)
- to intercede / to intervene / to interfere / to interpose / to meddle (ingerirse en)
- to mediate / to offer one's good offices / to arbitrate / to referee / to moderate / to facilitate / to be an honest broker
- mediator / arbitrator / settlor / broker / go-between / facilitator
- to expostulate / to expound / to explain
- to remonstrate / to admonish / to upbraid / to rebuke
- chain of events / sequence / concatenation / series / cycle / round / continuum
- to procrastinate / to temporize / to delay / to stall / to buy time (atermoiement)
- fast / swift / rapid / prompt / quick / fleet / speedy
- to endorse / to support / to back / to subscribe to (souscrire à)
- consistent with / consonant with / in keeping with / commensurate with / equal to / equal to the task of
- impediment / hindrance / obstruction / obstacle / hurdle
- in parallel / as a corollary / at the same time / by the same token
- hermetic / esoteric / enigmatic / recondite / apocryphal / anecdotal / arcane (apócrifo)
- a sequence of / a series of / a train of
- chain of events / spiral / vicious circle / roller-coaster / race to the bottom
- concatenation / chain of events / domino effect (effet d'entraînement)
- inexorable / relentless / unrelenting / unsparing / unremitting / implacable
- overwhelming / crushing / landslide (aplastante)
- supererogatory / superfluous / needless / unnecessary / surplusage / redundant

- bowed / cowed / browbeaten / intimidated (bafoué)
- to flout / to defy / to disregard (faire fi de)
- praise / tribute / commendation / plaudits / kudos / applause (encomio)
- to denounce / to condemn / to revile (denunciar)
- abuse / vituperation / insult / offense / acrimony / imprecation / indignity / taunt / barb / invective (improperio / injuria / injure)
- debate / polemics / discussion / exchange of views
- controversial / sensitive / divisive / disputed (polémico / controvertido)
- paramount / cardinal / essential / overriding / peremptory / overarching / imperative (perentorio)
- utmost / cardinal / chief / primary
- urgent / pressing / imperative (impostergable)
- site / location / venue / locality / place
- to forgo / to dispense with / to waive
- callous / cynical / uncaring / insensitive / contemptuous
- merciless / harsh / cruel / ruthless / wanton / heedless (cruento)
- rift / gap / chasm / gulf / interstice / lag (gouffre)
- cheap / inexpensive / economical / cost-effective (à moindres frais)
- economies / savings / efficiencies / efficiency gains
- splintering / fragmentation / atomization / Balkanization
- way / avenue / approach / path (voie)
- forecast / prediction / projection (pronostic / prognóstico)
- prognosis / diagnosis / assessment / outlook / perspective
- to grant / to bestow / to confer (octroyer)
- threshold / eve / doorstep / dawn (umbral)
- aftermath / wake / epilogue / post-mortem / twilight
- in profusion / in abundance / multitudinous
- crowd / mass / gathering / multitude / assembly
- handmaiden / lackey / flunkey / servant / camp-follower / creature / underling / hireling (lampiste)
- spawn / engender / generate / spark / trigger / prompt / set off / ignite
- proliferate / multiply / spawn
- dictatorship / despotism / tyranny / autocracy / totalitarian / authoritarian
- to counteract / to offset / to compensate / to check / to curb / to outweigh
- links / ties / bonds / contacts / relations (lazos / liens)

- to exceed / to surpass / to transcend / to overtake / to outstrip / to outperform / to outpace
- perfunctory / lackadaisical / to give something short shrift
- persuasive / convincing / conclusive / compelling / potent
- insightful / penetrating / incisive (atinado)
- illuminating / enlightening / instructive / illustrative / informative
- gradation / rank / grade / hierarchy / seniority / class / status / chain of command / precedence / priority (jerarquía / rango / prelación)
- speech / statement / presentation / remarks / comments / intervention / address / press conference
- disorder / disarray / chaos / riot / bedlam / upheaval / strife
- revolt / rebellion / resistance / uprising / revolution
- resilient / steadfast / staunch / dogged / persistent / determined / resolute / tenacious (empecinado)
- irate / angry / enraged / disgruntled (iracundo)
- concomitant / correlative / accompanying / attendant / ancillary / derivative / associated / consequent
- to expound / to expostulate / to propound / to advance / to put forward
- to happen / to occur / to take place / to supervene / to transpire (advenir)
- to take the opportunity to / to avail oneself of the opportunity to / to make use of the opportunity to / to seize the occasion to
- to constrain / to hobble / to shackle / to yoke / to hamper
- ossified / paralyzed / sluggish / fossilized / sclerotic (entumecido)
- inertia / inaction / paralysis / apathy / sclerosis / complacency
- to strengthen / to invigorate / to dynamize (agilizar)
- vigorous / robust / lively / brisk / dynamic
- obsolete / archaic / aged / time-worn / threadbare / anachronistic / ancient / hoary / old-fashioned / quaint / disused (périmé / anachronique / dépassé / vétuste)
- unwieldy / top-heavy / overgrown / ponderous / lumbering
- powerless / impotent / weak / feeble / timid / anemic / defenseless / prostrate (inerme)
- to undermine / to sap / to weaken / to drain (mermar)
- alloyed / diluted / watered down / adulterated
- blended / melded / mixed
- umbrella / portmanteau / omnibus / carry-all (fourre-tout)

- enabling / empowering / authorizing
- movement / campaign / drive / initiative / endeavor
- plan / program / agenda / platform
- goals / targets / aims / desiderata / purposes
- device / instrument / mechanism / apparatus / machinery / arrangements / structure (dispositif)
- to delve into / to go into / to dwell on
- to elaborate on / to embellish / to build up / to embroider / to gild
- to plan to / to intend to / to aim at (envisager de)
- concise / brief / laconic / unembellished / plain
- to embark on / to broach / to touch on / to refer to / to allude to / to mention / to advert to (aludir)
- to aver / to observe / to note / to point out / to touch upon (faire remarquer)
- model / mold / pattern / scheme / arrangement / framework (cadre)
- affiliation / affinity / allegiance / fealty / loyalty
- bookkeeper / accountant / auditor / actuary
- lawyer / attorney / advocate / solicitor / barrister / publicist / jurist (publicista)
- national / citizen / resident
- stranger / foreigner / alien
- state / government / nation / people / country
- patriotism / chauvinism / isolationism / neutrality / non-intervention
- posture / stance / position / mind-set / attitude
- to bolster / to shore up / to buttress / to undergird / to back
- progressive / gradual / incremental / phased (progresivo / paulatino)
- trepidation / misgivings / mixed feelings / ambivalence
- mixed results / inconclusive results / moderate success (résultats mitigés)
- intent on / bent on / determined to (s'acharner à)
- the sticking point / the bottom line / where the shoe pinches / the rub (là où le bât blesse)
- dissemble / concealed / veiled / covert / unspoken / unavowed / ulterior motive / hidden agenda
- to disavow / to repudiate / to retract / to jettison / to reject / to dissociate oneself from / waive (abandonar)
- to retreat / to backtrack / to climb down / to back away from
- unseemly / improper / inappropriate

- proper / fitting / suitable / to befit
- ribald / risqué / steamy / obscene / indecent / salacious / racy / sensational / tawdry / suggestive
- volatile / unstable / explosive / sensitive
- grass-roots / indigenous / endogenous / innate / inherent / native
- sacked / fired / dismissed / relieved of command / ousted / removed from office / separated / discharged / laid off / furloughed (renvoyé / révoqué / démis de ses fonctions)
- long-standing / permanent / secular / structural / enduring / time-honored / hallowed / age-old / lasting (secular / milenario)
- long-running / long-standing / ongoing / continuing
- prevalence / incidence / frequency / periodicity
- rate / pace / cadence / rhythm (taux / tasa)
- crescendo / climax / peak
- enticing / alluring / tempting / attractive / seductive
- widespread / endemic / chronic
- solace / consolation / relief / comfort
- titan / behemoth / mammoth / giant / gargantuan
- legendary / epic / saga / epochal / landmark / historic
- insidious / nefarious / sinister / notorious / pernicious (néfaste)
- pronounced / marked / distinctive / significant / substantial / salient / notable / noteworthy
- order / instruct / command / direct
- to tame / to master / to domesticate
- degrading / humiliating / demeaning / humbling / invidious
- to subdue / to subjugate / to suppress / to repress / to stifle / to quell / to put down (réprimer)
- leniency / laxness / clemency
- flexible / pliant / lax / amenable / understanding / sympathetic / compliant / deferential
- to proselytize / to recruit / to propagate / to disseminate / to propagandize
- seconded / assigned / detached / on loan
- hiatus / interlude / recess / moratorium / truce / cease-fire / pause / break
- to empower / to authorize / to enable / to delegate / to task / to mandate / to assign
- terms of reference / mandate / charter / warrant / authority / powers / remit / purview / brief / writ
- temporary / provisional / ad hoc / interim / transitional

- poor / impoverished / wretched / indigent / destitute / impecunious / penurious / needy (paupérrimo)
- mixed / varied / eclectic / diverse
- daunting / stiff / challenging / ambitious
- random / fortuitous / chance / fluke / unpredictable
- accidental / inadvertent / unintentional / fortuitous
- panache / brio / savoir-faire / aplomb / flair / presence of mind
- unsinkable / unflappable / imperturbable
- know-how / expertise / mastery / knack / skill (savoir-faire)
- to enthrall / to mesmerize / to spellbind / to dazzle
- to dwarf / to eclipse / to overwhelm / to overshadow
- to nullify / to cancel out / to bring to naught / to undo
- to urge / to exhort / to beseech / to appeal to / to call upon
- events / developments / incidents / trends (évolutions)
- experience / day-to-day life / course of events (el acontecer)
- unexpected / unprecedented / unheard-of / novel / a first / a case of first impression (inédit)
- pivotal / crucial / central / fundamental / critical
- salient / outstanding / remarkable / exceptional
- to impound / to seize / to attach / to confiscate / to levy / to garnish / to declare forfeit / to freeze
- to perform / to discharge / to acquit oneself of / to satisfy / to meet
- frivolous / flippant / facetious / tongue-in-cheek
- skeptical / realistic / cynical
- ironic / sardonic/ satirical
- capricious / arbitrary / inconsistent
- earnest / serious / responsible (sérieux / en serio)
- faltering / vacillating / unsteady
- peculiar / singular / distinctive / salient (singular)
- specificity / peculiarity / eccentricity / special feature (particularidad)
- fleeting / impermanent / transient / transitory / ephemeral / will-o'-the-wisp / evanescent (efímero)
- chimerical / illusory / imaginary / insubstantial / ethereal (chimérique)
- rout / defeat / disarray (débandade)
- travesty / sham / mockery / farce / charade / kangaroo court / dog and pony show / bogus (trompeur)
- injured / damaged / disadvantaged (perjudicado)
- prejudice / bias / favoritism (parti-pris)

- leeway / wiggle-room / margin / flexibility / room to maneuver / breathing space
- to tarnish / to stain / to sully
- esteem / repute / reputation / renown / held in high regard
- commonplace / banal / mundane / to play down / to trivialize (banaliser)
- abrupt / brusque / disruptive / sudden / drastic / untimely / unseasonable (intempestivo)
- unceremoniously / bluntly / without further ado (brusquement)
- unruffled / sedate / subdued / dispassionate
- objective / impartial / dispassionate / even-handed / open-minded (ouverture d'esprit)
- upper-echelon / ranking / senior / high-level / high-ranking
- top-of-the-line / first-rate / top-notch / upper-echelon / high-caliber (haut-de-gamme)
- in keeping with / consistent with / consonant with / commensurate with / to comport with / to tally with
- nettlesome / thorny / sensitive (névralgique)
- to nettle / to badger / to heckle / to harass / to be a thorn in the side of / to irk / to annoy / to chaff (gouailler)
- to boast / to showcase / to hold up / to dangle before the public eye / to feature / to flaunt / to highlight
- beholden / indebted / compromised
- proper / due / rightful / fitting (qui lui revient / debido)
- much touted / oft spoken of / famous / heralded (tant vanté)
- notorious / sad to recall / sadly famous (tristement célèbre)
- rejoicing / jubilation / celebration (júbilo)
- disengagement / cessation of hostilities / cease-fire / truce / demobilization / decommissioning / disarmament
- to copy / to clone / to imitate / to pattern after / to mimic / to ape (calquer)
- cacophony / babel / bedlam / chorus / clamor / outcry / uproar (remue-ménage / escándalo)
- to lose control / to spin out of control / to run amok (dérapage)
- unreliable element / loose cannon / weak link in the chain
- to parcel out / to carve up / to divide / to partition
- to allocate / to assign / to apportion / to earmark / to appropriate
- to rule / to judge / to decide / to hold (trancher)
- to monitor / to observe / to supervise / to oversee (vigilar)
- to heighten / to escalate / to raise / to ratchet up / to step up (incrementar)

- to trigger / to prompt / to incite / to cause / to unleash / to precipitate (incitar)
- to promote / to foster / to further / to advance (fomentar)
- to fuel / to feed / to nourish / to foment / to encourage (fomentar)
- to abet / to conspire with / collusion / to give aid and comfort
- steady / constant / persistent (constante)
- to take offense / to take umbrage / to feel slighted / to feel singled out (sentirse aludido / se sentir visé)
- target / goal / aim / objective (but / objectif)
- fundamental / subjacent / underlying (sous-jacent)
- hypothesis / eventuality / scenario / assumption / case / event / premise (hypothèse)
- to single out / to pick and choose / to be selective (singularizar)
- exacting / scrupulous / painstaking / meticulous / thoroughgoing
- deep-rooted / time-honored / well-established (arraigado)
- injured / victimized / attacked (agredido)
- damage / detriment / injury / hurt
- unwieldy / awkward / unmanageable / top-heavy (torpe)
- palliative / remedial / corrective
- to alleviate / to dampen / to abate / to cushion
- to reshuffle / to restructure / to reorganize / to streamline
- buoyant / sanguine / optimistic / hopeful
- to make amends / to make reparations / to make restitution
- to default / to abdicate / to yield / to step down
- ouster / overthrow / removal
- ploy / stratagem / device / scheme / plot (complot)
- to muster / to rally / to marshal / to galvanize / to gather / to garner (galvaniser)
- to prevaricate / to lie / to tell untruths
- steps / measures / procedures (gestiones / trámites)
- shelter / sanctuary / asylum / aid and comfort
- accomplice / collusion / complicity / accessory / aiding and abetting / giving aid and comfort (cómplice)
- to bring to book / to bring to justice / to prosecute
- scheme / plot / calculation (supputation)
- cabalistic / conspiratorial / partisan / factional
- specious / sophistry / Jesuitical / Talmudic / hairsplitting / a nicety / a distinction without a difference / a formalism / a semantic distinction / an esoteric distinction

- conjectural / speculative / theoretical / academic
- to concoct / to hatch / to devise (ourdir)
- to commend / to hail / to welcome / to congratulate / to celebrate
- entourage / retinue / delegation
- restrained / courteous / measured / moderate (retenue)
- moderation / tolerance / reserve
- naively / uncritically / ingenuously
- deliberate / premeditated / intentional / conscious / disingenuous
- malicious / willful / reckless / negligent / feckless
- guilty / liable / responsible
- unreserved / unqualified / unstinting
- to usurp / to take over / to seize
- culprit / perpetrator / doer / offender (el responsable)
- to kill / to murder / to assassinate / to do away with
- stealth / deviousness / guile / deception
- insidious / surreptitious / unseen
- deceitful / fraudulent / tortious (doloso)
- deceit / duplicity / hypocrisy (doblez)
- to commit / to perpetrate / to carry out
- attack / assault / attempt on (attentat)
- generosity / largess / extravagance
- vanguard / spearhead / pioneering / groundbreaking / standard-bearer
- hero / champion / avenger / protagonist (adalid)
- to claim / to demand / to make a case for (reivindicar)
- to divert / to distract / to derail / to sidetrack
- to diminish / to decline / to dwindle (menguar)
- situation / business cycle / circumstances (conjoncture / coyuntura)
- obsequiously / deferentially / respectfully
- crest / peak / summit / acme / zenith
- boomerang / backlash / reaction (contre-coup)
- cross-current / undertow / groundswell (lame de fond)
- sparse / spare / scarce
- fetter / shackle / yoke
- to bar / to ban / to prohibit / to exclude / to rule out
- figurehead / effigy / front man
- leader / pioneer / standard-bearer (figure de proue)
- straw man / front corporation / dummy corporation (prestanombres)

- camouflage / smoke-screen / cover-up
- to pay lip-service to / a cosmetic measure / on the surface
- clampdown / crackdown / dragnet
- recipe / formula / boilerplate
- unintended consequences / side-effects / collateral damage (effets collatéraux)
- to curb / to forestall / to avert / to contain (tenir en échec)
- grisly / macabre / eerie / hair-raising / gruesome (hallucinant / espeluzante)
- to be plunged in / to be immersed in / to undergo / to experience / to go through / to endure (traverser)
- benighted / uninformed / ignorant
- clearinghouse / focal point / switchboard / help desk
- profitability / cost-effectiveness / the bottom line (rentabilité)
- to process / to formalize / to take through proper channels (hacer trámites / tramitar)
- stakeholders / persons concerned / persons with an interest / those involved (les intéressés)
- untrammeled / galloping / uncontrolled / rampant (desenfrenado)
- to pool efforts / to act jointly / to act in concert (actuar mancomunadamente / conjuguer nos efforts)
- to bank on / to count on / to bet on / to rely on (miser sur / apostar sobre)
- to design / to lay out / to draw up (concevoir / diseñar)
- tailored to / geared to / suited to / adapted to / consonant with (adapté)
- grant / endowment / investment / fund (dotation)
- platitude / bromide / commonplace (lieu commun)
- bout / spell / period / lapse (lapso)
- onslaught / tide / wave / surge
- time line / deadline / time-frame / time limit / time horizon (fecha tope / date-butoir)
- calendar / schedule / timetable
- bold / courageous / valorous / dauntless
- predicated / based / founded
- concerned / apprehensive / worried
- duplication / redundancy / overlapping
- tense / trying / taut (éprouvant / éprouvé)
- dead giveaway / smoking gun / incontrovertible evidence
- serfdom / slavery / peonage / servitude / indentured servitude

- epitome / symbol / emblem / paradigm
- to epitomize / to symbolize / to typify
- legerdemain / sleight of hand / trickery
- matter / topic / question / issue / item
- posturing / grandstanding / posing
- trial balloon / feeler / probe
- plan / blueprint / master plan / battle plan
- conversant with / proficient in / knowledgeable about
- impending / imminent / clear and present
- refrain / leitmotif / repetition / recurring theme
- carping / harping / hectoring
- duet / duo / twosome (dupla)
- comparison / contrast / juxtaposition (cotejo)
- anomaly / disparity / discrepancy / irregularity / aberration / fluke
- dispute/quarrel / difference of opinion / controversy / debate / polemic (discrepancia)
- desired / yearned-for / long-sought (anhelado)
- generous / selfless / unselfish / altruistic / devoted / self-sacrificing / disinterested (abnegado)
- rendezvous / to meet again / to meet anew (retrouvailles)
- tough / hard-headed / unsentimental / realistic
- to take stock / to see where things stand / to pause for thought / to get one's bearings (faire le bilan / faire le point)
- abused / ill-used / mistreated (malmené)
- plundering / pillaging / looting / marauding
- treading water / making no headway / spinning one's wheels / running in place
- disaffected / dissatisfied / disgruntled
- predicament / crisis / imbroglio
- observance / compliance / satisfaction
- to dissolve / to abolish / to disband
- impact / prestige / notoriety / prominence (rayonnement)
- to disregard / to overlook / to ignore / to dispense with (passer outre à)
- mess / confusion / turmoil / upheaval (mare magnum)
- suitability / fitness / aptness / sufficiency (adéquation)
- slightly / somewhat / a little (marginalement)
- egregious / outlandish / preposterous / grotesque / outrageous
- to be in the fray / to be in the thick of it / to step into the breach

- gallantry / valor / guts / courage / intestinal fortitude
- important / vital / crucial / critical / momentous / epochal / earth-shaking (trascendente)
- appalled / dismayed / concerned / disconcerted
- discomfort / dissatisfaction / dismay / discomfiture
- to relieve / to alleviate / to lighten / to soothe (atténuer)
- rigid / strict / severe / stern / disciplined (rigoureux)
- proponents of / advocates of / adherents of / disciples of / devotees of (partisans de)
- partisans / guerrillas / fighters / combatants / militias / irregulars / mercenaries
- to ravage / to wreak havoc / to rain death and destruction
- volatile / explosive / unstable
- one-sided / biased / slanted / distorted
- telling / suggestive / symptomatic / speaks volumes about (en dit long sur)
- sidestep / circumvent / evade
- to snowball / to spiral / to escalate / to spin out of control / to spread (faire tache d'huile)
- volte-face / turnabout / reversal / 180-degree turn / about-face
- escape-valve / outlet / scapegoat / whipping-boy (exutoire)
- mollifying / soothing / reassuring (lénifiant)
- hype / media event / PR / publicity stunt (médiatique)
- foresight / vision / clear-sightedness (clairvoyance)
- insight / perceptiveness / keen intellect (lucidité)
- cheaply / on the cheap / at no cost (à bon compte)
- pattern / model / scheme / paradigm (schéma / parangón)
- to impair / to hurt / to injure / to harm / to detract from
- to jeopardize / to endanger / to threaten / to undermine / to imperil
- thought-provoking / stimulating / valuable (interesante)
- sweeping / extensive / plenary / unlimited
- backlash / pendulum swings back / tables turned (retour de bâton)
- example / illustration / case in point
- requires / involves / entails / demands (passe par)
- to rally / to pull together / to close ranks / to get behind (se rassembler)
- riposte / retaliation / countermeasure / retribution / revenge / reprisal / retorsion
- to step in between / to act as a buffer / to separate (s'interposer)
- to lead / to monitor / to supervise / to oversee (encadrer)

- liberal / kind-hearted / benevolent (bienveillant)
- volunteer / non-profit / charitable (bénévole)
- shaken / jolted / stirred (avoir un sursaut)
- fact / finding / observation / conclusion (constat)
- to note / to observe / to conclude (constater)
- admission of failure / resignation / abdication (constat d'échec)
- to settle / to decide / to rule / to resolve (zanjar / trancher)
- conjectural / conclusory / directive / assertive (volontariste)
- commotion / disturbance / outbreak / riot / upheaval / rebellion (conmoción)
- lithe / graceful / supple / flexible (souple)

(17) *Corruption.* A subject which was once taboo but is increasingly discussed in public fora, and which requires interpreters to exercise special care with nuances, is corruption. The interpreter must weigh words carefully when such references do occur, since there is a serious risk of giving offense by the wrong choice of words. It is a mistake to be blunt when the source-language speaker is clearly being euphemistic, or vice versa. The court interpreter must be especially careful to pin down the precise meaning of a specific allegation or charge of wrongdoing.

As with other sensitive or controversial subject areas (race, sex, religion, discrimination, gender, class, rank, status, etc.), the interpreter should strive to be faithful to the speaker's meaning whenever that meaning is unmistakably clear; however, when there is any doubt about the speaker's meaning or intent, it is wise to err on the side of caution and choose the more neutral or inoffensive word from those that are possible in the context. Among the famous mistakes interpreters have made is the case of the interpreter whose poor knowledge of Polish led him to use the word 'lust' in translating a speech by a US President expressing affection to his Polish audience. A more cautious choice of words (e.g. 'love' or 'affection') would have saved the day.

(a)   The translated article below provides an overview of forms of corruption around the world today and some of the words associated with them. It is important to understand the specific forms of conduct to which such words refer and to distinguish between expressions of moral disapproval and terms referring to illegal acts. They differ in both meaning and register, and they can be deceptive. For example, the US slang expression 'to be on the take', referring to bribery of public officials, has a euphemistic ring but refers to acts that are subject to severe penalties. Similarly, the term 'insider trading' does not sound like a crime but refers to one of the most well-defined forms of financial crime. By contrast, the slang terms 'payola' and 'kickback', referring to secret payments for commercial favors, sound like highly reprehensible acts but refer to practices that are not always considered illegal. Wrongdoing in everyday speech is different from wrongdoing as defined in the penal code. Consequently, an interpreter must be alert to the context, carefully discern the speaker's intended meaning, choose the word that refers to the specific conduct in question, and also strike the right register. Read the article, analyze and critique the translation from the standpoint of diction, then translate it into your other working languages.

Corruption Worldwide

We all remember those slightly faded black-and-white images of shadowy figures in dark glasses carrying attaché-cases full of cash in the seamy settings that befit shady deals. But for most of the world's inhabitants there is nothing of the grade-B movie about it. Corruption is an everyday affair, made all the more surrealistic by the fact that it happens all the time.

In China, along the highway from the city of Shenzhen to the industrial zone, the police set up a 'mandatory checkpoint' where drivers had to have their tires inspected for a modest 200 yuan. In Kenya, morgues grow rich charging decedents' families for bodies and school principals make ends meet by reselling used uniforms. In Russia you learn to pay for everything: a permit to live in Moscow and buy an apartment there will cost you $35,000.

In Egypt it's *baksheesh*, in Nigeria *dash*, in Mexico *la mordida*. Corruption is the one thing we all have in common. In Venezuela it has become the theme of a prime-time sitcom! There's no getting around it: this is now a part of everyday life all around the world. It may be a few electronic fund transfers between phantom corporations, a few petty deals here and there, a knack for keeping clients and constituents on the hook, or a dim trail leading to a Swiss bank account. But, wherever you look, you will find influence being bartered for money. . . .

Long considered the preserve of dictatorships of the South, the specialty of Marcos, Duvalier, Mobutu and other well-known kleptocrats, we have since learned that corruption can also thrive in industrialized democracies. The globalization of the economy seems to have brought about a globalization of corruption. Some see it as growing into an irreversible cancer.

Economist Alain Cotta describes one of the reasons: 'The drug trade generates mammoth profits, and corrupting anyone in power is the preferred way of reinvesting those profits.' That trend, everyone agrees, taints political life, ruins the citizenry and slows down development. According to the Luigi Einaudi research center, corruption is swelling the Italian government's debt by 15%, that is by $200 billion. According to the IMF, half of the $300 billion external debt of the world's 15 most heavily indebted countries is being held in private accounts transferred to tax havens.

So, in Rome and Beijing, in Buenos Aires and Moscow, anti-corruption campaigns are all the rage. Do they signal a resolve to fight what many consider a social scourge? Nothing could be less certain. 'Anti-corruption campaigns are an old tradition,' says political scientist Jean-Louis Rocca. 'They are a cloak of legitimacy that everyone uses. To win power, you have to portray yourself as being cleaner than all the others.' ...

And in many countries, at all levels of society, the government is the main source of wealth. A civil service job means, first and foremost, a salary, prestige, material benefits and the chance to help out one's kin. In that context, the black sheep is not the person with his hand in the till but the one who refuses to share the booty. A Chinese Communist Party cadre will work for the development of his village. An African businessman will donate millions of CFA francs to the *griots*. 'To Malians, accumulating wealth is not objectionable,' says Africa scholar Jean-Loup Amselle. 'What is objectionable is hoarding it. The practice of redistributive grabbing is the source of a vast patronage network that encompasses much of the population. Although only a minority of bureaucrats really profit from tapping the public coffers, the process of redistribution does reach a lot of people.' As a Czech proverb puts it, 'If you don't steal from the state, you're stealing from your family'. That proverb could serve as a slogan for many other countries.

Under those conditions, analyzing corruption in terms of good and evil becomes fairly meaningless. 'The main thing to understand is that, in most societies, economic accumulation involves an overlapping of the private and the public,' explains Jean-François Bayart. You use your position of power in government to accumulate wealth. And, contrary to a widespread opinion, that is not a peculiarly African habit.

Elsewhere, the economic miracles in Japan and Italy are there to remind us that corruption does not always go hand in hand with economic failure. 'There is no correlation between corruption and underdevelopment,' Bayart stresses. 'You can have productive corruption which generates growth, as in Japan, in most countries of East Asia, in Italy and even in France. In Africa, on the other hand, corruption hurts capitalism because it has been nothing but one more form of the income dependency that besets the sub-continent. The real problem is one of capital flight. But there can be corruption without capital flight, as in Asia, or with it, as in Africa.'

Economists have long emphasized that bribes are often a way to oil the machine. 'Corruption can be very functional,' explains specialist Jean Cartier-Bresson. 'The first Eastern European reformers who tried to eliminate corruption would have had a hard time of it because the practice was an essential complement to the barter system and conferred a little flexibility on economic transactions in the communist countries. Corruption kept those countries this side of total economic collapse.'

In the USSR under Brezhnev corruption virtually became an assembly-line process. Black market production, theft of state-allocated funds, use of state-run factory tools and inventory to produce goods that did not appear on the books and sell them illegally became that regime's daily fare. 'In terms of economic growth,' wryly notes American sociologist Samuel Huntington, 'the only thing worse than a society with a rigid, over-centralized, dishonest bureaucracy is a society with a rigid, over-centralized honest bureaucracy.'

In that case, why all the indignation? Why has corruption become the bugbear of every international conference, with leaders the world over vowing to end it? Why has Transparency International, a kind of Amnesty International against corruption, been created?

Because the machine is out of control. The economic deregulation of the 1980s seems to have brought in its wake a deregulation of corruption. Easy money has taken hold among the world's elites like a fever. And corruption through connections, providing ways to advance one's family or ethnic group, has replaced the commercial corruption whose sole purpose was personal gain.

In Eastern Europe, economic and political liberalization has opened the floodgates. 'Ethics has disappeared among the administrative nomenklatura,' notes Marie Mendras, a Russia specialist. 'The Soviet "ethic" mainly made it possible to maintain a pecking-order of corruption. A junior ministry employee could make a few thousand rubles a year in bribes, but no more. His higher-placed chief had bigger ambitions, although he could not compete with the top bosses in Moscow or the capitals of the republics. Those who broke the rules by trying to become local potentates faced reprisals.' Those good old days are over. Today, you can bribe and be bribed without a party membership card. The awareness that 'anything goes' is well entrenched, and any hope of help from the state has faded. As a result, 52,000 corruption-related crimes were reported in 1993. According to a recent report, a third of earnings from retail trade is being skimmed off by corruption. Every day the Russian press exposes cases of extortion, under-valuation of property slated for privatization, and embezzlement of funds for transfer overseas.

In the South, the decline of incomes of all kinds (whether from oil earnings, raw materials, international aid, major contracts, etc.) has triggered a sense of 'every man for himself'. It's a matter of survival. Corruption is spreading so fast that illegality has become the rule. Graft is feeding on graft. In Karachi, you buy your job as a policeman for 20,000 rupees ($800), and then pay yourself back over time by doing favors. . . .

Things are even more worrisome at the top. With structural adjustment and falling commodity prices, people seek out new sources of income: drug trafficking, storage of toxic wastes, diamond dealing. 'Crime in political life is the highest form of corruption,' explains Bayart. 'People in power use their political office to accumulate wealth drawn from parts of the world economy that are considered criminal. For example, the political-military class in Nigeria is investing in the drug trade. The war in Liberia is a drug conflict. Monrovia's banks, even before the war, specialized in money laundering. Today, there are even more banks in Monrovia than before, and their specialty is still the same.'

The same customs prevail in other climes. Thailand's chief of police, General Pratin Santiprapop, makes no secret of the information he has gathered about some 100 high-ranking Thais involved in drug trafficking, including quite a few political figures. But it seems there is not enough evidence to arrest them. And that is how corruption often helps criminal syndicates to gain control of the government. 'The underworld corrupts officials in local bureaucracies, representatives of legal economic organizations and even senior military officers,' claims Russian journalist Alexander Loima. Recently a Moscow intelligence officer was arrested for selling his services to criminal groups. . . . As one Mexican attorney general has said, 'In Mexico, we should no longer describe it as infiltration. Here, the government officials and the drug traffickers are the same people.' In Mexico, this is now being described as 'narco-democracy'. . . .

For those who are left out of the corruption loop, for all those who can't pay, for all those who can't buy their way in, all that's left is revolt. And young people left on the sidelines tend to become, depending on circumstances, 'soldiers' like Charles Taylor in Liberia, hooligans like those just about everywhere, or Islamists in the Arab world. Egyptian journalist Mohammed Sid Ahmed noted recently, 'Corruption is becoming so widespread that social relations are no longer defined by law or by the state, but by the covert practices of people dealing in influence, commissions, and bribes. Faced with that law of the jungle, those who lack the means to pay their way with bribery are tempted to resort to violence. Corruption and terrorism go hand in hand. During a particularly harsh phase of the economic cycle, with IMF structural adjustment policies wreaking havoc, the man in the street may well consider corruption more dangerous than terrorism.' In Algiers, following the 1990 electoral victory by the Islamic Salvation Front, one junior official offered me the following explanation: 'When *they* steal, they steal from God.' Corruption seems well on its way to becoming a major source of social and political violence. (Tolotti, 1995 (excerpts); trans. James Nolan)

(b)   Translate the following passage into English, French or your other working languages:

A la sazón, Octaviano tenía escasamente treinta años y se encontraba siendo dueño de toda la herencia de Cesar. El Senado no tenía ya ganas ni fuerza para disputársela, y sólo por cautela él no le pidió la investidura del trono. Se la hubiese concedido. Pero Octaviano conocía el peso de las palabras y sabía que la de rey era desagradable. Para qué despertar ciertas manías que ya no hacían sino dormitar en las conciencias entumecidas? Los romanos habían dejado de creer en las instituciones democráticas y republicanas porque conocían su corrupción, pero estaban apegados a las formas. Pedían orden, paz y seguridad, una buena administración, una moneda saneada y los ahorros garantizados. Y Octaviano se aprestó a darles estas cosas. (Montanelli, 1959; trans. Pruna, 1969)

(c) Translate the following passage into English, Spanish or your other working languages:

Carthage, devenue riche plus tôt que Rome, avait aussi été plus tôt corrompue. Ainsi, pendant qu'à Rome les emplois publics ne s'obtenaient que par la vertu et ne donnaient d'utilité que l'honneur, ... tout ce que le public peut donner aux particuliers se vendait à Carthage, et tout service rendu par les particuliers y était payé par le public. La tyrannie d'un prince ne met pas un Etat plus près de sa ruine que l'indifférence pour le bien commun n'y met une république. L'avantage d'un Etat libre est que les revenus y sont mieux administrés. Mais lorsqu'ils le sont plus mal, l'avantage d'un Etat libre est qu'il n'y a point de favoris. Mais quand cela n'est pas le cas, et qu'au lieu des amis et des parents du prince il faut faire la fortune des amis et des parents de tous ceux qui ont part au gouvernement, tout est perdu. (Adapted from Montesquieu, *Considérations sur les causes de la grandeur des Romains et leur décandence*)

(d) What do contemporary patterns of corruption have in common with the problem of corruption as viewed in ancient times? Has the nature of the problem changed significantly? What does 'ciertas manías' refer to in the above passage by Montanelli? Could the English expressions 'to rock the boat' and 'to pay lip-service' be used in translating that passage? Could the word 'merit' be used to translate 'vertu' in the above passage by Montesquieu?

(e) With the aid of a good dictionary, define the following terms. Then translate them into your other languages. Write illustrative sentences that bring out the distinctions between the terms. Explain differences in register or level of language. Which of the terms are standard vocabulary, which are slang and which are legal or administrative terms of art? Which would be considered acceptable usage in the context of a formal speech and which would be considered 'sub-standard' in register?

bribery / embezzlement / extortion / contraband / smuggling / bootlegging / trafficking / misappropriation of funds / graft / payola / payoff / kickback / slush-fund / loophole / dealings / maladministration / blackmail / dilapidation / waste / misuse of public funds / hoarding / abuse of power / abuse of authority / overreaching / misuse of public office / accumulation of powers / nepotism / duress / exactions / excesses / to pull strings / influence-peddling / racket, racketeer, racketeering / to suborn / subornation / unlawful delegation of authority / insider trading / white-collar crime / corporate crime / electoral fraud / lobby, lobbyist, lobbying / malfeasance / misfeasance / insubordination / impunity / to grease someone's palm / diversion of funds / creative accounting / to cook the books / misrepresentation / to pull strings / boondoggle / junket, junketing / featherbedding / pork-barrel politics / pork / the spoils system / patronage / a sinecure / a plum / venal / venality / crony, cronyism / old-boy network / accountability / transparency / unaccountable / co-conspirator / the mob / the underworld / non-disclosure

le piston / pistonner quelqu'un / le cumul / abus de pouvoir / exactions / délit d'initié / une planque / pot de vin / contrebande / traffic

la palanca / el soborno / la mordida / venalidad / tropelía / sinvergüencería / venalidad / abuso / contrabanda / tráfico / conducta delictiva / encubrimiento / enriquecimiento ilícito / desvío de recursos

(f) Are the local terms *backsheesh*, *mordida* and *dash* given in the article above (pp. 151–155) all translatable into English as 'bribery'? Are they translatable as 'graft'? Are they translatable as 'embezzlement'?

(g) The practice of rigging an election by 'stuffing' the ballot boxes with fraudulent votes is popularly known in Mexico as 'el taco'. How might you translate this idea into your other languages with a term of equivalent colloquial register?

(h) In an English article about corruption in Europe, the Italian bribery scandal *Tangentopoli* was rendered as 'bribe city'. Is this a good translation? Are the American political and financial scandals known as Watergate, Irangate, Whitewater and Enron translatable into other languages, or are the words easily recognizable in other languages and therefore best left in English?

(i) The US practice of 'gerrymandering' consists of drawing the boundaries of an electoral district in such a way as to guarantee victory for a given candidate or party. What is the derivation of this word? Is it based on a metaphor? How might you translate this concept into your other languages? How would you draw the distinction in translation between corrupt practices and the legitimate activities described by 'lobbying' and 'advocacy'?

(j)   An English-language history of European Christianity refers to the abuses committed by ecclesiastical authorities prior to the Reformation as 'exactions'. Is this a proper use of the term? How does 'exaction' differ from 'misuse of authority' or 'duress'? In French, 'exactions' is sometimes used in the general sense of taking undue advantage of the public under cover of authority. In that sense, is 'depredations' a good English equivalent?

(18) *Stereotypes.* Stereotypes are, by definition, concepts that do not correspond to reality. National or ethnic stereotypes (positive or negative) are 'loaded words' and, unless spoken humorously, are usually best avoided by interpreters working in an international setting, not only because they may offend some members of an international audience, but also because the intended meaning will often be obscured or lost in a too-literal translation. If the speaker's intent is distorted and gives offense, it is the interpreter, naturally enough, who will bear the blame.

Every modern language has an inherited stock of words based on stereotypes about real or imagined 'national characteristics'. But these words tend to be untranslatable because they are culture specific: each culture views others through the prism of its own value system, and such subjective perceptions may be difficult or impossible to convey accurately in translation.

Positive stereotypes like 'esprit Gaulois', 'Castizo' or 'Hellenic' refer to a whole cultural ethos which cannot easily be summed up. What an English speaker means when he speaks of 'Gallic humor' or 'Teutonic thinking' may be quite meaningless to a Frenchman or a German. Similarly, what is meant by the archaic adjective 'Oriental' is apt to be meaningless today to any person from the Far East, or indeed to anyone but another English speaker. What is meant in English by 'Latino' or 'the Latin temperament' has become, at best, rather elusive.

When a French speaker uses the word 'anglo-saxon', it is often meant merely as a synonym for 'anglophone', that is a general term for 'English speakers', and is not intended to carry ethnic, historical or racial connotations, so that it is often a mistake to translate it as 'Anglo-Saxon'. It has become rather inapt to use 'Anglo-Saxon' in reference to an English-speaking multicultural society like the United States. And the alternative expression 'Anglo-American' is also unsatisfactory in many cases because it is under-inclusive: it impliedly leaves out English-speaking people from Hong Kong to Nigeria.

When a Spanish speaker uses the word 'yanqui', he does *not* mean a person from the northeastern seaboard of the United States, which is what the word 'Yankee' normally means to an American audience. Conversely, when a Latin-American uses the adjective 'Norteamericano', he usually *does* mean 'from the United States', which is not what the word 'North American' normally means to an English speaker, for whom it is merely a geographical term including Canadians and Mexicans.

In all of these cases (and regardless of any express or implied value judgments, positive or negative) the specific meaning of the stereotype in the source language often has no accepted equivalent in the target language. The nearest equivalent stereotype in the target language is often over-inclusive or under-inclusive, and often carries a different connotation or resonance.

Consequently, it is important to distinguish between straightforward adjectives of nationality or ethnicity (e.g. 'Hungarian') and ethnic stereotypes (e.g. 'Hispanic'). The former are translatable, but the latter often are not and should be avoided if possible. When speakers consciously use stereotypes which are untranslatable, meaningless or misleading, but which are at least recognizable in the target language, a literal translation is perhaps safest because it at least has the merit of indicating to the listeners that a stereotype is being used.

(a) Read the following excerpt from an article about stereotyped perceptions of foreigners, paying special attention to the way metaphors are used to create or reinforce such perceptions:

> *Alien Expressions*
>
> In the United States, as in many European countries, one consistently neutral metaphor for immigration is water. Immigration is a flow, a flood, a tide, a wave, an influx, a stream, a tsunami, or, after restrictions, a trickle. Immigrants are drained from their homelands. They wash up like 'wretched refuse' on the shores. The country is inundated, swamped, submerged, engulfed, awash.
>
> Another common metaphor is the nation as a house and the immigrant as a visitor knocking at the door or the window, standing at the threshold or in the backyard.
>
> A more menacing metaphor, especially popular in the United States, is the military one. Two weeks ago during the candidates' debate in New Hampshire, Mr. Buchanan said, 'When you have one, two, three million people walking across

your border every year, breaking your laws, you have an invasion.' (Of course, it isn't an invasion if the 'people walking across your border every year' happen to be the 250,000 essential farm workers approved by the House Agriculture Committee last week.)

... British politicians, with a strong sense of their country as an island, also use water metaphors for immigration. But while those who wish to appear neutral talk about tides and waves and flows, those who oppose immigration use more insidious liquid metaphors.

In 1978, Margaret Thatcher commented that she could understand that British citizens might feel 'swamped' by immigration. Recently her words have been echoed by Tory extremist Stuart Millson: 'We have had an unnatural multicultural society imposed on us. Creeping into every part of our national life today is a wetness and weediness that would have been unimaginable 50 years ago.' ...

In China the uncomplimentary expression for a migrant laborer is 'zazi', meaning a young animal or whelp, but with the same feeling as 'bastard' in English. The implication: foreigners are, like bunny rabbits, promiscuous. ...

How people talk about perceived threats gives clues about how they view their homeland. As water metaphors reveal a nation-as-island, and filth metaphors reveal an obsession with purity, the French habit of discussing immigration with metaphors of disease reveals an implicit conception of France as a body, and particularly as a female body. (Christenfeld, 1996 (excerpts))

(b) Of the 'water' metaphors in the first paragraph above, which ones are actually 'neutral', as the author says? Does the choice of the metaphor used to describe a phenomenon tend to determine whether that phenomenon will be viewed in a positive or negative light? Are the 'house' metaphors used to describe immigration more neutral than the 'water' metaphors? Is the word 'influx' the most neutral one because of its seemingly technical resonance?

(c) Can one infer that one culture is more xenophobic than another because its language has more negative words referring to foreigners?

(d) Given the existence of English metaphorical expressions such as 'the body politic', would you agree with the author of the above comment that the conception of the nation as a 'body' is uniquely French?

(e) Is it unusual for one language to borrow derogatory words from another language? What problems does this present for the translator or interpreter?

(f) Translate the above excerpt into French, Spanish or your other working languages. Consider which, if any, of the images used are actually 'neutral' enough in the target language not to give offense.

10 Formal Style

Rhetoricians sometimes say that the register and diction (choice of words) of a speaker must satisfy three criteria: they must be appropriate to (1) the subject, (2) the occasion and (3) the audience. This, of course, applies with equal force to the writer's translator or to the speaker's interpreter. The translator or interpreter, as the speaker's echo, must reflect the speaker's *sense of occasion*, and the more important the occasion the more accurate and complete should the reflection be.

For the translator, it is the original writer who dictates the register, diction, style and color. The translator:

> is to exhibit his author's thoughts in such a dress of diction as the author would have given them, had his language been English: rugged magnificence is not to be softened; hyperbolical ostentation is not to be repressed, nor sententious affectation to have its points blunted. A translator is to be like his author: it is not his business to excel him. (Johnson, Samuel (1779) *Lives of the English Poets: Dryden*. London: Faber & Faber)

Similarly, for the interpreter, it is primarily the speaker who dictates the register, diction, style, tone and color of the speech, regardless of the occasion or the audience's expectations. The speaker is sovereign, and may choose to deliver a speech quite different from what the audience expected on a particular occasion. For example, the crowds who flocked to the burial ground of the Battle of Gettysburg expecting to hear President Abraham Lincoln deliver one of the long, colorful orations for which he had become famous were disappointed to hear only a brief eulogy. Yet that brief speech was so well suited to the historic solemnity and gravity of the occasion that it is widely regarded as one of the finest speeches in the English language. The speaker's tone, it should be recalled, may be as important as the content of the speech. To sound abrasive or blunt when the speaker is being delicately diplomatic, or to sound incisive when the speaker is being deliberately evasive, are also forms of misinterpretation.

The problem faced by French or Spanish interpreters working from English is that they are often forced to use a wordier style than that of the source language in order to strike the right note of formality, which makes it more difficult to keep up with the speaker. But the English interpreter working from Spanish or French faces a stylistic dilemma where formal oratory is concerned. Contemporary English speaking style, even on formal and solemn occasions, is marked by relative simplicity and straightforwardness. However, much formal oratory in Spanish and French even today bears the stamp of the Baroque: eloquence, deliberate complexity, richness of vocabulary, verbal ornamentation and the use of a wider range of rhetorical devices than it is fashionable to use in modern English. Thus, the English interpreter may find that, if the style of the Spanish or French speech is tracked *too* closely, the English interpretation will not sound 'solemn' but, on the contrary, ridiculous. So the English interpreter must find ways of striking a delicate balance: conveying the stylistic richness of the original without lapsing into excesses which are silly or anachronistic to the English ear.

Plain speech, the interpreter's 'safety net', should not become a crutch or a formula for reducing brilliance to monotony. When a speaker has labored long and hard to give a major address to an important audience an epic quality, the interpreter who reduces the speech to pedestrian 'plain words' is not doing justice to the speaker. Simple ideas are sometimes obscured by unnecessarily complex or turgid constructions, and an interpreter who can clarify them in the act of interpreting is doing a service to both himself and the audience (see Chapter 3). But not all ideas are simple. When a speaker makes a complex argument or reaches a high pitch of oratory, an interpreter who has acquired enough experience, confidence and skill should climb out of the safety net and try to follow the speaker's movements on the trapeze, without making a fool of himself.

Exercises

(1) To preserve at least some of the flavor of French or Spanish formal oratory, it is useful to draw on the rhetorical devices used by the great orators of ancient Greece and Rome (e.g. English translations of the speeches of Cicero) or English speakers of the 19th century and earlier times. For example, one good, reasonably modern source is the speeches of Abraham Lincoln. The speech quoted below, 'The Perpetuation of Our Political Institutions' (1838) is a speech about the danger which mob rule represents to the rule of law.

At the beginning of the speech, Lincoln paints a somewhat idyllic picture of America in order to create a stark contrast between the many advantages and blessings Americans enjoy and the atrocious incidents he goes on to describe later in the speech. He then likens the specter of mob rule to an 'enemy' as being as dangerous to the Republic as a foreign invader:

> *The Perpetuation of Our Political Institutions*
> We find ourselves in the peaceful enjoyment of the fairest portion of the earth, as regards extent of territory, fertility of soil, and salubrity of climate. We find ourselves under the government of a system of political institutions conducing more essentially to the ends of civil and religious liberty than any of which the history of former times tells us. We ... find ourselves the legal inheritors of these fundamental blessings ... a legacy bequeathed us by a once hardy, brave, and patriotic but now lamented and departed race of ancestors. Theirs was the task (and nobly they performed it) to possess themselves, and through themselves, us of this goodly land; and to uprear upon its hills and valleys a political edifice of liberty and equal rights; 'tis ours only to transmit these, the former unprofaned by the foot of an invader, the latter undecayed by the lapse of time and untorn by usurpation, to the latest generation that fate shall permit the world to know. **This task gratitude to our fathers, justice to ourselves, duty to posterity, and love for our species in general, all imperatively require us faithfully to perform**. (Lincoln, 1991a: 1 (excerpts))

A useful construction appears in the last sentence: the object comes first, the subject(s) next and the verb last (as sometimes occurs in formal speeches in French or Spanish, and as often happens in other languages). Notice that, although it has a slightly archaic flavor to the modern ear, this inverted word order nevertheless does not sound un-English and has a certain soaring elegance. The same sentence put in the normal English word order sounds flat and uninteresting by comparison: 'Gratitude to our fathers, justice to ourselves, duty to posterity, and love for our species in general all imperatively require us faithfully to perform this task.'

A similar inverted construction appears in the second sentence of the fifth paragraph of the speech:

> there is, even now, something of ill-omen amongst us. I mean the increasing disregard for law which pervades the country; the growing disposition to substitute the wild and furious passions, in lieu of

the sober judgment of Courts; and the worse than savage mobs, for the executive ministers of justice. This disposition is awfully fearful in any community; **and that it now exists in ours, though grating to our feelings to admit, it would be a violation of truth, and an insult to our intelligence, to deny**.

Here again, the verb is placed at the end, creating an element of suspense within the sentence that is only resolved when the *crescendo* has reached its peak. No similar impact is achieved by the 'usual' word order: 'It would be a violation of truth, and an insult to our intelligence, to deny that it now exists in ours, though it be grating to our feelings to admit it.'

Note the function in the following sentence of the adverbial phrase 'Abstractly considered ...': 'Abstractly considered, the hanging of the gamblers at Vicksburg was of but little consequence.' Since the main point is made in the remainder of the sentence and the adverbial phrase merely sets the scene, this construction has the merit of getting the secondary point neatly out of the way. (Compare 'The hanging of the gamblers at Vicksburg was of but little consequence, viewed in the abstract' or 'The hanging of the gamblers at Vicksburg, in the abstract, was of but little consequence'.) Using this construction in interpretation will enable you to focus all your attention on the main point in the sentence (see Chapter 5). Notice also the extraordinary pithiness of the word 'abstractly', which (in only three syllables) would be adequate to render such wordy phrases as 'considéré en tant que tel' or 'considéré en dehors de ses conséquences plus larges', etc.

In the next passage, several words appear that are useful for translating various contemporary ideas: perpetrators, bane, forebodes, averse, bulwark, vicious, at pleasure and with impunity. Note their meaning in context. In addition, Lincoln coins a word of his own, 'mobocratic':

By such examples, by such instances of the **perpetrators** of such acts going unpunished, the lawless in spirit are encouraged to become lawless in practice. ... Having ever regarded Government as their deadliest **bane**, they make a jubilee of the suspension of its operations. ... While, on the other hand, good men, men who love tranquility, who desire to abide by the laws ... seeing their property destroyed, their families insulted, and their lives endangered ... and seeing nothing in prospect that **forebodes** a change for the better, become tired of and disgusted with a Government that offers them no protection and are not much **averse** to a change in which they imagine they have nothing to lose. Thus, then, by the operation of

> this **mobocratic** spirit ... the strongest **bulwark** of any Government
> ... may effectually be broken down and destroyed – I mean the
> attachment of the People. Whenever this effect shall be produced
> among us; whenever the **vicious** portion of population shall be per-
> mitted to gather in bands ... and burn churches, ravage and rob
> provision-stores, throw printing presses into rivers, shoot editors,
> and hang and burn obnoxious persons **at pleasure**, and **with impu-
> nity**, depend on it, this Government cannot last. (Lincoln, 1991a: 4)

'Perpetrator' is useful synonym for 'offender' when the speaker is expressing strong disapproval but not a technical legal judgment about guilt or innocence (which is implied by terms like 'criminal' or 'culprit'), and also when the deed is particularly horrendous, as in the case of grave human rights violations. It can also be used to translate 'responsable' or 'malfaiteur' in the proper contexts.

'Bane' is a useful alternative for 'scourge' in translating the frequently used 'fléau'.

Notice how Lincoln uses 'forebodes' in the neutral sense of 'heralds' or 'foreshadows'. Although 'forebodes' would today generally be used in the sense of foreshadowing some negative future event, is there any reason why it should not also be used in that neutral sense if the rest of the sentence makes it clear that the future event is positive?

Notice the use of 'averse' as a somewhat more elegant alternative for 'resistant to' or 'object to'.

'Bulwark' is a concept that frequently occurs in formal speeches, especially at the UN (e.g. 'The Charter is a bulwark of peace.'). Notice that Lincoln is using it here much as a synonym of 'pillar' or 'cornerstone' or 'mainstay'. It can sometimes be used with 'against' to translate the French verb 'endiguer' in the sense of holding back something bad.

Notice the rather Victorian but still plausible use of 'vicious' in '... the vicious portion of the population ...' to refer to people given to violence. Could 'une foule déchaînée' be translated as 'a vicious mob'?

'At pleasure', as used here by Lincoln, could be used to translate 'comme bon leur semble' or 'suivant leur gré'.

'With impunity', as used here by Lincoln, is precisely what is meant in a sentence like 'Les militaires, agissant *impunément*, ont fait disparaitre des centaines de personnes.'

As regards the coinage 'mobocratic', note that, while it is often considered taboo for translators to create new words that are not in the dictionary, interpreters are allowed more license and could use this device where it is useful and appropriate.

The next passage also contains a number of words, constructions and phrases of interest to the translator or interpreter:

We hope all dangers may be overcome, but to conclude that no danger may ever arise would itself be extremely dangerous. There are now, and will hereafter be, many causes, **dangerous in their tendency**, which have not existed heretofore. . . . **That our government should have been maintained in its original form from its establishment until now, is not much to be wondered at**. It had many **props** to support it through that period, which now are decayed, and **crumbled away**. Through that period, it was felt by all to be an **undecided experiment**; now, it is understood to be a successful one. (Lincoln, 1991a: 6)

Notice the following:

- the use of 'in their tendency' in the phrase 'dangerous in their tendency' as an intensifier with the same meaning as 'de nature' in 'de nature dangereuse'.
- '. . . is not to be wondered at' as a possible translation of '. . . n'est guère surprenant'.
- Another example of emphasis achieved through inverted construction, with the verb at the end: **That our government should have been maintained in its original form from its establishment until now, is not much to be wondered at**.
- The use of 'props' (one syllable) in the sense of 'underpinnings' (four syllables).
- The use of 'crumbled away', a good possible translation for phrases like 'se sont écroulés' or 'se sont évanouis'.
- The use of 'undecided experiment', a good possible translation for phrases like 'une expérience incertaine' or 'une tentative incertaine' (the word 'experiment' by itself sometimes sounds too scientific).

(a) Can you think of any adverbs ending in -ly which you could use to abbreviate more wordy phrases in French or Spanish? For example, could you translate 'Regardant en face les faits devant nous, . . .' as 'Realistically, . . .'? Could you translate 'Sin ir más allá de lo que los datos nos permiten suponer . . .' as 'Speaking conservatively . . .'?

(b) Translate the following sentences first into the 'normal' English word order (subject–verb–object), then into inverted word order with the verb at the end:

Example: Debo recalcar la urgencia de actuar inmediatamente. = I must stress the urgent need to act immediately. = That we take immediate action is an urgent need I must stress.

- Nous ne saurions manquer une opportunité si rare.
- Une si rare opportunité ne saurait pas être manquée.
- Agir de la sorte serait trahir nos plus beaux idéaux.
- Ce serait trahir nos plus beaux idéaux que d'agir de la sorte.
- Nous devons à tout prix défendre ce droit.
- C'est là un droit à défendre à tout prix.
- C'est un impératif incontournable que de sauver l'environnement.
- La vida no valdría la pena en un mundo sin dolidaridad.
- En un mundo sin solidaridad, no valdría la pena vivir.

(2) Compare the style, tone and content of Lincoln's political speech above (pp. 164–166) with the following excerpts from a political speech by Mikhail Gorbachev. Both speeches are concerned with the same general theme: the problem of establishing or strengthening institutional legitimacy and preserving the rule of law. However, whereas Lincoln relied more on negative examples of lawlessness, Gorbachev relies more on the motivational appeal of 'pep talk'. Notice the expressions in bold type.

I should like to express a fundamental thought. We have adopted a number of deeply considered and crucial decisions. But if we **drag our feet** in carrying them out ... much of what we have accomplished will **fall by the wayside**. This should be said **loud and clear**. Let's **get rid of our weaknesses** and begin immediately to **tackle the work ahead** of us **without waiting** for additional decrees, injunctions, instructions and explanations. ... Naturally, intensive organizational work to **translate this reform into reality** lies ahead. We will have to discuss everything thoroughly in our Party and in our society. But now we know how we should go about reforming the political system; we have arrived at a **common viewpoint** and articulated it in the form of policy guidelines. ... As concerns the key landmarks of the discussion on the issues, the point is above all that after the Conference we must **get down in earnest** to the **job of dismantling the mechanisms holding us back**. Representatives of virtually all delegations said that the bureaucracy was still **showing its teeth**, resisting and trying to sabotage our efforts. As a result, the reform is **hitting snags** in many areas. ... What we need is not **blind faith in a bright future** but scientific projections based on a profound and precise knowledge of the **inexhaustible potential** inherent in a citizen of socialist society, in his work and **creative spirit**. That is exactly why we refer to a **new and humane image of socialism** as the objective of perestroika. ... And one more issue, comrades, raised shortly before and at the Conference: that of building a monument to the **victims of the repressions**. ... As noted in the Report, **restoring justice** with regard to the **victims of lawlessness** is our political and moral duty. Let us **perform that duty** and build a monument in Moscow. (Speech by Mikhail Gorbachev to the 19th Conference of the Communist Party of the Soviet Union, 1 July 1988)

(3) Study the following examples of modern English formal oratory. Read the speeches aloud into your tape recorder, giving your delivery and tone of voice a seriousness and solemnity appropriate to the occasion. Play back your recording at a later time and consider whether your performance conveyed the purpose and conviction of the speaker. Then translate the speeches into your other languages and perform the same exercise with the translated versions.

Neutrality is no longer feasible or desirable where the peace of the world is involved and the freedom of its peoples, and the menace to that peace and freedom lies in the existence of autocratic Governments, backed by organized force which is controlled wholly by their will, not by the will of the people. ... A steadfast concern for peace can never be maintained except by a partnership of democratic nations. ... The world must be made safe for democracy. Its peace must be planted upon the tested foundations of political liberty. We have no selfish ends to serve. We desire no conquest, no dominion. ... We are but one of the champions of the rights of mankind. ... It is a fearful thing to lead this great, peaceful people into war, into the most terrible and disastrous of all wars, civilization itself seeming to be in the balance. But the right is more precious than the peace, and we shall fight for the things which we have always carried in our hearts – for democracy, for the right of those who submit to authority to have a voice in their own Governments, for the rights and liberties of small nations, for a universal dominion of right by such a concert of free peoples as shall bring peace and safety to all nations and make the world itself at last free. (Speech by President Woodrow Wilson upon the entry of the United States into World War I)

The real complaining party at your bar is Civilization. In all our countries it is still a struggling and imperfect thing. It does not plead that the United States or any other country has been blameless of the conditions which made the German people easy victims to the blandishments of the Nazi conspirators. But it points to the dreadful sequence of aggressions and crimes I have recited, it points to the weariness of flesh, the exhaustion of resources, and the destruction of all that was beautiful or useful in this world, and to greater potentialities in the days to come. It is not necessary among the ruins of this ancient and beautiful city with untold numbers of its civilian inhabitants buried in its rubble, to argue the proposition that to start or wage an aggressive war has the moral qualities of the worst crimes. ... Civilization asks whether law is so laggard as to be utterly helpless to deal with crimes of this magnitude by criminals of this order of importance. It does not expect that you [the Tribunal] can make war impossible. It does expect that your juridical action will put the forms of international law, its precepts, its prohibitions and, most of all, its sanctions, on the side of peace, so that men and women of good will, in all countries, may have 'leave to live by no man's leave, underneath the law'. (Opening address by Justice Robert H. Jackson to the Nuremberg War Crimes Tribunal)

However close we sometimes seem to that dark and final abyss, let no man of peace and freedom despair. For he does not stand alone. If we all can persevere, if we can in every land and office look beyond our own shores and ambitions, then surely the age will dawn in which the strong are just and the weak secure and the peace preserved. ... Never have the nations of the world had so much to lose or so much to gain. Together we shall save our planet or together we shall perish in its flames. Save it we can, and save it we must, and then shall we earn the eternal thanks of mankind and, as peacemakers, the eternal blessings of God. (Speech by President John F. Kennedy, address before the General Assembly of the United Nations, New York City, 15 September 1961)

If we cannot end now our differences, at least we can help make the world safe for diversity. For, in the final analysis, our most basic common link is that we all inhabit this planet. We all breathe the same air. We all cherish our children's future. And we are all mortal. This generation of Americans has already had enough – more than enough – of war and hate and oppression. ... We shall do our part to build a world of peace where the weak are safe and the strong are just. We are not helpless before that task or hopeless of its success. Confident and unafraid, we labor on – not toward a strategy of annihilation but toward a strategy of peace. (Speech by President John F. Kennedy, commencement address, American University, Washington, 10 June 1963)

Unfortunately, as all of us are painfully aware, our modern world is still witnessing terrible armed conflicts and political and economic tensions which give rise to unspeakable offenses against human life and freedom. Against that background, how can we fail to remember, and commend to God's loving mercy, all those who have given their lives in the service of the United Nations and its ideals, especially those who have fallen in peace-keeping and humanitarian missions. Their sacrifice is an integral part of United Nations history. In the face of continuing tragedy and evil, however, *we do not lose hope with regard to the future.* For we witness the sincere efforts of nations striving to work together, actively pursuing policies of partnership and joint responsibility in addressing problems both old and new. ... In the context of the community of nations, the Church's message is simple yet absolutely crucial for the survival of humanity and the world: *the human person must be the true focus of all social, political and economic activity.* This truth, when effectively put into practice, will point the way to healing the divisions between rich and poor, to overcoming the inequality between the strong and weak, to reconciling man with himself and with God. For men and women are made in the image and likeness of God. So people may never be regarded as mere objects, nor may they be sacrificed for political, economic or social gain. We must never allow them to be manipulated or enslaved by ideologies or technology. Their God-given dignity and worth as human beings forbid this. ... I wrote that it was difficult to say what mark the year 2000 would leave on the face of human history, to know what it would bring to each people, nation, country and continent. It is no easier to foretell those things today; but I do know that your dedicated work here at the United Nations is a promising sign that the new millennium will see *a flowering of true humanity in compassion, openness and solidarity between peoples and nations.* My prayers are with you and your families. May Almighty God bless you always and strengthen you with his grace and peace, that you may continue to serve him in the service you give to the whole human family! (Address by His Holiness Pope John Paul II to the United Nations Staff, 5 October 1995 (excerpts))

(4) Study the following English translations of formal speeches delivered at the solemn commemorative meeting marking the 50th anniversary of the United Nations. Read the speeches aloud into your tape recorder, giving your delivery and tone of voice a seriousness and solemnity appropriate to the occasion. Play back your recording at a later time and

consider whether your performance conveyed the purpose and conviction of the speaker.

Mr President:

Special and unforeseen circumstances have prevented His Excellency, President Gonzalo Sánchez de Lozada of Bolivia, from being present here today.

I therefore have the honor to make this statement paying tribute to the United Nations and conveying the cordial greetings of the Head of State of Bolivia to Your Excellencies, the Heads of State and Government of the world, to you, Mr President of the General Assembly, and to the Secretary General of the United Nations.

For Bolivia, this solemn ceremony symbolizes an act of faith in the capacity of human beings to live together in harmony. It represents a renewal of our commitment to work on in the conviction that freedom and equality will prevail on this earth.

In Bolivia we remember with admiration the ability and vision of the distinguished figures who laid the foundations of the United Nations, and we pay special tribute to our fellow countrymen who attended the historic San Francisco Conference, under the guidance of then President of the Republic, Colonel Gualberto Villaroel.

The contribution of the Bolivian delegates to that debate was particularly important. And so, 50 years later, we reiterate the conviction that permanent peace on earth requires justice in international relations and within each country.

Our delegates maintained that, if harmony were to prevail among nations, solutions had to be found to situations that impede fraternal relations between peoples. Only justice will be the foundation of a true peace.

Someday in the not too distant future there will be an end to situations of oppression and dependency, just as colonialism will come to an end, extreme poverty will disappear, friendship among peoples will flourish, and the free and sovereign presence of Bolivia on the Pacific Ocean will be possible.

The power politics of yesterday will have to give way to brotherhood and cooperation as central instruments in the new international relations.

Bolivia cultivates friendship among countries and calls for cooperation based on dignity, sovereign equality, respect for diversity, and understanding of the needs and legitimate concerns of peoples.

Good-neighborly relations require sincerity by all but, most especially, respect for others and the desire to contribute to the welfare of our brother peoples, to raise standards of living, to promote opportunities for work, and to reach definite objectives in the area of health, education, and housing, widening access to financing, technology, and world markets.

Based upon those principles all countries will be active members of the world community, capable of making sustainable development possible, of capitalizing and creating enterprises to respond to the challenges of the day, of eradicating consumption and trafficking of harmful substances, of releasing mankind from the arms spiral and nuclear peril, of consolidating political stability and participatory democracy, of respecting cultural and ethnic diversity, and of creating real conditions for all men and women, the elderly, youth, and children, to live in a better world of true solidarity.

Thus, Mr President, the agenda of the United Nations for the years to come has been laid out.

In Bolivia we have learned that stagnation corrodes institutions and paralyzes ideologies, while change is a wellspring of life and the key to social transformation.

Therefore, in order to protect the worldly and spiritual heritage of nations, we must change attitudes, discover new dimensions of development, modify the international system, and adopt dynamic forms of cooperation, tolerance, and universal understanding.

We shall also have to strengthen the role of the General Assembly, make the Security Council more functional and representative, confer effective authority on the Economic and Social Council, and ensure that Law will be the instrument by which international Justice is secured.

Bolivia, that multi-cultural and multi-lingual country we are building across our Andean highlands and our plains, is preparing honorably to fulfil the role that falls to it in the universal community of the future.

Thank you, Mr President. (Edgar Camacho-Omiste, statement to the United Nations on its 50th anniversary on behalf of the President of Bolivia, Mr Gonzalo Sánchez de Lozada, 1995; trans. James Nolan)

A United Nations for the 21st Century
Mr President:
There is a fact which has become so apparent to the common man the world over that there is no need to insist upon it: we are witnessing far-reaching changes that have definitively eclipsed the frame of reference within which international life was led over a period of more than half a century during which the United Nations Organization was created.

Undoubtedly, the immense consequences of those changes will extend beyond the turn of the century. We are living in a time of global change in which mankind as a whole is entering a truly universal era, in which the intensity of global exchanges and the new conditions governing the balance of world power foreshadow, for the first time in history, a chance to build a new international order based more on the rational imperative of cooperation than on the use of force.

There has been a substantive change in the nature of the conditions that determine the complex fabric of international security. In this scenario of great changes, if the United Nations wishes to remain faithful to the purposes and principles that presided over its birth and thus constitute a useful instrument of peace and harmonious development for the planet, rather than a merely symbolic institution, the Organization will undertake a profound renewal of its structures in order to achieve the efficiency that all countries of the world are clearly calling for.

The inseparable dimensions of peace and development, although recognized by all in official statements and turned into a cliché in every technical report of the system, nevertheless go unnoticed when the time comes for commitments and have only a faint impact upon the real practice of international politics. However, it has never been clearer that the principal threats to peace and security come from the deterioration of social or institutional structures whose most stubborn and dangerous expression is the persistence of extreme poverty over broad areas of the planet.

A United Nations Organization for the 21st century will be one which, with moral steadfastness and political conviction, faces up to the challenge of development and the eradication of poverty in the world, a daunting task which involves an integrated conception of security and development that responds to the concrete demands of society, the ultimate recipient of our collective efforts. It is time to pave the way for international cooperation as the new paradigm governing United Nations activities, as a guarantee of a new era of peace and solidarity in the world.

It is therefore indispensable for a strictly democratic perspective to prevail in the very structures of the United Nations, ensuring authentic representativity in organs of vital importance such as, for example, the Security Council.

That is the precondition for the United Nations, that great creation of this waning century, to marshal the strength of mankind as its sets a course into the coming century.

Thank you, Mr President. (Alberto Fujimori, President of Peru, message and greetings to the United Nations on its 50th anniversary, 1995; trans. James Nolan)

(5) Study the following excerpts from speeches delivered at the solemn commemorative meeting marking the 50th anniversary of the United Nations in 1995. Read the speeches aloud into your tape recorder, giving your delivery and tone of voice a seriousness and solemnity appropriate to the occasion. Play back your recording at a later time and consider whether your performance conveyed the purpose and conviction of the speaker. Translate the passages and repeat the exercise using the translation(s).

Cinquante années se sont écoulées depuis la création, en 1945, de l'Organisation des Nations Unies à San Francisco. C'est dire que la présente session nous offre une occasion unique de mesurer l'importance du geste historique qui a conduit les dirigeants de l'époque à créer l'organisation, mais également de renouveler notre foi aux idéaux et principes contenus dans sa Charte, qui constitue, sans aucun doute, l'un des documents les plus importants dont dispose l'humanité pour construire le monde de demain. Pour les jeunes états, comme le Niger, qui a accédé à la souveraineté internationale il y a de cela 35 ans, il serait injuste de ne pas mentionner ici le rôle moteur que l'Organisation des Nations Unies a joué en faveur de l'émancipation des peuples et son apport inestimable au progrès de l'humanité en tant que creuset de la coopération internationale dans les domaines politiques, économiques, sociaux et culturels. (Address by Mohamed Bazoum, Minister of Foreign Affairs and Cooperation of the Republic of Niger)

Dans le cheminement historique de l'Humanité vers l'accomplissement de ses idéaux, le cinquantième anniversaire des Nations Unies représente un moment privilégié pour l'introspection collective et pour l'aménagement des conditions prometteuses d'un nouveau point de départ au bénéfice de notre Organisation: une introspection collective qui permette de s'instruire de l'état des lieux de la maison planétaire commune; un nouveau point de départ à organiser au moyen d'une saine réhabilitation des valeurs et des idéaux fondateurs des Nations Unies. A travers cette commémoration, ce sont ces valeurs et ces idéaux qui correspondent aux aspirations de tous les peuples à la paix, à la sécurité et à une prospérité partagées qui sont célébrées avec d'autant plus de foi que l'espérance incarnée par les

Nations Unies a été longtemps contrariée et que leur œuvre demeure inaccomplie. (Address by Liamine Zéroual, President of the People's Democratic Republic of Algeria)

No tendría sentido que llegáramos hoy al más alto foro mundial, solo para inventariar los éxitos políticos que la ONU ha logrado en estos 50 años – que sin duda los ha tendio, a partir de la globalización de la idea de la libertad y la democracia, a lo que contribuyó en forma decisiva – y no enfatizáramos los aspectos que hacen al desarrollo sustentable de la humanidad, que en ese mismo lapso no solo no se han solucionado sino que en vastas áreas del Planeta se han agravado considerablemente. ... El hambre, la miseria y las condiciones infrahumanas de vida, han cobrado más víctimas en el mundo que todas las guerras juntas. Han diezmado, y siguen diezmando, pueblos enteros en diversas regiones del mundo. ... La libertad y la democracia son frutos vulnerables, y su estabilidad está constanetmente amenazada si las naciones no logran contemporáneamente un adecuado y justo entorno económico y social. ... Haber logrado el silencio de los cañones en diversos teatros de conflicto; haber contribuido a la eliminación del apartheid y a destruir la sólida estructura colonial de casi cinco siglos son – sin duda – grandes conquistas de la Comunidad Internacional, y la ONU puede sentirse orgullosa a justo título. Pero hoy la Organización debe repensarse a sí misma, para emplear todos sus recursos ... en la gran empresa de resolver los injustos desequilibrios económicos y sociales y los problemas conexos de medio ambiente, en la convicción de que no sólo es un imperativo moral, sino que también es la forma idónea para consolidar la paz. (Address by Dr Hugo Batalla, Vice-President of the Republic of Uruguay)

Los portentosos avances de la ciencia y la tecnología se multiplican diariamente, pero sus beneficios no llegan a la mayoría de la humanidad, y siguen estando en lo fundamental al servicio de un consumismo irracional que derrocha recursos limitados y amenaza gravemente la vida del planeta. Hasta cuándo habrá que esperar para que haya racionalidad, equidad y justicia en el mundo? ... Queremos un mundo sin hegemonismos, sin armas nucleares, sin intervencionismos, sin racismo, sin odios nacionales ni religiosos, sin ultrajes a la soberanía de ningún país, con respeto a la independencia y a la libre determinación de los pueblos, sin modelos universales que no consideran para nada las tradiciones y la cultura de todos los componentes de la humanidad, sin crueles bloqueos que matan a hombres, mujeres y niños, jóvenes y ancianos, como bombas atómicas silenciosas. Queremos un mundo de paz, justicia y dignidad, en el que todos, sin excepción alguna, tengan derecho al bienestar y a la vida. (Address by Dr Fidel Castro Ruz, President of the Republic of Cuba)

El nacimiento de la Organización, tan ligado al final de una trágica guerra, consagró unos principios base del esfuerzo común para lograr los anhelos de la Humanidad: la paz, la libertad, la dignidad del ser humano y el progreso económico y social. Los grandes sufrimientos causados en Europa por las guerras que en este siglo nos enfrentaron, nos hicieron buscar en los principios y propósitos de la Carta de San Francisco, la inspiración necesaria para aunar nuestras voluntades. ... El mundo de hoy no puede imaginarse sin la contribución de las Naciones Unidas al proceso descolonizador, al medio ambiente, al desarrollo, y a la consagración de conceptos innovadores como el patrimonio común de la humanidad. Esa universalidad y fuerza legitimadora explican la contribución fundamental de la Organización a la paz y seguridad internacionales, al desarme y prevención de la proliferación de las armas de destrucción masiva, a la codificación del Derecho Internacional y a la protección y fomento de los derechos humanos. (Address by Felipe González, President of Spain and President of the European Union)

(6) Read the following excerpts from a judge's instructions to the jury at a murder trial. Then read the passage aloud into your tape recorder, giving your delivery and tone of voice a seriousness, clarity and solemnity appropriate to the occasion. Play back your recording at a later time and consider how convincing your performance was. Translate the passage, and repeat the exercise using the translation(s).

Jurors, you're not to discuss this case, any aspect of this case, with anyone during the course of this trial, and that means exactly what I said. It means among yourselves while you're waiting upstairs in the jury room to be called back down to the courtroom to resume the trial, away from the courthouse. If you have lunch together or breakfast together or you travel back and forth together, you are not to discuss the case among yourselves. At night when you're away from the courthouse, in the morning, on weekends, you're not to discuss the case with your family, your friends and neighbors. ... Of course, you may tell them you're on a case, and they're going to ask you what type of case it is. It's a criminal case. You stop at that ...

you're not to discuss any aspect of the case. . . . You're not to form an opinion with respect to the guilt or innocence of this defendant . . . until you've heard all of the evidence in the case, and the law from the Court. You are not to read, watch or listen to any media reports on the trial of this indictment. . . . Keep in mind during the course of the trial the Court's statements yesterday when you first came to this courtroom concerning the burden of proof, the defendant's presumption of innocence, the fact that you are to use your common sense and your life's experience in evaluating the credibility of all witnesses who will testify here during the course of this trial. . . . Those are your instructions. You are to comply with them. Have a pleasant evening. Report back tomorrow morning.

(7) The solemnity that attaches to a speech is not only a matter of tone and choice of words. It is also a matter of circumstances – in which chance or fate may take a hand. One cannot tell when and why a speech will go down in history. Consequently, whatever the occasion, no speech by an important public figure should ever be taken lightly. The following simple speech to a rally must have seemed at the time like just one more political speech. But it was delivered only moments before the speaker, Yitzakh Rabin, was assassinated, and it turned out to be the last words of a great statesman and peacemaker. Read the speech aloud into your tape recorder, giving your delivery and tone of voice a seriousness appropriate to the occasion. Play back your recording at a later time and consider whether your performance conveyed the purpose and conviction of the speaker. Translate the speech and repeat the exercise using the translation(s).

> The government, which I have the privilege to head with my friend Shimon Peres, decided to give peace a chance – a peace that will solve most of the state of Israel's problems. I was a military man for 27 years. I waged war as long as there was no chance for peace. I believe there is now a chance for peace, a great chance, and we must take advantage of it for those standing here, and for those who are not here – and they are many. I have always believed that the majority of the people want peace and are ready to take a chance for peace. And you, by coming to this rally, prove . . . that the people truly want peace and oppose violence. Violence erodes the basis of Israeli democracy. It should be condemned and wisely expunged and isolated. It is not the way of the state of Israel. There is democracy. There can be disputes but the outcome will be settled by democratic elections. Peace is not only in prayers . . . it is the desire of the

Jewish people. There are enemies of people. They are trying to attack us in order to torpedo peace. I want to tell you: we found a partner for peace among the Palestinians, the PLO, which used to be an enemy, and stopped terrorism. This rally must broadcast to the Israeli public, to the world Jewish public and to many in the western and outside world that the people of Israel want peace, support peace. (Yitzhak Rabin, Israeli Prime Minister, address to a peace rally, Tel Aviv, 4 November 1995 (excerpts); trans. Reuters)

11 A Policy Address

In addition to the usual difficulties of translation and interpretation, a formal policy address – of the kind now delivered routinely by 192 member states every year at the UN General Assembly's general debate – poses some additional challenges.

The first of these is the political status of the speech. A policy address is an official public statement of position, for the record. Such an address is usually delivered by a plenipotentiary ambassador, a foreign minister or the head of state or government. Consequently, as regards the content, nearly perfect accuracy is required. Each and every idea must be correctly rendered.

Second, there is the challenge of length. Such speeches tend to be very lengthy and detailed, since ambassadors, foreign ministers and heads of state will usually take the opportunity of a general debate to cover a great deal of ground. Moreover, even speeches of this kind are now subject to time limits, which force the speaker to speak fast or at least to speed up at certain points. This can severely tax the interpreter's endurance.

A third challenge is posed by the timeliness and diversity of the subject matter. In one and the same address, the speaker may cover everything from environmental and demographic issues to human rights crises and regional conflicts in several parts of the world. This requires the interpreter to keep abreast of the latest developments in world affairs, as well as any related new concepts, technical terms, neologisms and jargon generated by the issues (e.g. 'ethnic cleansing' / 'épuration ethnique' / 'limpieza étnica' as a newly coined term for genocidal practices, or 'ozone hole', the latest environmental threat). In addition, a formal policy address will sometimes include a 'vision' or a 'mission statement' articulating a certain perception of the state of the world or a set of principles or goals to be pursued.

Exercises

(1) Study the following speech by Canadian Foreign Minister André Ouellet. (The speech has been slightly abridged.) As you read, jot down each topic covered. Consider what changes in structure, phrasing, tone, etc. were necessary in translating the speech in order to produce equally accurate English and French versions of equivalent register and elegance. Notice especially how the words and structures highlighted in bold type have been treated, and take special note of those instances where the equivalent expression used in one language is more concise than that used in the other language (example: 'tirer profit de' = 'harness'). Speeches in other languages may be found in the final section of the Bibliography.

> **Mr Ouellet**: It is a great honour to represent Canada **here** today as we celebrate the fiftieth anniversary of the United Nations during this general debate.

> **M. Ouellet**: Alors que nous célébrons le cinquantième anniversaire des Nations Unies durant ce débat général, c'est un insigne honneur pour moi de représenter le Canada aujourd'hui **dans cette enceinte**.

> Canada has always been among the **strongest** supporters of the United Nations, not only in word but also in deed. In 1945 we were, through Canadian Prime Minister Mackenzie King, **an original signatory** of the United Nations Charter. Ambassador John Humphreys helped write the 1948 United Nations Universal Declaration of Human Rights. Successive Canadian Ambassadors to the United Nations have distinguished themselves in the service of the Organization, as have countless Canadian negotiators **in areas ranging from** disarmament to trade to development. **In addition**, Lester B. Pearson won a Nobel Peace Prize for his contribution to the success of the United Nations in establishing the first peace-keeping operation, in 1956.

> Notre pays a toujours été l'un des **plus ardents** défenseurs de l'ONU, en paroles comme en actes. En 1945, le Canada, en la personne du Premier Ministre canadien, Mackenzie King, a été **l'un des premiers pays signataires** de la Charte des Nations Unies. L'Ambassadeur John Humphreys a participé à la rédaction de la Déclaration universelle des droits de l'homme de l'ONU, en 1948. Les ambassadeurs successifs du Canada auprès de cette organisation

se sont distingués dans leur travail au service de l'Organisation, tout comme l'ont fait d'innombrables négociateurs canadiens **dans des domaines allant** du désarmement au commerce et au développement. M. Lester B. Pearson, **quant à lui**, s'est vu décerner le prix Nobel de la paix pour avoir contribué au succès de la première opération de maintien de la paix montée par l'ONU en 1956.

All these Canadians had a **unifying purpose**: to promote progress in implementing the United Nations Charter, which enshrines the **commitment** of the people of the United Nations **to the advancement** of humanity.

Tous ces Canadiens avaient un **objectif commun**: promouvoir le progrès en mettant en œuvre la Charte des Nations Unies, laquelle exprime la volonté des peuples des Nations Unies à **s'employer à favoriser l'avancement** de l'humanité.

Of course, there have been criticisms of the Organization; many are legitimate and require attention. It is clear, however, that the international community remains committed to the goals of the Charter and to the United Nations as the primary instrument **for global problem solving**.

Bien sûr, l'Organisation a fait l'objet de critiques. Un grand nombre d'entre elles sont fondées et méritent qu'on leur prête attention. Il est clair cependant que la communauté internationale demeure résolue à atteindre les buts de la Charte et voit dans l'ONU un excellent instrument **pour régler les problèmes mondiaux**.

The United Nations deserves our continued support. **If we look at the record of just** the last few years, the United Nations has conducted successful peace-keeping operations in Cambodia, Mozambique and Haiti. Thanks to the United Nations, in this decade alone 5 million children will grow up normally, children who would otherwise have been paralysed by polio. This year the United Nations is working, as it does every year, to ensure a better life for the almost 23 million refugees in the world.

Les Nations Unies méritent que nous continuions de leur accorder notre soutien. **Si l'on fait seulement le bilan** des dernières années, on constate que l'Organisation a mené des opérations de maintien de la paix fructueuses au Cambodge, au Mozambique et en Haïti. Dans cette seule décennie, cinq millions d'enfants grandiront normalement, alors que sans l'ONU ils auraient été paralysés par la polio. En 1995, l'ONU œuvre pour offrir à près de 23 millions de réfugiés dans le monde une meilleure vie.

Global resolve to support the United Nations and to advance the interests of the international community has recently been underscored by such successes as the indefinite extension of the Treaty on the Non-Proliferation of Nuclear Weapons. At the Halifax Summit in June, chaired by our Prime Minister, Jean Chrétien, the P-8 (Political Eight) leaders reaffirmed their strong commitment to the United Nations system of international institutions and added their ideas for **revitalizing** it.

La volonté de tous d'appuyer l'ONU et de promouvoir les intérêts de la communauté internationale a été récemment soulignée par des succès comme la prorogation indéfinie du Traité de non-prolifération nucléaire (TNP). En juin, au Sommet de Halifax, présidé par notre Premier Ministre, Jean Chrétien, les leaders du Groupe des Huit ont réaffirmé leur ferme engagement envers le système onusien d'institutions internationales et ont proposé des idées pour le **revitaliser**.

The **central** message is clear: we must take this **momentous** opportunity to confirm and renew our commitment to the United Nations. To do so, we require a renewed vision for the next 50 years. This vision must be centred on **not just striving for, but achieving**, human security on the basis of the freedom of people everywhere to **live in peace and without fear**, to be prosperous and enjoy equality, justice before the law and knowledge. The Members of the United Nations must work together now to renew the Organization and its agencies and programmes and to help make this vision a reality.

Le message **fondamental** est clair: nous devons profiter de cette occasion **solennelle** pour confirmer et renouveler notre engagement à l'égard de l'ONU. À cette fin, nous avons besoin d'une vision renouvelée pour les 50 prochaines années. Cette vision doit être centrée **non seulement sur les efforts pour assurer** la sécurité humaine, **mais aussi sur la réalisation** de cette sécurité fondée sur la liberté de tous les peuples à **vivre en paix sans connaître la peur**, à être prospères et à bénéficier de l'égalité, de la justice devant la loi et du savoir. Les Membres des Nations Unies doivent collaborer maintenant afin de renouveler l'Organisation, ses institutions et ses programmes, pour aider à faire de cette vision une réalité.

In Canada's view pursuing this vision **requires a focus on** three interlinked objectives: preventing conflict; responding quickly when conflict occurs; and supporting peace-building efforts on an ongoing basis. I will **address** each objective **in turn**.

Le Canada estime que, pour réaliser cette vision, **il faut atteindre** trois objectifs intimement liés: empêcher les conflits, réagir rapidement quand un conflit éclate, et appuyer en permanence les efforts d'édification de la paix. Je **parlerai de** chacun de ces objectifs **l'un après l'autre**.

The first priority must be to help the United Nations better protect people from conflict. The United Nations has had important successes in the past few years but, unfortunately, **there have also been setbacks**. If the United Nations is to adapt to a changing world, **if confidence** in the Organization **is to be restored**, we must learn from the failures of Bosnia, Somalia and Rwanda and build on the successes of Cambodia, Namibia and El Salvador.

La grande priorité doit être d'aider l'ONU à mieux protéger les personnes des conflits. L'ONU a connu d'importants succès depuis quelques années, mais malheureusement, **elle a aussi essuyé des échecs**. Si l'on veut que cette organisation s'adapte à un monde en changement, **si l'on veut rétablir la confiance** à son égard, il faut tirer une leçon des échecs essuyés en Bosnie, en Somalie et au Rwanda et s'appuyer sur les succès remportés au Cambodge, en Namibie et en El Salvador.

Preventive action, as the Secretary-General has laid out so well in 'An Agenda for Peace', **takes** many forms, from economic development programmes to mediation, to the preventive deployment of personnel – as, for example, in the Former Yugoslav Republic of Macedonia – from the investigation of human rights violations to the conclusion of agreements limiting the spread of weapons of mass destruction. Prevention **saves** lives, **forestalls** untold human suffering and **makes** the best use of limited resources.

L'action préventive, comme le Secrétaire général l'a si bien exprimé dans l' 'Agenda pour la paix', **revêt** de nombreuses formes, qui vont des programmes de développement économique à la médiation et au déploiement préventif de personnel – comme par exemple dans l'ancienne République yougoslave de Macédoine –, et des enquêtes sur les violations des droits de la personne à la conclusion d'accords limitant la prolifération des armes de destruction massive. **La prévention sauve** des vies; **la prévention prévient** d'innombrables souffrances humaines; **et la prévention permet** de faire le meilleur usage possible des ressources limitées.

Last year I announced at this podium that Canada was providing a list of Canadian experts available to the United Nations for preventive diplomacy missions. We are also taking advantage of our membership in La Francophonie, in the Commonwealth and in regional organizations such as the Organization of American States (OAS) and the Organization for Security and Cooperation in Europe (OSCE) **precisely in order to work towards enhancing** the ability of these organizations to prevent conflicts. Our Prime Minister, Jean Chrétien, is currently pressing for an expanded Commonwealth role in democratization and **good governance**, which are two key elements of conflict prevention. I recently convened a meeting of La Francophonie in Ottawa to generate recommendations for it **to strengthen its role** in conflict prevention, particularly in Africa. These recommendations will be presented to the leaders, the Heads of State and Government, gathered at the Francophone Summit to be held in Cotonou, Benin, in December of this year.

L'année dernière, j'ai annoncé à cette tribune que le Canada fournirait une liste de ses experts prêts à participer à des missions de diplomatie préventive. De plus, nous mettons à profit notre appartenance à la Francophonie, au Commonwealth et à des organisations régionales telles que l'Organisation des États américains, l'Organisation pour la sécurité et la coopération en Europe, **pour justement renforcer et favoriser** cette capacité de prévention des conflits au sein de ces organisations. Le Premier Ministre du Canada, Jean Chrétien, incite actuellement le Commonwealth à jouer un rôle plus important en matière de démocratisation et de **bon gouvernement**, qui sont deux éléments clefs de la prévention des conflits. J'ai récemment convoqué une rencontre de la Francophonie à Ottawa en vue de formuler des recommandations **pour élargir le rôle que joue** cette organisation dans la prévention des conflits, particulièrement en Afrique. Ces recommandations seront présentées aux chefs d'État et de gouvernement réunis au sommet de la Francophonie, qui aura lieu à Cotonou, au Bénin, en décembre prochain.

Prevention also **means** deterring crimes against humanity. Canada strongly supports the **early** establishment of an international criminal court, which will, **we hope**, deter such crimes in the future but, **should they occur**, would punish the perpetrators. The recently approved Platform for Action at the United Nations Fourth World Conference on Women in Beijing **lends further impetus** in this area.

La prévention **permet** aussi d'empêcher les crimes contre l'humanité. Le Canada est très partisan de la création **prochaine** d'une cour criminelle internationale, qui empêchera – **du moins, nous l'espérons** – de commettre de tels crimes dans l'avenir et qui punira les auteurs **si jamais il s'en produisait**. La Plate-forme d'action approuvée récemment à la quatrième Conférence de l'ONU sur les femmes, tenue à Beijing, **donne une nouvelle impulsion** dans ce domaine.

One of the priorities of Canada's foreign policy and one of the best ways to renew commitment to the United Nations consists of adopting a coherent approach to **the prevention and management of complex emergencies**. **Averting** crisis requires more flexibility and speed in decision-making and in implementation. . . .

Une des priorités de la politique étrangère du Canada, et aussi un des meilleurs moyens de renouveler les engagements envers l'ONU, consiste à adopter une démarche cohérente à l'égard de **la prévention et de la gestion des urgences complexes**. **Afin d'éviter** les crises, nous devons faire preuve de plus de souplesse, mais aussi prendre des décisions et les mettre en œuvre plus rapidement. . . .

Our recent experiences in the former Yugoslavia and in Rwanda emphasize the link between security and human rights. The United Nations' many human rights mechanisms produce **a wealth of** information that could help us **identify** and understand potential areas of conflict. The United Nations High Commissioner for Human Rights has a role to play in **enhancing** the **early warning functions** of the United Nations. The experience of the Human Rights Field Operation in Rwanda **revealed** the need for the more effective coordination of United Nations field missions. Canada has **commissioned work** on the human rights components of field operations and on **stand-by arrangements** for them. This work will **yield** recommendations on ways to integrate human rights into United Nations field operations,

in a way consistent with the approach outlined in 'An Agenda for Peace'.

L'expérience que nous avons vécue récemment dans l'ex-Yougoslavie et au Rwanda met en relief les liens qui existent entre la sécurité et les droits de la personne. Les nombreux mécanismes onusiens de défense des droits de la personne produisent **une abondance** d'informations, qui pourraient nous aider à **repérer** et à comprendre les domaines potentiels de conflit. Le Haut Commissaire des Nations Unies aux droits de l'homme a un rôle à jouer pour **rehausser** les **fonctions d'alerte rapide** de l'ONU. L'expérience de l'Opération des Nations Unies pour les droits de l'homme au Rwanda a **mis en lumière** le besoin d'une coordination plus efficace des missions de l'ONU sur le terrain. Le Canada a **commandé des travaux** sur la place des droits de la personne dans les opérations sur le terrain et sur les **arrangements relatifs aux forces en attente**. Ce travail **produira** des recommandations sur la façon d'intégrer les droits de la personne aux opérations de l'ONU sur le terrain, **conformément à** l'approche esquissée dans l' 'Agenda pour la paix'.

Another **major focus** of Canada's preventive action is arms control and disarmament, especially concerning nuclear weapons. The historic decision to extend the Treaty on the Non-Proliferation of Nuclear Weapons (NPT) indefinitely provides a foundation for further important gains on nuclear disarmament. We must now complete the comprehensive test-ban treaty negotiations **as early as possible** in 1996 in order to permit its signature at the General Assembly next September. An agreement to begin negotiations on a treaty to ban the production of fissionable material for nuclear weapons **is currently held up**. We **squander** such opportunities **at our peril**. Canada calls on all members of the Conference on Disarmament to **proceed urgently** with the cut-off negotiations.

Un autre **grand axe** de l'action préventive du Canada est le contrôle des armements et le désarmement, particulièrement en ce qui concerne les armes nucléaires. La décision historique de proroger indéfiniment le Traité sur la non-prolifération des armes nucléaires (TNP) ouvre la voie à d'autres progrès notables en matière de désarmement nucléaire. Nous devons maintenant terminer **dès que possible**, en 1996, les négociations relatives à un traité sur l'interdiction complète des essais nucléaires afin qu'il soit signé lors de l'Assemblée générale en septembre prochain. Un accord portant sur le début des négociations en vue de la signature d'un traité sur l'interdiction de la production de matières fissiles pour les armes nucléaires **n'a pas encore eu lieu**. C'est **à nos risques et périls** que nous **laissons passer** de telles occasions. Le Canada prie tous les membres de la Conférence sur le désarmement d'**amorcer de toute urgence** les négociations sur l'arrêt de la production.

Regrettably our efforts to take preventive action are **eroded** by the continued **global imbalance** between spending on armaments and spending on human development. Multilateral institutions should take trends in military and other **unproductive** spending into consideration. All States Members of the United Nations should comply with the United Nations Register of Conventional Arms which will, we hope, be expanded soon to include military holdings and **national procurement activities**. Together, interested countries could develop criteria to identify excessive military expenditures and appropriate **international responses**. Canada has taken some initiatives in this regard in recent months and **we look forward to** productive negotiations with many Member States here.
  Il est regrettable que les efforts de prévention que nous déployons soient **contrecarrés** par le **déséquilibre qui perdure à l'échelle mondiale** entre les dépenses consacrées aux armements et celles consacrées au développement humain. Les institutions multilatérales devraient tenir compte des dépenses militaires et des autres dépenses **improductives**. Tous les États Membres de l'ONU devraient se conformer au Registre des armes classiques de l'ONU, qui, nous l'espérons, sera prochainement élargi pour inclure les avoirs militaires et **l'approvisionnement sur le plan national**. Les pays intéressés pourraient, d'une part, élaborer ensemble des critères qui permettraient d'identifier les dépenses militaires excessives, et d'autre part, prévoir des **réactions internationales** appropriées. Le Canada a pris des initiatives à cet égard ces derniers mois, et **nous avons bon espoir de mener** des négociations productives avec de nombreux États Membres.

When a United Nations preventive diplomacy operation **stumbles** and **efforts** to prevent conflict fail, Member States all too often criticize the United Nations. But much of the blame for the failures of the Organization **lies with** the Member States themselves who **do not provide it with the tools** needed for success. These tools are never needed more than when a crisis erupts.

Lorsqu'une opération de diplomatie préventive de l'ONU **trébuche** et que **les efforts déployés** pour prévenir un conflit échouent, les États Membres n'hésitent pas à critiquer l'Organisation des Nations Unies. Or une grande partie du blâme concernant les échecs de l'Organisation **revient aux** États Membres eux-mêmes, qui **ne lui fournissent pas les outils** du succès. Ces outils sont particulièrement essentiels au moment où la crise se déclenche.

Last year I discussed the problems the United Nations has encountered in mobilizing its peace operations to respond to crises. **Canada's long experience with** peace-keeping has convinced us that improvements are possible. The international community's slow response to the horrible and **deeply distressing** events in Rwanda was **very much in our mind**. It was in this context that I announced that Canada would examine ways to improve the **capacity** of the United Nations to react quickly to such events.

L'année dernière, j'ai discuté des problèmes qu'a connus l'ONU lorsqu'il s'est agi de mobiliser ses opérations de paix en réaction à des crises. **La longue expérience qu'a le Canada du chapitre du** maintien de la paix nous a convaincus que des améliorations sont possibles. La lente réaction de la communauté internationale aux événements horribles et **profondément bouleversants** survenus au Rwanda était **très présente à notre esprit**. C'est dans ce contexte que j'ai annoncé que le Canada examinerait les moyens d'améliorer **l'aptitude** des Nations Unies à réagir sans tarder à de tels événements.

Today I have the honour of presenting to the Assembly Canada's report entitled 'Towards a Rapid Reaction Capability for the United Nations' as a special Canadian contribution to the United Nations during its fiftieth anniversary year. It presents practical proposals for enhancing the United Nations rapid reaction capability in the field of peace operations. I believe the proposals **will both help** save lives **and** conserve scarce resources.

Aujourd'hui, j'ai l'honneur de présenter à cette assemblée le rapport intitulé 'Towards a Rapid Reaction Capability for the United Nations', qui constitue une contribution spéciale du Canada à l'ONU pour son cinquantenaire. On y trouve des propositions pratiques en vue d'améliorer la capacité d'intervention rapide des Nations Unies dans le domaine des opérations de paix. Je crois que ces propositions **permettront à la fois de** sauver des vies **et d'**économiser des ressources rares.

The report expresses the view of the Government of Canada, but **considerable care was taken** to consult with other Governments, non-governmental organizations and intergovernmental institutions. We are also deeply grateful to the many experts from many countries who have **lent us their time and wisdom**.

Le rapport exprime le point de vue du Gouvernement du Canada. Mais **nous avons pris bien soin** de consulter d'autres gouvernements, des organisations non gouvernementales et des institutions intergouvernementales. Nous sommes également profondément redevables aux nombreux experts qui **nous ont dispensé leur temps et leur sagesse**.

The main proposal of the report is the 'Vanguard Concept'. This concept will permit the United Nations to **assemble**, from Member States, a multifunctional force of up to 5000 military and civilian personnel, and, with the authorization of the Security Council, quickly deploy it **under the control of an operational-level headquarters**. This operational headquarters would be responsible for the advance preparations **that are crucial if** rapid reaction is to work. Forces will be provided **under** enhanced standby arrangements with Member States. Our other proposals seek to enhance training, to create more efficient logistics and transportation and to strengthen the planning efforts of the entire United Nations system. **Let me say that** none of the 26 recommendations in the report requires Charter reforms.

La principale proposition du rapport est celle du 'concept des groupes d'avant-garde'. Elle permettrait à l'ONU de **réunir** dans une force multifonctionnelle jusqu'à 5000 civils et militaires des États Membres et, avec l'autorisation du Conseil de sécurité, de la déployer rapidement **sous le commandement d'un état-major opérationnel**. Ce dernier serait chargé des préparatifs préliminaires, **dont l'exécution est cruciale pour** le succès d'une réaction rapide. Les forces seraient fournies **aux termes d'**arrangements améliorés conclus avec les États Membres relativement aux forces en attente. Nos autres propositions visent à améliorer la formation, à accroître l'efficacité de la logistique et des transports, et à renforcer les activités de planification de l'ensemble du système de l'ONU. **Je précise qu'**aucune des 26 recommandations du rapport n'appelle une réforme de la Charte.

But the search for immediate, practical solutions must not preclude more visionary possibilities. In this regard, the report looked at longer-term questions, such as **advanced technology in support of** the United Nations peace operations, the feasibility of a permanent group of civilian police, the idea of a United Nations Standing Emergency Group, a permanent force as has been considered by our colleague from the Netherlands; and the question of independent sources of revenue for the United Nations system.

Cette quête de solutions immédiates et pratiques ne doit cependant pas exclure l'examen d'options plus visionnaires. À cet égard, le rapport se penche sur des idées à plus long terme comme **la mise des technologies de pointe au service des** opérations de paix de l'ONU; la création d'un groupe permanent d'instructeurs de la police civile; la constitution d'un groupe d'urgence permanent au sein de l'ONU, idée émise par notre collègue des Pays-Bas; et la mobilisation de sources indépendantes de revenus pour le système onusien.

I believe that the recommendations in the report, if implemented, will strengthen the United Nations capacity for more rapid, **effective and successful** peace operations. They will help restore confidence in the ability of the United Nations to respond to crises.

Je crois que les recommandations du rapport, si on leur donne suite, accroîtront la capacité de l'ONU de mener des opérations de paix plus rapides et plus **fructueuses**. Elles contribueront à rétablir la confiance dans la capacité de l'ONU de réagir aux crises.

We are conscious of the fact that words are not enough. **In the words of** a former military adviser to the United Nations: 'We can't deploy studies.' For Canada this report is only the first step **in translating ideas into action**. To meet the growing need for civilian personnel during crises, Canada will offer the United Nations **secondment or the loan** of civilian personnel on a short-term urgent basis to help in the **development of** a fully trained capacity in the areas of human rights, legal advice, humanitarian assistance and other aspects of a rapid civilian response to crises.

Nous savons bien que les mots ne suffisent pas. **Comme l'a dit** un ancien conseiller militaire de l'ONU, 'nous ne pouvons pas déployer des études'. Ce rapport n'est, pour le Canada, qu'un premier pas **sur la voie qui mène des idées aux actes**. Afin de répondre au besoin croissant de personnel civil durant les crises, le Canada offrira à l'ONU **de lui détacher ou de lui prêter** du personnel, en situation d'urgence et pour de courtes périodes, afin de l'aider à **se doter d'**un effectif bien formé dans les domaines des droits de la personne, des conseils juridiques et de l'assistance humanitaire, et dans d'autres aspects également de l'intervention civile rapide face à une crise.

Last week Canada sent the Secretary-General an updated inventory of Canadian personnel and equipment on standby to the United Nations, including technical information that would be crucial to rapid response. We are now prepared to negotiate with the United Nations a more detailed **memorandum of understanding** on standby arrangements, which would include more information on **readiness** and **capability standards**.

La semaine dernière, le Canada a fait parvenir au Secrétaire général un répertoire à jour du personnel et du matériel que notre pays tient à la disposition de l'ONU, y compris les renseignements techniques essentiels à une réaction rapide. Nous sommes maintenant prêts à négocier avec l'ONU un **protocole d'entente** plus détaillé sur les arrangements relatifs aux forces en attente, qui contiendrait plus d'informations sur l'**état de préparation** et les **normes de capacité**.

Our report devotes special attention to the creation of an operational-level headquarters **as the heart** of the 'Vanguard' concept. Canada is prepared to help in establishing its headquarters should the United Nations decide to accept this recommendation. We have already made **a significant number** of military personnel available to the United Nations on secondment or on loan. We are prepared to make available additional personnel, both civilian and military, in order to bring this idea closer to realization.

Nous avons consacré une attention particulière dans le rapport à la mise en place d'un état-major opérationnel, qui **serait au cœur du** concept des groupes d'avant-garde. Si l'ONU devait décider de retenir cette recommandation, le Canada serait disposé à participer à la création de cet état-major. Notre pays a déjà mis à la disposition de l'ONU **un nombre important** de militaires, par voie de détachements ou de prêts. Nous sommes disposés à détacher du personnel supplémentaire, tant civil que militaire, afin de favoriser la concrétisation de cette idée.

The time for moving towards fundamental improvements in the way the United Nations responds to crises **is now**. A number of countries have advanced proposals similar to Canada's and there are many new and interesting proposals for change **coming** also **from** the non-governmental sector.

Le moment est venu d'apporter des améliorations fondamentales à la façon dont l'ONU réagit aux crises. Un certain nombre de pays ont avancé des propositions semblables à celles du Canada. Les propositions de changement **issues du** secteur non gouvernemental sont aussi nombreuses et intéressantes.

Follow-up is of key importance. We need to **marshal our energies**, to determine the most promising areas of action, and to move quickly towards putting words into action. **Over the coming** weeks and months, Canada intends to work closely with **like-minded** countries from around the world, and, of course, with the United Nations Secretariat to this end.

Le suivi est donc d'une importance cruciale. Nous devons **rassembler nos énergies**, déterminer les secteurs d'intervention les plus prometteurs, et passer de la parole aux actes sans plus tarder. **Au cours des** jours, des semaines **à venir**, le Canada a l'intention de travailler en étroite collaboration avec des pays **de même opinion**, partout dans le monde, et, bien sûr, avec le Secrétariat des Nations Unies afin d'atteindre cet objectif.

The **ongoing work** of peace-building **must continue** alongside preventive diplomacy and now rapid reaction operations. Indeed, peace-building **involves a wide range** of activities. Much of the work needed for articulating a broad vision of human security has already been done in the series of United Nations conferences in the economic and social fields, culminating in the Platform for Action recently adopted at the United Nations Conference on Women. It **sets out a comprehensive view** of sustainable development, which **balances** economic and social agendas for the purpose of promoting the well-being of society. This global consensus offers an opportunity to restore confidence in the work of the United Nations system in these fields, and to **dispel the perception of aimlessness and drift**. The United Nations can continue to play an invaluable role in **forging global agreements** on development goals, in advocating core values, and in responding to humanitarian and development needs.

Nous **devons poursuivre nos efforts permanents** en vue de l'édification de la paix, tout en pratiquant une diplomatie préventive et en maintenant les opérations de réaction rapide. En fait, l'édification de la paix **comporte tout un éventail** d'activités. Une grande partie du travail nécessaire pour en arriver à une vision globale de la sécurité humaine a déjà été accompli dans la série de conférences tenues par l'ONU dans les domaines économique et social et couronnées récemment par l'adoption de la Plateforme d'action élaborée dans le cadre de la Conférence mondiale de l'ONU sur les femmes. Elles ont permis de **tracer le portrait général** d'un développement durable, qui **établit un équilibre** entre les priorités économiques et sociales afin d'accroître le bien-être de l'humanité. Ce consensus planétaire nous offre l'occasion de rétablir la confiance dans le travail du système des Nations Unies dans ces domaines, et de **dissiper l'impression de désœuvrement et de dérive**. L'ONU peut continuer de jouer un rôle de premier plan dans **l'élaboration d'accords internationaux** sur les buts du développement, dans la défense des valeurs fondamentales et dans la satisfaction des besoins humanitaires et de développement.

We must seek to **anchor change in** a commitment to people-centred sustainable development. A strong emphasis must be placed on the reduction of poverty and on the integration of the poorest countries into the world economy. **However, no single country, or even group of countries, can** achieve global results alone. We are, therefore, determined to work with all Member States to pursue these goals sufficiently and effectively. **Let me take this opportunity to set out** some ideas on the way to renew commitment to the economic and social work of the United Nations.

Nous devons chercher à **fonder les changements sur** un engagement envers un développement durable axé sur la personne. Il faut carrément mettre l'accent sur la réduction de la pauvreté et l'intégration des pays les plus pauvres à l'économie mondiale. **Aucun pays, cependant, ni même aucun groupe de pays, ne pourra** parvenir seul à des résultats pour l'ensemble de la planète. Nous avons donc la ferme intention de collaborer avec tous les États Membres afin d'atteindre ces buts avec efficacité et le plus rapidement possible. **Je profite de cette occasion pour énoncer** quelques idées sur la façon de renouveler notre engagement envers le travail économique et social de l'ONU.

First, there is a need to **achieve the right balance** between wide-ranging debate and decisions on which programmes should be adopted. The **justified breadth of debate** does not mean that

United Nations programmes should be established to address every problem. There are many other actors who play important roles. The United Nations should **focus on what it is uniquely equipped to achieve**.

Tout d'abord, il faut **trouver le juste équilibre** entre les débats de portée générale et les décisions au sujet des programmes qui devraient être adoptés. **L'ampleur du débat, quoique justifiée**, ne signifie pas pour autant que l'ONU doive créer des programmes pour régler tous les problèmes. D'autres acteurs ont des rôles importants à jouer. Et l'ONU devrait **miser sur ses atouts distinctifs**.

Secondly, there is a **need for a fresh sense of** the real goals of development. The outcomes of the major conferences are at the core, and their distillation and coordinated follow-up should **be a touchstone for** the United Nations in the economic and social fields.

Deuxièmement, il faut **réaffirmer** les vrais buts du développement. Les résultats des grandes conférences en sont le noyau; la diffusion de leurs conclusions et leur suivi coordonné devraient **servir de pierre de touche à** l'ONU dans les domaines économique et social.

The roles and functions of organizations and agencies should be examined and **refocused** to ensure that they are **oriented to future needs**. The Agenda for Development is an important opportunity to initiate the institutional change **required**.

Il y a lieu d'examiner et de **repenser** le rôle et les fonctions des organisations et des institutions afin de les préparer à **répondre aux besoins de l'avenir**. L'Agenda pour le développement présente une excellente occasion d'amorcer les changements institutionnels **jugés nécessaires**.

Improving cooperation with and among specialized agencies is essential **to give limited resources some impact**. The Economic and Social Council must take more responsibility for policy coordination within the United Nations system. **A start was made** this summer in Geneva. The recent establishment of the United Nations Programme on AIDS is a promising example. There, the executive heads of agencies and programmes must demonstrate leadership, particularly in coordinating the follow-up to international conferences and **ensuring that** duplication, overlapping and needless spending are eliminated as far as possible.

II est essentiel d'améliorer la coopération avec et entre les institutions spécialisées pour **que nos ressources limitées exercent un certain effet**. Le Conseil économique et social (ÉCOSOC) doit assumer davantage de responsabilités pour ce qui est de la coordination des politiques au sein du système de l'ONU. **Le coup d'envoi a été donné** à Genève l'été dernier. La création récente du Programme des Nations Unies de lutte contre le sida constitue un exemple prometteur. Sur ce chapitre, les chefs des institutions et des programmes doivent absolument faire preuve de leadership; en particulier, ils doivent coordonner le suivi des conférences internationales et **veiller à** éliminer, autant que possible, les doubles emplois, les chevauchements et les dépenses inutiles.

We must effectively **harness** the complementary roles of the United Nations and the Bretton Woods institutions. **To ensure a smooth transition** from emergencies to rehabilitation, improved cooperation in crises **must be an immediate priority**. I urge the Secretary-General and the leaders of the World Bank and the International Monetary Fund (IMF) to propose new arrangements for post-crisis assistance. They could also establish a high-level working group to consider how to **strengthen cooperation**, both at the Organization's Headquarters and elsewhere, in areas such as data collection, analysis and reporting. The World Trade Organization (WTO) should also participate in relevant **aspects** of this work.

Nous devons arriver à **tirer profit des** rôles complémentaires de l'ONU et des institutions de Bretton Woods. Il faut **en toute priorité** améliorer la coopération en temps de crise **afin de passer en douceur** d'une situation d'urgence à une situation de redressement. Je prie le Secrétaire général et les dirigeants de la Banque mondiale et du Fonds monétaire international de proposer de nouvelles modalités pour l'aide postérieure aux crises. Ces personnes pourraient aussi créer un groupe de travail de haut niveau chargé d'étudier les moyens de **resserrer la coopération** tant au Siège de l'Organisation qu'à l'extérieur, dans des domaines tels que la collecte des données, l'analyse et les rapports. L'Organisation mondiale du commerce devrait également participer aux **volets** pertinents de ce travail.

We **have all come to** understand the extent to which human security is indivisible from environmental security. More and more conflicts are arising following disagreement over the use of **finite** natural resources. The United Nations therefore has a key role to play in promoting sustainable development. Canada welcomes the recent success of United Nations conferences in some areas of **international resource-management operations**, such as the United Nations Conference on Straddling Fish Stocks and Highly Migratory Fish Stocks. **Our goal is** concrete, **internationally sanctioned** conservation measures. The same objective applies to our efforts to ensure the sustainable management of forests and arable land.

Nous **en sommes tous venus à** comprendre à quel point la sécurité humaine est indissociable de la sécurité de l'environnement. De plus en plus de conflits sont attribuables à des désaccords touchant l'exploitation de ressources naturelles **limitées**. Le rôle des Nations Unies dans la promotion du développement durable est donc primordial en cette matière. Le Canada se réjouit du récent succès des conférences des Nations Unies dans certains secteurs des **opérations internationales de gestion des ressources**, comme la Conférence de l'ONU sur les stocks de poissons chevauchants et les stocks de poissons grands migrateurs. **Nous visons** l'adoption de mesures de conservation concrètes **à l'échelle internationale**. Et nos efforts en vue d'assurer la gestion durable des forêts et des terres arables visent exactement le même objectif.

The Rio Summit **achieved landmark** agreements on climate change and biodiversity. Canada welcomes the progress made by the Commission on Sustainable Development and by the United Nations Environment Programme (UNEP), in **clarifying** their respective roles **in following up** these agreements in collaboration with Member States.

Le Sommet de Rio a **débouché sur** la signature d'accords **historiques** sur le changement climatique et la biodiversité. Le Canada se réjouit des progrès réalisés par la Commission du développement durable et par le Programme des Nations Unies pour l'environnement en vue de **préciser** leurs rôles respectifs **en ce qui concerne le suivi de** ces accords, de concert avec les nations membres.

In speaking about the three elements – preventive action, rapid reaction and peace-building – I wish to emphasize the need to see them as mutually reinforcing. United Nations Member States **must be committed to all three** in order for any one to be successful.

À propos des trois éléments, à savoir l'action préventive, la réaction rapide et l'édification de la paix, j'insiste sur le fait qu'il faut les considérer comme se renforçant les uns les autres pour que chacun d'entre eux porte des fruits. Les États Membres de l'ONU **doivent apporter aux trois une importance égale**.

To ensure a renewal of the United Nations vision through these actions, we must also **reassert** our commitment to assuring the effectiveness of its key bodies. Although I could speak of many United Nations agencies in this regard, because of its critical role **in promoting the vision** of the next 50 years, I will limit my remarks to the Security Council.

Pour que ces actions permettent de concrétiser la vision renouvelée de l'ONU, nous devons aussi **réaffirmer** notre engagement en vue d'assurer l'efficacité de ces principaux organismes. À cet égard je pourrais mentionner un grand nombre d'organismes de l'ONU, mais mes propos porteront uniquement sur le Conseil de sécurité, à cause du rôle essentiel qui lui revient **s'agissant de promouvoir** la vision des 50 prochaines années.

The Security Council's **mandate** to help prevent disputes and to resolve conflicts confers on it unique responsibilities. The binding nature of some decisions **adds** further weight to its deliberations.

Le Conseil de sécurité a des responsabilités uniques, **à titre d'organe chargé d**'aider à prévenir les différends et à résoudre les conflits. Le caractère exécutoire de certaines de ses décisions **confère** encore plus de poids à ses délibérations.

In recent years the Council has experienced a period of intensified activity. It has also experienced **setbacks** from which we can all learn. One **lesson** of particular importance is that members of the Security Council, especially the permanent five, **need to demonstrate a firm commitment to the implementation of** their own decisions.

Ces dernières années, le Conseil a connu une période d'activité intense. Il a aussi connu des **revers** dont chacun peut tirer la leçon. Un des grands **enseignements** à tirer est que les membres du Conseil de sécurité, en particulier les cinq membres permanents, **doivent se montrer résolus à faire appliquer** leurs décisions.

For Canada, the need for more open, transparent and collegial decision-making **is crucial**. There must be closer consultations with countries contributing personnel and equipment in order to help implement Council decisions. Here, real progress has been achieved of late, which Canada **warmly welcomes**. This progress needs to be institutionalized.

   Le Canada estime essentiel de mettre en place des mécanismes de décision plus ouverts, plus transparents et plus collégiaux. L'on doit consulter plus étroitement les pays qui fournissent équipement et personnel pour faciliter la mise en œuvre des décisions du Conseil. À ce titre, le Canada **ne peut que se réjouir** des progrès notables accomplis dernièrement. Ces progrès doivent être institutionnalisés.

The credibility and effectiveness of the Council in promoting international peace and security is also a key element. Although we do not regard expansion of its membership as a panacea, **it is clear that** composition plays a role in fostering credibility and effectiveness. The Council is no longer as representative as it once was. Its legitimacy, and perhaps also the quality of its decisions, would be greatly enhanced by more representation from those countries that contribute the most to the maintenance of international peace and security and to the broad purpose of the Organization – that is, the **key** criterion for non-permanent membership **enshrined** in Article 23 of the Charter.

   La crédibilité et l'efficacité du Conseil en matière de promotion de la paix et de la sécurité internationales sont également essentielles. Même si l'augmentation du nombre de ses membres ne nous apparaît pas comme une panacée, **il n'empêche que** la composition du Conseil influe sur sa crédibilité et son efficacité, et qu'il n'est pas aussi représentatif que naguère. Sa légitimité, et peut-être aussi la qualité de ses décisions, profiteraient d'une meilleure représentation des pays qui contribuent le plus au maintien de la paix et de la sécurité internationales et à la poursuite des grands buts de l'Organisation, critère **déterminant** de l'appartenance des membres non permanents **énoncé** dans l'Article 23 de la Charte.

Perhaps it is time to reflect together on those purposes to which Article 23 refers. They would surely include participation in United Nations peace operations, commitment to arms control and disarmament, support for good-neighbourly relations, humanitarian assistance, human rights, development cooperation and the promotion of civil society. **An understanding among Member States along these lines** would help in the selection of non-permanent Council members, whether on the existing basis or on a modified basis.

Il est peut-être temps de réfléchir ensemble aux buts auxquels se réfère l'Article 23. Ils comprendraient sûrement la participation aux opérations de maintien de la paix de l'ONU, l'engagement à l'égard du contrôle des armements et du désarmement et l'appui aux rapports de bon voisinage, à l'aide humanitaire, aux droits de la personne, à la coopération en matière de développement et à la promotion de la société civile. **Si les États Membres arrivaient à s'entendre sur ces questions**, il serait plus facile de choisir les membres non permanents du Conseil, que ce soit selon les modalités en vigueur ou selon une nouvelle formule.

A recurring theme throughout my remarks has been the need for the United Nations to **marshal** its scarce resources **more effectively**. There is simply no other option if we are to restore confidence in this Organization and in the specialized agencies. As the Secretary-General has stressed, the Organization's financial crisis is crippling its effectiveness and its credibility. We cannot allow this to happen.

Un thème que je reprends sans cesse dans mes propos concerne la nécessité pour l'ONU **d'utiliser à meilleur escient** les rares ressources qu'elle possède. Il n'y a tout simplement pas d'autre solution si l'on veut rétablir la confiance dans l'Organisation et les institutions spécialisées. Comme l'a souligné le Secrétaire général, la crise financière de l'ONU compromet son efficacité et sa crédibilité. Nous ne pouvons pas permettre que cela se produise.

The answer lies in addressing both expenditure and revenue. Many Governments, including Canada's, are facing difficult budgetary decisions. We have had to **live with** expenditure reductions in real terms while maintaining priority programmes. International organizations must respect the same pressures as domestic Governments. The United Nations and its agencies must focus on key objectives and reduce overhead spending in order to protect priority programmes. . . . Canada strongly supports the proposal put forward by the Secretary-General for an efficiency task force to address these issues. We are prepared to contribute both expertise and personnel **to get it started soon**.

La réponse consiste à viser à la fois les dépenses et les recettes. De nombreux gouvernements, dont le Canada, doivent faire des choix budgétaires difficiles. Nous avons dû apprendre à **composer avec** des réductions de nos dépenses en termes réels tout en maintenant les programmes prioritaires. Les organisations internationales doivent obéir aux mêmes contraintes que les gouvernements nationaux. L'ONU et ses organismes doivent privilégier les objectifs essentiels et réduire leurs frais généraux afin de protéger les programmes prioritaires. ... Le Canada appuie fermement la proposition du Secrétaire général de créer un groupe de travail sur l'efficacité pour faire face à ces questions. Nous sommes prêts à fournir à la fois des compétences et du personnel **pour qu'il voie le jour bientôt**.

While the United Nations needs to do more to limit spending and to promote efficiency, its financial crisis would be significantly alleviated if its Member States were to meet their financial obligations in full, on time and without conditions. Canada calls on all Member States to do so. We cannot accept that Member States, some of which **rank** among the richest countries in the world, **fail to meet** their financial obligations to this institution. This is **even more difficult to accept when we consider that** a number of the poorest countries in the world meet their payments in full and on time. **Indeed, among the merely** 60 Member States that had met their regular budget obligations to the United Nations fully by 31 July of this year, 32 were developing countries. Unfortunately, 71 other Member States had made no payment at all. Almost 100 countries still owe money from previous years, including, I have to say, several members of the Security Council. The majority of Member States appear content to approve programmes, appropriations and **assessments** without honouring the obligations to which they are committed. **This is unacceptable** and cannot be allowed to continue.

Certes, l'ONU doit faire davantage pour maîtriser ses dépenses et favoriser l'efficacité, mais les États Membres pourraient atténuer sensiblement la crise financière s'ils respectaient pleinement leurs obligations financières, en temps opportun et sans condition. Le Canada engage tous les États Membres à le faire. Nous ne pouvons accepter que des États Membres, dont certains **comptent** parmi les pays les plus riches de la planète, **échappent à** leurs obligations financières envers cette institution. Cela est **d'autant plus difficile à accepter que** certains des pays les plus pauvres du monde paient leur dû intégralement et à temps. **En fait, à peine** 60 États Membres avaient pleinement respecté leurs obligations budgétaires ordinaires envers l'ONU le 31 juillet dernier; 32 étaient des pays en développement. Malheureusement, 71 autres États Membres n'avaient effectué aucun paiement. Près de 100 États Membres, dont plusieurs membres du Conseil de sécurité – je dois le dire –, ont encore des contributions d'années passées à payer. La majorité des États Membres semblent se contenter d'approuver les programmes, les crédits budgétaires et les **prélèvements** sans respecter les obligations qui leur incombent. **Voilà qui est inacceptable** et ne peut plus être toléré.

The General Assembly's High-level Working Group **considering** the United Nations financial plight should begin looking at the establishment of incentives to pay. . . .

Le Groupe de travail de haut niveau de l'Assemblée générale **qui se penche sur** les difficultés financières de l'ONU devrait commencer à chercher des moyens d'inciter les États Membres à payer. . . .

In conclusion, let me say that I have sought to pay tribute to this Organization's achievements, and to emphasize that Canada strongly supports the United Nations. We are prepared to contribute concretely and actively to its revitalization and renewal. **But confidence will be restored and commitment renewed only through** a partnership in which Member States live up to their commitment and focus on key priorities that respond to human-centred goals for sustainable security and development. If we are successful, and **frankly I truly believe that we will** be successful, I have no doubt that 50 years from now our successors will be able to praise, without hesitation or qualification, the record of our Organization's first 100 years.

Pour conclure, je dirai que j'ai cherché à mettre en valeur les réalisations de l'Organisation et à souligner le fait que le Canada appuie fermement les Nations Unies. Nous sommes prêts à contribuer concrètement et énergiquement à sa revitalisation et à son renouveau. **Mais la confiance ne sera rétablie et l'engagement renouvelé que par** un partenariat au sein duquel les États Membres honoreront leurs engagements et se concentreront sur les grandes priorités qui correspondent aux objectifs de sécurité et de développement durables centrés sur la personne. Si nos efforts sont fructueux – et **j'ai tout lieu de croire qu'ils le seront** –, il ne fait aucun doute que dans 50 ans nos successeurs pourront faire sans hésitation ni restriction l'éloge des réalisations de l'Organisation au cours de son premier centenaire. (André Ouellet, Minister of Foreign Affairs of Canada, statement to the UN General Assembly, UN Official Records, A/50/PV7)

(2)   Without looking at the official English version, do a sight-translation of the speech paragraph by paragraph from French into English, speaking aloud to your tape recorder. Then check your sight-translation, as

recorded, against the official English version. Next, do a written translation. Then check your translation for accuracy against the official English version. Repeat this exercise working from English into French.

(3)   Relying on both the original French and English versions to discern the meaning, translate the speech into your other working languages paragraph by paragraph. Later, check your translation for accuracy and style against the official versions at www.un.org/en/documents/ods/.

(4)   Go through the English version of the speech paragraph by paragraph and try to see what sentences and phrases could be edited, abridged or combined in such a way as to make them shorter, without losing any of the meaning, if the speech were delivered at high speed. In particular, look for any redundancies or examples of verbosity or 'elegant variation'. Repeat this exercise with the French version.

(5)   Go through the speech paragraph by paragraph and summarize in writing, in as few words as possible, the main point(s) of each paragraph. When you have completed this, link together your paragraph summaries with appropriate transitional phrases and read out the text to your tape-recorder just as if you were delivering a consecutive interpretation of the speech to an audience. Listen to the recording and check it for completeness against the original.

(6)   Read out the speech in French to your tape-recorder, at a moderate speed, marking your recording with a cue-word (e.g. 'change') wherever the speaker changes the subject. Then play the speech back for yourself. When you hear the cue-word, stop the recording and try to give a complete consecutive interpretation into English (or your other working languages) of the section of the speech you have just heard, recording your performance. When you have completed this, play the recording of the original speech again and consider whether the points at which the speaker changed the subject would have been the appropriate points at which to interrupt him for consecutive interpretation, or whether you would have had to do so more often in order to be complete in your interpretation. In real life, the speaker's own 'thematic pauses' are the ideal points at which an interpreter may step in but, if they are too far apart, the effort may strain the interpreter's short-term memory beyond its limits, and that is to be avoided even if it means interrupting the speaker in the middle of a topic.

(7)   (a)   Read out the entire speech in English or French at moderate speed into your tape recorder, then play it back and interpret it simultaneously into the other language. Stop the recording to catch your breath if necessary. Repeat the exercise until you are able to get through the whole speech without stopping, and without any

major slips or omissions. When you have reached that point, record your performance and check it paragraph by paragraph for completeness and style against the French or English version given above. Give yourself a grade (A, B or C) for completeness and a grade for style. (Do not judge yourself too harshly if your interpretation seems less complete and smooth than the official version: remember that what you are reading in the official version is a translation, not a simultaneous interpretation.) Repeat this exercise, trying to improve your grade.

(b)   Repeat exercise (a) but, this time, try interpreting the speech one full sentence at a time. Get out one complete sentence before you tackle the next one, and leave no sentence hanging. For purposes of this exercise, do not be concerned if you miss an entire sentence: you are only 'stretching', that is trying to increase your lag.

(c)   For recordings of speeches in other languages, see final section of Bibliography.

12 Quotations/Allusions/ Transposition

When a speaker quotes from one of the conference documents, the interpreter should always try to use the official translation of the quotation in the target language if the document is available in that language. When a speaker has provided a text of his speech in advance of delivery and the speech contains a literary quotation, the interpreter should try to write out a translation at least of the key parts of the quotation in advance, so that it will come out more smoothly during the interpretation of the speech.

When a speaker quotes from a literary work and the written text has not been provided, the interpreter can usually handle it by translating the quotation. For example, an American delegate once argued against the Berlin Wall by quoting a well-known line from a poem by Robert Frost: 'Something there is that does not love a wall'. The French interpreter could simply translate this as 'Il y a en nous quelque chose qui répugne à un mur', and the Spanish interpreter could say 'Hay algo que no quiere a los muros', or similar words. No one expects an interpretation (as opposed to a translation) of a quotation to be a literary masterpiece, and the idea is usually sufficiently clear. Many famous quotations, such as 'to be or not to be', have set translations in most languages, and an interpreter should strive to learn them by heart.

When the quotation is originally from a work in the target language, it is, of course, desirable to avoid retranslation and use the original quotation if you know it. If not, try at least to use language that reflects the style, register and period of the author. For example, if a Frenchman quotes Shakespeare in French and you have to translate it back into English but do not remember the quotation, try at least to give your retranslation something of the flavor of Shakespeare. If the quotation is lengthy and this is impossible, an acceptable alternative approach is to paraphrase the quote in simple, modern

English in a way that makes it plain to the listeners that what they are hearing is merely a paraphrase, not your feeble attempt to rival Shakespeare.

However, an *allusion*, an indirect reference to literature, culture, geography or history, often given without attribution, poses a more difficult problem than the quotation. The speaker may be using the indirect reference for a particular effect, or as a kind of shorthand to convey a complex or multi-level message, or to dramatize a situation; for example 'The rock we are pushing up the hill like Sisyphus always seems to roll back a little' (Klaus Kinkel, speech to the UN General Assembly, 25 September 1996). If no attribution is given, there is an unspoken implication (as with antonomasia) that the quote is so quotable, the source so authoritative, the message so important and universal that the speaker expects even a multicultural audience to be familiar with the source. So the interpreter should try to do the same, or he will seem to be 'speaking down' to the audience.

For example, during the Cold War, a French-speaking Eastern-European delegate in an arms-control discussion unexpectedly made an attempt to break the ice by using a literary allusion drawn from La Fontaine in a humorous and self-deprecating way. He said that the East should not treat the West as 'Ce pelé, ce galeux, d'où venait tout le mal'. This is a reference to La Fontaine's fable *Les Animaux Malades de la Peste* (La Fontaine, 1962: 179–180), a tale in which a group of animals stricken by the plague decide that one of their number must be sacrificed to atone for everyone's sins and placate the gods. The lion, king of beasts, admits that he has killed and eaten several sheep, and even some shepherds. The rabbit, to save his own skin by flattering the lion, says it doesn't matter because sheep are worthless creatures anyway and it is just as well that the lion ate them. Thereupon, the foolish donkey publicly confesses that he once ate some grass that did not belong to him from a field at the monastery. All the other animals immediately set upon him and decide that the hapless donkey, 'Ce pelé, ce galeux, d'où venait tout leur mal', is the one that must be sacrificed. (The actual moral of the fable is that societies have a double standard of guilt, one standard for the strong, the lions, and one for the weak or foolish, the donkeys. But the meaning of the line quoted is roughly 'don't blame others for the problems of everyone'.)

As used, in context, by the Eastern-European disarmament negotiator, this allusion was intended to convey approximately the following message: 'We are foolishly wasting our time in these disarmament negotiations if all we ever do is blame each other for problems that are common to us all. The arms race is like the plague in the fable, an evil that affects all of us. And by wasting our time in unproductive mutual recriminations, we are just behaving like those foolish animals in the fable who took shelter in assigning misplaced guilt rather than looking at their problems squarely.' (Notice how densely packed with meaning an allusion can be.) Even more important was the style and *tone* of the allusion: it was humorous and conciliatory, meaning to convey a willingness to compromise.

How could the English interpreter, in the short time available, convey such a complex message? The easy way out was to translate the allusion and hope that everyone in the intended audience (Western experts in chemical and biological weapons) was familiar with La Fontaine's fables and would therefore recognize the allusion and get the point. But that seemed unlikely. And, given the importance of the message, it was better not to take the chance. So the interpreter opted for *transposition*: looking for an approximately equivalent reference drawn from English literature which would preserve, if not the full import of the French allusion, at least its main point and essential flavor, humorously portraying the mutual paranoia of the arms-race deadlock as absurd and counterproductive. The interpreter decided to use a caricature of 'Evil incarnate' from *The Wizard of Oz* to convey this idea and translated the La Fontaine allusion as follows: 'We should not treat our opponents here as the Wicked Witch of the West'.

In other words, the English interpreter used a stereotype from modern American literature to transpose a stereotype from classical French literature. Given the constraint of brevity, this strategy worked, and it at least preserved the most important element in the original French message: its humorous and self-deprecating tone.

Exercises

(1) Do you agree with the solution arrived at by the English interpreter in the example above? Given more time to think about it, can you devise a better solution?

(2) If the speaker does not give the attribution, should the interpreter do so, if it helps the audience to identify the quotation or its meaning?

(3) If an interpreter's transposition is 'on the mark' and appropriate in other respects, does it matter whether he transposes into a different body of literature? In the above case, is a transposition from a fable to a fairy-tale appropriate?

(4) How would you handle the following quotations or allusions in translation or interpretation? Use them in illustrative sentences, then translate the sentences into your other working languages.

> 'It would be Quixotic to attempt that.' / 'Ask not what your country can do for you; ask what you can do for your country.' / 'That is an utterly Orwellian suggestion.' / 'We are well on our way to a brave

new world.' / 'I have a dream.' / 'The meek shall inherit the earth.'
/ 'Let's not tilt at windmills.' / 'What the third world needs is a New
Deal.' / 'I came, I saw, I conquered.' / 'Conditions for workers in
Haiti are becoming Dickensian.' / 'Look on my works, ye mighty,
and despair!' / 'Walk softly and carry a big stick.' / 'The mother of
all battles.' / 'Will no one rid me of this troublesome monk?' / 'Lend
me your ears.' / 'The die is cast.' / 'Oh what a tangled web we weave
when first we practice to deceive!'

'C'est là un travail Herculéen.' / 'Il faut faire droit aux damnés de la
terre.' / 'L'audace, toujours l'audace.' / 'Pour parler en prose plutôt
qu'en vers …' / 'Après moi, le déluge.' / 'Ces mesures représentent
les Thermopyles de l'ére écologique.' / 'L'UNESCO est pour les arts
une véritable Catherine la Grande.' / 'Le peuple n'a pas de pain?
Qu'il mange du gâteau!' / 'L'État, c'est moi.'

'Eradicar la pobreza es un trabajo de Sísifo.' / 'Los poderosos no se
acuerdan de los olvidados.' / 'La vida de un refujiado es una verdadera
Odisea.' / 'Estos proyectos son utópicos.' / 'Venceréis pero no con-
venceréis.' / 'El respeto al derecho ajeno es la paz.'

'Se non è vero, è molto ben trovato.' / 'Lasciate ogni speranza, voi
ch'entrate!' / 'E pur si muove!'

(5) Translate the following allusion into Spanish, French or your other
working languages:

Mr Chairman: To invoke a different image, related to your country,
an attempt to establish a Code of Crimes omitting the crime of
aggression would be like trying to stage a production of Hamlet
without the Prince. Having said that, my delegation would acknowl-
edge that, in Shakespeare at least, the character and disposition of
the Prince of Denmark are not always easy to circumscribe and
define. (Statement by representative of Ireland)

(6) La Fontaine's fable *La Besace* (La Fontaine, 1962: 40) contains the following proverb (line 30):

On se voit d'un autre oeil qu'on ne voit son prochain.
(a)   What is the meaning of this verse?
(b)   Can it be translated?
(c)   Would the following verses by Robert Burns be an exact equivalent?

Oh would some bard the gift he gi'e us
To see ourselves as others see us!

(d) Can you think of a better English equivalent, or of equivalents in other languages?

(7) Which of the following is the better transposition into English of the Spanish quotation 'La vida es sueño':

> Life is but a dream. (verse from children's song *Row, Row Your Boat*)
> Life's but a walking shadow. (verse from *Hamlet*)

(8) Could an allusion to the ancient Greek myth of Phaeton be translated by a paraphrase of the expression 'Don't play with fire'? Could it be translated by the expression 'The higher they fly, the farther they fall'? Could the same idea be conveyed by the biblical proverb, 'Pride comes before disaster, and arrogance before a fall' (Proverbs, ch.16: v.18)? How does the myth of Phaeton differ from the legend of Daedalus and Icarus?

(9) Sometimes a famous name or literary allusion has acquired nuances in one language which it did not originally have or which it lacks in other languages. Consider the following:

(a) Can the word 'Quixotic' as it is usually used in English (meaning foolishly idealistic) be used to translate the allusion *quijotesco* as used in the following context?

> No hay en la literature universal ... una página más cercana del *Quijote* que estos capítulos primeros de *La cartuja de Parma* ... el episodio en que una mujer obliga a Fabricio a estrechar la mano de un soldado muerto, *qué quijotesco es*! (Azorín, 1958: 56–57)

(b) Toward the end of the reign of the first Roman emperor, Augustus (63 BC–14 AD), it appears that the native Roman population was in relative decline. From what you know about Malthus and his ideas, can the word 'Malthusianism' as it is usually used in English be used to translate the allusion *maltusianismo* as used in the following context?

> Divorcios y *maltusianismo* habían matado a la familia, y el tronco romano estaba casi extinguido. El último censo revelaba que las tres cuartas partes de ciudadanos eran libertos o hijos de libertos extranjeros. (Montanelli, 1959; trans. Pruna, 1969: 191)

(c) Do the following mean the same thing in each of your working languages?

> Quixotic / Malthusian / Cartesian / Confucian / Homeric / Machiavellian / Hobbesian

(10) In a televised interview on 26 October 1995, President Jacques Chirac of France, discussing exchange rates and monetary stability, used an allusion by antonomasia when he mentioned that *'le Général'* had been a strong supporter of a stable franc. To whom was he alluding?

Not mentioning the famous person's name carried at least two implications: (1) 'the general' was a man of such unique stature that there was no need to mention his name; and (2) President Chirac himself identified with 'the general' in an affectionate or deferential way.

(a) The English interpreter translating this interview decided that preserving these two unspoken implications was more important than spelling out the identity of the mysterious historical figure for those younger members of the English-speaking public who might not immediately guess it. Do you agree?

(b) If this had been an interpretation of an interview with a conservative Spanish president and the antonomasia had referred to 'el caudillo' instead of 'the general', would you have kept the antonomasia or spelled out the reference? To maintain the antonomasia in English, would you say 'el caudillo' or use an English equivalent such as 'the chief' or 'our leader'? This involves a judgment about the speaker's intentions and about how well known the unnamed person is to the target audience.

(11) (a) The following French sentence contains an idiom based on allusion to Homer. Would 'Homeric', used in this sense, be clear to most speakers of English or Spanish? Translate the sentence into idiomatic English and/or Spanish by transposing the French idiom into an equivalent English or Spanish idiom:

A ces mots, Bill Clinton a été pris d'un *fou rire homérique* et difficilement contenu. (*Le Monde*, 1995a)

(b) In the following sentence, a geographical allusion is used to evoke a similar kind of laughter. What idea does the word 'Florentine' usually evoke in the mind of an English speaker? Is that what the author means here? Translate the sentence into idiomatic English and/or French by transposing the Spanish idiom into an equivalent English or French idiom:

Su *carcajada florentina* resonaba en el patio como un carillón. (Benedetti, 1992)

13 Political Discourse

Political ideas and assumptions pervade the discourse of international conferences, even when the subject matter is not as such political. An interpreter must therefore have a fairly well-developed sense of current political trends and the vocabulary associated with them, as well as a knowledge of the standard procedural jargon of deliberative and decision-making bodies and fora.

Exercises

(1) One significant international political trend nowadays is the dissolution and formation of national entities and states, into which the following article provides some insights. Notice the meaning of the underlined words in the article, in the context where they appear. Is the choice of words a good one? How many synonyms can you think of which would carry approximately the same meaning? Are any of them more appropriate in context than the word used by the author?

> *How Yemen is Coming Undone*
> Aden, Yemen. – A few days before full-scale war broke out this month in Yemen, **armored** <u>brigades</u> from the north and the south clashed. ... The entanglement left scores of dead and wounded, and the usual <u>detritus</u> of battle. And in its wake, hundreds of armed mountain tribesmen, partisans of neither side, descended on the camp and made off with <u>stockpiles</u> of weapons and other combat <u>gear</u>.
>
> If the battle was a <u>prelude</u> to the vicious civil war now engulfing this country ... **the stripping** of the dead may be a <u>signpost</u> of what will follow. What Yemen entered, even before the south formally seceded, is a struggle not only between regular armies ... but among the tribes, militias, clans and families that rule <u>patches</u> of

territory as if there were no federal government – **as** if the Middle Ages had never ended.

Such <u>internecine</u> battles characterized most of the Arabian Peninsula a century ago, before Europeans arrived in force to reorganize it according to their own interests, drawing <u>boundaries</u> where there were no distinct <u>nations</u>. And as conflicts in Somalia and Rwanda show, tribal <u>warfare</u> could well characterize much of the <u>bloodletting</u> in the developing world well into the next century. For the decline of the Europeans, followed by the <u>disintegration</u> of one superpower and the <u>retreat</u> of the other, has left governments such as those in Sana and Aden <u>bereft</u> of the outside backing that once allowed them to hold warring factions <u>in check</u>. . . .

The bulk of the outside support ended with the <u>collapse</u> of the Soviet Union, and in 1990 north and south <u>merged</u> in order to <u>stave off</u> economic collapse in the south. But the hope for a bright future has now been <u>extinguished</u>. The war that began on May 5 is often <u>portrayed</u> as the extension of a long-running <u>feud</u> between President Ali Abdullah Saleh, who is from the north, and his former Vice President, Ali Salim al-Badih, who is from the south. Many Yemenis <u>sardonically</u> called this 'the war of the Alis'.

Neither side rules, however, without the backing of dozens of powerful tribal leaders. Tribes in Yemen often rule over small <u>fiefs</u> that Sana and Aden have been <u>loath</u> to challenge. This is because nearly half of the country's people live in villages of fewer than 250 inhabitants, and in those places the tribal leaders are often the only ones who can exercise direct authority. Civil war has only reinforced this, since **many** Yemenis, especially in the northern capital Sana, have fled back to their villages.

Back in 1990, the <u>merger</u> of north and south had the support of many tribal leaders because **the dream** of a united Yemen had been <u>current</u> in both regions for decades, and because unity seemed to offer a way to <u>reverse</u> a steady deterioration in Yemen's standard of living. If the south was offered a chance to survive the <u>withdrawal</u> of Soviet aid, the central government in the north got a much larger <u>land mass</u> over which to rule. Later, as a result of new oil exploration in the south, it also turned out that it had obtained access to additional production of 140,000 barrels a day. . . . But whatever economic benefit <u>accrued</u> from unity was <u>smashed</u> by **one** of the Government's first decisions – to sympathize with Iraq in the Gulf War. . . . Now, with the merger <u>in tatters</u>, **the** northern and southern political leaderships have exhausted much of their credibility.

So, as the two ruling parties, which never integrated their armed forces, tear themselves apart, the tribal leaders could well emerge as the new <u>power brokers</u>. Already the fighting has left hundreds, if not thousands, of casualties. It is destroying what little modern communications and transportation Yemen had, and it is exhausting the country's <u>meager</u> resources.

Yemen has long been home to dozens of tribes, many of which have formed powerful tribal <u>confederations</u>. ... Sheikh Abdullah al-Ahmar, who leads the hashid <u>coalition</u> of tribes and is a member of Parliament, is already said to have 50,000 men <u>under arms</u>, more than the entire northern army of about 40,000. There are **persistent** rumors that if the war goes badly for the north, President Saleh, a member of the Hashid tribe, will find himself out of a job.

In addition, tribes have **increasingly** entered the struggle for <u>diminishing</u> resources, <u>kidnapping</u> oil workers, tourists, foreign diplomats and even Chinese road workers and <u>holding them ransom</u> for a share of the oil profits, new weapons or social services. ... Whatever the outcome of the war, **Yemen**, already the Arab world's poorest nation, will be worse off. The <u>reach</u> of the central governments (if two, or even one, of them remain) will be weaker. And many Yemenis seem certain to <u>award</u> their first loyalties not to the state, which has failed them, but to the tribe, which so far has not. (Hedges, 1994 (excerpts))

(2)   Using a dictionary and thesaurus, identify the nuances that distinguish the following related words:
   • brigades / units / detachments / squads / bands
   • boundary / frontier / frontiers / border / border-line / demarcation / confines
   • warfare / fighting / strife / unrest / turmoil / upheaval
   • disintegration / collapse / crumbling / break-up
   • merge / combine / marry / unite / join forces / federate
   • retreat / withdrawal / pull-back / waning / dwindling
   • extinguish / end / snuff out / dash / put out
   • detritus / waste / rubble / remains
   • sardonically / wryly / ironically / smilingly / sarcastically / bitterly
   • feud / quarrel / spat / fight
   • gear / equipment / materiel
   • signpost / harbinger / omen / sign
   • loath / reluctant / trepidation / disinclined
   • fief / preserve / home ground / sanctuary

- patches / lots / tracts / areas
- internecine / fratricidal / in-fighting
- bloodletting / bloodshed / carnage
- bereft / stripped / devoid
- in check / at bay / under control
- stave off / forestall / avert
- portrayed / depicted / presented
- current / prevalent / widespread
- reverse / turn around / roll back / check / curb
- land mass / territory / expanse
- accrued / gained / arisen / derived
- in tatters / in pieces / in shreds
- power brokers / kingpins / key players
- meager / scant / paltry
- confederation / conglomerate / alliance / coalition
- under arms / in arms / up in arms
- outcome / result / denouement
- reach / scope / extent / outreach
- award / grant / tender
- patch / lot / plot / swath / strip / tract / belt
- smashed / dashed / annihilated / canceled out / nullified
- diminishing / dwindling / drying up
- kidnap / seize / abduct / hold to ransom / take hostage

(3) What is the difference between the following words, and what are their equivalents in French, Spanish or your other working languages?

tribe / clan / people / nation / ethnic group / minority

In the context of the above article on Yemen, would 'clan' be a functional synonym for 'tribe'? When would you say 'the Huron nation' rather than 'the Huron tribe', and why? How would a political scientist define 'tribe' and 'nation'? Which English term is closest to the French terms **une peuplade** and **une ethnie**? What, if any, is the difference between a 'tribesman' and a 'clansman'? What is the origin of the word 'tribe'?

Why do Puerto Rican nationalists sometimes refer to themselves as 'a national minority' rather than just 'a minority'? Is the term 'minority' a numerical concept? Consider the following:

Paradoxically, a minority may have nothing to do with numbers: take the case of black South Africans in the apartheid era. A minority is simply a cultural group that has limited or no possibility to influence its own future within the state. The definition also has a historical dimension: a minority is in general indigenous, and has been in the country since the beginning of time, or at least since the state was established. I think that in most cases this excludes immigrant groups. (Magga, 1995: 9)

What differences in nuance distinguish the terms 'separatism', 'secession' and 'self-determination'? Is it a difference of perspective rather than content? Why is self-determination usually called 'libre autodeterminación' in Spanish?

What is the meaning of the current expression 'failed state'? What is a 'rogue state'? What is a 'sub-national conflict'? What does the expression 'regional conflicts' usually refer to?

(4) Where a word in the above article on Yemen (pp. 211–213) appears in bold type, rewrite the sentence starting with that word, changing the meaning of the sentence as little as possible.

> *Example*: 'Now, with the merger in tatters, the northern and southern political leaderships have exhausted much of their credibility.' > 'The northern and southern political leaderships have exhausted much of their credibility now that the merger itself lies in tatters.'

(5) Read the following translation of an article about Yemen from *Le Monde*. Then translate the *Le Monde* editorial, 'Le Yémen réunifié par les armes', which follows. Make your translation as concise as possible. Lay it aside, reread it the following day and try to rewrite it in a way that is even more concise.

An Ill-fated Union

From our special correspondent: Estranged by History – Ottoman occupation in the North and British colonization in the South – Yemen's 14 million people (11 in the North and three in the South) will not get a chance to celebrate the fourth anniversary of the marriage from which they expected so much. The union was sealed on 22 May 1990 by Colonel Ali Abdallah Saleh, head of state in the North since 1978, and Ali Salem El Bid, leader of the Yemeni Socialist Party, who has been in power in Aden since the British left in November 1967. But the marriage could not withstand the claims by each of them to wield sole power.

Through this union, President Saleh sought to allay the military caste on which his power rests and Mr El Bid wanted above all to find a way out of the economic plight left by the end of Soviet aid.

But the union only temporarily masked the mistrust prevailing between two centers of power with different aims and the schism between two societies that have developed along different lines. It looked good on paper, but the union never became a reality if we bear in mind that the armies and the powerful security services were never merged and that, up to the eve of the war now under way, the two countries each kept their own airlines and their own means of propaganda, television, and radio.

Formal democracy. It was a hasty marriage between a military-tribal power with an Islamic hue in the North and the Arab world's only Marxist-Leninist party, which had governed for 23 years, in the South. It was at best an unlikely match and it became impossible when each sought to take from the other without giving anything in return – not to mention the fact that 'the union was still led by men who were separatists', as a staunch advocate of unity, Omar El Ghaoui, observes.

Although it had given up to Sanaa the status of capital city with everything that implies in terms of prestige, employment, and business, Aden did remain the country's economic capital. But the promise, especially the creation of a duty-free zone, was never realized, and Yemen remained one of the world's poorest countries, with a per capita income of $700.

Oil mirages. The democracy which was to form the basis of the new state was purely formal. The mushrooming of political parties – about 40 of them – and a profusion of newspapers and publications enjoying freedom of expression during the first legislative elections of 27 April 1993, created only a momentary illusion. The election results showed that each side was still holding its own ground. The PSY (Yemen Socialist Party) carried all the seats for the six southern governorates, while the CPG (General Popular Congress) led by President Saleh and the Yemeni Reform Movement (*El Islah*), an Islamic-tribalist party, took virtually all the seats in the North as contenders bowed out by mutual agreement.

The division of power between three major parties in fact weakened the PSY, which had shared power with the CPG since unification. Feeling short-changed by the union, none of whose promises – a modern state and liberal economy – had been kept, the PSY, the sworn enemy of *El Islah*, which accuses it of atheism, demanded a redefinition of the union along federalist lines – a polite way of remaining the boss in your own home.

The southerners' fears and frustrations were compounded by a wave of Islamic zeal waving Yemeni colors, and the southerners are now playing that card to get into the good graces of the West and of Arab countries beset by Moslem extremism. It is hard to say whether oil, which was discovered in the North in the early 1980s and later in the South, has been a factor in the separation, as many believe. The parties primarily concerned deny it. But President Saleh, who held out the prospect of overcoming underdevelopment thanks to oil resources, no doubt gave his people unfounded hopes that have fuelled envy in various quarters – especially since it now appears that the South has bigger reserves than the North.

According to specialists, Yemen is apparently not among the major oil states. Its current production is about 320,000 barrels per day, roughly equally divided between the Mareb oil fields of the North, operated by the US company Hunt, and the Massilah fields of Hadaramout in the South, operated by the Canadian company Canoxy. Net of operating costs and domestic consumption, the oil revenues are only about $300 million per year, which is enough to service a foreign debt reckoned at $6.5 billion. That falls well short of a windfall. Still, all eyes are focused on the province of Shabwa, where the biggest reserves are thought to exist, at the junction between the old border between the two Yemens and along the undefined border between Saudi Arabia and South Yemen. Last year, Riyadh issued a warning to oil-prospecting companies that they were operating in Saudi territory. The fighting now raging in the area, currently to the North's advantage, is aimed at controlling some potentially rich territory. One cannot rule out the possibility that the PSY, seeking allies, may accept a power-sharing arrangement with the League of the Sons of Yemen party, since its leaders hail from that disputed province of Shabwa.

In a part of the world where the concept of the state does not exist and where only clan interests count, the PSY is finding it hard to gain support. After having done all it could to break the power of the tribes, they are not eager now to come to its aid. Mohsen Farid, Secretary General of the League of the Sons of Yemen and now deputy prime minister of the new Democratic Republic of Yemen, admits, 'In this region we have a lack of political, military, and tribal leadership'. A tribal leader says: 'The tribes do not feel involved and are not ready to commit themselves to a fight with an uncertain outcome.'

A key piece on the political chessboard, the tribes are more sympathetic to the appeals of the North, which still have more resonance in this region, than they are to the heirs of a Marxist regime which stood against them. Opposed to the political confederation of the Hasheds, to which President Saleh belongs and whose leader is parliamentary chairman and *El Islah* leader Sheik Abdallal El Ahmar, the tribal confederation of the Bakhils is being showered with deference by the southerners.

But an expert admits that the southerners 'would be naive to believe that the Bakhils will help them against the North, with which they are bound. They will use the southerners to throw a scare into the President and gain favors from him, but they will act only according to their interests.' The Bakhils control the territory crossed by the oil pipeline that carries oil from Mareb to Hodeya, and they might therefore play a role in any oil war.

Huge waste. Sanaa and Aden blame each other for the breakdown of the union. While the northerners are unquestionably responsible for starting the war that sealed the separation, the independence which Mr El Bid declared on 21 May had been in the works since he last returned to his home ground in Aden on 19 August while he was still Vice President of a united Yemen.

The reconciliation agreement signed on 20 February in Amman under the sponsorship of Jordan and developed by a committee of dialogue involving all the parties largely satisfied the demands of the South as regards decentralization and establishment of a modern state based on the rule of law. But it merely postponed the outbreak of the crisis since, as one actor in the conflict has put it, 'it is clear neither of the main protagonists had the intention of putting it into practice'. The new rulers of Aden are trying to use that document as a guidepost while at the same time stressing that unity has become impossible so long as President Saleh's regime lasts. Sanaa has already gone a step farther: its first demand is the repeal of a declaration of independence which it deems 'illegitimate'.

As things now stand, it is hard to see anything but a military solution to the crisis. This is all the more true given the fact that the numerous mediators are not completely neutral and that Yemen is now, in a sense, paying for its pro-Iraq position during the Gulf War.

Saudi Arabia, which was hostile to Yemeni unity, has cut off aid and sent home some 700,000 Yemenis, thus complicating matters for its neighbor. Riyadh, which has kept its links with both North and South, could play a more constructive role if it wanted to. But that is far from certain.

Egypt, which has bitter memories of its military adventure in Yemen in Colonel Nasser's days, is being cautious too, although the southerners like to claim Egyptian support. President Saleh has put himself in the dock by rejecting any form of mediation out of hand. But 'President' El Bid no doubt put his supporters in an awkward position by his declaration of independence.

As one opposition figure ruefully notes, 'the war comes from the North, the separation comes from the South. It all amounts to one huge waste for Yemen and a deep disillusionment for all Yemenis still committed to unity.' (Françoise Chipaux, *Le Monde*; trans. James Nolan)

Le Yémen réunifié par les armes

Objet de si nombreuses convoitises, la péninsule arabique vient de connaître une nouvelle guerre meurtrière qui n'a pourtant suscité que peu d'intérêt. Le Yémen n'est pas le Koweit. La victoire des nordistes du président Saleh tient notamment au fait qu'il a compris beaucoup plus vite que son adversaire sudiste que la communauté internationale interviendrait mollement dans cette affaire. En accompagnant soigneusement son effort militaire de pressions diplomatiques, le chef de l'Etat a pu s'assurer une victoire complète sans encourir aucune sanction.

Les pays du Golfe, Arabie saoudite en tête, qui, dès l'ouverture des hostilités, avaient manifesté leur soutien implicite aux dirigeants sudistes, ne peuvent aujourd'hui que constater leur défaite. Face aux 'Grands' du Conseil de sécurité, les Etats-Unis en particulier, ils n'ont pu imposer leur volonté et faire triompher par un arrêt des combats et une reconnaissance de la nouvelle république sudiste, ce qu'ils considèrent être leur intérêt: une nouvelle division du pays. Avec ses quatorze millions d'habitants et ses ressources pétrolières, même limitées, un Yémen unifié a toujours fait peur aux Etats du Golfe dont la population totale est à peine supérieure.

La victoire du président Saleh est d'autant plus amère pour eux qu'ils ne lui ont toujours pas pardonné son attitude lors de la guerre du Golfe, Sanaa s'étant opposé à l'intervention occidentale contre Saddam Hussein. Or, paradoxalement, c'est avec les seuls soutiens avoués de l'Irak et du Soudan, deux pays mis quasiment au ban des nations par les Etats-Unis, que les nordistes ont gagné la partie. Avec l'aide aussi des islamistes yéménites, autres 'ennemis' potentiels qui, dans cette affaire, n'ont sans doute pas dit leur dernier mot.

Cette conjoncture a priori défavorable pour les nordistes ne les a toutefois pas desservis dans la mesure où les intérêts des 'Grands' n'étaient pas véritablement en jeu, le conflit yéménite ne risquant pas apparemment de déborder au-delà des frontières et d'affecter la sécurité de la région. En se contentant d'appeler à un cessez-le-feu garanti par des observateurs arabes et islamiques, les Etats-Unis on très vite marqué la limite de leur engagement. Ancien allié des sudistes, Moscou a tenté de son côté d'obtenir un arrêt des combats alors que les nordistes étaient déjà quasiment victorieux.

Cette victoire, le président Saleh devra toutefois très vite la consolider dans le domaine politique. C'est là que l'on peut nourrir les plus grandes craintes. Isolé diplomatiquement dans la région, il lui faudra beaucoup d'habileté pour renouer avec ses voisins, qui ne vont sans doute pas lui faciliter la tâche. Dans un pays aux structures étatiques très fragiles, toutes sortes d'ingérences sont possibles, comme par le passé, ce qui laisse augurer une longue période de turbulences. (*Le Monde*, 1994: Editorial)

(6) (a) Read the following translated article on Quebec from *Le Devoir*. Then read the French original, which follows. Critique the English translation from the standpoint of diction and style. Can you improve upon it? Make a new translation of your own and compare it to the English version given.

No, Quebec Didn't Lose!
'A defeat is a defeat,' the de facto leader of the sovereignty movement Lucien Bouchard shrewdly reminded us last week, refusing to celebrate a premature 'moral victory'. For those of us who voted Yes, the hair's-breadth margin that tipped the balance for the No vote left our hopes intact but did not give us space in which to hide from reality. The people of Quebec, one of the healthiest and most vigorous democracies in the world, made a decision. Political life will go on, with the same institutions, because a frail majority still supports them.

Quebec must still live within these institutions, which are both Quebecer and Canadian institutions. And yet, as we all know, something changed decisively during the extraordinary debate we have just gone through. Without going so far as to break away from Canada, Quebec – through the enormous leap of the Yes vote, from 40.5% in 1980 – now holds a central place in a country which, for nearly 15 years, had been coolly denying Quebec that place since the referendum of 1980. In the eyes of Canadians, for whom the last two weeks have been a wake-up call, Quebec must finally be recognized as the 'people' it is, as it has just affirmed. Never again will Quebec be a negligible factor, as it was in 1982, or 'one problem among others', as it became in 1990 and 1992 during the Lake Meech and Charlottetown agreements [on changes in constitutional arrangements]. If Canadian leaders do not take notice of this fact, if the 'change' they were muttering about toward the campaign's end does not amount to Quebec resuming its central place in the Canadian experience, everyone knows that from now on the march toward sovereignty will go ahead with unquestionable legitimacy.

These things need to be said and acknowledged before we can talk about reconciliation, since the real reconciliation will depend on them. Tensions between individuals will die down, as both sides have often understood and shared the same concerns, the same dilemmas, and the same dreams. Our quarrel is an old one, which creates empathies as deep as the confrontations. But today we can, we must, hold out our hands without closing our eyes. There will be no real, lasting reconciliation through mere words of comfort after a vote like this one. The task that lies before Canada is an enormous one. Many said that Canada would have trouble speaking with a single voice and joining its scattered ranks if the Yes vote had won. But the challenge is the same when the No vote won thanks to half-hearted promises of change. Where will that change come from? By what means? The months to come will tell.

Quebec's internal reconciliation also calls for necessary and radical changes. Analysts are often warned against the temptation to emphasize the linguistic split in the vote, with a French-speaking majority which voted a definite Yes, and minorities of English speakers and speakers of other languages who voted overwhelmingly for the No, and whose choice thus decided the winning side. Here we have to distinguish between analysis and blame. All the votes had the same weight, no one challenged their validity, and no one should, if the 'people' of Quebec is what we want it to be – a modern, pluralistic people who stand for inclusiveness now and in the future. But to make a taboo out of the linguistic cleavage would be a serious moral error. The issue of identity for French-speaking Quebecers is no longer the only issue that fuels the sovereignty movement, but it has historically been at its core. To disregard the wishes of the majority within the majority, to do nothing in response to them, would be to perpetuate the blindness from which Canada has finally been striving to heal itself in recent days. A democratic country cannot be a prison for those who 'built' the country, as has so often been said.

The No vote of 1995 is not the No vote of 1980. It does not stand on the same political footing, or on the same demographic premises. That is why the real reconciliation is yet to come. It lies at the end of a road along which we must understand the full meaning of the Yes and the No that have just been added up to force Canada finally to answer the Quebec question. (Bissonnette, 1995; trans. James Nolan)

Non, le Québec n'a pas perdu!
'Une défaite est une défaite', nous disait la semaine dernière le leader de facto du mouvement **souverainiste**, Lucien Bouchard, qui, lucide, refusait de **se complaire** d'avance dans une 'victoire morale'. Pour ceux d'entre nous qui ont voté oui, l'**infime marge** qui a donné la victoire au non laisse l'espoir intact, mais ne saurait être un refuge d'où nier la réalité. Le peuple du Québec, l'une des démocraties **les plus saines et les plus vives** au monde, a pris une décision. Avant tout, elle exige respect. La vie politique reprendra donc son cours, au sein d'institutions inchangées parce qu'une fragile majorité les appuie toujours.

Le Québec doit encore **vivre à l'intérieur de ces institutions**, qui sont québécoises et canadiennes. Pourtant, tous le savent, quelque chose a changé de façon décisive durant l'extraordinaire débat que nous venons de vivre. Sans aller **jusqu'à la rupture** avec le Canada, le Québec s'est redonné – par le progrès énorme du oui – une place centrale dans un pays qui la lui niait **allègrement**, depuis près de quinze ans, après le **verdict référendaire** de 1980. Aux yeux des Canadiens qui ont vécu les deux dernières semaines **comme un électrochoc**, le Québec doit être enfin reconnu comme le '**peuple**' qu'il est, qu'il vient d'affirmer. Jamais plus il ne sera **une quantité négligeable** comme il l'a été en 1982, ni 'un problème parmi d'autres' où on le noyait, en 1990 et en 1992, durant les épisodes de Meech et de Charlottetown. Si les leaders canadiens **ne prennent pas acte** de ce fait, si le 'changement' dont ils ont **balbutié** le mot en fin de campagne ne marque pas un retour au rétablissement de cette place centrale du Québec dans l'expérience canadienne, tous savent, désormais, que la marche vers la **souveraineté** continuera avec une **légitimité** incontestable.

Ces choses doivent être dites et reconnues avant de parler de réconciliation puisque la vraie réconciliation en dépend. Les

tensions entre individus de convictions différentes **se résorberont**, car les deux camps ont partagé et compris les inquiétudes, les **déchirements** et les rêves de **leurs vis-à-vis**. Notre querelle est ancienne, elle crée des **empathies** aussi profondes que ses **affrontements**. Mais on peut, ont doit aujourd'hui **se donner la main sans fermer les yeux**. Il n'y aura pas de **retrouvailles** réelles, durables, avec de simples mots d'apaisement au lendemain d'un **scrutin** pareil. La tâche qui attend le Canada est énorme: on a beaucoup dit qu'il aurait eu de la difficulté à **parler d'une voix**, à **regrouper ses rangs** dispersés si le oui l'avait emporté, mais le défi est le même au lendemain d'un non qui s'est appuyé sur **une molle promesse** de changement. D'où viendra-t-il? Par qui et par quels moyens? Les prochains mois seront décisifs.

La réconciliation interne du Québec tient aussi à ces changements radicaux et indispensables. On met souvent les analystes en garde contre la tentation de faire ressortir **le clivage linguistique** du vote, la majorité francophone qui a voté oui et clairement, les minorités anglophones et allophones qui ont voté non et massivement, et dont le choix a donc déterminé le camp victorieux. Il faut distinguer ici entre le devoir d'analyse et la **mise en accusation**. Tous les votes avaient le même poids, nul n'a mis en doute leur validité et nul ne le devrait, si le 'peuple' du Québec est celui que nous voulons, celui de la **modernité pluraliste**, de **l'inclusion** présente et future. Mais faire de ce clivage linguistique un tabou serait **une négligence morale** grave. La **question identitaire**, chez les Québécois de langue française, n'est plus la seule à nourrir le mouvement souverainiste mais elle a été historiquement son centre. Ignorer les vœux de la majorité au sein de la majorité, ne rien faire pour en **prendre acte**, serait perpétuer l'aveuglement dont le Canada prétendait, au cours des derniers jours, vouloir enfin se guérir. Un pays démocratique ne saurait accepter d'être une **prison** pour ceux dont on a dit et répété qu'ils l'ont 'bâti'.

Le non de 1995 n'est pas le non de 1980. Il ne repose ni sur les mêmes **données politiques**, ni sur les mêmes **données démographiques**. C'est pourquoi la vraie réconciliation **se fera attendre**. Elle est **au bout de la démarche** qui reconnaîtra le plein sens du oui et du non, **qui viennent de s'additionner** pour obliger le Canada à répondre, enfin, à la question québécoise. (Bissonnette, 1995)

(b) Consider the words highlighted in bold in the article and try to think of possible ways of translating them into your other languages.

(c) Treating the article as a speech, do a sight translation of the French version into English, or the English version into French, or either version into your other languages.

(d) Treating the article as a speech, make a recording of one version and practice interpreting it into the other or into another of your working languages. Record your performance and review it at a later time.

(e) Repeat the above exercises using the article presented in Annex IV.

14 Economic Discourse

Writings and oral presentations on economics can be highly technical. The translation and interpretation of those specialized technical materials is beyond the scope of this book. However, much of the vocabulary of business and economic commentary consists not of technical terms (e.g. 'demand elasticity') but of conventional descriptors (e.g. 'a sluggish market'). And many general presentations, especially in international fora, include a good deal of economic description, often as the basis of or justification for a statement of position or a policy argument. Translators and interpreters must therefore have at their fingertips a good basic vocabulary for economic description.

Exercises

(1) Use words from the list of common economic descriptors in Table 14.1 in sentences describing the current state of an industry or business with which you are familiar.
(2) Look for examples of the use of the words in the table, and similar descriptive words, in *The Economist, The Wall Street Journal, The Financial Times*, the business section of *The New York Times*, or your local newspaper. Then look for equivalents in newspapers in your other languages.
(3) Using a dictionary and a thesaurus, identify the different shades of meaning of the words in each column of Table 14.1, paying special attention to those with which you are least familiar.

    Notice that most economic descriptors derive from mechanistic or organic analogies. These are not, strictly speaking, technical terms. But they do usually convey a specific nuance. The important thing in describing economic conditions and trends is to choose a word that conveys the right *degree* of positive or negative movement. Whether you use an image or figure of speech derived from a mechanistic or organic

Table 14.1

decline	slump	rise
dwindle	stagnate	increase
decrease	paralysis	growth
fall	inertia	gain momentum
shrink	freeze	pick up
dip	wane	surge
weaken	anemic	boom
lose steam	stopped	boost
lose impetus	blocked	peak
retreat	waste away	level off
deteriorate	plateau	set record
bust	hold steady	inching up
all-time low	soft landing	soar
drop	flattened out	skyrocket
plummet	jammed	thrive
collapse	sharply	flourish
crash	steeply	develop
implode	gaping	unfold
slide	hit bottom	strengthen
peter out	bottom out	vigor
contract		expand
loser		winner
lose ground		gain ground
lag behind		advance
cooling off		forge ahead
ailing		banner year
nosedive		bolster

analogy, or from some other source, is not as important as striking the right note. For example, a market may 'soar' or 'skyrocket' (mechanistic analogies) or it may 'thrive' or 'flourish' (organic analogies). Or, on the negative side, an industry might be described as being 'anemic' or 'sluggish' (organic analogies) or it might be described as 'treading water' or 'in a state or inertia' (mechanistic analogies). But it would be wrong to translate 'la demande du coton **est en chute libre**' or 'la demanda de algodón **está en caída libre**' as 'demand for cotton is **slipping**', as this would be too weak.

Economic description also freely draws analogies or metaphors from a wide range of other fields, for example from graphics ('margin'), geometry ('spiral'), navigation ('in its wake'), transport ('engine of growth'), medicine ('shock therapy', 'symptoms', 'diagnosis', 'on the mend'), architecture ('foundation', 'cornerstone'), meteorology ('stormy', 'calm'), sports ('level playing field') and aviation ('take-off point').

Example:

To the extent that the debt has increased deficit spending by **syphoning** taxes to maintain itself, and may continue to increase merely to maintain the **status quo**, the debt provides ... a relatively risk-free **haven** for the investment of unproductive **accumulations** of capital. Investment capital **tied up** financing the debt, year after year, amounts to **dead weight** in the economy. ... But it remains true that if the government had no need to borrow to cover its past borrowing, those capital funds would be available as economic **muscle** rather than being used to maintain otherwise unproductive **poundage**. ... It appears to be too late for fiscal '**health and exercise**' program cuts and tax increases alone to do the job. Stronger **medicines** or even **surgery** must be considered. Adopting a balanced budget amendment to the Constitution may be the **strong medicine** that will enable Congress to **balance** future deficits. As contended by the proposed amendment's opponents, the adoption of an amendment may turn out to be **as drastic, painful and uncertain as gastric bypass surgery** would be to the seriously **overweight**. (Mount, 1995: 606–609 (excerpt))

(a) Translate the above passage preserving the same images as in the original.
(b) Translate the above passage using different images which express the same nuance or the same degree of positive or negative meaning.

(4) Read the following translated articles on the economy of South Africa, paying special attention to the words highlighted in bold type. Try to think of possible alternatives for those words.

Can South Africa Avoid IMF Shock Therapy?

Embarked on an ambitious and costly program of economic reconstruction and development, the South African government's **room to maneuver** is steadily **shrinking**. On the horizon looms the **straight and narrow road** charted by the Bretton Woods agencies.

To draw investors, Nelson Mandela's country needs a **brisk, transparent** socio-economic climate. Otherwise, capital flight could **speed up** and leave **in its wake** a shortfall of capital and foreign exchange – a scenario that would **push** South Africa right **into the arms** of the International Monetary Fund (IMF). Unless the South Africans **run a tight budgetary ship**, they will find it hard to escape the **shock therapy** prescribed by the Bretton Woods agencies, which is already in force throughout the rest of the continent. And 'the IMF should not be blamed for the hardships of that adjustment,' a European official of the World Bank told *Jeune Afrique Economie*.

IMF officials are not yet drawing any conclusions. After all, South Africa's leaders are still trying to see how they can restore macro-economic equilibria and rebuild on a **healthier** economic **foundation**. 'It is clear that South Africa is trying hard not to **fall under the thrall** of the Bretton Woods agencies, and the dialogue is taking place between responsible people,' a World Bank spokesman said.

Beyond that, one senses that IMF and World Bank officials are somewhat on the lookout, eager to see more definite indicators about 'South Africa Inc.' before they arrive at a more definite **diagnosis**, one that would determine what sort of **therapy** the **giant** of southern Africa should undergo.

That seems to leave South Africa's leaders on the spot. For reasons of social justice, and to meet the basic needs of a disadvantaged population, investments have to be found, and soon. That could lead to mistakes, and then **the door would be wide open** for the international financial institutions.

The Economic Reconstruction and Development Program (RDP), which the African National Congress estimates at $11 billion over five years, will **forge ahead** under the twofold **pressure** of 30.4 million blacks who, while supporting the program, are already showing some signs of impatience, and the IMF and World Bank, which are awaiting only a false step before pulling out their charts and prescribing their now-famous 'adequate remedies'.

Nelson Mandela's government knows that it will be **walking** a **tightrope** and **juggling** the hopes of voters, the criticisms of the opposition and the prudence of donors. Mandela got a taste of that sense of caution in September during his recent state visit to the United States, when he contacted US financial circles. After taking losses during the apartheid era, US investors had been **retreating in waves** from South Africa.

To make for a more attractive financial **landscape**, the South African President is first trying to keep the budget deficit **within bounds** by cutting waste. Any budgetary laxness would show up in the growth rate of GNP and the economy would immediately have to deal with an increase in public debt, which already accounts for 6.4% of GDP.

Since it cannot count on an immediate return of the 10 billion rand that fled the country's banks, the government is currently subscribing a series of loans and taxing corporations at a high rate (up to 30%), which makes South African products more expensive on the world market. Hence the risk that the Bretton Woods agencies may begin urging that South Africa **restore its macro-economic equilibria** and, failing that, turn to structural adjustment.

True, South Africa, given its productivity, export capacity and sound monetary system, can adopt an attitude toward IMF/World Bank '**shock therapy**' more like the attitude of some Asian countries than like that of other African countries (especially as regards time-frames and results). However, it does face one **obstacle** which could prove to be insurmountable: high labor costs, especially when compared with those of Asia.

The government's economic and social program therefore needs support from South Africa's 'true friends', those who know that the RDP, while not a **panacea**, is crucial, particularly when it comes to development and human resources and fighting unemployment. Those are **stages** that the country must go through to enhance productivity. For many economists, the new South African administration will have to contend with two things: the fact that the country has not **reached a threshold** of development enabling it to escape the need to import capital goods; and the fact that large-scale investments might **deepen** the trade deficit and affect the balance of payments.

According to a World Bank working paper, 'It is essential to follow a cautious monetary policy. To **overstep the confines** of a strict budgetary policy would lead to inflation and balance of payments problems.' Investors will surely perceive the (anticipated) budget deficits in the early years under the new government as a negative signal. And, since structural adjustment policies pertain in part to the balance of payments, it seems a safe bet that South Africa will sooner or later have to go through a drastic **cure** under the **watchful eye** of the World Bank and the IMF.

As for monetary policy, which on the whole has been capably handled so far, there are two noticeable **symptoms**. First, it does not seem very reasonable to stimulate the economy through the (negative) device of setting an attractive exchange rate for the financial rand used by foreign investors. If South Africa wanted to fall into the grasp of the Bretton Woods institutions, it could not choose a better way. That choice would lead to an increased flow of capital, increasing investment ratios in production and **exerting stronger pressure** on the balance of payments without having any corresponding effect on employment.

And it would also be disastrous for the administration to apply a **monetary fix** to the budget deficit. That policy would **speed up** inflation. The social consequences would be severe, since the whole **burden of adjustment would then be shifted** to the population. In any event, the only way South Africa will escape adjustment is by '**tightening its belt**', as Nelson Mandela urges, and by raising its growth rate from the current 3% to 6%, as the President hopes.

It will be an **uphill road**. Nelson Mandela prefers to warn people that the reconstruction program will not be able to satisfy the basic needs of the population. Is South African public opinion ready to accept that kind of candor? The seven million people still without decent housing are **swelling the ranks** of the disillusioned. And there's the fact that, as the President himself admits, 'the acute problem is not so much foreign investments, although we do need them, but investing at home'. There is great insight in that remark, because, if Mandela's appeal goes unheeded, there is every chance that external indebtedness will be the only alternative.

That fallback solution would initially take the form of a 'standby' credit, later followed by a letter of intent signed with the IMF. Mandela seems to be setting deadlines to force his fellow citizens to face their responsibilities: either domestic investment **picks up** or we will go looking for money wherever we can find it, he seems to be saying. Some Western economists fear that South Africa may be **on the brink** of **plunging** into a 'Latin American-style infernal **spiral** of debt', even though other observers agree that South Africa is 'not just any African country, not one **to give up without a fight**'. (Ndir, 1994; trans. James Nolan)

South African Conglomerates
London, from our correspondent: 'We must encourage participation by South African blacks in mining and financial companies. It can

only benefit all concerned.' For the cartel known as the Anglo-American Corporation, the **dismantling** of its affiliate, the Johannesburg Consolidated Investment Company (JCI), was a historic **stride** toward a 'new South Africa'. This time it was a **new departure**, really it was! Anglo-American executives swore that the **break-up** of the industrial giant comprising several independent units – gold, coal, agro-industry, press, breweries – would create many jobs **at all levels** which could be available to blacks.

But the more knowledgeable London analysts of the South African economy are not fooled: 'All they are doing by changing the legal structure and opening up a few companies is to **throw a bone** to Mandela. It is a false dismantling that does not redistribute national wealth in any way to black entrepreneurs,' says a City expert. And it is true that Julian Ogilvie Thompson, the current chairman of both Anglo-American and De Beers, took the precaution beforehand of buying up JCI's very profitable platinum division and its 16% share in the world's leading diamond concern, De Beers.

As part of the remarkable **high-wire act** being performed by major South African multi-nationals with an eye to the first multiracial elections, both English-speaking and Afrikaner entrepreneurs have just coined a new byword: '**unbundling**'. Are we seeing a cultural revolution among white businessmen consenting to share economic power and being **patterned by a new mold**? Or is it a **sleight of hand** that enables a handful of conglomerates to **retain their hold** on thee conomy? Appearances tend to support the former explanation, but the latter is probably closer to reality.

Giants. Anglo-American, De Beers, Rembrandt Group, Old Mutual Sanlam, Liberty Life ... Looking at the South African economy, one is always tempted to **boil it down to** those five groups, which, like an **all-embracing octopus**, between them control 80% of the stocks listed on the Johannesburg stock exchange. They are **five giants** whose presence is felt everywhere and which grew by means of acquisitions.

The very strict exchange-control regulations – through a **two-tier** market for the rand – long prevented them from investing abroad and forced these giants to **branch out** into sectors quite different from their initial business. The result was a **pyramidal structure** which, through a holding company at the top, enabled a few big families, like the Oppenheimers, the Ruperts or the Gordons, to **keep a grip on** their assets without owning a majority of the shares of affiliated companies. Those who favor the system say that it defends companies against hostile LBO bids, reassures the banking community and makes it easier to raise the capital needed for major investment projects, especially in mining exploration and operation.

Until recently, Brian Gilbertson was in control of a conglomerate with **nebulous outlines** called Gencor. A year ago, Sankorp, the investment holding company, itself an affiliate of the insurance company Sanlam, granted independence to four Gencor affiliates: Malback (pharmaceuticals), Sappi (forest products), Engen (oil refining) and Genbel (financial services).

That **'vertical' dismantling** was designed to enable Gencor, the world's leading producer of platinum and number-two producer of gold, to **concentrate** its efforts on mining. To hear its chairman, the operation had a financial aim: correcting the fact that the stocks of the different companies were undervalued on the stock market as compared with the performance of the conglomerate as a whole.

The **reshuffling of the cards** was also meant to reassure major US and UK institutional investors, who are afraid of very complex conglomerates. 'These giant, very centralized conglomerates are like real **dinosaurs**. They no longer have any place in the **economic arena** of today because the management is not accountable to the shareholders,' stresses Steve Oke of Smith New Court.

But the most salient aspect of the restructuring has been its political **dimension**. Sankorp also sold its 10% share in an insurance company to Methold, an insurance group belonging to black interests. The ANC was discreetly consulted by Finance Minister Derek Keys, who was Gencor's boss from 1986 to 1991, and it **gave the green light**.

Offshore. This would seem to **paint a rosy picture** of the South Africa of tomorrow. But, as commentators are pointing out, most of the recent corporate **break-ups** – with the exception of Gencor – led to the creation of extraterritorial **offshore vehicles** intended primarily to protect assets abroad. That goes for Anglo-American, which controls nearly 40% of De Beers, which, in turn, controls about 30% of the capital of Anglo-American. In October 1993, Anglo-American transferred all of its non-South African interests to a **dummy corporation**, Minorco, 75% of whose capital is held by the Oppenheimer family. Minorco has gone from a holding company created about 20 years ago to a mining company like the others. 'A good move!', says an observer, 'Thanks to Minorco becoming Anglo-American's **right arm** abroad, Anglo-American can now present itself as an African company. Anglo-American can tell Mandela that it now invests only in the local economy or in neighboring companies.'

Skepticism. What has De Beers done? It formed De Beers Centenary AG, based in Zurich, which has assumed control of the diamond stocks of the Central Selling Organization in London, the synthetic diamond plants and the financial shares in certain holdings. For its part, De Beers Consolidated Mines now owns purely South African interests. The two companies have the same boss, Julian Ogilvie Thompson, the same board of directors, and their shares cannot be traded separately on the stock exchange.

South Africa's second-largest industrial fortune, the Ruperts, has the Swiss holding company Richemont, created in 1988. This company controls the foreign assets, particularly Rothmans cigarettes and the Cartier and Alfred Dunhill luxury trademarks. The South African assets are managed by a different company, Rembrandt. Johann Rupert, the founder's son, bears the purely honorific title of director of Richemont. But he **keeps a close eye** on the world-class luxury-product companies he owns. He is always moderate and prepared for dialogue with the ANC, but he firmly and even doggedly defends his group's interests. The same goes for Nicky Oppenheimer, who is only a vice-president of Anglo and De Beers, but who **keeps a tight leash** on Julian Ogilvie Thompson, the official director.

These white capitalist maneuvers have been received in London with a skeptical reaction. Some recall that, although the word nationalism is not now part of the ANC's vocabulary, Nelson Mandela's party did commit itself to **breaking up** the mining oligopolies through anti-trust legislation. But it is anybody's guess when and how such legislation will force these national 'institutions' to give up any of their assets.

Economic **paralysis** would spell great danger for the republic. The new government faces daunting tasks and possesses few financial resources. Potential black stockholders have little business experience. All in all, analysts say, it's a safe bet that we have not seen the last of South Africa's giant cartels. (*Le Monde*, 1995a; trans. James Nolan)

(5) Read the following translated passage about the world wheat market, paying particular attention to the parts in bold type. Then answer the questions that follow.

Global Wheat Shortage
The year 1994 was **a bad year** for world wheat harvests, which will mean a **substantial and worrisome decline** in reserves in the

months to come. The **latest estimates** by the International Wheat Council **point to** a harvest of only 526 million tons, compared with 558 million last year. The **drop** is largely due to the very poor harvest in Russia (32 million tons compared to 43.2 million in 1993) and in the Ukraine, where the **decline** was over 27% due to an abnormally dry, hot summer.

For the European Union as a whole, production is **barely over** 80 million tons and the exportable surplus is 20 million, although GATT agreements authorized EU **subsidized exports** of 31 million tons for the 1995–1996 season.

World consumption is **reckoned at** 554 million tons, which will make it necessary **to tap reserves**. The reserves of the European Union, which **stood at** 15 million tons in July 1993, are already below 4 million and **could drop** to 2.5 million by the end of the present season. Worldwide, reserves are currently sufficient, but some experts fear they may **dwindle** enough by the third quarter of 1995 **to create serious tensions on the market**.

Substantial price rises are already being noted on world markets, and prices are expected **to rise further** in 1995. That has no implications for us here at home, since our prices are **still higher (but nolonger by much)** than world market prices. Moreover, the **producer price** for wheat now **accounts for** barely 10% of the price of our daily bread.

But for countries that have to import, it could be **disastrous**. The FAO is talking about the risk of **a major, widespread famine** in several places, especially in Africa, where political instability, civil wars, drought and locust infestations could continue **wreaking havoc** with Southern Hemisphere crops. (Hannart, 1994; trans. James Nolan)

(a) In the above context, would the terms suggested in Table 14.2, column (ii) serve as acceptable alternatives to the expressions listed in column (i)? If so, which is better, (i) or (ii)? If not, why not? Can you think of other expressions that would work as well or better?

(b) If the wheat harvest had gone from 558 million tons not to 526 million tons but only to 555 million tons, would it have been correct to describe it as a **drop**? What would the correct description have been? If it had gone from 558 million tons to 225 million tons, could it have been described as a **collapse**?

Is the word **drop** suitable to describe the decline in European Union wheat reserves from 4 million tons to 2.5 million tons?

Table 14.2

(i)	*(ii)*
bad year	poor / disappointing year
substantial decline	significant fall / dip
latest estimates	latest forecasts
point to	suggest / augur
drop	dip / downturn
decline	fall-off / dip / downturn
barely over	just over / just exceeds
reckoned at	estimated at / put at
tap reserves	draw on / draw down
stood at	were
dwindle	decline
create serious tensions on the market	put serious strains on the market
substantial price rises	major price hikes
rise further	climb higher
still higher (but not by much)	higher (but only just)
accounts for	is responsible for
disastrous	calamitous / chaotic
wreaking havoc	ravaging

(6) Translate the following passage into English, Spanish or your other working languages, taking special care with the words in bold type:

> La **conjoncture** allemande ne devrait pas, au cours des mois qui viennent, être une **puissante locomotive** pour les autres économies européennes. En **dressant un pronostic** de croissance de 2,25% pour 1995 et de 2,5% pour 1996, les six principaux **instituts économiques** allemands, qui présentaient leur traditionnel rapport d'automne mardi, 24 octobre à Bonn, tirent les conséquences du **fléchissement** de l'activité économique constaté **outre-Rhin** depuis le printemps 1995.
>
> Les prévisions de croissance du ministère de l'économie – dont le rapport mensuel **de conjoncture** a été rendu public lundi 23 octobre – sont elles aussi **révisées à la baisse**: alors que le pronostic de croissance officiel était de 3% pour cette année, Bonn s'en tient aujourd'hui à des prévisions de +2,5% du PIB pour 1995 comme pour 1996.
>
> L'appréciation du deutschemark et les **fortes hausses** de salaires intervenues cette année ont entraîné un **ralentissement** sensible. Alors que les exportations avaient permis à l'Allemagne de **sortir** de la récession en 1994, le principal **facteur d'espoir** pour 1995 et

surtout 1996 est la reprise de la **consommation intérieure** (celle-ci devrait augmenter de 3% en 1996).

Le ministère fédéral de l'économie souligne que 'l'année 1996 devrait avant tout être celle de la **consommation privée**'. A la suite de baisses d'impôts et de la suppression de la **taxe charbonnière** (le *Kohlepfennig*), les **ménages** allemands disposeront d'un **supplément** de revenus de 20 milliards de marks l'an prochain. Autre facteur **encourageant**, selon le ministère de l'économie: la reprise de l'**investissement des entreprises**, encouragée par la stabilité des prix et le niveau modéré des taux d'intérêt allemands. (*Le Monde*, 1995a (excerpt))

(suggested words: engine / think-tanks / slump / occasional / revised downward / steep increases / slow-down / bright spot / domestic consumption / coal tax / households / corporate investment)

(7) Translate the following passage into English, French or your other working languages, taking special care with the words in bold type:

En un importante discurso pronunciado en noviembre pasado, Trotman **retó** a los ejecutivos de Ford: 'Fabricamos cinco de los 10 mejores vehiculos de Estados Unidos. ... Todavía **nos quedan** cinco'. También observó que con las plantas que cuenta actualmente, Ford podría **aumentar** su **participación de mercado** en Europa al 15%, de un 12% de hoy en día, y en EE.UU. al 30%, de un 26,5% **en estos momentos**.

En momentos que GM mantiene una **cuota de mercado** del 13.3% en Europa, más el 32,3% en EE.UU., una combinación de las ganancias de Ford y las pérdidas de GM colocaría a ambas empresas en **una posición muy pareja**. En una conversación con los reporteros después de la reunión anual de Ford de 1994, Trotman destacó que **sobrepasar** a GM 'es una posibilidad si nos preparamos debidamente, hacemos lo correcto ya al consumidor le gustan nuestros automóviles'. (*Wall Street Journal Americas*, 1995 (excerpt))

(suggested words: challenged / have ... to go / boost / market share/ current / equal footing / outperform, overtake)

(8) Translate the following excerpts into English, Spanish or your other working languages, taking special care with the economic terms and idiomatic expressions:

Le **réseau** de librairies de notre pays est assez réduit. ... Ce sont des librairies **de taille moyenne** (de 6 à 30 employés) **qui se cherchent**

encore. . . . La Grande Librairie, après **une période faste**, est en voie de **restructuration**. . . . Le Tchad n'ayant pas de façade maritime, le libraire Tchadien doit faire face à un **coût de transport** élevé, ce qui **grève** lourdement le **prix de revient** et **pénalise** le **consomma-teur.** . . . Cet **environnement commercial** déjà **austère** est rendu **drastique** par la **dévaluation** du franc CFA. . . . La **clientèle s'amenuise** au fil des ans, **frappée de plein fouet** par la **crise salariale**, les salaires étant payés à des intervalles de plusieurs mois. . . . Aussi est-il aisé de comprendre que les livres scolaires se vendent très peu, alors que les journaux (européens surtout) **ont pignon sur rue.** . . . **Il va de soi** que pour les manuels scolaires, les parents **font des pieds et des mains** pour trouver quelques bouquins à leur progéniture. (Koï Pierrot Ganda, 'L'insoutenable prix de l'écrit', *N'Djamena Hebdo* (excerpts))

(9) The following sentences contain expressions that were used by commentators on popular television programs about investment, finance and economic issues. Translate the sentences given. Then form additional sentences with each expression and translate them as well.

- This year we have been seeing a **slow-growth economy**.
- Investors shy away from an **oscillating market**.
- I am confident this is a **secular bull market**.
- It's a case of **dollars chasing stocks**.
- Retailers are **euphoric about general-merchandise sales**.
- There's been some **pick-up** in the wholesale sector.
- The cautious will stand by during the market **catch-up**.
- This stock is an **attractive turnaround situation**.
- The overall economy shows strong **secular growth prospects**.
- High-tech firms have good **internal growth characteristics**.
- Localization services have become a **hot item**.
- High-end durable goods are showing a **turn toward quality**.
- The fur **business is dead**.
- Wall Street is hiring **top-performing mutual fund managers**.
- Hardware stores are losing their **market niche** to **superstores**.
- Financial markets are only just recovering from the **tequila effect**.
- This month we've had a **stealth bull market**.
- Every now and then we get a **horrendous correction**.
- Innovations have **thinned the ranks of the competition**.
- There is **overcrowding of supply** in this sector, producing some **margin pressures**.
- Retail is having **soft sales**.

- Supply is expanding to meet demand **and then some**.
- These stocks have **solid, tappable earnings**.
- If **the fundamentals deteriorate**, we'll get out.
- This is an **interest-sensitive sector**.
- It's been a **sterling performance** for technology stocks.
- He is one of the year's **standout stock pickers**.
- The holiday season was less than a **sales bonanza**.
- There were enough **rumbles** of continuing economic growth to **unnerve** the bond market, which **wrapped up** its worst year since 1969 with another **losing week**.
- The **faltering** new-homes market suggested that higher interest rates were beginning to **bite into** the economy's **momentum**.
- New York Stock Exchange trading **dipped below** a billion shares, and the Dow Jones Industrial Average **barely budged**.
- It's been a year of down 2%. A **milquetoast bear**, really.
- The key feature of the year was a **stupendous margin call**.
- What's **propelling** the bond market is not just the strength of the economy, but also **the unwinding of a lot of leverage**.
- I think long-term rates will **pop up** again.
- We're in the final phases of a **typical four-year stock market cycle**.
- For most of the year we were **locked into a fairly narrow trading range**.
- I think the market will **break out on the upside**.
- It was an **abysmal year** for bond investors.
- The Dow Jones managed to **eke out an 80-point gain**.
- We're trying to **build a strong brand presence** in that market.
- It's hard to **balance the push-pull elements of marketing**.
- The merger involves **cash, stocks and assumed debt**.
- It was a **wacky session** on Wall Street today.
- That's when the Stock Exchange **uptick rule** comes in.
- Technology stocks **rallied through the session**.
- International global funds **got kicked around pretty badly**.
- We use both **trailing and forward measures** in forecasting stock performance.
- We're seeing activity **perk up**.
- How do you **translate those trends into asset allocations**?
- Companies may be **reversing past write-offs this year**.
- The week's **selloff** is over.
- The **trend spotters** foresee a sharp downturn in **earnings momentum**.

- There's a lot of downward pressure on the **short end of the yield curve**.
- Even allowing for the **GDP price deflator** there may be **inflation scares** early in the year.
- There's been some **liquidation in industrial commodities**.
- In some sectors, there is **chronic overcapacity**.
- Some stock areas are **oversold**.
- Inflation would be a problem if we saw some **broad-based signs** of inflation, not just **a commodity blip in selected markets**.
- People are taking **giant bets on hedge funds**.
- Existing bond earnings might be **grandfathered** if a flat tax law is passed.
- Nobody **bats 1000** in financial predictions.
- Gold has boomed, but **its days are numbered**.
- The **misery index** is at a three-year low.
- A wave of **downsizing** has eliminated thousands of jobs.
- The market will have a **soft landing**.
- The senator said that only in some **supply-side fantasy-land** could the budget be balanced at the expense of health and education.
- This is a one-time opportunity for **big players**.
- Mutual funds are **spawning** new shareholders.
- The stock exchange provides **auction agency market representation, transparency and price discovery**.
- Equities trade locally but **gold follows the sun**.
- The aim of **counter-cyclical policy** is to **dampen the business cycle**.
- It's hard to **wring inflation out** of the economy when you have **entrenched inflationary expectations**.
- The **rational expectationist** school of thought believes people will anticipate and counteract policy moves.
- The trade deficit is due to an **overly strong dollar**.
- The tax cut is producing an **economic stimulus** but much of it is **going overseas**.
- We have a **ballooning merchandise deficit**.
- You can't separate **stabilization policy** from **international trade policy**.
- From **fine-tuning** of the economy we have moved to a policy of **coarse-tuning**.
- A **hiccup** in interest rates sent a **shudder** through the market.

- We are entering an age of **mega-competition**.
- Japan needs to make its labor market amenable to **entry-level and mid-course movement**.
- The Japanese government's **Jusen bailout plan** will be costly.
- This company is a **cash cow**.

(10) (a) Read the following passage on the European Union economy, paying special attention to the terms in bold type and to the figures and quantitative concepts. Try to think of possible alternatives for the terms in bold type.

EU Economic Outlook For 1996–1997

The pace of the EU's economic recovery has slowed down in 1995, but **healthy fundamentals** should lead to a **pick-up** in growth late in 1996 according to the Commission's economic forecasts for 1996–97. **Slower growth** in 1995 (EU GDP growth is expected to be 2.7% instead of the earlier 3.1% forecast) is primarily attributable to **currency fluctuations**, particularly against the U.S. dollar, but also to the lack of credible **budgetary consolidation** in some member states. Nevertheless, fundamental factors (continued growth in world trade, improved **business profitability**, **wage moderation** and a good **economic policy mix**) augur well for **steady GDP growth**, which should reach 2.6% in 1996 and accelerate to 2.9% in 1997. After **peaking** at 11.4% in March 1994, the EU's **jobless rate** will **drop** to around 9.5% by the end of 1997, through the **net creation** of 2.4 million jobs in 1996 and 1997. Implementation of the European strategy for employment ... could further improve the situation in the labor market. As regards inflation, the forecast is for continued good performance: the inflation rate in most member states is around 2% or less, and **average EU inflation** will fall from 3.1% this year to 2.7% in 1997. Moderate increases in **nominal wage levels** will restrain increases in **unit labor costs**, and import prices will not **feed inflation**. This trend represents a degree of consensus across the EU found in no other **policy area**: price stability is considered essential to face the challenges of the **real economy**, especially unemployment. **Budget deficits** will fall across the EU in 1996 and, assuming unchanged policies, also in 1997. The **aggregate EU public deficit**, which stood at 6.2% of GDP in 1993, will drop to 3.8% in 1996. For 1997, the forecasts show that eight member states (Denmark, Germany,

France, Ireland, Luxembourg, the Netherlands, Finland and the UK) should be **running a deficit** of less than 3% of GDP, the Maastricht criterion for the **single currency**. **Average public debt** across the EU is expected to **stabilize** at around 71% of GDP over the forecast period. At present, only four countries (Germany, France, Luxembourg and the UK) have a **public debt to GDP ratio** of less than 60%. (*Eurecom*, 1995)

(b) Translate the passage into Spanish, French or your other working languages.

(c) Read the passage aloud into your tape recorder at moderate speed. Play it back, take notes on what you hear, and reconstruct the passage from your notes. Check the reconstruction against the original. Repeat the exercise until you can get all of the economic terms, numbers and numerical concepts right.

(d) Play back the passage again, and interpret it simultaneously into Spanish, French or your other working languages.

(e) Read out your translations into your tape recorder at moderate speed. Then play back the recording and interpret it simultaneously into your other languages. Record your interpretation and check it for accuracy against the original.

(11) (a) Read the following excerpt from an article about funding of scientific research in Canada, paying special attention to the highlighted words:

Funding Crisis Grips Genome Research
Canada's genome program, which **leapt out of the starting blocks** with great promise 4 years ago, is suddenly **struggling** to **stay on its feet**. It was **plunged into crisis** this summer as the Canadian government **followed through** on a 4-year plan to cut research budgets, a policy that will extend through 1999. In keeping with **the new austerity**, the chief contributor to the Canadian Genome Analysis and Technology program (CGAT) – a ministry called Industry Canada – said it cannot give CGAT any more support. Without a **big backer**, the $22-million, 5-year program ... will soon run out of grant money. ... The Canadian National Cancer Institute has offered $1 million, as has the Social Sciences and Humanities Research Council, but so far, CGAT's leaders haven't found anyone **with deep pockets** willing to **kick in** the rest of the money. The result: an effort that rivalled the U.S. and British genome projects in quality is **about to hit the wall**. (Marshall, 1996: 867 (excerpt))

(b) Find possible alternatives or synonyms for the highlighted words, for example: **leapt out of the starting blocks** = **took off**.

(c) Translate the excerpt into your other working languages.

(d) Read out the original and your translations into your tape recorder at moderate speed. Then play back each recording and interpret it simultaneously into your other languages. Record your interpretation and check it for accuracy against the original. Repeat the exercise until you have gotten all of the economic and numerical concepts right.

(12) The following terms were used at a presentation by the Managing Director of the International Monetary Fund (IMF). Find possible equivalents for them in your other languages and write sentences illustrating their meaning.

> dépenses inutiles / faux frais / assainissement / croissance soutenue/ taux de croissance / volatilité financière / gérer la crise / d'un seul chiffre (inflation) / perte de revenu

> peak of the cycle / to subside / to retard growth / propelling role played by developed economies / to derail the process of recovery / the stock of debt / debt overhang / capital flight / preferred creditor status / structural unemployment / draw maximum benefit from/ local windfalls

(13) The following terms and phrases relating to international business and finance were used by various speakers at the 1995 Wall Street Journal/ Dow Jones Co. Annual Conference on the Americas (New York, 28–29 September 1995). The Spanish equivalents given are those arrived at by the Spanish interpreters at the conference. Do you agree with these equivalents? Can you think of others? Find appropriate equivalents for the terms which are not translated in French, Spanish or your other working languages. Write sentences illustrating the meaning of the terms.

> pass-through – valor de transferencia de ingresos / bondholder – obligacionista / equity securities – valores patrimoniales / unsecured debt – deuda sin garantía / asset-based structure – conversión basada en activos / rating agency – organismo de clasificación de valores / receivables – deudas por cobrar / spread – margen / drive – empujón / crash – quiebre / bellwether – indicador / let down – defraudar / bloom – florecer / bullish – en alza, optimista / factor – agente / welfare state – estado de beneficiencia social / senior-rated paper – efectos prioritarios / origination – tramitación / tranches – tramos / fast track accession (to NAFTA) – adhesión acelerada / spur – impulsar / floating rate – taza flotante / crawling peg exchange rate– taza de cambio de

paridad móbil / spin – revuelo / liquidity – liquidez / squeeze – contracción / runs – salidas, pánicos / fire sale prices – precios de remate / trade – transarse / surge – auge / gains – logros / abrupt – sorpresivo / wedge – diferencial / commensurate – correspondiente

stripped of value / transaction costs / hidden costs / guest worker / interest waiver / consolidation / free remittance of profits / market-led development strategy / unintended consequences / social overhead capital / market-oriented / debt relief / replenishment / teledensity / bubble / emerging market debt / turndown / run-up of prices / price / wage spiral / local supplier industries / reaction time / a local shareholder majority approach / non-tradeables (products saleable only locally) / securitization (issue of securities in exchange for debt) / disclosure and transparency requirements / compression of current-account debt / the private capital-oriented development model / discretionary timing of releases (of information) / a run (on a bank) / world lender of last resort / moral hazard problems / volatility / unit of account / highest use / debased currency / exchange rate system driven by balance of payments / currency backing / anchor currency country / irksome constraint / real depreciation / outlier / optimal current account balance / fiscal pump priming / a bias in the spin / external drains of resources / country risk / tax wedge / 400 basis point risk premium / tequila effect / pegged regime / flashpoint / spillover / the latest derivative (product) / to debunk / fair market value / money supply / monetary aggregates / the fallout in the bond market / propensity to consume / herd-instinct pattern of behavior / to propagate inflation / band system (of exchange rates) / unit labor costs / foreign-currency denominated amortization / non-performing assets / rollover of external liabilities / the future and forward market / risk-weighted assets / mandatorily convertible subordinated debt

(14) The terms listed in Table 14.3 were used at the International Conference on Financing for Development (Monterrey, Mexico, 18–22 March 2002). Note the relative brevity of some of the English terms as compared with their Spanish and French equivalents.
   • If the context makes clear what kind of 'spread' is in question, is it necessary to give the full French or Spanish terms given above, or could the word 'marge' or 'margen' stand alone?
   • Is there any real difference between 'être productif au regard des sommes dépensées' and 'être rentable'? Could the latter serve as a functional synonym?

Table 14.3

buy-sell spread	marge entre taux à l'achat et taux à la vente	margen entre el tipo de compra y el de venta
to call in one's capital	exiger le remboursement de ses capitaux	reclamar el reembolso de sus capitales
highly leveraged transaction	opération à fort coefficient d'endettement	operación con alto coeficiente de deuda
to yield value for money	être productif au regard des sommes dépensées	tener un rendimiento proporcional al dinero invertido
flight capital	capitaux expatriés	capitales expatriados
management fees	commissions de courtage	comisiones de administración
netting system (banking)	système de compensation (bancaire)	sistema de compensación (bancaria)
performance requirements	prescriptions de résultat	requisitos de desempeño
tariff escalation	progressivité des droits	progresividad arancelaria
transfer pricing	fixation de prix de cession interne	precios de transferencia
hot potato trading	mouvements fébriles	comercio de 'patata caliente'
global public goods	biens collectifs mondiaux	bienes públicos mundiales

- Note how the English equivalent of 'progressivité des droits' uses a mechanistic analogy: tariff *escalation*.
- Note that the Spanish term for 'hot potato trading' ('trading in which traders shuffle positions around following an initial large foreign exchange transaction until a new short-run equilibrium position is established a few minutes later') has simply borrowed the image used in the English term, while the French term uses no image but rather attempts to describe the phenomenon. Given the complexity of the phenomenon, which works better, the description or the image?
- Would 'exode des capitaux' work as a synonym for 'capitaux expatriés'?

(15) From the list of proverbs in Chapter 7 (pp. 64–110), select those which embody a principle of economics or business and restate them in straightforward non-figurative terms.

> *Example*: 'A bird in the hand is worth two in the bush.' = A smaller asset that is secure is worth more than a larger asset that is speculative.

15 Humor

Humor is difficult to translate and even more difficult to interpret. For a simultaneous interpreter to draw a laugh from the audience at the same time as those hearing the original joke burst into laughter is a rare feat.

An interpreter must be attentive to the purpose of the humor. Many speakers will begin a speech on a humorous note just to be clever or simply to establish rapport with the audience. For example, a British Ambassador acting as President of the UN Security Council once began a meeting with a limerick dedicated to the Russian ambassador, who had just come back from Florida with a handsome tan while the other Security Council members had weathered a bitter New York snowstorm:

> Serguei is a difficult name
> To slip in the limerick game
> But we have to admit
> That he looks so fit
> That he puts the whole Council to shame.

Needless to say, it is extremely difficult, if not impossible, for simultaneous interpreters to render a complex verse form like a limerick into French, Spanish, Arabic, Russian and Chinese while preserving the humor.

In such cases it is helpful but not indispensable for the joke to be accurately translated; the joke is merely an 'opening gambit'. On the other hand, jokes are sometimes used to convey a key point of the speech. In those cases, the message is more important than the humor, and it is the content of the message, not the humorous 'sugar coating', that the interpreter should strive to translate.

Although the joke must sometimes be sacrificed to the message, it is of course preferable to preserve the humor whenever possible, since it can often be *part* of the message. Moreover speakers sometimes use humor to revive a somnolent debate or to break the ice when a negotiation has come to a deadlock. In such situations the humor is not incidental to the speaker's substantive intent; it *is* the speaker's intent. And an interpreter who fails to get across the humor has failed to get across the point. Consider the following all-too typical situation:

Lost in Translation
In his toast at a State Department luncheon honoring President Yeltsin, Vice President Al Gore, dead-pan, told a typically shaggy story about his job's lack of clout.

When he had his left leg operated on recently, he said, he was under general anesthesia for 90 minutes. During that time, he surrendered his Constitutional prerogatives to the person next in the line of succession, House Speaker Thomas S. Foley.

When he came to, Mr. Gore re-claimed his powers, which, he said, restored Mr. Foley to his usual position of authority.

The Americans in the room weaned on tales of Vice Presidential superfluousness, laughed. But when the story was translated, most of the Russians sat stone-faced.

Defense Secretary William J. Perry did the best he could to help. He leaned to his left and told the Russian Defense Minister, General Pavel Grachev, 'That's a joke.' No laugh. Then he tried to explain. No laugh.

Maybe the Russians were saving their senses of humor for their boss. A little later, Mr. Yeltsin noted with approval that the United States was relaxing its trade restrictions linked to the emigration of Jews. Everyone in his country, he said, would be pleased; in Russia, 'even schoolchildren know who these people are – Jackson and Vanik'.

Finally, the Russians laughed. (*New York Times*, 1994)

At the other extreme from jokes that fall flat in translation is the temptation some interpreters may feel to go rather *too* far in conveying the speaker's wit or charm. For instance, at a joint news conference given by Presidents Clinton and Yeltsin, the latter humorously chastised the journalists present for their grim predictions about the inevitable failure of the presidential talks. The interpreter rendered Mr Yeltsin's remark as 'It is *you* who are a disaster!' This was a bit too strong for Mr Clinton's taste and, in his embarrassment, he immediately quipped to the press, 'Be sure you get the attribution right!' However, it turns out that what Mr Yeltsin actually said in Russian was simply 'It is you who fell through' (i.e. not the meeting that fell through), which is not particularly witty or funny, but certainly more charitable toward journalism than the word 'disaster' and well short of causing Mr Clinton any discomfort in his relations with the press. It would have been better if the interpreter had not tried so hard to be clever and had handled this simple point more cautiously.

As the above episodes suggest, part of the problem of translating humor stems from the fact that 'humor is in the eye of the beholder', and what is funny in one language or culture is not necessarily funny in another. But another aspect of the problem is the fact that much humorous speech is by definition *fast* speech: repartee is amusing because it is quick and lively, and many jokes are funny mainly because of the split-second timing of the punch-line. Consider, for example, the following rapid exchange (which the French interpreter handled quite well):

Speaker:	Mr President, I have made so many concessions on this resolution that I feel I am sticking my neck out.
President:	Well, I will do all I can to make sure it doesn't get chopped off. (laughter)
(French interpreter:	Je ferai de mon mieux pour que vous ne soyez pas décapité! (laughter))

A speaker often has to 'lay the groundwork' for a humorous punch-line in much the same way that a lawyer examining a witness has to lay a foundation which shows the relevance of the question to which he is leading up. This is helpful to the interpreter, because it gives some advance warning that a punch-line is coming. In order to sense when a joke is in the works, it is helpful to study different types of humor and joke-telling techniques, and to practice trying to translate jokes and puns. A recommended source is Isaac Asimov's anthology of jokes, which analyzes and categorizes jokes by type (Asimov, 1971).

One of the most widely used types of humor in formal speeches is 'deadpan' or 'straight-faced' sarcasm. This caustic form of humor does not require as much finesse as irony. Apparently it was even within the reach of the mad and notoriously unfunny Roman emperor Caligula who, during lucid moments, is said to have been pleasant and cordial and once replied to a shoemaker who had the audacity to call him a sycophant to his face, 'It's true, but my subjects are no better'. Dry sarcasm was also a style for which Abraham Lincoln was famous. Once accused by a critic of being two-faced, he earnestly replied, 'Ladies and gentlemen, if I had two faces, would I be wearing this one?'

Exercises

(1) *Sarcasm*

Sarcasm is irony raised to a high pitch. If irony is like a dagger, sarcasm is more like a sword. Read the excerpts below from Lincoln's speech on 'The Presidential Question' (1848), a campaign speech given on behalf of the Whig presidential candidate General Zachary Taylor and against the Democratic candidate, General Lewis Cass. The speech is a good example of skillful political sarcasm. Lincoln mocks Cass's record in the military and in public service. But notice how, despite the intense passions and acrimony involved in the issues, Lincoln's style never lapses into anger or the petty nastiness of the modern campaign 'sound-bite'. Although he does engage in an *ad hominem* attack on his political opponent, he does so with such an elaborate and formal display of 'evidence' of General Cass's misdeeds that one is hardly aware of how personal the attack actually is.

> The other day, one of the gentlemen from Georgia, an eloquent man, and a man of learning, so far as I can judge, not being learned myself, came down upon us astonishingly. He spoke in what the Baltimore American calls a 'scathing and withering style'. At the end of his second severe flash I was struck blind, and found myself feeling with my fingers for an assurance of my continued physical existence. **A little of the bone was left**, and I gradually revived. He eulogized Mr. Clay in high and beautiful terms, and then declared that we had deserted all our principles, and turned Henry Clay out, **like an old horse, to root**. This is terribly severe. It cannot be answered by argument; at least, I cannot so answer it. I merely wish to ask the gentleman if the Whigs are the only party he can think of who sometimes turn old horses out to root. Is not a certain Martin Van Buren an old horse, which your own party have turned out to root? and is he not rooting a little to your discomfort about now? ... But the gentleman from Georgia further says, we have deserted all our principles, and taken shelter under General Taylor's **military coat tail**; and he seems to think this is exceedingly degrading. Well, as his faith is, so be it unto him. But can he remember no other military coat tail under which a certain other party have been sheltering for near a quarter of a century? Has he no acquaintance with the ample military coat tail of General Jackson? Does he not know that his own party have run the last five Presidential races under that coat tail, and that they are now running the sixth under that same cover? Yes, sir, that coat tail was

used, not only for General Jackson himself, but has been **clung to with the grip of death** by every Democratic candidate since. You have never ventured, and dare not venture, from under it. ... Mr. Speaker, old horses and military coat tails, or tails of any sort, are not figures of speech such as I would be the first to introduce into discussions here; but as the gentleman from Georgia has thought fit to introduce them, he and you are welcome to all you have made, or can make, by them. If you have any more old horses, **trot them out**; any more tails, **just cock them**, and come at us. ... Yes, sir, all his [Cass's] biographers (and they are legion) have him in hand, tying him to a military tail, **like so many mischievous boys tying a dog to a bladder of beans**. True, the material they have is very limited; but they drive at it, might and main. He *in*vaded Canada without resistance, and he *out*vaded it without pursuit. As he did both under orders, I suppose there was, to him, neither credit nor discredit in them; but they are made to constitute a large part of the tail. He was a volunteer aid to General Harrison on the day of the battle of the Thames; and, as you said in 1840, Harrison **was picking whortleberries** two miles off, while the battle was fought, I suppose it is a just conclusion, with you, to say Cass was aiding Harrison to pick whortleberries. ... By the way, Mr. Speaker, did you know I am a military hero? Yes, sir, in the days of the Black Hawk war, I fought, bled, and came away. Speaking of General Cass's career reminds me of my own. I was not at Stillman's defeat, but I was about as near it as Cass was to Hull's surrender; and, like him, I saw the place very soon afterwards. ... If General Cass went in advance of me in picking whortleberries, I guess I surpassed him in charges upon the wild onions. If he saw any live fighting Indians, it was more than I did, but I had a good many bloody struggles with the mosquitoes; and although I never fainted from loss of blood, I can truly say I was often very hungry. ... Mr. Speaker, I adopt the suggestion of a friend, that General Cass is a general of splendidly successful charges – charges, to be sure, not upon the public enemy, but upon the public treasury. He was Governor of Michigan Territory, and, *ex officio*, superintendent of Indian affairs, from 9 October 1813 till 31 July 1831 – a period of seventeen years, nine months, and twenty-two days. ... First, he was paid in *three* different capacities. ... Second, during part of the time ... he was paid in *four* different capacities. ... Third, during *another* part of the time ... he was also paid in *four* different capacities. ... Fourth, still another part of the

time ... he was paid in *six* different capacities. ... But I have introduced General Cass's accounts here chiefly to **show the wonder-
ful physical capacities of the man**. They show us that he not
only did the labor of several men at the same time, but that he
**often did it in several places many hundred miles apart at
the same time**. (Lincoln, 1991b: 9)

(a) Isaac Asimov observes in his joke anthology that all types of humor
depend for their effect on an anomaly or an absurdity. Lincoln's
attack on Cass uses the technique of *reductio ad absurdum*. Does the
fact that humor depends on absurdity make humor harder or easier
to translate? Is absurdity the same in every language? Is Lincoln
also using a form of parody when he takes up the figures of speech
used by his opponents and elaborates on them?

(b) Try to freely translate Lincoln's campaign speech into Spanish, French
or your other working languages in a way that preserves the humor.

(2) *Puns*

Paronomasia, or punning, is the exploitation of different meanings of
words that sound similar, for example 'The ancient Greek maiden was
tired of listening to lyres' (juxtaposition of 'lyres' and 'liars'). These
conceits may or may not be translatable, depending on the cultural references of the two words involved. If the play on words depends solely on
like *sounds* or *spellings* of two different words, as is the case with most
puns, it will rarely be translatable, since two similarly spelled or similar-
sounding words with humorously contrasting meanings will rarely be
found in the target language. But if the play on words depends on at
least one word which has a cultural reference that is recognizable across
language barriers, it may be translatable.

For example, of the following two puns, (a) is not translatable into
French or Spanish because there is no French or Spanish word corresponding to 'idle', but (b) is translatable because any educated audience
will have heard of the Brandenburg Concertos:

(a) Show me an unemployed movie star, and I'll show you a movie idle.

(b) I make no apologies for punning. I have been at it for a long time,
and a small, if anonymous place in history belongs to me because of
a pun. In December 1945, I called a speech on Soviet–American relations by Secretary of State James F. Byrnes 'The Second Vandenburg
Concerto' because of its similarity to a speech made by Senator
Arthur Vandenberg a short time before. (Newman, 1962: 211)

Puns based on a single word with multiple meanings in the source language should generally not be attempted by interpreters or translators,

as the result will probably not be funny. Consider the following two puns, both of which are based on some of the possible meanings of the word 'chip' (a gambling token/a French-fried potato/a computer processing component):

> The monks in a down-at-the-heels monastery, envious of the success neighboring monasteries were having selling cognac or cheese, decided to open a fish-and-chips business. It was a great success, and the news spread far and wide. A business reporter came to interview the monastic entrepreneurs, knocked at the monastery door, and asked the monk who answered, 'You must be the **fish-friar**?' 'No,' the brother replied, 'I'm the **chip-monk**!'

> Intel ... discovered ... that there was a certain danger in the marketing of modern technology to openly pursuing a policy of 'let the **chips** calculate where they may'. (Rukeyser, 1994: 3)

Even assuming the word 'chip' itself existed as a borrowing in the target language, it would still be impossible to translate either of these puns, because the English word chipmunk and the English idiom 'Let the chips fall where they may' would not exist as such in the target language. (Moreover, borrowings are often given a different meaning, for example the word 'chip' *is* used in French, but it is used to refer to a crisp potato chip, not to the British 'chip' that goes with fish and chips, which is called a 'frite'.)

Occasionally, by sheer coincidence, a pun based on homophones may be roughly translatable because a meaningful related pun can be produced in the target language. The alert interpreter may be able to spot those cases.

> *Example*: The devout lady asked her minister, 'Please pray for my pancreas'. The minister replied, 'We are not usually so specific in our prayers'. And she said, 'Oh yes, last week you prayed for loose livers.' = Une dame pieuse demande au curé, 'Priez pour mon pancréas'. A quoi le curé répond, 'Nous ne prions pas d'habitude pour des choses si concrètes'. Et la dame de répondre, 'Mais si, la semaine dernière nous avons prié pour ne pas perdre la foie!'

Off-color puns. A particularly ticklish problem is posed by off-color puns used in a formal context. Speakers occasionally use this technique to lend warmth or color to an otherwise staid presentation. When translated, such puns may be offensive without even being funny, because taboos and standards of propriety in formal speech can vary greatly from one language and culture to another. Consider the following two instances of off-color puns used in a formal context:

(a)   In a joke Henry Wallace, not usually a humorous man, told in my hearing in 1943, FDR could keep all his balls in the air without losing his own. (Schlesinger, 1973: 409)

(b)   Ladies and Gentlemen, he who rests on his laurels is wearing them in the wrong place. (Abraham Lincoln)

Notice that, even assuming the words of both puns are translatable, only pun (b) would fall within the limits of propriety in a formal Spanish speech. The second element of pun (a) might be translated in a 'sanitized' version by the Spanish expression 'hacerse bolas' (to get mixed up), but otherwise pun (a) would probably offend a Spanish-speaking audience without even amusing them, and the *substantive content* of the remark would thereby be lost or obscured. Consequently, for pun (a), it would be wiser for a Spanish interpreter to sacrifice the humor and simply spell out the message: 'El Presidente Roosevelt era capaz de atender a muchos intereses y problemas sin comprometer sus principios.' In French, pun (a) would probably not raise too many eyebrows, but it would not be fully translatable literally because the usual colloquial French word used for the male sexual organs has nothing to do with 'balls', and the play on words would be lost. The best a French interpreter could do would be something like, 'Le Président Roosevelt était capable de maîtriser un grand tableau sans mélanger ses pinceaux', which would be adequate, although not as funny as the original. In short, a Spanish interpreter would have to censor pun (a) in order to save the message, while a French interpreter would merely have to tone it down.

Pun (b), on the other hand, would be well within the limits of propriety for both French and Spanish audiences, and a French or Spanish interpreter would simply have to judge whether the expression 'to rest on one's laurels' was sufficiently familiar to the audience.

Unintentional puns. Finally, there is no need for an interpreter to take the risk of attempting to translate a pun which is unintentional, especially if the pun is due to the speaker's lack of mastery of the language he or she is speaking. A famous example is President John F. Kennedy's statement 'Ich bin ein Berliner', which, to his German audience, literally meant 'I am a jelly doughnut'. Another striking example was the very tall Swedish delegate who announced to an international committee that he would be brief by saying 'I will make myself short'. In both of these cases the intended meaning was clear, the humor was unintentional and harmless and any attempt to render the pun, even if successful, would only have served to heighten the speaker's embarrassment.

(3) *Irony*

Irony, the most trenchant form of humor, is usually reserved for serious subjects. It is a way of saying in a palatable way what is almost too painful or too bitter to say in any other way. Like 'deadpan humor', its effect, for both the speaker and the interpreter, depends on preserving a cool and even tone. Irony is sometimes so low key that it is almost an 'undertone' or a 'sub-text' that may go unnoticed if the interpreter is not sensitive to its presence.

One must also be alert to irony because an easy error for an interpreter to commit is to make a speaker sound ironic when no irony is intended.

Consider the following example, translated from French, in which a desperate Sarajevan ironically asked the world: if you will not help us, how can we help you?

Sarajevo: What Can We Do to Help Out the West?
A day like any other here in Sarajevo. It's been a long time since we've been able to leave the house. The town is terrorized by snipers and shelling, a day-in-day-out fear, as the world looks on with its usual weariness. We are now shut-ins, with only four walls to look at and no contact with the world outside. Behind locked doors, crouching in hallways and bathrooms (which seem to be the safest place in an apartment, though nobody knows why), the people of Sarajevo strain to hear the sound of shells exploding in their streets and news exploding on the world.

The bursting bombs mean that death is in the neighborhood again. The bursts of news mean that something important is finally happening. For Sarajevans, explosions have become an everyday sound. But the bursts of news have long since stopped getting the world's attention. Deaths in Tuzla? What else is new? The umpteenth violation of the ultimatum? It can't be. Phosphorus bombs falling on Sarajevo? Come now, let's be serious.

For quite some time things that seem important to the rest of the world have been leaving men and women of Sarajevo cold. This town no longer believes in anyone. ... No, Sarajevo does not believe in 'smart bombs' or in men who think only of themselves and never of others. For, since the beginning of our tragedy, the world has always put its own interests ahead of ours. ...

Today, people are afraid of the madman of Pale because he wants to kill them. In their fear, they are staging a show in which Sarajevo does not want to play any role. At best, **we could help them not be so afraid. We could ask them in to share what we have. One should always help people who have problems. That's what our parents told us when we were little.** Unfortunately, that's all we have to offer. It's too late for a great friendship. (Dizdarevic, 1995 (excerpts); trans. James Nolan)

(4) *Critique*

Humor is often used in various forms of artistic criticism, from literary reviews to theater, film or sports criticism. In this context, it requires a deft touch. Consider the following example, in which a light 'deadpan' humor is used to criticize the somewhat unprofessional styles and habits of Spain's new breed of young bullfighters.

Bullfighting Makes a Comeback
Hailed by the crowds, scorned by the mavens.

A new generation of **toreros** is revolutionizing the art of bull-fighting by playing not to the inner circle of **aficionados** but to the masses. Bullfighting is back in fashion. Television is broadcasting more bullfights than ever, and the bullrings are bursting with crowds of young women who come to cheer 'handsome **toreros**' like movie idols or rock stars.

The list of young matadors grows long: Jesulín Ubrique, El Cordobés [presumably the son of the famous **matador** of that name], Chamaco ['The Kid'], Enrique Ponce, Finito de Córdoba, Julio Aparicio, Pedrito de Portugal, etc. They are handsome and well-dressed, rich and famous, and are seen every day on television and in the press. The list includes some older figures: Joselito, El Litri and Rafael Camino, not to mention such veterans as Espartaco, Ortega Cano, César Rincón, the brothers Campuzano, and, of course, the 'Pharaoh' from Camas, Curro Romero, whose name has long been in lights.

Into this panoply of stellar figures the very young Francisco Rivera Ordóñez, grandson of the great Antonio Ordóñez, swept like a hurricane. He has become the 'great hope' of the **aficionados**. He scored a major triumph in Seville on 23 April at his **alternativa** [ceremony of becoming a full-fledged bullfighter], where he won four ears in two corridas. It is true, however, that he did not face very stiff competition at that event.

No one quite understands the reasons for this renewed interest in bullfighting. Some critics say it has much to do with television, which is broadcasting more bullfights than ever. Others say it is thanks to bullfighters like Jesulín de Ubrique, whose performances reveal more showmanship than true mastery of the art. Last year, Jesulín did 153 bullfights and killed 260 bulls, seemingly bent on entering the *Guinness Book of Records*, which he finally did. But going overboard in that way is bad for bullfighting, says critic Fernando Carrasco. Another critic, Juan Manuel Albendea, believes that having a lot of bullfighters who can fill the stands does not spell a heyday for bullfighting. The critics see two very different breeds among this new batch of bullfighters: the serious ones, and the not-so-serious ones, the orthodox bullfighters and the eccentrics. But that is not new. For as long as anyone can remember, some bullfighters have played to the galleries while others have bowed to the rules of the art.

Among the 'serious' bullfighters, the leading figure is Valencien Enrique Ponce. He stands firm in front of the bull, is in full command of his technique and makes no concessions to the audience. He is squarely in the tradition of such veterans as Espartaco, a leading figure of the years 1985–1991, or his seniors Paco Camino and Antonio Ordóñez. In the same line is Emilio Muñoz, a masterful and resourceful bullfighter now seen as the best exponent of the Seville school.

To this family of true bullfighters also belong Julio Aparicio, a matador of very supple movements and a true artist, Francisco Rivera Ordóñez, who is bold and technically proficient.

Then come the **tremendistas**, the bullfighters who specialize in showmanship. This is the specialty of Chamaco and El Litri, masters in the art of the **desplante**, the display of bravado. You will see them getting down on their knees in front of the bull or throwing their cape to the ground to face the animal unarmed. This type of **torero** is almost as popular with big audiences as the antics of Jesulín de Ubrique or El Cordobés, and it is not unusual to see a bevy of girls crowding the entrance to a hotel to catch a glimpse of the dashing El Litri. **Toreros** beloved of the crowd are snubbed by the real **aficionados**. But they are the only ones who can fill the bullrings in places as obscure as Olot, Catalonia.

Last year, Jesulín de Ubrique managed to fill Las Ventas, the big bullring of Madrid, for his famous 'ladies only' bullfight. Scandalously, the arena was littered with panties, bras and sundry undergarments.

His goal, of course, is to make more money than the others, but also to be in more bullfights than the others. He does not mind a small town requiring him in his contract to put in an appearance at the local night-club and allow his underwear to be raffled off. Like El Cordobés, Jesulín knows what he is doing in the bullring. The problem is, he doesn't care. He does this job for money, and playing the clown is the way to cash in. This controversial matador is quite frank: he does not appear for the connoisseurs, whose numbers might just fill one mini-van. During the last fair in Seville, one **aficionado** yelled out 'Buffoon!' as he entered the arena. Yet, to satisfy a Seville audience, Jesulín put in a more orthodox performance than usual, even though, at the end of the second bull, he included some of the usual stunts for the gallery. Outraged fans who say that **toreros** like him will never make the big time at the top bullrings are forgetting that in the late 1960s El Cordobés won a tail at La Maestranza for feats as unorthodox as the 'frog jump'. Jesulín has invented a routine he calls '**la tortilla**' ('the omelet'), a kind of double flourish of the cape which suggests an omelet being flipped over in a pan. That is the kind of stunt which leaves purists appalled.

The young matadors have in common several characteristics that are unusual in the world of bullfighting. With few exceptions, none of them has ever been hungry and none are illiterate. On the contrary, they are sons of well-to-do families who have never had to steal chickens or risk life and limb jumping fences in order to practice bullfighting by the light of the moon. They were welcomed as guests of honor into the best **tentaderos** [corrals where the mettle of thoroughbred fighting bulls is tested].

Many of them, like Rivera Ordóñez, El Litri or Chamaco, come from old bullfighting dynasties. They had famous teachers, enjoyed a comfortable environment and had all the time they needed to train. Some have degrees earned abroad and refined hobbies, like Chamaco, who plays the oboe. Living a life of ease may have influenced their style, says the critic J.M. Abendea. In his view, many of these young toreros lack professional drive, as if they had never had to prove themselves in the arena. They are bold, skillful and even artful, but one often has the feeling they do not want to take any risks.

This lack of passion is perhaps also due to the fact that, today, the cast of a bullfight is billed long in advance, whereas formerly it depended on the results of the last feria. Jesulín says he already has

170 engagements scheduled for this year. So it hardly matters what he does once he is in the arena. He is sure to beat his own record regardless, and that is all he is interested in. (José Bejarano, *La Vanguardia*; trans. James Nolan)

(5) *Social criticism*
Humor is often used for social criticism, as an alternative to outrage, indignation or polemics, and this form of humor sometimes surfaces in speeches in international fora. A good sense of humor can be an effective instrument of social change. Here again, a light touch, in keeping with the seriousness of the problem, is called for. Consider the following examples, translated from German and French, in which an 'edge' of tongue-in-cheek humor is used to question the excesses of the tourism industry and to mock and caricature the unscrupulous practices of swindlers who prey on the unemployed.

The 'Slave Route': A New Tourist Attraction?
Tourism seems to have a finger in every pie! The World Tourism Organization (WTO) and UNESCO are even calling one of their projects 'The Slave Route'. Are people even now finding a way to cash in on that calamity of bygone times?

The question is not all that simple. Certainly one goal of the project is to foster cultural tourism in Africa (especially West and Central Africa) and to open up places that have been associated with the slave trade.

Discovering roots. 'But the Slave Route may also provide a motivation for foreign visitors to become more thoroughly acquainted with the history of Africa and to discover their roots,' said Ousmane N'Diaye, WTO Regional Representative for Africa, at a meeting in Ghana.

The same idea lies behind the adoption of the so-called 'Accra Declaration', which says, among other things: 'By virtue of its scale and duration, the slave trade is today viewed by historians as the greatest tragedy in human history. The Program will therefore forge a close link between ethical imperatives, preserving the memory of the slave trade, and the contemporary demands of economic and social development'.

Money and memorials! But money will indeed be needed in order to restore and preserve the monuments, such as the forts and strongholds along the coast of Ghana and on the Senegalese island of Gorée that have recently been added to UNESCO's list of sites that comprise the 'heritage of mankind'.

High hopes. And money will also be needed to carry out plans to catalogue the monuments, to build visitors' centers, to produce video-films and to train special tour guides. There is also work to be done with tour organizers to develop special package tours. But the African countries themselves will also have much to do.

'We have high hopes for this project and we expect that it will swell the influx of tourists to Africa from all over the world,' WTO Spokesperson Deborah Luhrman told *Die Presse.*

When future tourists find themselves standing before the monuments, squares, forts and other landmarks all along the Slave Route listening to the explanations of specially trained guides, many a foreigner will begin to hear more and see more of this chapter of history, to understand it better and to give more thought to it. Perhaps some will even begin to feel, to sense what it must have been like. (Richter, 1995; trans. James Nolan)

Fleecing the Jobless

This is the story of a swindle as old as the hills. The trick is only too well known, but it was enough to dress it up a bit in order for 180 unfortunate victims to have fallen for it last month. Disarmed by the anxiety of searching for a job, they let down their guard and replied to an ad which promised '$1000 and more per week for stuffing envelopes with advertising' in exchange for a $30 'processing fee'. Naturally, all they got was the inevitable card in the mail advising them ... to stuff envelopes. Does one have to be awfully naive to be taken in by that kind of trick? Perhaps. But some very sensible people fall for scams that are almost as transparent.

Take the one that has just cost $20,000 at the ANPE (National Employment Service) unemployment office in Paris's 16th *arrondissement.* It took the form of 80 employment fees paid to the self-styled boss of a non-existent company: $20,000 embezzled in the form of 80 applications submitted and fees accepted before the fraud was disclosed thanks to the complaints of the 80 defrauded, discouraged and humiliated job-seekers. And for each such swindler who gets arrested (as did the one with the $30 fee, jailed in February), how many are still in business, their listings in the phone book and the Minitel? How long will it be before we have to set up paid workshops for job seekers just to train them to be on the lookout?

'In my group I don't know anybody who hasn't fallen for it at least once,' says 30-year-old Sylvie, a secretary who has been job-hunting for a year.

One readily believes her. All you have to do is turn on your Minitel terminal or open the want-ads to realize how big a market unemployment is creating for peddlers of false hopes.

First, let's see what's happening on the Minitel. As of 7 February there were 31 'job offer' services officially listed. (If you want the list, to compare their rates, key in 3615 MGS.) Most of them, under very different names and with different rates ranging from 0.36 to 3.42 francs per minute, advertise exactly the same services, with no indication of origin or expiry date. We even noted (occasionally?) that some of them provided nothing more than an empty screen once you had paid for the call. One way of sorting them out: the least expensive are the most reliable. And the least expensive of all, since it is free, is still the ANPE screen, which some of the other services simply copy in whole or in part, with a time-lag that renders the information completely useless.

'The Minitel is a fraud,' affirms Annick, who has been enrolled at the Chambéry ANPE office for a year. 'The connection takes forever. The pages scroll by slowly. And when you finally find something you're interested in, you get nothing specific. Sometimes it even asks you for a secret code to continue. Or the connection suddenly cuts off. In the end, you spend a good five minutes on average, run up a huge phone bill, and get nothing for it.'

Annick has also gone through the 'certificates' experience. 'I answered an ad that offered training to become an advertising agent, with an exclusive contract for a concept. The cost was $1300. In fact, it was three days of training at the end of which they gave me a "certificate of completion" saying I was in advertising. Three days! As for the exclusive concept, all it amounted to was preparing a brochure that listed doctors, a kind of directory. But since doctors are not allowed to advertise, and since all publications about them are official, the so-called "concept" was useless. Not to mention the expenses, which were about $6000 for printing, that you would have had to spend anyway to put the concept to use.'

Sham training courses (whether reimbursable (as job-search costs) or not) at exorbitant prices have become commonplace in every field. You can pay $3280 for an 'accelerated' secretarial course, or $2180 to go to business school two evening hours for three months (with a loan that jacks up the bill to over $4000 for those who don't pay cash). Those are two of the deals offered by a 'training institute' in Strasbourg about which the local ANPE official says,

'These courses have no educational credibility. On your résumé they count for zero.'

But some offers are more fun, less expensive or less complicated. Take the ad that came out in January in a reputable specialized publication: 'Training course in crepe-making. Want to start your own business? Looking for work? Become a professional in this field! (*sic*) Training: 50 hours. Maximum class size: two. Cost: $360. Housing can be arranged. Training costs may be paid for by social services.' There followed the address of a 'training site', which was a small-town crepe restaurant that probably takes in students during the off season. An ideal way to keep the kitchen fires going at two times $360 per week (rooming costs not included). A good recipe indeed – and surely more profitable than the recipe for crepe dough.

But it's not all that hard to sort out the phony offers from those that can actually lead to a job. You absolutely must select only approved training courses that issue an official diploma. Above all, figure out a way to get in touch with former graduates. They alone can give you reliable information on how serious the course is.

But, whether armed with a diploma or not, you can never be too wary of alluring want-ads. Elementary caution should prompt you to rule out any ad that asks for money – however small the amount – to find out more. The January issue of the magazine *Rebondir* pointed out the example of 'luxury cruises for the unemployed'. The ad (published widely, but from overseas, to prevent prosecution) cast a wide net: 'Luxury cruises offering jobs of all kinds for men and women. With or without qualifications.' You had to mail in $30 (yes, it was just the sea-going version of the usual scam, plus the sea-sickness), for which you received a list of the 50 or so companies around the world that operate cruise ships, none of which by the way were hiring.

Be wary also of the host of so-called 'psychologists', 'handwriting experts', 'employment specialists' and 'sophrologists' who offer not to find you a job but to put you in an 'optimal' physical or mental condition to find one. The least dangerous ones will just take your money without giving you anything in return. But the worst ones will take just as much from you and attempt to recruit you into a sect to boot.

Be wary too of all those who wave the flag of 'compassion' a bit too wildly. Increasingly, you must take a hard look at 'spontaneous' proposals made in lofty tones of 'solidarity'. Watch out especially for the new credit schemes offered to the unemployed. Those dubious favors can end up costing the poorest people a lot of money. A washing-machine with a list price of $500 can end up costing $1200. You're better off borrowing your relatives', or finding your way to the nearest laundromat.

Finally, be at your most alert when you feel most discouraged. There is an army of charlatans lying in wait for you. Above all, don't squander your valuable savings on the corner 'reader-advisor'. If you admit your age and you happen to be about 50, she will magically inform you that you're having 'employment problems'. But one hardly needs to be a visionary to guess that, when 50% of people who come to gaze into the crystal ball today are beset by concerns of that kind.

At the rate of $10 per 'prediction', you're better off buying yourself a nice pair of shoes. They'll come in a lot handier when you need to take to your heels. (Clémence Dulac, *Le Figaro Magazine*; trans. James Nolan)

(6) Since joke-telling ability can improve with practice, an interpreter should cultivate this art in order to improve his or her chances of being able to interpret humor. Listen to stand-up comedians who specialize in the art and famous punsters like Raymond Devos. From a book of jokes, choose two or three that you find especially funny. Practice telling them to friends or relatives, to yourself in the mirror or to a tape recorder. The next time you are with a group of friends, try telling the jokes in a way that will draw a smile from even the most serious of them. If you fail the first time, consider how the jokes might be adapted in order to make them even funnier or more appealing, and then try again on another occasion. In light of this experiment, do you find it true that 'humor is in the eye of the beholder'?

16 Latinisms

Speakers, especially in formal statements and in some technical contexts, may use Latin expressions. It is therefore advisable for interpreters to know some Latin, but this is not always possible because mastering modern living languages is far more important to an interpreter. As a general rule, it is safe simply to repeat a Latin expression you hear when you are interpreting a speech. That is certainly the best course when you do not know what a particular Latin expression means. Presumably the intended audience will know what it means if you have heard it and repeated it accurately.

However, it is also important to understand that there are at least three different kinds of Latinisms: (a) 'assimilated' Latinisms, which have become part of the standard lexicon in the language that has adopted them (e.g. *a priori* in French, *ex profeso* in Spanish or *seriatim* in English); (b) literary or scholarly phrases, maxims, quotations, etc., which are sometimes used not as technical terms but interspersed in a speech mainly for rhetorical effect (e.g. *'Sic semper transit!'* or *'Tempus fugit!'*); and (c) Latin expressions used as terms of art, which occur most often in the legal, medical and scientific contexts (e.g. *pacta sunt servanda* or *corpus delicti*). (This classification also applies to foreign words and phrases borrowed from languages other than Latin.)

Notice that type (a), the assimilated Latinism, does not have to be left in the Latin. It can be treated in much the same way as any other foreign-language term or expression. If you know what it means, it may be better to translate it. The French sentence 'Je ne sais pas *a priori* si mon gouvernement acceptera cette proposition' means simply 'I cannot readily say whether my government will accept this proposal'. Since we do not use *a priori* in that way in everyday English, it is stylistically preferable to put the speaker's meaning into plain English. To use a Latinism (even if it exists in the English lexicon) where an ordinary English speaker would not normally use Latin makes a simple statement sound odd and affected. It is probably for this reason that George Orwell urged writers never to use a Latin word when an English word would do.

Type (b), the literary Latinism, poses a different problem. A Latin phrase or quotation of this type is usually best left in Latin, since the intent of the speaker is to impress the audience with his erudition, or that of the source he is quoting. Sometimes, the speaker will spell out the meaning of the Latin quotation for the audience, in which case you will have the opportunity to interpret the explanatory translation into the target language. But if the speaker does not do the audience that favor, you need not feel that it is your job as an interpreter to translate the Latin phrase. The speaker is assuming a certain level of learning in the audience, which you must respect, or you may seem to be speaking down to the audience when the speaker is not. In interpreting a speech, you would not explain a Latin maxim to an audience of international lawyers any more than you would explain a Freudian term to an audience of psychoanalysts.

Type (c), the technical Latinism, poses yet a different problem. When used as a term of art, a Latin expression is being used in the same way as an English technical term like 'hydrocarbon' or 'metal fatigue'. It has a specific technical meaning, and sometimes there does not exist any word in the target language that will convey that precise meaning. In fact, in some technical contexts, the Latin term is the only practical choice for a multinational audience. The names of fish, for example, vary greatly from one country to another even within the same language, so that the only way an international meeting of marine biologists or fisheries experts can be sure of understanding each other is to use the Latin term for the species of fish they are discussing. Similarly, astronomers use only Latin names for certain stars or galaxies.

Here, your job as an interpreter (especially if the Latin term of art is unfamiliar to you) is simply to repeat it as accurately as you can, turning up the volume to your earphones if necessary so that you can hear the exact pronunciation. The worst problem with this type of Latinism is not to hear it right. For example, in a debate about jurisdictional immunity of states, one interpreter (due to poor sound quality) did not correctly hear an English speaker's reference to the distinction between *jure imperii* and *jure gestionis* (sovereign acts as opposed to commercial acts of states) and reiterated the latter in French as *juridictionis*, an interpretation which did not make sense. Such errors may not be very serious, since a specialist audience will probably not be misled and will usually forgive errors by non-experts. However, there is a potential for misleading some members of the audience for whom the Latin term is less familiar.

Exercises

(1)   At a fisheries conference, the discussion turns to three species of fish that the speakers refer to as *Trachurus mediterraneus*, *Trachurus picturatus*

and *Trachurus fallax*. You know, having read the conference documents, that all three of these species are commonly referred to by fishermen in English-speaking countries as 'Horse Mackerel'. Would you translate all three as 'Horse Mackerel' or use the Latin terms as you heard them?

(2) Is the Latinism in the following sentence (translated from French) being used as a term of art?

Until that time, the various technical approaches followed by most specialized research teams had consisted of identifying the different molecules of the principal malarial parasite, *Plasmodium falciparum*, which should go into the composition of a vaccine according to the logic of molecular chemistry.

(3) You are interpreting at a trial. The defendant, a Spanish speaker who understands neither English nor Latin, appears without a lawyer. The judge asks him, 'Are you appearing *pro se*?' Should you interpret the question using only the Latin term or spell it out for the defendant in Spanish?

(4) At a meeting of international lawyers, a French speaker refers to 'l'autorité de la chose jugée', and it is clear from the context that he is referring to the fact that a decision of a court concerning a given case should be considered definitive and binding. You know that this idea is usually known to English-speaking lawyers by the Latin term *res judicata*. Could you use this Latin term in your English interpretation even though the French speaker did not use Latin?

(5) An exasperated French speaker at a very long committee meeting exclaimed, 'Nous n'allons pas discuter de ceci *ad vitam eternam*!' Since English speakers seldom use that Latin expression, would it be correct to interpret this statement as, 'Are we going to discuss this forever'? Would it be possible to use a Latin expression that is in current use in English, for example *ad nauseam*?

US Secretary of State Adlai Stevenson once responded to Soviet reluctance to answer questions about the Cuban missile crisis with the famous comment, 'I am prepared to wait *until hell freezes over*'. Could the French interpreter have used *ad vitam eternam* to render this English idiom into formal French? Could he also have used the French expression 'jusqu'à la fin des temps'?

Could a French interpreter also use *ad vitam eternam* to render the English idiom 'till the cows come home'?

(6) A Latin term current in the target language can sometimes be used to render a non-Latin expression in the source language.

Examples: en flagrant délit = in flagrante delicto / le corps du délit = corpus delicti / de son propre mouvement = proprio motu /

pour la forme = pro forma / selon les règles de l'art = secundum artem / à plus forte raison = a fortiori

The Latin term may be more concise than the non-Latin term, and hence more useful in interpretation. For example, the somewhat wordy French term *le principe de la légalité des peines* (the principle that crimes and criminal penalties must be defined by law) can be concisely translated in English (and other languages) by the Latin maxim *nulla poena sine lege*:

> 'Toutefois, une approche très restrictive ne répondra pas à l'objectif de la Cour, ni *au principe de la légalité des peines* qui veut que les crimes et les sanctions dont ils sont punissables soient énumérés avec précision.' (Statement by representative of Algeria) = However, a highly restrictive approach will not satisfy the purpose of the Court, or the principle *nulla poena sine lege*, which requires that crimes and punishments be clearly defined.

Could you translate 'Le tribunal a agi *de son propre gré*' into English with the concise Latin expression *sua sponte*?

The opposite is also true: a Latin term in the source language can sometimes be translated by an equally accurate non-Latin term of art in the target language.

(a) You know that English-speaking lawyers often use the term 'settled law' to refer to a rule of law that has been firmly established by a long series of cases. You also know that this idea is known to international lawyers as *lex lata* (by contrast with *lex ferenda*, or 'law-in-the-making'). At a conference of lawyers where French or Spanish speakers used the term *lex lata*, would you be bound to use the Latin term in your interpretation, or could you also use 'settled law' as a synonym where it would tend to clarify the meaning of the sentence?

(b) A French speaker describing a change of policy used the Latin expressions *ex ante* and *ex post* simply to mean 'before' and 'after' the change. Would an English speaker have used those expressions in such a case? Is there any need to do so in interpretation?

(c) Translate the following excerpt from a speech into English, French or your other working languages, first with the Latinism (see list below), and then with a non-Latin expression of equivalent meaning:

Sin embargo, el Gobierno de México estima que la sola aprobación, y sobre todo la firma del Tratado contribuirá a deslegitimar las armas nucleares, a reforzar la *opinio juris* respecto a la obligación de eliminarlas, e inhibirá la suspensión de las moratorias de ensayos que han declarado las cinco naciones poseedoras de armas nucleares. (Statement by representative of Mexico)

(7) You cannot hope to have at your fingertips all of the myriad Latin words and expressions that are used in legal, medical and scientific discussions. But the more familiar you become with the most common ones, the less likely it is that you will mishear or misinterpret them. The following are some of the Latinisms more frequently used, especially at conferences and in legal materials:

- ab absurdo – by reduction to absurdity
- ab initio – from the beginning
- absente reo – the defendant being absent
- Abusus non tollit usum. – Abuse is no argument against proper use.
- Actus non facit reum nisi mens sit rea. – The act does not make the doer guilty unless his mind is guilty.
- actus reus – criminal act
- ad damnum – the amount of damages demanded
- ad hoc – for a special purpose
- ad hominem – against the person (not on the issue)
- ad infinitum – forever
- ad interim – meanwhile, temporary
- ad litem – for the suit (as in 'guardian *ad litem*')
- ad nauseam – to a sickening degree
- ad nutum – by inherent authority at any time
- ad usum – according to custom
- ad valorem – according to value (as in '*ad valorem* tax')
- a fortiori – with even stronger reason
- alieni juris – not possessing full legal power (e.g. a minor)
- alter ego – another self
- amicus curiae – friend of the court
- a minima – reduced to a minimum
- Anno Domini (AD) – year of Our Lord
- ante bellum – before the war
- a posteriori – after the fact
- apsit omen – 'knock on wood'
- arguendo – for the sake of argument
- Ars longa, vita brevis. – Art is long and time is short.
- assumpsit – he promised (name of an action at common law)
- audi alteram partem – hear the other side
- aut dedere, aut judicare – 'extradite or prosecute'
- bona fide – in good faith, genuine

- bona vacantia – goods of unknown ownership
- Carpe diem. – Seize the day.
- casus belli – cause of war
- causa mortis – by reason of death
- Caveat emptor. – Let the buyer beware.
- cestui que trust (Anglo-French) – he who benefits by the trust
- Communis error facit jus. – Popular prejudices become law.
- contra bonos mores – against good morals
- contra pacem – against the peace
- corpus delicti – the basic elements of the offense
- corpus juris – a body of law
- Credo ut intelligam. – I believe in order that I may understand.
- damnosa hereditas – an inheritance carrying obligations
- damnum absque injuria – harm caused without violation of law
- de facto – in fact, actually
- de jure – as a matter of law, as of right
- de jure gestionis – relating to commercial acts by a state
- de jure imperii – relating to sovereign acts of a state
- de lege ferenda – law in the making
- de lege lata – settled law
- de minimis – insignificant
- De minimis non curat lex. – Law does not deal with trifles.
- de novo – afresh, anew
- desiderata – things desirable, ideals, aims
- deus ex machina – the god from the machine (a suddenly intervening force that sets things aright)
- dies irae – the wrath of the gods
- divortium aquarum – watershed (used in border demarcation)
- dixit – says
- doli capax – capable of crime
- doli incapax – incapable of crime
- duces tecum – bring with you (as in subpoena *duces tecum*, a court order that a person must bring evidence into court)
- ejusdem generis – of the same kind
- erga omnes – toward everyone (e.g. an obligation erga omnes)
- ergo – therefore
- et sequentes / et seq. – and the following
- Ex abundantia cordis os loquitur. – Out of the abundance of the heart the mouth speaketh.
- ex aequo et bono – based on equity and right
- ex delicto – arising from a tort

- ex gratia – as a gift
- ex mero motu – of one's own free will, without compulsion
- ex nihilo – out of nothing
- ex officio – by virtue of his office
- ex parte – on one side or for one party only
- ex post facto – after the fact (as in 'an *ex post facto* law')
- Expressio unius est exclusio alterius. – A thing expressly listed implies that other things not expressly listed are meant to be excluded (a rule of statutory interpretation).
- ex profeso – on purpose, for the purpose
- ex relatione / ex rel. – upon relation or report of
- ex testamento – by will
- Fiat justitia, ruat coelum. – Let justice be done even if the sky should fall.
- forum non conveniens – inconvenient court (doctrine under which a court with jurisdiction may defer to another better suited to try a case)
- forum prorogatum – extension of a court's normal jurisdiction to a case by the consent of the litigants
- habeas corpus – you have the body (name of a writ)
- honoris causa – honorary
- hostis humani generis – enemy of humankind
- Ignorantia legis non excusat. – Ignorance of the law is no excuse.
- in extremis – in extremity, in the last illness
- in fine – specifically
- in flagrante delicto – in the act of committing an offense
- in forma pauperis – as a poor person
- infra – below
- in fraudem legis – in circumvention of the law
- in loco parentis – in the place of a parent
- in medias res – in the midst of things
- in pari delicto – in equal fault
- in pari materia – on like subject matter
- in personam – relating to the person (by contrast with in rem)
- in re – in the matter of
- in rem – relating to a thing
- in rerum natura – in nature
- in situ – in its original position
- in statu quo – in the condition in which it was
- in sua causa – in one's own cause
- in terrorem – in terror
- inter se – among themselves

- inter vivos – between living persons
- in toto – completely
- in vitro – within glass, as in a test tube
- ipse jure (jurisdiction) – (jurisdiction) by law
- ipso facto – by the fact itself
- ipso jure – by operation of law
- jus gentium / iure gentium – the law of nations
- jus sanguinis – a doctrine of nationality based on descent
- jus soli – a doctrine of nationality based on place of birth
- jus tertii – the right of a third person
- lapsus calami – error committed in writing
- lapsus linguae – error in language
- lex loci – the law of the place
- lex loci delicti – the law of the place of the offense
- lex mercatoria – the law merchant
- lex talionis – the law of retribution ('an eye for an eye')
- lis pendens – litigation on a pending suit
- litera legis – the literal wording of the statute
- locus delicti – the place of a crime or tort
- locus standi – legal grounds to be heard
- malum in se – evil in itself
- mea culpa – my fault, an admission of guilt
- mens rea – guilty mind, criminal intent (required, together with actus reus, to constitute a crime)
- mirabile dictu – marvelous to say
- mobile vulgus – the changing crowd
- modus operandi – manner of operation
- mortis causa – by reason of death
- mutatis mutandis – all other necessary changes being made
- nec plus ultra – the very best, the ultimate
- nolle prosequi – (decision) not to prosecute
- nolo contendere – I will not contest it (name of a plea)
- non bis in idem – rule against double jeopardy
- non compos mentis – not of sound mind, mentally deficient
- Non est factum. – a plea alleging that one was mistaken about the character of a document
- non obstante veredicto / NOV – notwithstanding the jury verdict
- non sequitur – it does not follow
- non sui juris – not by one's own authority or legal right
- Noscitur a sociis. – A word is known by the company it keeps (i.e. a word is to be understood by its context) (rule of statutory interpretation).

- Nullum crimen sine lege. – There is no crime without a law.
- nunc pro tunc – now for then (an action taken in the present that should have been taken before)
- obiter dictum – remark by the way
- opinio juris sive necessitatis – the belief by a nation that a rule of international law must be followed by it
- Pacta sunt servanda. – Agreements are binding.
- parens patriae – (acting as) parent to the community
- pari delicto – in equal guilt
- Par in parem imperium non habet. – Sovereigns have no jurisdiction over each other.
- pari passu – at the same pace, in parallel
- passim – here and there
- pax Romana – the peace of Rome (by analogy: pax Americana, etc.)
- pendente lite – pending the suit
- per capita – per person
- per curiam – by the court
- per stirpes – by representation (in distribution of an estate)
- pleno jure – with full authority
- post hoc – after the fact
- post mortem – after death
- post partum – after birth
- prima facie – at first sight
- primus inter pares – first among one's peers
- pro bono publico – for the public good
- pro hac vice – for this occasion
- pro rata – in proportion
- pro se – for oneself
- pro tempore – for the time being
- quantum meruit – as much as deserved
- quare clausum fregit – wherefore he broke the close (a form of trespass)
- quid pro quo – something in exchange for something
- Quis custodiet ipsos custodes? – Who will guard the guards?
- qui tam – (suit) brought by private citizen on behalf of the government
- Quod erat demonstrandum. – that which was to be demonstrated
- ratio decidendi – the reason for the decision, the principle which the case establishes
- ratio legis – the spirit or purpose of the statute
- rebus sic stantibus – as matters stand

- reductio ad absurdum – reducing to absurdity (a way to disprove)
- Rem tene, verba sequentur. – Grasp the facts, and the words will follow.
- requiescat in pace – rest in peace
- res – the thing, the subject matter
- res ipsa loquitur – the thing speaks for itself (a theory of tort liability)
- res judicata – a matter adjudicated, an issue previously decided
- respondeat superior – doctrine that an employer is responsible for acts of the employee
- sanctum sanctorum – the holy of holies
- satisfecit – approval, endorsement
- Scripta manent, verba volant. – Writing remains, spoken words fly.
- secundum artem – according to the rules of the art
- sedes materiae – the substantive basis
- seriatim – severally, separately
- Sic semper transit. – So it always happens.
- Sic utere tuo in alienum non laedas. – Use your property in such a way as not to damage that of others.
- sine die – without a day appointed, indefinitely
- sine qua non – prerequisite
- stare decisis – to abide by decided cases
- sua sponte – on one's own initiative
- sub judice – under consideration
- sub silentio – under silence
- sui generis – unique
- sui juris – of his own right
- supra – above
- Tempus fugit. – Time flies.
- terra incognita – unexplored land
- terra nullius – land belonging to no one
- tu quoque – you too
- ultra vires – beyond the powers of
- uti possidetis – as you possess, state of present possession (one of the theories used to define a nation's territory)
- Vade in pace. – Go in peace.
- vade mecum – a handbook
- vel non – or not
- via media – middle course
- voir dire (Anglo-Norman) – to speak the truth (name of preliminary examination to determine competency of jurors)
- vox populi – the voice of the people

17 Numbers

Figures given by speakers are generally offered either as an order of magnitude or as a technical measurement. It is important to distinguish these because an interpreter has considerable leeway in rendering the former and very little leeway with the latter. For example, if the figure 52.3% is offered as an order of magnitude, an interpreter having trouble with speed can simply say 'roughly half'. However, if the figure '873.5 milligrams' were given in a statement to an audience of pharmacologists, the interpreter does not have that option: giving the wrong measurement may be a more serious mistake than giving no figure at all. At the very least, the interpreter should strive to accurately render the quantitative or quantitative *concept* correctly, that is to use the right unit of measurement or make clear whether the speaker is talking about an increase or a decrease, for example.

Exercises

(1) In the following reports, consider whether the numbers given are technical measurements or orders of magnitude:

> To date, about 45,000 people have been vaccinated with SPf66. On average, the results in Latin America show that the vaccine is 30% to 65% effective among adults. It seems to be much more effective among children under age five. The side-effects are apparently minor. Out of 35,000 people vaccinated in Colombia, there were at most 5.6% who showed adverse reactions, and these were in any case minimal and required no medication.

> A scientist in Australia reports that he has found evidence that the speed of light is slowing. ... The measurements taken showed that a 12 billion-year-old stream of light had properties which appeared to violate accepted laws of physics. He said the only possible explanation for the unusual data was that the speed of light had

been faster 6 to 10 billion years ago than its current speed of around 300,000 kilometers per second.

(2) (a) Make a recording of the following list of numbers, reading them out at moderate speed in French, Spanish or your other working languages. Then play back the recording and try to interpret what you hear into English without falling behind. Record your performance and check it against the list.

20 80 90 60 70 62 72 82 92 7 17 77 50 55 65 75 85 67 68 78 160 170 110 280 290 260 270 277 298 278 297 777 666 555 24 80 80,000 80,880 90,000 90,880 99,824 97,670 678 678,424 678,480 4,888,677 80,777,167 88,675,177 98,675,110 167,767 67,177 76,771 188.2 276.7 359.98 458.22 329.99 787.87 484.84 988.8 98.9% 99.8% 48.8%

(b) Once you are able to interpret the complete list without mistakes or omissions, make a new recording at progressively faster speeds and repeat the exercise. Repeat the exercise working from English into your other languages.

(c) Write down the numbers on index cards. Shuffle the deck. Then use the newly randomized numbers to repeat exercises (a) and (b) above.

(d) Reshuffle the deck, begin drawing cards from the top and try to simply call the numbers out in each of your languages as fast as possible.

(e) Play your recording of numbers again, and try to simply jot them down as fast as possible. As you do this, work out a simple symbol of your own that can be used to represent two zeros and another to represent three zeros. (see Chapter 18)

(3) The extra effort required to interpret figures accurately sometimes distracts the interpreter's attention from the numerical concept, the unit of measurement or the item to which the figure refers. For example, an interpreter hearing the phrase '15 kilos par mètre carré' (a technical measurement of the density of manganese nodules on the sea floor) in a high-speed speech mistranslated it as '15 kilos per square kilometer', that is she got the number right but the interpretation was wrong because the unit of measurement was wrong. A correct number is of little use to the audience if its referent is wrong. To help overcome this problem, it is helpful to practice interpreting numbers in conjunction with their referents.

(a) Make recordings of the following passages read out at a normal speed, then at progressively faster speeds. Play back the passages and practice repeating from memory as much of each passage at a time as you can.

(b)   Then practice interpreting the passages until you can get all of the numbers and quantitative concepts right.

(c)   Next translate the passages, make a recording of the translation and practice interpreting them three times into another language. The first time, concentrate on the numerical concepts or referents (the item to which the figure refers). The second time, concentrate on the figures themselves. The third time, try to capture both. Record your performances and compare them to the original text. Repeat the exercise until you get all the numbers and their referents right.

Global Warming

In Uganda, record rains of 1997 destroyed 40 per cent of its 9,600 kilometre feeder road network. Between 1997 and 1998, a prolonged drought in the Seychelles led to the closure of the Seychelles Breweries and the Indian Ocean Tuna Company. . . . Emissions of carbon dioxide, the main global warming gas, have risen eightfold in Africa since 1950 to 223 million metric tons. However, those are still less than the emissions of a developed country such as Germany or Japan. South Africa accounts for 42 per cent of these emissions, while Egypt, Nigeria and Algeria combined account for 35.5 per cent. (*UN Chronicle*, 2002)

Vehicle Sales

New vehicle sales jumped nearly one quarter last year to 376,362 units, latest figures from the National Association of Automobile Manufacturers of South Africa show. New car sales rose 22.9% to 235,686, light commercial vehicle sales were 26% higher at 128,634, medium-sized vehicle sales were 23.1% up at 4,135 and heavy truck sales 34.9% up at 7,607. Higher sales, together with an average 8% price rise, boosted vehicle manufacturers' turnover 33% to 28 billion Rand. Sales not represented by NAAMSA would have added about 15,000 to the figures. December sales were also above average compared with the same month a year before. New car sales increased 15.5% to 17,015, LCV sales increased 13.9% to 9,028, while MCV and heavy truck sales increased 14.7% and 11.6% respectively over December 1994. (*News Highlights from the South African Media*, 1996)

The Suez Canal

Opened to world navigation in 1869 (and nationalized in 1956), the Suez Canal has become one of the country's main foreign-exchange earners, behind oil but ahead of tourism. 1992 and 1993 were excellent years in financial terms, with 1992 earnings reaching $1.9 billion and 1993 earnings expected to exceed $2 billion (the exact figure is not yet known), which is twice as much as the canal earned in the early 1980s. More than 17,000 vessels used the canal in 1993, representing a total of nearly 400 million tons. By way of comparison, 4,200 vessels totalling 25 million tons used the canal in 1945. Since then, the number of users has grown steadily, except for the years when the canal has been closed due to various local conflicts. The last closing was for eight years, from 1967 to 1974, during the war with Israel. . . .

With the exception of the 'Sumed' Suez-Mediterranean pipeline across Egypt (a joint venture of Egypt, which holds 50% of the equity, Saudi Arabia, Kuwait, and United Arab Emirates, and Qatar), whose capacity is expected to grow from 80 to 120 million tons by 1994, the five pipelines in the region have gradually shut down. The Kirkuk-Haifa pipeline has been closed since 1948. The Kirkuk-Baniyas-Tripoli pipeline was closed in 1982 due to souring relations between Syria and Iraq. The Kirkuk-Saida pipeline, whose capacity had been doubled to make up for the closing of the previous pipeline, was closed by Turkey during the Gulf War. And the 'Tapline' between Ras Tanura in Saudi Arabia and Tripoli in Lebanon has gradually shut down since 1983. . . .

Specialists foresee that Middle East production may rise from 880 million tons per year today to 1,450 million tons by the year 2000 and 1,600 million tons by the year 2005. Absent other solutions, there is no doubt that part of that production will reach the West through the Suez Canal.

The following are the major characteristics of the canal:
Length of canal: 195 kilometers
Width between buoys: 180 meters
Maximum draft allowed: 53 feet
Maximum weight allowed: 140,000 tons
Transit allowed day or night
Daily capacity: 55 vessels
Mode of transit: vessels go through daily in 3 convoys

Average duration of crossing: 15 hours
Speed permitted: 11 to 15 km per hour
Tolls: sliding scale determined by weight of ship. Example: Suez Canal Authority demands 7.21 SDR (Suez Due Rate, i.e. $1.35) per ton for the first 5000 tons, then 4.02 for the next 5000 tons, 3.61 for the next 10,000 tons, etc. The lowest tariff (1.32 SDR per ton) applies to weights over 70,000 tons.

Ownership: The canal belongs to the Suez Canal Authority, a public corporation comprising eight companies and employing 25,000 people. (Françoise Paoletti, *Jeune Afrique Economie* (excerpts); trans. James Nolan)

La Guerre du Golfe en chiffres

La guerre du Golfe qui s'est déroulée du 17 janvier au 28 février compte parmi les plus grandes concentrations de troupes de l'histoire. Quelque 580,000 Irakiens ont fait face aux 750,000 hommes de la coalition organisée autour du corps expéditionnaire américain – fort de 510,000 soldats. Celle-ci, outre les Etats-Unis, a regroupé trente-deux pays: Arabie saoudite (67,500 hommes), Grande-Bretagne (36,000), Egypte (35,600), Syrie (20,800), France (15,600), Conseil de coopération du Golfe – Qatar, Bahrein, Emirats Arabes Unis, Oman et troupes koweitiennes en exil – (14,000), Pakistan (10,000 hommes, plus 2,000 moudjahidines afghans), Canada (2,200), Bangladesh (2,000), Italie (1,300), Maroc (1,200), Australie (600), Espagne, Sénégal et Niger (500 hommes chacun), Pays-Bas et Belgique (400 chacun), Argentine (300), Grèce et Sierra Leone (200 chacun), Honduras (150), Turquie, Danemark, Bulgarie, Nouvelle-Zélande et Norvège. (Valladao, 1992: 27)

Pensiones

Aunque es difícil comparar directamente la cuantía de las pensiones de jubilación de los diferentes países, la OIT ha intentado establecer lo que un asalariado medio puede esperar recibir como fracción de sus ingresos. Según los Convenios antes mencionados, por regla general esta cantidad no debe ser inferior al 40 por ciento (Convenio número 102) o al 45 por ciento (Convenio número 128) del promedio de los salarios cuando ha cotizado o ha estado emplado durante treinta años en un régimen de seguro social, o tiene veinte años de residencia en un régimen de asistencia social universal. (ILO, 1995)

Ganancias

Los analistas estiman que durante el segundo trimestre las firmas de valores ganaron US$ 900 millones después de impuestos, un aumento del 26% respecto a los US$ 710 millones que declararon el primer trimestre. Pero esta cifra ni siquiera se acerca a los US$ 1,400 millones después de impuestos que ganaron las casas de valores en cada trimestre de 1993, e incluso representa una caída respecto a los US$ 965 millones de ganancias trimestrales de 1991, un año que, al igual que este, se caracterizó por mercados fuertes pero no espectaculares.

(*El Comercio/Wall Street Journal Americas*, 1995)

18 Note-taking

A personal system of note-taking is very useful not only in consecutive interpretation but also in simultaneous interpretation (e.g. to jot down the jargon of a meeting as it is taking place, or to jot down figures, names or proposed wordings in a drafting group), as well as for translators (who, in some jobs, are required to write summary records from notes). Developing a personal system of notes also helps to form the habit of summarizing and symbolizing words and phrases, which is an important aspect of the interpretation process.

Note-taking is most important to the consecutive interpreter. Consecutive interpretation relies mainly on short-term memory. Psychological studies have shown that short-term memory fades very rapidly. However, they have also shown that, although it is very difficult to remember a large number of *words*, it is not so difficult to remember a series of *ideas* (Garretson, 1981: 244).

Consequently, a successful note-taking technique for consecutive interpretation calls for a method of reducing words to ideas and putting the ideas into symbols that can then be re-expressed in another language. An interpreter must not try to write down word for word everything the speaker says because a hundred words may contain only one idea, while one word may imply several ideas.

A classic book on this subject is *La prise de notes en interprétation consécutive* by Jean-François Rozan (1970). Study of Rozan's book is a good way to begin developing one's own note-taking system.

There are some basic guidelines on note-taking that should be followed:

- Your note-taking system must be your own. It must be one that *you* can easily use, based on your own style of handwriting.
- It is helpful to learn a stenographic system such as shorthand, or a note-taking system such as Speedwriting, or to invent your own way of 'writing phonetically' (representing sounds as well as words or ideas).

English, for example, has only about 40 sounds. But it is not helpful to get into the habit of trying to write down everything a speaker says verbatim.

- Adopt and use symbols that are useful for the subjects you are dealing with.
- Always use a symbol to mean only one thing in a given context.
- Use pictorial or graphic devices like circles and squares or lines and arrows. You are not 'writing out the speech'; you are 'drawing a picture for yourself' of the speech.
- Arrange your notes on the page in a meaningful way (e.g. with the main points at the top and minor points at the bottom). Use indentations logically and consistently.
- Learn and use conventional abbreviations and acronyms (e.g. the telegraphic business abbreviation 'cak' meaning 'contract', or the Morse-code acronym SOS to mean 'help').
- Adopt a simple, one-stroke symbol which, whenever you write it, will mean 'the main subject of the speech'.
- Adopt a simple sign which will mean 'three zeros', so that you can write down large numbers quickly (e.g. if – means 'three zeros', then 89 – – means '89 million'). Adopt another symbol to represent two zeros.
- Adopt or coin abbreviations or acronyms for often-used phrases (examples: asap = as soon as possible; iot = in order to; iaw = if and when).
- Invent symbols for common prefixes and suffixes, such as 'pre-', 'anti-' or '-tion', '-ment'.
- When you write out words, do not double any consonants, and delete any vowels that are not necessary to make the word recognizable or to distinguish it from another similar word.
- When interpreting consecutively, write your notes as much as possible in the target language.
- Always have enough sharp pencils or functioning pens at hand.

Notice that all of the words in Table 18.1 are recognizable in the column on the left even though the consonants are not doubled and even though some or all vowels are missing.

Once you have adopted a symbol and assigned it a specific meaning, you can then build other symbols from it. For example, if the symbol x is used to mean 'time', numerous variations on it are possible, as shown in Table 18.2.

There are many sources of symbols. You will find them all around you, even on signs in the street. It does not matter from what source you borrow

Table 18.1

zbr	zebra
arpln	airplane
hstry	history
cmtee	committee
elfnt	elefante
ptrlo	petroleo
bmb	bomba
invrn	invierno
cnrd	canard
Mrsl	Marseille
phlsphie	philosophie
asmblé	assemblée

Table 18.2

x–	timeless, eternal
xx	many times, often
xx+	many times more
xx–	many times less
x t x	from time to time, occasionally
=x	equal time
+x	more time, longer time
–x	less time, shorter time
2x	twice
3x–/	three times less than
100x	a hundred times
100x+	a hundred times more
Ltdx	a limited time
oldx	old-time, old fashioned
x!	It's time, the time has come
x̲	now, this time
gdx	a good time
xly	timely, on time
unxly	untimely, late
x)	time limit, deadline
x>	future
<x	past
ovrx	overtime
xng	timing

Table 18.2 *Continued*

sumrx	summertime
xtbl	timetable, schedule
prtx	part-time
x,x	time after time, repeatedly
x.	time period
wrx	wartime

your symbols, so long as you use them consistently in your own note-taking system. Look for symbols that can be written quickly and easily, with few pencil-strokes. The following are a few possible sources of symbols:

- proofreader's marks (see, e.g. back matter of dictionaries)
- symbols or abbreviations from dictionary entries, like ~
- mathematical and algebraic symbols, like √ or >
- books on semiotics
- ancient writing systems, like Norse or Cuneiform
- conventional business and commercial symbols and abbreviations, like @, £, c.i.f. or a.s.a.p.
- foreign-alphabet letters
- pictographs borrowed from languages with pictographic script, like Chinese (e.g., ⊥ to mean 'standing')
- pictographs and pictographic devices borrowed from ancient hieroglyphic scripts (e.g., runes, or the ancient Egyptian device of enclosing the proper names of important people in a 'cartouche')
- punctuation marks, like ! or ? or / (e.g., you could use +/ to mean 'and or', and the ampersand (&) to mean 'and')
- signs of the zodiac
- pronunciation symbols, accents, diacritical marks
- capital letters used for a specific meaning, like P to mean president or F to mean France; or single letters used for a specific meaning, like c to mean 'country'
- children's 'picture-writing' (e.g. ^ to mean 'house' or 'shelter', or ☺ (to mean 'happy' or 'pleased', or ♥ to mean 'love')
- symbolic logic
- scientific symbols, like for 'man' and for 'woman'
- musical signs
- legal symbols, like § to mean 'section'
- monograms (combinations of letters, such as Æ)

Exercises

(1) Compare the difficulty of the following pairs of mental tasks and the speed with which they can be performed.

- Describe a spiral. Draw a picture of a spiral.
- Describe a cone. Draw a picture of a cone.
- Describe an ellipse. Draw a picture of an ellipse.
- Describe the route you take from home to work. Draw a sketch of the route you take from home to work.
- Define the word 'notwithstanding'. Invent an abbreviation for it.
- Define the word 'motion'. Invent a symbol for it.

(2) On a single, large sheet of paper, represent the story of 'the tortoise and the hare' using only symbols, lines, shapes, pictures and abbreviations. Then, using the same set of graphic devices and following the guidelines above, make notes on the following news items:

Wayward Tortoise
Thirty-five years after Chester disappeared from his master's back-yard in Lyde, England, the escaped tortoise turned up a mere 500 feet from his original home. Chester was discovered ambling along a roadside by a local resident who cleaned him up and set out to track down the owner. Malcolm Edwards, 44, who still lives in his boyhood home, recognized his long-lost pet immediately because of a white paint mark his father had put on the shell in 1960 to make the creature easier to spot in the grass. Edwards, who failed to say how Chester got away, hopes the turtle 'might decide to stay home a little longer this time'. (*The Earth Times*)

Snail Mail
E-mail has such a reputation for speed that technophiles have long sneered at the inefficient 'snail mail' delivered by the Postal Service. But while E-mail zips along at nearly the speed of light, sometimes the snail gets there first. An electronic message between two Manhattan offices a dozen blocks away, last month, for example, took two days to reach its destination. The reply took seven hours, which is faster than the post office's overnight delivery, except that the recipient had gone home and didn't see the message until the next day. (*New York Times*, 1996a)

(3) Draw pictures of the following ideas:

the aircraft is taking off / the value of the dollar is rising / the runner has crossed the finishing line / troops have crossed the border / four speakers have spoken / this is the fourth conference held on this same subject in 10 years / the president has entered the room / the assembly welcomes the President of France / the water level has risen twice as high / the percentage of women employed in industry has doubled / there are 70,000 people in the country / there are 70,000 displaced persons in refugee camps in 24 countries / the witness is speaking / the witness for the prosecution is lying / the group is growing / the organization has grown too large / the level is declining / the level of funding has fallen too low / three times more people / there are 10 times more poor people in the southern hemisphere than in the northern hemisphere / I said this before / I have repeated this point many times before / the ship is sailing / the ship made its way through the archipelago

(4) Using mainly abbreviations, pictures, lines and symbols, make notes of the following news items:

> Près de 150 chefs d'Etat et de gouvernement convergeant sur New York. On s'attendait à une belle pagaille pour le cinquantième anniversaire des Nations Unies. Mais chacune et chacun y mettant du sien, les choses se passèrent plutôt bien et dans la bonne humeur.

> 'Il nous faut aujourd'hui concentrer nos efforts sur l'adaptation de notre organisation, sur sa rénovation et d'abord lui donner les moyens de fonctionner,' a dit Jacques Chirac à l'occasion des cérémonies du 50e anniversaire des Nations Unies à New York. ... 'Thank you, Larry, and see you soon.' C'est par ces mots que le président français a conclu plus tard dans la journée son interview, en anglais, dans l'émission du journaliste-vedette Larry King sur CNN. ... Le président français, qui maîtrise bien l'anglais, n'a dû que rarement se tourner vers son interprète pour solliciter son aide.

> One of the most powerful temblors to strike Sumatra in decades left at least 80 people dead, and tens of thousands of homes wrecked in and around Sungai Penhu. The magnitude 5.8 quake was felt as far away as Singapore and southern Malaysia.

> The environment program will convene participants in Washington to adopt a plan for enhancing the international Montreal Guidelines on the Marine Environment, agreed to in 1985. The conference runs from October 23 to November 3. The meeting is planned to finalize agreements on promoting better waste-water treatment and management, more control over pollution and protection of wildlife, among other goals.

Over the 1987–94 period, US exports to the BEMs (Big Emerging Markets) grew $65 billion, or 177%, for an average annual compound gain of 16%. US exports to the rest of the world grew by 95% over the same period, for an average annual compound gain of 10%.

El noviembre pasado, las fuerzas armadas brasileñas se unieron a la policía de Río de Janeiro para poner fin a una ola de criminalidad que parecía haber llegado a un nivel insoportable. Seis meses después, la escalada de violencia sigue irrefrenable y su víctima es la población civil, principalmente la que vive en las favelas.

El gobierno boliviano privatizará las 78 empresas estatales del país en lo que queda de 1995, vendiéndolas por 2,050 millones de dólares, informó el subsecretario de Promoción Económica de Bolivia. .... La enajenación de los seis colosos fiscales aportará 2,000 millones de dólares al fisco y otros 50 millones de dólares ingresarán a las arcas estatales gracias a la venta de otras 72 empresas de menor envergadura.

(5) Read out the above news items into your tape recorder at a moderate speed. Play them back one at a time, make notes for them, and try to orally reproduce the gist of each item from your notes, first in the same language, then in a language other than the source language. Record your performance and check it against the original for accuracy and completeness. Repeat this exercise regularly with other news items of your choice from recent newspapers, in each of your languages.

(6) (a) The following is a simplified passage on HIV/Aids written for a high-school audience. Read it out into your tape recorder at a moderate speed. Play it back, make notes, and try to orally reproduce the entire passage from your notes, first in the same language, then in your other languages. Record your performance and check it against the original for accuracy and completeness. While the wording may vary, all of the ideas should be present. Repeat the exercise at progressively faster speeds.

Le SIDA

Le SIDA est la phase finale d'infection par le virus VIH. Le virus attaque et affaiblit le système immunologique de la victime. Ainsi, certaines maladies qui normalement ne se manifesteraient pas, comme la pneumonie *Pneumocystis carinii* ou le sarcoma Karposi, peuvent menacer la vie du malade. Chez certaines personnes, le virus peut s'attaquer aux cellules du cerveau, précipitant des problèmes psychiatriques.

Selon les chiffres de l'OMS, environ 6,000 personnes sont contaminées par le VIH chaque jour. Le SIDA ou VIH peut être transmis de trois façons: transmission par les rapports sexuels; transmission par le contact direct avec le sang infecté, c'est à dire, lorsque des toxicomanes partagent des seringues, ou bien accidentellement durant des interventions médicales; et transmission par une femme infectée au foetus qu'elle porte, ou à son bébé. En 1991 il y avait environ 3 millions de femmes infectées en âge d'avoir des enfants, et les experts prévoient que, d'ici l'an 2000, il y aura entre 5 et 10 millions d'enfants en dessous de 5 ans porteurs du virus VIH.

Selon les dernières observations, environ 50% des personnes qui portent le virus tomberont malades du SIDA dans les 10 ans après la première infection.

Un aspect remarquable de cette maladie est le fait qu'une personne infectée de VIH peut vivre entre 2 et 12 ans sans symptômes. Donc, on peut être infecté sans le savoir, et ainsi transmettre le virus sans le savoir.

Le SIDA est une maladie inguérissable. Comme avec toute maladie inguérissable, la seule démarche logique est la prévention. Comment s'y prendre pour que cette maladie ne se répande pas?

Pour empêcher la transmission du virus, le contact sexuel avec toute personne qui porte la maladie ou qui pourrait la porter doit être évité. La méthode préventive la plus efficace est l'abstinence, ou de limiter le contact sexuel à une seule personne non-infectée.

L'éducation des gens dans les écoles et dans la communauté est devenue la stratégie principale pour éviter l'infection. Beaucoup d'écoles ont établi des cliniques de santé qui distribuent des prophylactiques aux étudiants. Mais ce programme est controversé car beaucoup de gens estiment que de discuter en classe l'emploi des méthodes contraceptives implique le consentement à la sexualité en dehors du mariage.

Empêcher l'abus des drogues et renseigner les toxicomanes sur le danger de ce virus est aussi une démarche importante pour contrôler l'épidémie. Parmi les mesures utilisées pour éduquer les toxicomanes sont des programmes d'information sur le sexe et la santé, aussi bien que des programmes permettant aux toxicomanes d'échanger leur seringue usée pour une nouvelle stérilisée.

Cependant, la stratégie idéale pour empêcher la propagation du SIDA devrait comprendre plusieurs volets: désamorcer la question, de façon à ce que l'on puisse en parler plus librement; persuader le public à ne pas pratiquer la discrimination contre ceux qui sont déjà atteints de la maladie; faire comprendre aux enfants, aussi bien qu'aux adultes, comment le SIDA se répand et comment ne pas l'attraper; et encourager les gens à obtenir régulièrement une prise de sang.

(b) Translate the above passage into English, Spanish or your other working languages. Using whichever version you prefer, do the following exercise step by step:
- Read out the entire passage aloud.
- Try to repeat the first full paragraph from memory, and record yourself. Play it back and check against the original. Jot down any errors and/or omissions.
- Try to repeat the first two full paragraphs from memory, and record yourself. Play it back and check against the original. Jot down any errors and/or omissions.
- Proceed as above through the entire passage.
- Examine the list of errors and/or omissions, and work out a notation sign or symbol that would enable you to quickly jot down each concept you missed or got wrong.
- Record the full passage at moderate speed, play it back, and make notes on it, using the new signs or symbols you have devised. Try to reproduce the full passage from your notes, and record yourself. Check yourself against the original.
- Repeat this exercise with other passages of your own choosing, trying gradually to use longer and more difficult ones.

(7) Create simple symbols to represent some of the common economic descriptors listed in Chapter 14 (p. 226). Try to draw pictures or symbols of some of the items listed in the 'potpourri' of figures of speech in Chapter 7 (pp. 81–89).

(8) Translate the following symbolic statements into verbal ones, first orally and then in writing:
- vlu £ = ¥ all '93 but in '94 ¥ > £
- ± 90% child ♥ choclt
- ± 95% UK ♥ tea
- In F wrkr mvmt united but in UK Lbour ÷ed

- Pres Bnk: Cttee reprt was music to ears!
- Pres Clint: Free "is crnstn of dmcy
- Pres Tuns: un-dev was #1 src of pol vlnce
- Bundsbnk Pres: If $ ^ +, we buy DM
- Bsnia Gen: We pro peace but n @ any prx!

(9) Create a symbol, sign or abbreviation for each of the frequently used technical concepts listed below. Update the list periodically by adding concepts you encounter in your work or reading. List your symbols on cards or on a separate sheet of paper and go over the list periodically to see whether you recognize them all and can restate them in each of your working languages.

ozone layer / ozone depletion / ozone hole / global warming / drift-net fishing / straddling fish stock / allowable catch / by-catch / highly migratory species / endangered species / climate change / geo-stationary orbit / remote sensing / epidemic / pandemic / endemic / chemical precursors / the green revolution / improved seed varieties / locust infestation / desertification / erosion / environmental degradation / ecosystem / dual-use technology / acid rain / new and renewable energy source / non-renewable resource / resource endowment / sustainable development / gene pool / genetic diversity / genetic engineering / ecology / cybernetics / cyberspace / electronic data processing (EDP, informatics) / robotics / optical fiber / enriched plutonium / nuclear fuel reprocessing / fast-breeder reactor / ultraviolet radiation / megaton / kiloton / megabyte / kilobyte / byte / sea level / real time / archipelagic state / small island state / least-developed country (LDC) / liquid crystal display (LCD) / air quality / emissions / effluents / mass transit / the demographic transition / superconductor / structural adjustment / structural unemployment / gross national product (GNP) / gross domestic product (GDP) / biomass / biomass energy / geothermal energy / photovoltaic energy conversion / the water table / groundwater / aquifer / arable land / nuclear power source / user-friendly / on-line / off-line / the information revolution / the information superhighway / local area network (LAN) / mainframe computer / central processing unit / server / national technical means / life expectancy / infant mortality / fertility / fecundity / morbidity / biodegradable / non-biodegradable / artificial intelligence / virtual reality / marginalization / digital

(10) To help extend your short-term memory, do the memory drill presented in Annex II at regular intervals.

Annex I: Additional Reformulation Strategies

Reformulation is expressing an idea in different words or in a different form so as to make it more concise, clear or manageable. There are many ways to do this. Several have already been covered in this book, e.g. general adverbial clauses (Chapter 5). The following are some additional reformulation strategies.

Using Appositives to Combine, Shorten and Clarify Sentences

An appositive is a noun, noun phrase or noun clause which follows a noun or pronoun and renames or describes it. In composition, appositives are often set off by pauses or commas. Appositives make it possible to avoid repeating certain words or phrases. An interpreter should learn to recognize and use appositives.

Example: The italicized words are appositives:
We visited the home of Herman Melville, *the author of <u>Moby Dick</u>*.
Our city hall, *that building on the corner*, was built in 1930.

Appositives can often be used to combine two or more sentences into one sentence that is relatively shorter, and often clearer. An appositive can usually go in different positions in the sentence, depending on the desired emphasis:

The city comptroller is Ed Smith. The city comptroller was appointed last year.
The city comptroller, Ed Smith, was appointed last year.
Ed Smith, the city comptroller, was appointed last year.
The city comptroller, appointed last year, is Ed Smith.

We received a flood of mail in April. April is the busiest month of the year.
We received a flood of mail in April, the busiest month of the year.
In April, the busiest month of the year, we received a floor of mail.

Exercise

Combine the following sentences using appositives.

- Your car's alternator is the round, gray device at the back of the engine. Your alternator is badly worn and needs replacing immediately.
- The documents from the hospital comprise all the evidence that the Defense has to offer. The Defense completed submission of its evidence today.
- Dr Jones is an experienced diplomat. Dr Jones led the negotiations to a successful conclusion.
- The headline of the story appears in bold capitals. The headline of the story is 'ALIENS INVADE EARTH!'

Using the Gerund to Create a Concise Subject Phrase

Sometimes the subject of a sentence may be a phrase conveying an abstract idea, a situation or a description, such as '**The sight of the children at play** made me happy.' If that phrase seems wordy or awkward, try reformulating the phrase with a gerund (-ing) instead: '**Seeing the children play** made me happy.' Such a gerund phrase can also be personalized by using a possessive adjective: '**When we eat** too much candy, it worries Mom.' > '**Our eating** too much candy worries Mom.'

Example:
'**The fact that we are based** in Rio provides an excellent opportunity to educate legal and business professionals in the region about the full range of our services.'
'**Being based** in Rio provides us an excellent opportunity to educate legal and business professionals in the region about the full range of our services.'

Exercise

Rewrite the following sentences more concisely by using a gerund phrase instead of the phrase in bold.

- **When we responded to his letter** with more details, it gave rise to a long exchange of correspondence.

- **Since she was late for work several times** during the month, it prompted her supervisor to have a word with her.
- **The tendency to drink too much** coffee during working hours is what gives many people insomnia.
- **If you show trust in your fellow players**, it will build up team spirit.
- **The determination of whether or not** a claim is valid is the task that takes longest.
- **The preparation and division into batches** of all the letters took several days.
- **When the trawler caught too much fish**, it caused the coast guard to issue a citation.
- **The dissolution of the company and the return of assets** to the partners took a year.
- **You asked her the same question three times** and that is what annoyed her.
- **The maintenance of an unyielding position** by the conservative party is what brought about the failure of the negotiations.
- **The disruption of the proceedings by the defendant** prompted the judge to adjourn the hearing.

Avoiding Nominalizations

The key word in a sentence or phrase is usually the verb. In English, the purest verb form is the base verb, like *decide, complain, buy, state*. This form of the verb is clear and concise. It usually gives a simpler structure to a sentence or phrase. Try to avoid turning base verbs into nouns, like *decision, complaint, purchase, statement*. If an SL sentence contains many nouns, the TL rendition in English will usually be clearer and shorter if you turn some of those nouns into verbs. Similarly, avoid using abstract nouns (such as 'validity') when the corresponding adjective ('valid') will convey the meaning.

Example:
The applicant should **make a decision** about whether he is filing his claim under Case ABC or Case XYZ.
The applicant should **decide** whether he is filing his claim under Case ABC or Case XYZ.

The submission of proper documentation will show the **validity** of your case.
Submitting proper documents will show that your case is **valid**.

Give us the date on which you **made the purchase** of the vehicle.
Give us the date when you **bought** the vehicle.

Exercise

Clarify the following by using verbs for the words in bold.

- They should clarify the reason why they are **lodging an appeal**.
- Please make clear whether **it is your intention** to appeal this determination.
- **Producing an improvement** in our educational system **has as a requirement** the **termination** of sub-standard curricula.
- **In the event of your refusal** to **effect a modification** of your position on this issue, we will **be led to the conclusion** that **the completion** of the contract with your company is impossible.
- Please **send a statement** of why we should **perform a correction** of the calculation. You should **make a submission** of your personal contact information and **provide documentation** of the purchases you reported.

Avoiding Strings of Prepositional Phrases

Too many prepositional phrases in a sentence can be confusing, both to the interpreter trying to keep ideas clear in his mind and to the audience listening to him. Try to rephrase such sentences in a simpler way, with fewer prepositions, or to break up the sentences into shorter ones.

Example:
Confusing: The November 20 deadline **for** submitting printed application forms **in** response to the notice you received **from** us **by** mail also applies **to** applicants who wish to file their applications **by** e-mail.
Better: The deadline for submitting applications in response to the notice, both on paper and by e-mail, is November 20.

Confusing: In entering information **on** the form, please place names **within** the boxes indicated **for** that purpose and not **over** the lines with legends **beneath** them.

Better: When filling in the form, please write names in the boxes, not on the lines.

Exercise

Simplify and clarify the following sentences by using fewer prepositional phrases.

- One of the objectives in our policy statement on the development of customer relations skills in the campaign for business expansion is putting transparency in tone over persuasiveness in content.
- While considerable progress has been made over the last two years on training within departments and, more recently, in support of external training on the Internet, a number of new technical and policy issues have come up in the cross-departmental training and online information access context.
- Declining prices in the market for health insurance products is of concern to the industry, due to increases in the costs of covered prescription drugs and doubts over the effectiveness of alternative medications sold over the counter.
- As more students in the department find their grades coming out under the passing mark after going through the statistics course in the spring semester after the first year, they give up on the program and drop out of the running before getting over the hump.

Keeping Modifiers Close to the Words They Modify

Just as it is important in writing to express ideas clearly, it is important for an interpreter to keep the speaker's ideas clear in her mind and convey them with equal clarity in the target language. One important aspect of this is the proper use of modifiers, which should be kept close to the words they modify.

Exercise

Read the correct wording (in italics), then explain why the alternatives are incorrect or misleading.

Don't process these applications until we have finished formatting them. *The applications to be processed must* **first** *be put into the proper format.*

- The applications processed **first** must be put into the proper format.
- The **first** applications to be processed must be put into the proper format.

The settlement terms were complicated and the parties were confused. *All the explanatory documents they received were wrong.*

- The explanatory documents they received were **all** wrong.

Don't pay these claims yet. *If claims are filed **late**, we cannot pay them without the company's approval.*

- We cannot pay claims **late** without company approval.
- We cannot pay **late** claims without company approval.

*We **randomly** sampled invoices from the database and checked them for errors.*

- We sampled invoices from the database and checked them for errors **randomly**.
- We sampled invoices from the database **randomly** and checked them for errors.

Exercise

Rephrase the sentences below, putting modifiers in their proper place and making clear who is doing what.

Example: Running along the back fence, Grandma chased the cat. > Grandma chased the cat that was running along the back fence.

- Estimating the losses for the incidents, Cathy's computer crashed.
- While buying gas at the gas station Phil's car broke down.
- Eating cookies in bed, Mom said I would not do a good job on my homework.
- Answering calls from clients put on hold, they got impatient and hung up.
- With insufficient postage, the packages did not reach the addressees.
- Forgetting the batteries, the calculator did not work.
- Kept after working hours, the boss said he would be paid overtime.
- 'The lawsuit accused the Wall Street banks of netting huge profits during the technology boom of the late 1990s by artificially inflating the share prices through various means of newly public companies after they went public.' (*New York Times*, 2006)

Annex II: Memory Drill

This exercise, which is said to help strengthen short-term memory, can be done by two interpreters working together.

Make a list of 50 words chosen at random (e.g. from various pages of a dictionary or newspaper). The list should include different parts of speech (nouns, verbs, adjectives, adverbs, etc.) and words of varying length and difficulty. If written on index cards, these can be shuffled and re-used in a different random order.

Person A reads out the first five words from the list at the rate of approximately one word every two seconds. Person B has to repeat the complete list of words in the same order.

Person A puts an X next to each mistake (wrong word or wrong order). If Person B succeeds with five words, the number of words is increased to six, and so forth.

The drill goes on until Person B can recite all 50 words correctly, or until he reaches his maximum recall without errors. Then A and B exchange places.

Variation 1

Same as above, except that Person A does not read out the whole list each time. He reads out only the one additional word, and Person B is expected to recall the whole list plus the additional word.

Variation 2

Same as above, except that Person A does not read out the whole list each time. He reads out only two, or three, or four additional words, etc., and Person B is expected to recall the whole list plus the additional words.

Variation 3

Same as above, except that the list of words is taken from different languages, or from a particular subject area, such as economics, science, law or medicine, or from vocabulary of a particular type, such as jargon, formalities, technical terms, figures of speech, proper names, numbers, etc.

Variation 4

Same as above, except that the words are read out faster, for example one per second, or at an accelerating rate, or at fluctuating rates.

Variation 5

Same as above, except that Person B is allowed to take notes.

Variation 6

Same as above, except that Person B has to remember every other word, or every third word, or every fourth word, etc.

Annex III: Patterns in Speech

One of the hallmarks of a good interpreter or note-taker is the ability to adjust to the organizational pattern of the speech. Just as writers use patterns to structure and organize the material they are writing about, speakers also use patterns to structure a speech. For example, a speaker may use the inductive pattern – that is, identify a number of incidents and then draw a conclusion from them. Different source-language patterns permit an interpreter to render the message in the target language in different ways, sometimes allowing greater flexibility. This is important because it is generally more difficult to interpret in linear fashion. The following are some of the more commonly used speech patterns.

Cause and Effect

Consider the following statements:

The nail is bent; you cannot hammer it in.
You cannot hammer in that nail, it's bent.
Because the nail is bent, you cannot hammer it in.
You cannot hammer the nail in because it is bent.
That bent nail can't be hammered in.
Hammering in that bent nail is impossible.
Since the nail is bent, you cannot hammer it in.
You cannot hammer in that nail, as it is bent.
It's impossible to hammer in a bent nail.
Don't try to hammer in a bent nail.

In all 10 of these possible variants, the cause–effect relationship is clear regardless of whether the cause or the effect is stated first, and regardless of whether a logical connector (e.g. because, since, as) is used. In other words, the sequence is not important because the logical relationship comes through clearly from the contents of the two parts of the statement. When the logic of the pattern is this clear, the interpreter has greater flexibility in phrasing, re-phrasing or paraphrasing the TL statement.

General to Specific (deductive)

Consider the following statements:

Almost everyone at this hospital works late hours; for example, the nurses, nursing aides and anesthesiologists.
At this hospital, almost everyone, like nurses, nursing aides and anesthesiologists, works late hours.

Does the general statement have to come before the examples?

Specific to General (inductive)

Consider the following statements:

The nurses, nursing aides and anesthesiologists at this hospital work late hours; almost everyone works late hours.
Whether it's the nurses, nursing aides or anesthesiologists, almost everyone at this hospital works late hours.

Do the examples have to come before the general statement?

Simple Listing

Consider the following statements:

(a) Our branch employs three kinds of staff: editors, clerks and text-processors.
(b) The produce area features items like vegetables, fruits, nuts, salad mixes, salad dressings, etc.

If the list is exhaustive, as in (a), are you free to omit an item in the TL? If the list is illustrative, as in (b), would it be a serious error to omit an item?

Chronological

An interpreter should strive in the TL rendition to keep a series of items in the same order if they refer to a chronological sequence, that is a series of steps. But note that events or past time periods are sometimes referred to in order of importance or relevance and the TL rendition in that case need not necessarily be linear, the important thing being not to leave out any items.

Consider the following statements:

(a) Our gallery features mediaeval, renaissance and modern landscapes.
(b) Dr Smith will anesthetize you, make an incision, and remove your gall bladder.

Which statement actually describes a chronological sequence? Is it imperative to render the items in (a) in the same sequence? Would a TL rendition in reverse chronological order be equally satisfactory? Is it important to render the items in (b) in the same sequence?

Exercise

The following news report ranked the events by their newsworthiness. Reorganize it, putting the events in chronological order.

Port of Seattle commissioners gave the go-ahead Tuesday for the final $220 million needed to complete the third runway project at Sea-Tac Airport, approving the last piece of the $1.1 billion project. It has been a long time coming. After much wrangling with opposition, the port approved the initial plan in 1996, about a decade after the subject was first officially considered. In 1997, the commission authorized the third runway project's cost – at $587 million, due to be completed in 2004.

Classification

In a statement classifying items of a similar kind, the items can usually be rendered in the TL either in the same order or in a different order if it is easier to remember them that way. Consider the following statements:

This airfield allows fixed-wing and rotary-wing aircraft but **not balloons**.
This forest is a habitat for many insects, birds and lizards, but **few mammals**.
Our town has several Thai and Chinese restaurants but no **Vietnamese restaurants**.

Exercise

Recast the statements above, putting the phrase in bold at the beginning of the list.

Comparison/Contrast

Consider the following statements:

English spelling tends to be irregular while Spanish spelling is more consistent.
German pastry is heavy while French pastry is light.
Our seacoast is rainy but our hinterland is dry.

If the two parts of the comparison are on equal footing and of parallel construction, does it matter which one comes first in the TL rendition?

Thesis – example

Note that the logic of this speech pattern does seem to require a linear rendition; although paraphrases are possible, they would turn out to be wordier.
Consider the following statements:

Global warming seems to be affecting the weather, for example, more frequent flooding.
Travel has become more affordable; for example, airfares are getting cheaper.
We often run short of school supplies, such as pencils, erasers and notebooks.

Problem – solution

Consider the following statements:

With unemployment rising in the provinces, investment in agriculture is needed.
Investment in agriculture is needed to address rising unemployment in the provinces.
As unemployment rises in the provinces, what is needed is agricultural investment.

Note that the word order and sequence of phrases here implies a choice about emphasis. Since the last words in a sentence usually get the most attention, placing the solution or the problem at the end will give more emphasis to that element. Consequently, although paraphrases are possible, it is better to follow the speaker's sequence in order to respect her choice about which item to emphasize.

Annex IV: Political Discourse – Additional Exercise

Europe Divided Over Palestinian State, by Julio Godoy

BERLIN, 18 September 2011 (IPS) – Divisions that have **surfaced** within the European Union over recognition of the Palestinian Authority as an independent and **sovereign** state are unlikely to be resolved ahead of a **crucial** vote in the United Nations next week.

A two-state **settlement** is part of the **long-term** official EU line on the Palestinian–Israeli conflict. But while several European countries, led by France, are **partially** supporting the PA claim, four countries, particularly Germany, are likely to oppose the move.

Germany, Italy, the Netherlands and the Czech Republic are risking an open **schism** within the EU that would undermine the group's ability to **decisively** intervene in **conflicting** geopolitical issues. The European schism surfaced prominently at a meeting of EU foreign ministers in the Polish city Sopot on 3–4 September.

'European governments currently opposing recognition of a Palestinian **state** should reconsider their **attitude** and work instead within the EU framework to **pursue** the European line of consistently supporting a two-state settlement,' Muriel Asseburg, head of the research division on Middle East and Africa at the Berlin-based German institute for International and Security Affairs (SWP, after its German name), told IPS.

French foreign minister Alain Juppé called on his **peers** to act unanimously in order to ensure that 'neither Israel nor the PA suffers a **defeat**, nor the US be forced into isolated support of Israel.'

But Germany is **reluctant** to support the PA demand for recognition as an independent state. German foreign minister Guido Westerwelle said in Sopot that 'Germany has a particular responsibility towards Israel' as a **consequence** of the German Nazi persecution and obliteration of the European Jewish population during World War II. Asseburg points out that EU member states, including Germany, have supported 'the building of a Palestinian state with **considerable** financial and technical **assistance**' since the 1993 Oslo peace accords between the Palestinian Liberation Organization (PLO) and Israel.

'In 1999, towards the end of the end of the interim period agreed in Oslo, the EU announced that it would consider recognizing a Palestinian state "**in due course**",' Asseburg told IPS. 'The German government, the largest European **donor** to the Palestinians, agreed last May that the PA was already "operating above the **threshold** of a **functioning** state in key areas".'

Opposing the PA claim for statehood now would not only be inconsistent, but also represent 'a **severe** blow to EU credibility in the Arab world – and far beyond too.'

Juppé said at the foreign ministers' meeting that it would be a '**catastrophe**' if the PA gathers a favorable vote from a large majority of states at the UNGA, but such a vote be vetoed by the US at the United Nations Security Council (UNSC).

To avoid such a 'catastrophe', the French, supported by several European countries including Austria, Belgium, Finland, Luxemburg, Poland, Slovenia, Spain and Sweden, have been **persuading** the PA to seek an **upgrade** to observer **status** similar to that of the Vatican. A draft resolution for an upgrade would only require a simple majority in the 193-member General Assembly. But the United States and Israel's allies are expected to either vote against such a resolution or **abstain**.

Despite the small number of negative votes, however, the Palestinians are assured of the **enhanced** status in the General Assembly – if they decide to take that route. But the PA has so far rejected such **semantic** upgrading on the grounds that it would not bring any major change to its present **status**.

On Friday, Palestinian President Mahmoud Abbas announced PA plans to go for complete statehood, which is certain to be vetoed by the United States. Any draft resolution on statehood has to be approved by the Security Council (nine votes and no vetoes) and subsequently by a two-thirds majority in the General Assembly.

Westerwelle argued that the declaration of 'a **viable** Palestinian state can only be the result of negotiations' with Israel.

Asseburg says such an argument is not **sustainable**. The PA application for recognition 'can hardly be termed unilateral. What the PA actually wants is to **crystallize** the support of the international community and **internationalize** the resolution of the conflict.'

'Given that the peace process has made no **meaningful** progress since 1995, the US and the Middle East quartet (formed by the EU, Russia, the UN and the US government) have also been **discredited** as **mediators**,' Asseburg added. 'It is **high time** to find new ways to **arrive at** the two-state settlement.'

Sarah Hibbin, researcher at the Hotung programme for law, **human rights** and **peace building** at the School of Oriental and African Studies (SOAS) in London, says that a UN General Assembly vote declaring that it '**collectively recognized**' Palestine would be more **symbolic** than legal, if vetoed by the UNSC.

In a study on the legitimacy of the Palestinian **bid** for recognition as a sovereign state, Hibbin and other international law experts at the University of London noted that the PLO was **granted** observer status in the UN back in 1974, and was invited to participate in all sessions and attend all international conferences **convened** under the **auspices** of the UN.

This status granted the PLO a unique **position** in the UN with more **extensive** rights of participation than other entities participating in an observer capacity.

In 1998, the UNGA granted the Palestinian **representation** additional rights and **privileges** of participation. As consequence, Palestine is invited to participate in UNSC debates on the situation in the Middle East.

This status is similar to that accorded to UN member states not members of the UNSC, to participate in debates when the UNSC considers that the **interests** of those members are specially affected by a matter on its agenda.

The **overwhelming** majority of states formally recognize the PA or the PLO as the representative of the Palestinian people, and maintain bilateral relations, some to the **level** of full diplomatic **relations**. The PA also maintains permanent **representative** offices in more than 70 countries. More than 114 nations recognized Palestine following its 1988 Declaration of Independence. Palestine has observer status in international organizations such as UNESCO and the World Health Organization, and is a full member of the Non-Aligned group, the Islamic Conference, the Group of 77 and China, and the League of Arab States.

Bibliography

Works Consulted

The following were consulted in the preparation of this book.

Asimov, Isaac (1971) *Treasury of Humor*. Boston, MA: Houghton Mifflin.

Crystal, David (1971) *Linguistics*. London: Penguin Books.

Garretson, Deborah A. (1981) A psychological approach to consecutive interpretation. *Meta* 26 (3), September.

Gémar, Jean-Claude (1990) La traduction est-elle civilisatrice? Fonctions de la traduction et degrés de civilisation. *Meta* 35 (1).

Herbert, Jean (1952) *Manuel de l'interprète*. Geneva: University of Geneva.

Johnson, Samuel (1779) *Lives of the English Poets: Dryden*. London: Faber & Faber.

Miller, George A. (1981) *Language and Speech*. New York: W.H. Freeman.

Rheingold, Howard (1988) *They Have a Word For It*. Los Angeles: Jeremy P. Tarcher/St Martin's Press.

Rozan, Jean-François (1956, 1970, 1973) *La prise de notes en interprétation consécutive*. Geneva: Georg.

Strang, Barbara (1968) *Modern English Structure*. London: Arnold.

Illustrative Materials Used

The following are quoted or excerpted in the exercises to illustrate features of language, aspects of oratory or problems of translation and interpretation.

Speeches

Batalla, Hugo, Vice-President of the Republic of Uruguay. Address, UN 50th Anniversary, 1995.

Bazoum, Mohamed, Minister of Foreign Affairs and Co-operation of the Republic of Niger. Address, UN 50th Anniversary, 1995.

Camacho-Omiste, Edgar. Statement on behalf of the President of the Republic of Bolivia, Mr Gonzalo Sánchez de Lozada. UN 50th Anniversary, 1995.

Castro Ruz, Fidel, President of the Republic of Cuba. Address, UN 50th Anniversary, 1995.

Castro Ruz, Fidel, President of the Republic of Cuba. Speech, Abyssinian Baptist Church, New York, 22 October 1995.

Clinton, Hillary Rodham. Address, UN Fourth World Conference on Women, Beijing, China, 5 September 1995.

Fujimori, Alberto. 'A United Nations for the 21st Century', message and greetings of the President of the Republic of Peru, UN 50th Anniversary, 1995.

George, Lloyd. Speech, London, 19 September 1914.

González, Felipe, President of Spain and President of the European Union. Address, UN 50th Anniversary, 1995.

Gorbachev, Mikhail. Speech, 19th Conference of the Communist Party of the Soviet Union, 1 July 1988.

Jackson, Robert H. Opening address, Nuremberg War Crimes Tribunal.

John Paul II. Address to UN Staff, 5 October 1995.

Kennedy, John F. Speech, American University, Washington, 10 June 1963a.

Kennedy, John F. Statement, UN General Assembly, 25 September 1963b.

Kinkel, Klaus. Speech, UN General Assembly, 25 September 1996.

Lincoln, Abraham (1991a) Perpetuation of our political institutions. In A. Lincoln, *Great Speeches*. New York: Dover Books.

Lincoln, Abraham (1991b) The presidential question. In A. Lincoln, *Great Speeches*. New York: Dover Books.

Lincoln, Abraham (1991c) Address at Cooper Institute. In A. Lincoln, *Great Speeches*. New York: Dover Books.

Ouellet, André, Minister of Foreign Affairs of Canada. Statement, 50th session of the UN General Assembly. Official Records, A/50/PV7.

Rabin, Yitzhak, Prime Minister of Israel. Address, peace rally, Tel Aviv, 4 November 1995 (trans. Reuters).

Wilson, Woodrow. Speech, Pueblo, Colorado, 25 September 1919.

Wilson, Woodrow. Speech upon entry of the United States into World War I.

Zéroual, Liamine, President of the People's Democratic Republic of Algeria. Address, UN 50th Anniversary, 1995.

Books

Azorín (1958) *De un transeúnte*. Madrid: Espasa-Calpe.

Benedetti, Mario (1992) *La Borra del café*. Montevideo: Arca.

Einstein, Albert (1949) The Disarmament Conference of 1932. In A. Einstein, *The World As I See It*. New York: Philosophical Library.

ILO (International Labour Organization) (1995) *Seguridad Social*. Geneva: ILO.

La Fontaine (1962) *Fables Choisies Mises en Vers*. Paris: Classiques Garnier.

Montanelli, Indro (1959) *Storia di Roma*. Milan: Rizzoli; translated by Pruna, Domingo (1969) *Historia de Roma*. Barcelona: Ediciones G.P.

Montesquieu (1734) *Considérations sur les causes de la grandeur des Romains et leur décadence*.

Newman, Edwin (1962) The vicious cycle of reality. In Art Moger (ed.) *The Complete Pun Book*. Secaucus, NJ: Citadel Press.

Schlesinger, Arthur (1973) *The Imperial Presidency*. Boston, MA: Houghton Mifflin.

Taylor, Telford (1992) *The Anatomy of the Nuremberg Trials*. New York: Little, Brown & Co.

Triolet, Elsa (1959) *Luna Park*. Paris: Gallimard.

Valladao, Alfredo (1992) La Guerre du Golfe en chiffres. In *L'état du monde: annuaire économique et géopolitique mondial.* Paris: Editions La Découverte.

Yutang, Lin (1960) *Translations from the Chinese.* Cleveland, OH: World Publishing.

Articles

Amalric, Jacques (1996) Vengeance et justice. *Libération* (Paris), 27 February.

Asahi Shimbun, Swimming against the current. *Asahi Shimbun* (Tokyo).

Bejarano, José, Bullfighting makes a comeback. *La Vanguardia* (Spain).

Bissonette, Lise (1995) Non, le Québec n'a pas perdu! *Le Devoir* (Montréal), November; (trans. James Nolan, 'No, Quebec Didn't Lose', 6 December 1995).

Chipaux, Françoise, An ill-fated union. *Le Monde* (Paris).

Christenfeld, Timothy (1996) Alien expressions. *The New York Times*, 10 March.

El Comercio/Wall Street Journal Americas, 19 July 1995.

Conason, Joe (1995) Police mayor in fire city. *The Nation* (USA), 18 December.

(1995) *Courrier International*, 261, 2–8 November.

Dizdarevic, Zistko (1995) Sarajevo: what can we do to help out the west? *Courrier International*, 1–7 June.

Dulac, Clémence, Fleecing the jobless. *Le Figaro Magazine* (Paris).

Earth Times.

Egurbide, Peru (1996) La Padania, ¿dónde está? *El País*, 19 May.

Ganda, Koï Pierrot, L'insoutenable prix de l'écrit. *N'Djamena Hebdo* (N'Djamena).

Giscard d'Estaing, Valéry (1995) Algeria: at arm's length. *L'Express* (Paris), 2 November.

Hamilton, David (1988) Another Option. *Opera News*, May.

Hannart, Max (1994) Global wheat shortage. *La Libre Belgique*, 29 December.

Hedges, Chris (1994) How Yemen is coming undone. *The New York Times*, 29 May.

Magga, O.H. (1995) Interview. *UNESCO Sources* 74, November.

Marshall, Eliot (1996) Funding crisis grips genome research. *Science* 273, 16 August.

Le Monde (1994) Le Yemen réunifié par les armes. *Le Monde* (Paris), 9 July.

Le Monde (1995a) *Le Monde* (Paris), 25 October.

Le Monde (1995b) South African conglomerates. *Le Monde* (Paris), 25 October.

Le Monde (1995c), *Le Monde* (Paris), 29 November.

Mount, Joe (1995) Reprieving the debt. *Urban Lawyer* 27 (3), Summer.

Ndir, Mansour (1994) Can South Africa avoid IMF shock therapy? *Jeune Afrique Economie* (Paris), November.

New York Times (1994) Lost in translation. *The New York Times*, 28 September.

New York Times (1995a) *The New York Times*, 5 March.

New York Times (1995b) *The New York Times*, 30 November.

New York Times (1995c) *The New York Times*, 1 December.

New York Times (1996a) *The New York Times*, 7 January.

New York Times (1996b) *The New York Times*, 9 January.

New York Times (1996c) *The New York Times*, 14 January.

New York Times (2006) *The New York Times*, 12 June.

Noblecourt, Michel (1993) Paradoxes et records. *Le Monde: Bilan Economique et Social 1993* (Paris).

Nordell, Göran, The lyricism of Same. *Stockholm News.*

Paoletti, Françoise, The Suez Canal. *Jeune Afrique Economie* (Paris).

Richter, Claudia (1995) The slave route: a new tourist attraction? *Die Presse* (Vienna), 2 September.

Rubio, Luis (1992) El Dilema Liberal. *Vuelta* (Mexico), October.
Rukeyser, Louis (1994) *Wall Street Week* 2427, 30 December.
Schori, Pierre (2002) What we need is a cooperative America. *The International Herald Tribune*, 6 August.
Simonnot, Philippe (1995) Hypercapitalisme américain. *Le Monde* (Paris), 1 December.
Singer, Daniel (1995) Election '95: Fractured France. *The Nation* (USA), 29 May.
Slama, Alain-Gérard (1995) Le nostra culpa du Président. *Le Point* (Paris), 22 July.
Tolotti, Sandrine (1995) Le cancer mondial. *Croissance* (Paris), April.
UN Chronicle (2002) Global warming'. *UN Chronicle* 4.
UNEP (United Nations Environment Programme) (1993) *Industrial Development* 16 (4), October–December.
Wall Street Journal Americas, 19 July 1995.

Other

British Media Review. British Information Services, 18 January 1996.
Diploma de Español como Lengua Extranjera, practice test. Education Office, Embassy of Spain, 1995.
Eurecom (Monthly Bulletin of European Union Economic and Financial News) EU Economic Outlook for 1996–97, December 1995.
News Highlights from the South African Media 03/96, 11–16 January 1996.
Proceedings of the International Conference on Finance for Development, Monterrey, Mexico, 18–22 March 2002.
Proceedings of the Wall Street Journal/Dow Jones Co. Annual Conference on the Americas, New York, 28–29 September 1995.
Treaty on intermediate-range missiles between the US and the USSR of 8 December 1987 (French version). *Désarmement* 11 (1), Winter 1987–1988, p. 209.
UNEP (United Nations Environment Program). News Release, 1996/49.

Resources

The following are suggestions for further reading, study and reference.

Articles and Documents

Adamopoulos, Spindon (1989) La spécialisation en interprétation. *Parallèles* 11, Fall.
Anon. (n.d.) *Interpreters: Occupational Outlook Reprint* No. 1875-130. Washington, DC: Superintendent of Documents, US Government Printing Office.
Anon. (n.d.) *Interpreters and Translators: Occupational Brief* (3rd edn), DOT 137.268.288. Moravia, NY: Chronicle Guidance Publications.
Bester, John (1991) The other art of the possible. *Japan Quarterly*, January–March.
Chaves, Jonathan (1976) Notes on the translation of a Chinese poem. In *Translation in the Humanities*. New York: State University of New York Press.
Chute, J.B. (1971) The necessity of translation. In *The World of Translation: Proceedings of the Conference on Literary Translation, New York, May 1970*. New York: P.E.N. American Center.
Daly, A.F. (1980) The growth of conference languages – is there a limit? *AIIC Bulletin* 3 (1), May.

Goleman, Daniel (1991) For stage fright, rehearsal helps. *The New York Times*, 12 June, C1.
Grosjean, Francois (2011) Those incredible interpreters. *Psychology Today*, blog of 15 September 2011.
Hedges, Chris (1990) In a polyglot place, the most welcome voices. *The New York Times*, 11 October.
Hewitt, Michael J. (1994) Language translating on the net. *Link-Up*, September–October, 20.
Hillenbrad, Barry (1989) Trying to decipher Babel. *Time*, 24 July, 62.
Horn, Pierre (1975) Vocational opportunities for foreign language students. *The Modern Language Journal* 59, 1–2 January.
James, Barry (1991) Interpreting: perils of palaver. *International Herald Tribune*, 11 January.
Macanderson, Andrew R. (1966) The hazardous art of mistranslation. *Harper's*, May, 94–102.
Malaurie, Philippe (1965) Le droit français et la diversité des langues. *Journal du Droit International* 92, 1–26.
Manguel, Alberto (1991) Prisoner in a modern Babel: The barriers to intimate glimpses and astounding revelations. *World Press Review* (New York), November.
McCarney, Rosemary A. (1983) Language politics: doing business in Quebec. *International Lawyer* 17, 553.
Nolan, James (2010) Translatability and untranslatability in simultaneous interpretation (or overcoming the mot juste syndrome). *ATA Chronicle*, July, 25.
Rabassa, Gregory (1971) The ear in translation. In *The World of Translation: Proceedings of the Conference on Literary Translation, New York, May 1970* (p. 82). New York: P.E.N. American Center.
Teichmann, Hans, T. General aspects of translatability. *Parallèles* 11, Fall 1989.
Waldman, Peter (1994) Message lost in translation: population conference adopts U.S.-supported concepts that remain foreign in every sense of the word. *The Globe and Mail*, 14 September.
Winston, Richard (1950) The craft of translation. *The American Scholar* 19 (2), 179–186.
Winter, Werner (1961) Impossibilities of translation. In W. Arrowsmith and R. Shattuck (eds) *The Craft and Context of Translation*. New York: Doubleday.

Books

Albertini, J.-M. (1971) *Les rouages de l'économie nationale*. Paris: Éditions économie et humanisme.
Archer, Peter (1956, 1963) *The Queen's Courts*. London: Penguin.
Bertrand, Raymond (1971) *Economie financière internationale*. Paris: P.U.F.
Charlot, J. (1968) *Les Anglais devant la loi*. Paris: Armand Colin.
Clark, Herbert H. and Clark, Eve V. (1977) *Psychology and Language: An Introduction to Psycholinguistics*. New York: Harcourt Brace Jovanovitch.
Colin, Joan and Morris, June (1996) *Interpreters and the Legal Process*. Winchester: Waterside Press.
De Jongh, Elena M. (1992) *An Introduction to Court Interpreting: Theory and Practice*. New York: Lanham.
Delattre, J., Vernisy, G. and Schwarz, R.P. (1961) *The Economy Through Boom and Slump: A Short French–English Dictionary*. Geneva: Georg.
Delisle, Jean. (1993) *La traduction raisonnée: manuel d'initiation à la traduction professionnelle de l'anglais vers le français*. Ottawa: University of Ottawa Press.

Delisle, Jean and Woodsworth, Judith (eds) (1995) *Translators Through History*. Amsterdam, PA: John Benjamins; French version: *Les traducteurs dans l'histoire*.

Edwards, Alicia Betsy (1995) *The Practice of Court Interpreting*. Amsterdam, PA: John Benjamins.

Edwards, John (1994) *Multilingualism*. London: Penguin Books.

Epping, Randy Charles (1992) *A Beginner's Guide to the World Economy*. New York: Random House.

Gaiba, Francesca (1998) *The Origins of Simultaneous Interpretation: the Nuremberg Trial*. Ottawa: University of Ottawa Press.

Gallais-Hamonno, Janine (1971, 1974) *The Language of Macroeconomics* (2nd edn). Paris: Dunod.

Gile, Daniel (1995) *Basic Concepts and Models for Interpreter and Translator Training*. Amsterdam & Philadelphia: John Benjamins.

Gillies, Andrew (2004) *Conference Interpreting: A New Students' Companion*. Cracow: Tertium.

González, Roseann D., Vásquez, Victoria F. and Mikkelson, Holly (1991) *Fundamentals of Court Interpretation: Theory, Policy and Practice*. Durham, NC: Carolina Academic Press.

Hattenhauer, Hans (1987) *Conceptos fundamentales del derecho civil*. Barcelona: Ariel; Spanish translation by Gonzalo Hernández of Hattenhauer, H. (1982) *Grundbegriffe des bürgerlichen Rechts*. Munich: H. Beck'sche Verlagsbuchhandlung.

Hayakawa, S.I. (1962) *The Use and Misuse of Language*. Greenwich, CT: Fawcett.

Herbert, Jean (1952, 1966) *Manuel de l'interprète: comment on devient interprète de conférence*. Geneva: Editions Georg; also Dutch (1968), English (1952, 1968), and German (1952) translations.

Hibbitt, George W. (ed.) (1965) *The Dolphin Book of Speeches*. New York: Doubleday.

James, Philip S. (1989) *Introduction to English Law* (12th edn). London: Butterworths.

Lambert, Sylvie and Moser-Mercier, Barbara (eds) (1994) *Bridging the Gap: Empirical Research in Simultaneous Interpretation*. Ottawa: University of Ottawa/University of Geneva.

Lefranc, A. and Sladen E. (1981) *The World of Commerce*. Paris: Gallimard.

Leliard, J.D.M. (1968) *Terminologie judiciaire*. Anvers: Uitgeverij S.M. Ontwikkeling.

MacNeil, Robert (1990) *Wordstruck*. London: Penguin.

Martienssen, Anthony (1953) *Crime and the Police*. London: Penguin.

Merryman, John Henry (1969) *The Civil Law Tradition: An Introduction to the Legal Systems of Western Europe and Latin America*. Stanford, CA: Stanford University Press.

Miller, George A. (1973) *Communication, Language, and Meaning*. New York: Basic Books.

Morris, Marshall (1995) *Translation and the Law*. ATA Scholarly Monograph Series, VIII. Amsterdam, PA: John Benjamins.

New York State Bar Association (1993) *The Courts of New York: A Guide to Court Procedures, with a Glossary of Legal Terms*. New York: NYSBA.

Obst, Harry (2010) *White House Interpreter – The Art of Interpretation*. Bloomington: Author House.

Radcliffe, Geoffrey and Cross, Geoffrey (1971) *The English Legal System*. London: Butterworth.

Ritchie, Graeme and Moore, James (1931) *Translation from French*. London: Cambridge University Press.

Robinson, Marshall A., Morton, Herbert C. and Calderwood, James D. (1956, 1967) *An Introduction to Economic Reasoning*. Garden City, NY: Doubleday.

Rónai, Paulo (1976) *Guía práctico de traducao francesa* (2nd edn). Rio de Janeiro: EDUCOM.

Rozan, Jean-François (1956, 1970, 1973) *La prise de notes en interprétation consécutive*. Geneva: Georg.

Samuelson, Paul A. (1976) *Economics* (3rd edn). International Student Edition. Tokyo: McGraw Hill Kogakusha.

Schibsbye, Knud (1969) *A Modern English Grammar*. London: Oxford University Press.

Seleskovitch, Danica (1978) *Interpreting for International Conferences*. Washington, DC: Pen and Booth.

Steiner, George (1975) *After Babel*. London: Oxford.

Trabig, Eta (1979) *Manual for Judiciary Interpreters: English–Spanish*. Houston, TX: Agri-Search International.

Trudgill, Peter (1974) *Sociolinguistics: An Introduction*. Middlesex: Penguin.

Truffaut, Louis (1974) *Exercises de stylistique*. Munich: Hueber Verlag.

Vinay, J.-P. and Darbelnet, J. (1958, 1996) *Stylistique comparée du français et de l'anglais*. Paris: Didier; English version: Juan C. Sager and M.-J. Hamel (trans. & ed.) (1995) *Comparative Stylistics of French and English: A Methodology for Translation*. Amsterdam, PA: John Benjamins.

Weldon, T.D. (1953) *The Vocabulary of Politics*. Baltimore, MD: Penguin Books.

Collections of Essays, Monograph Series, and Conference Proceedings

American Translators Association. Scholarly Monograph Series. Published periodically at the State University of New York at Binghamton by the Center for Research in Translation.

Arrowsmith, William and Shattuck, Roger (eds) (1964) *The Craft and Context of Translation: A Critical Symposium*. Garden City, NY: Doubleday.

Balibar-Mrabli, Antoinette (1995) *Langue Française*, No. 105, février. Paris: Larousse.

Crawford, James (1992) *Language Loyalties: A Source Book on the Official English Controversy*. Chicago, IL and London: University of Chicago Press.

P.E.N. (1971) *The World of Translation: Papers delivered at the Conference on Literary Translation held in New York City in May 1970 under the auspices of P.E.N. American Center*. New York: P.E.N.

Dictionaries, Glossaries and Thesauruses

An effort has been made to include here a cross-section of dictionaries and glossaries which can be especially useful to conference and court interpreters. However, because they would be too numerous to list, this section for the most part omits dictionaries of quotations, dictionaries of synonyms and antonyms, geographical and place-name dictionaries, dictionaries of abbreviations and acronyms, and specialized technical dictionaries.

Aglion, Raoul (1947) *Dictionnaire juridique anglais-français*. New York: Brentano's and Librairie générale du droit et de jurisprudence.

Anderlo, Georges and Schmidt-Anderlo, Georgette (1979) *Delmas Business Dictionary: English–French, French–English* (2nd edn). Paris: Delmas & Cie.

Anon. (1964) *Petit Larousse* (19th edn). Paris: Larousse.

Anon. (1981) *Diccionario básico Espasa* (5 vols). Madrid: Espasa-Calpe.

Appleby, Barry Léon. (1980) *Elsevier's Dictionary of Commercial Terms and Phrases*. Amsterdam: Elsevier.

Atkins, Beryl T., Duval, Alain and Milne, Rosemary (1978) *Collins-Robert French–English and English–French Dictionary*. London: Collins.

Babcock Grove, Philip (ed.) (1966) *Webster's Third International Dictionary of the English Language, Unabridged*. Springfield, MA: G. & C. Merriam.

Banque de terminologie du Québec (BTQ) (n.d.) *Terminology Bulletins* on construction, electricity, tourism, etc. Québec: Editeur officiel du Québec.

Benmaman, Virginia, Connolly, Norma C. and Loos, Scott Robert (1991) *Bilingual Dictionary of Criminal Justice Terms (English/Spanish)* (2nd edn). Binghamton, NY: Gould Publications.

Bergeron, Léandre (1980) *Dictionnaire de la langue québécoise*. Montréal: VLB Editeur.

Bernard, Yves and Colli, Jean-Claude (1976) *Vocabulaire économique et financier* (3rd edn). Paris: Seuil.

Black, Henry Campbell (1968) *Black's Law Dictionary*. St Paul, MN: West.

Bladsoe, Robert L. and Boczek, Boleslaw A. (1987) *The International Law Dictionary*. Santa Barbara, CA and Oxford: ABC-CLIO.

Cabanellas de las Cuevas, Guillermo and Hoague, Eleanor C. (2001) *Diccionario Jurídico/ Law Dictionary (English/Spanish)* (2 vols). Buenos Aires: Editorial Heliasta.

Cabanellas de Torres, Guillermo (1979) *Diccionario jurídico elemental*. Buenos Aires: Heliastra.

Capitanat, Henri *et al.* (1930) *Vocabulaire juridique*. Paris: PUF; Spanish translation: Guaglianone, Aquiles Horacio (n.d.) *Vocabulario Jurídico*. Buenos Aires: Depalma.

Castillo, Carlos and Bond, Otto F. (1977) *University of Chicago Spanish Dictionary* (3rd edn). Chicago, IL: University of Chicago Press.

Corbeil, Jean-Claude and Archambault, Ariane (1987) *Visual Dictionary: French–English*. Montreal: Québec-Amérique.

Crabb, George (1966) *Crabb's English Synonyms*. London: Routledge and Kegan Paul.

Cuyas, Arturo (1956) *Appleton's Revised Cuyas Dictionary* (Spanish–English) (2 vols). New York: Grolier, Appleton-Century Crofts.

de Gámez, Tana, Forbath, Guido N. and Page, Clive D. (1975) *Simon and Schuster's Concise International Dictionary: English–Spanish, Spanish–English*. New York: Simon and Schuster.

Denoeu, François, Sices, David and Sices, Jacqueline B. (1982) *2001 French and English Idioms*. Woodbury, NY: Barron's.

Di Benedetto *et al.* (1977) *New Comprehensive Spanish–English/English–Spanish Dictionary*. Madrid: EDAF.

Dixson, Robert J. (1951) *Essential English Idioms in English for the Foreign-Born*. New York: Regents.

Dubois, Claude (ed.) (1979) *Dictionnaire encyclopédique Larousse*. Paris: Larousse.

Ehrlich, Eugene *et al.* (1980) *Oxford American Dictionary*. New York/Oxford: Oxford University Press.

Flexner, Stuart and Flexner, Doris (1993) *Wise Words and Wives' Tales*. New York: Avon.

Fowler, W.S. (1972) *Dictionary of Idioms*. London: Nelson.

Freeman, William (1951, 1975) *A Concise Dictionary of English Idioms* (3rd edn). Boston, MA: The Writer Inc.

García-Pelayo y Gross, Ramón *et al.* (1983) *Gran Diccionario Español Inglés*. Paris: Larousse.

Gifts, Steven H. (1975) *Law Dictionary*. Woodbury: Barron's Educational Series.

González Gutierrez, Orlando (1971) *Diccionario de expresiones idiomáticas y modismos ingleses*. Buenos Aires: Editorial Universitaria de Buenos Aires.

Guarnieri, Juan Carlos (1977) *Diccionario del lenguaje rioplatense*. Montevideo: DLSA.

Guerrero, Antonio Perol (1942) *New Technical and Commercial Dictionary*. New York: Editorial Tecnica Unida.

Guillen, Raymond and Vincent, Jean (1988) *Lexique de termes juridiques*. Paris: Dalloz.

Guinagh, Kevin (1965) *Dictionary of Foreign Phrases and Abbreviations*. New York: Pocket Books.

Guralnik, David B. (ed.) (1984) *Webster's New World Dictionary: Second College Edition*. New York: Simon and Schuster.

Hammond, N.G.L. and Scullard, H.H. (1970) *The Oxford Classical Dictionary* (2nd edn). London: Oxford University Press.

Hathaway, D.E. (1985) *Harrap's French and English Science Dictionary*. London: Harrap.

Herbert, Jean (1962) *Conference Terminology* (2nd edn). Amsterdam: Elsevier.

Horn, Stefan (1965) *Glossary of Financial Terms*. Amsterdam: Elsevier.

Howatson, M.C. (1989) *The Oxford Companion to Classical Literature* (2nd edn). Oxford: Oxford University Press.

Kaplan, Steven M. (1993) *Wiley's English–Spanish and Spanish–English Legal Dictionary*. New York: Wiley Law Publications.

Kettridge, J.O. (1939, 1970) *French Idioms and Figurative Phrases* (2nd edn). London: Routledge & Kegan Paul.

Kleiser, Luis Martínez (1978) *Refranero general ideológico español*. Madrid: Hernado.

Laurendeau, Françoise, Pratt, Jane and Collin, Peter (1981) *Harrap's French and English Business Dictionary*. London and Paris: Harrap.

Little, William, Fowler, H.W. and Coulson, J. (1933. 1955) *The Oxford Universal Dictionary on Historical Principles*. London: Oxford University Press.

Malgorn, Guy (1972) *Dictionnaire technique anglais–français*. Paris: Gautheir-Villars.

Mansion, J.E. (1934, 1956) *Harrap's Standard French and English Dictionary* (2 vols). London: Harrap's.

Mansion, J.E. (1967, 1977) *Harrap's Modern College French and English Dictionary*. New York: Scribener's.

Mathews, Mitford M. (1951) *A Dictionary of Americanisms on Historical Principles*. Chicago, IL: University of Chicago Press.

Mawson, Sylvester (1975) *Dictionary of Foreign Terms*. New York: Thomas Y. Crowell.

McMoride, W. (1913, 1972) *English Idioms and How to Use Them* (3rd edn). London: Oxford University Press.

Mieder, Wolfgang (1986) *Encyclopedia of World Proverbs*. Englewood Cliffs, NJ: Prentice-Hall.

Mieder, Wolfgang, Kingsbury, Stewart A. and Harder, Kelsie B. (eds) (1992) *A Dictionary of American Proverbs*. New York and Oxford: Oxford University Press.

Mingot, Tomás de Galliana (1983) *Pequeño Larousse de ciencias y técnicas*. Buenos Aires: Larousse.

Moliner, María (1991) *Diccionario de uso del español*. Madrid: Gredos.

Monterde, Francisco (1976) *Diccionario Porrua de la lengua española* (9th edn). Mexico City: Porrua.

Morris-Brown, Vivien (1993) *The Jamaica Handbook of Proverbs*. Mandeville, Jamaica: Island Heart.

Nolan, James (2008) *Spanish–English/English–Spanish Pocket Legal Dictionary*. New York: Hippocrene Books.

Ortiz, Fernando (1985) *Nuevo catauro de cubanismos.* Havana: Editorial de Ciencias Sociales.

Pichardo, Esteban (1985) *Diccionario provincial y casi racionado de vozes y frases cubanas.* Havana: Editorial de Ciencias Sociales.

Pradez, E. (1970) *Dictionnaire des gallicismes les plus utilisés.* Paris: Payot.

Prieto, Jorge Mejía (1978) *Así habla el mexicano: diccionario básico de mexicanismos.* Mexico City: Panorama.

Proteau, Lorenzo (1982) *La Parlure québécoise.* Boucherville, Québec: Publications Proteau.

Real Academia Española (1984) *Diccionario de la lengua española* (2 vols). Madrid: Espasa-Calpe.

Renoux, Yvette (1970) *Glossary of International Treaties.* Amsterdam: Elsevier.

Robb, Louis A. *et al.* (1955) *Dictionary of Legal Terms: Spanish–English, English–Spanish.* New York: Wiley.

Robert, Paul (1971) *Dictionnaire alphabétique et analogique de la langue française* (6 vols). Paris: Société du Nouveau Littré.

Robert, Paul (1976) *Dictionnaire alphabétique et analogique de la langue française* (2 vols). Paris: Société du Nouveau Littré.

Rodale, J.I. (1978) *The Synonym Finder.* Emmaus, PA: Rodale Press.

Rofer, Francisco (1989) *Sinónimos españoles* (4th edn). Mexico City: Editores Mexicanos Unidos.

Roget, Peter Mark (1941) *Thesaurus of English Words and Phrases.* Cleveland, OH: World Publishing.

Rogive, Ernest (1965) *Le musée des gallicismes* (2nd edn). Geneva: Georg.

Rolland, Henri and Boyer, Laurent (1983) *Dictionnaire des expressions juridiques.* Lyon: L'Hermès.

Rosenzweig, Paul (1965) *The Book of Proverbs.* New York: Philosophical Library.

Roy-Debove, Josette and Gagnon, Gilberte (1980) *Dictionnaire des anglicismes.* Paris: Robert.

Santamaría, Andrés (1975) *Diccionario de sinónimos, antónimos e ideas afines.* Barcelona: Sopena.

Santamaría, Francisco J. (1983) *Diccionario de mejicanismos.* Mexico City: Porrua.

Saudibet, Tito (1978) *Vocabulario y refranero criollo.* Buenos Aires: Sainte-Claire.

Servotte, J.V. (1964, 1978) *Dictionnaire commercial et financier.* Brussels: Brepols/Antwerp: Marabout.

Sisson, A.F. (1978) *Sisson's Word and Expression Locator.* West Nyack, NY: Parker.

Smith, Colin, Marcos, Manuel B. and Chang-Rodríguez, Eugenie (1971, 1977) *Collins Spanish–English/English–Spanish Dictionary.* London/Glasgow: Collins.

Smith, William George (1970) *The Oxford Dictionary of English Proverbs.* London: Oxford University Press.

Thomson, Francis J. (1979) *Elsevier's Dictionary of Financial Terms.* Amsterdam: Elsevier.

Tracey, William R. (1991) *The Human Resources Glossary.* New York: Amarcom.

Trautman, Carl O. *The Language of Small Business.* Dover, NH: Upstart Publishing Co.

Tull Boatner, Maxine and Gates, John Edward (1975) *A Dictionary of American Idioms.* Woodbury, NY: Barron's.

United Nations, Department of Conference Services, Translation Division, French Service (1980) *Lexique général anglais–français, avec suppléments espagnol–français et russe–français* (2nd edn). New York: United Nations.

United Nations, Terminology and Reference Section (1999) *Development Glossary* (English–Spanish), Document TN/1999/1. New York: United Nations.

United States Department of State, Language Services Division (1976) *English–French Glossary*. Washington, DC: US Department of State.

University of Ottawa, Faculty of Law (1980) *Vocabulaire juridique bilingue canadien*. Ottawa: University of Ottawa Press.

Velásquez de la Cadena, Mariano *et al.* (1974) *New Revised Velásquez Spanish and English Dictionary*. Chicago, IL: Follet.

Wentworth, Harold and Berg Flexner, Stuart (1960) *Dictionary of American Slang*. New York: Crowell.

Whiting, Bartlett Jere (1989) *Modern Proverbs and Proverbial Sayings*. Cambridge, MA: Harvard University Press.

World Bank, Language Services Division (1981) *The World Bank Glossary: English, French, Spanish*. Washington, DC: World Bank.

Wyckoff, Peter (1973) *The Language of Wall Street*. New York: Hopkinson and Blake.

Handbooks of Usage

Alonso, Martín (1982) *Ciencia del lenguaje y arte del estilo* (12th edn). Madrid: Aguilar.

Etiemble (1964) *Parlez-vous franglais?* Paris: Gallimard.

Fowler, H.W. (1965) *A Dictionary of Modern English Usage*. London: Oxford University Press.

Gowers, Ernest (1948) *Plain Words*. London: Her Majesty's Stationery Office.

Gowers, Ernest (1975) *The Complete Plain Words*. London: Penguin.

Grevisse, Maurice (1969) *Le Bon Usage*. Paris: Hatier.

Hornby, A.S. (1954) *A Guide to Patterns and Usage in English*. London: Oxford University Press.

McArthur, Tom (ed.) (1992) *The Oxford Companion to the English Language*. Oxford: Oxford University Press.

Partridge, Eric (1947, 1973) *Usage and Abusage*. London: Penguin.

Thomas, Adolphe (1956) *Dictionnaire des difficultés de la langue française*. Paris: Larousse.

Directories and Guides

Congrat-Butlar, Stefan (ed.) (1979) *Translation and Translators: An International Directory and Guide*. New York and London: R.P. Bowker.

Harris, Brian and Kingscott, Geoffrey (eds) (1997) *Language International World Directory of Translation and Interpreting Schools*. Amsterdam: Language International/John Benjamins.

Hendry, J.F. (1969) *Your Future in Translating and Interpreting*. New York: Richard Rosen Press.

Honig, Lucille J. and Brod, Richard I. (1979) *Foreign Languages and Careers*. New York: MLA Publications.

Koek, Karin E. (ed.) (1989) *Encyclopedia of Associations: International Organizations* (2 vols). Detroit, MI: Gale Research.

Translation Research Institute (n.d.) *Translation Referral and Translation Services Directory*. Philadelphia, PA: Translation Research Institute.

UNESCO (1948–) *Index Translationum: Répertoire international des traductions/International Bibliography of Translations*. Paris: UNESCO Press.

Periodicals, Journals and Series

Abrates. Associaçao Brasileira de Tradutores, Brazil.

L'Antenne. Bulletin d'information de la Société des Traducteurs du Québec, Canada.

The ATA Chronicle. American Translators Association, USA.

Babel. International journal of translation – quarterly journal devoted to information and research in the field of translation. Akadémiai Kiadó, Budapest, Hungary.

Bulletin. Association suisse des traducteurs et interprètes.

Bulletin de l'Ecole de traducteurs et d'interprètes, University of Ottawa, Canada.

Equivalences. Institut Supérieur des Traducteurs et Interprètes, Bruxelles, Belgium.

Forum. International journal of interpretation and translation. Presses de la Sorbonne Nouvelle. Paris, France.

Författaren. Organ för Sveriges Författarförbund.

Incorporated Linguist. Journal of the Institute of Linguistics, UK.

informaATIO. Association of Translators and Interpreters of Ontario, Canada.

L'Interprète. Bulletin de l'association d'interprètes et traducteurs – Groupement des diplômés de l'Ecole de traduction et d'interprétation de l'Université de Genève, Genève, Switzerland.

Langue et société. Commissaire aux langues officielles, Ottawa, Canada.

Langues et linguistique. Département de langues et linguistique, Université de Laval, Canada.

Lebende Sprachen. Zeitschrift für fremde Sprachen in Wissenschaft und Praxis, zugleich Fachblatt des Bundesverbandes der Dolmetscher und Übersetzer, Berlin.

The Linguist. The Institute of Linguists, London, UK.

Le Linguiste. Organe de la Chambre Belge des Traducteurs, Interprètes et Philologues, Belgium.

Meta. Organe d'information et de recherche dans les domaines de la traduction, de la terminologie et de l'interprétation. Les Presses de l'Université de Montréal, Montréal, Canada.

Mitteilungsblatt. Österreicher Übersetzer- und Dolmetscherverband, Austria.

Mitteilungsblatt für Dolmetscher und Übersetzer. Germany.

Le mot. Centre de traduction et de terminologie juridique, Ecole de droit, Centre universitaire de Moncton, Canada.

Parallèles. Cahiers de l'Ecole de traduction et d'interprétation de l'Université de Genève, Genève, Switzerland.

PMLA: Publications of the Modern Language Association of America. New York, USA.

Representative American Speeches (annual). Owen Peterson (ed.), H.W. Wilson Co., New York, USA.

Revue de l'Association québécoise de linguistique. Québec, Canada.

Terminogramme. Bulletin de la Direction de la terminologie, Gouvernement du Québec, Office de la langue française, Québec, Canada.

Traduire. Revue française de la traduction – information linguistique et culturelle, Paris, France.

Il Traduttore. Rivista trimestrale a cura dell'Associazione Italiana Traduttori e Interpreti, Italy.

Translation News. International Translations Center, Delft, Netherlands.

Translation Review. The University of Texas at Dallas, Richardson, Texas, USA.

Translatoren. Translatorforeningen, Kobenhavn, Denmark.

Van Taal Tot Taal. Nederlands Genootschap van Vertalers, Netherlands.

Vital Speeches of the Day. A selection of speeches by prominent persons on current issues (twice monthly). City News Publishing, Mount Pleasant, South Carolina, USA.
Working Papers on Translatology. University of Ottawa, Canada.

Internet Resources

Speeches

Government of Spain: text & audio
http://www.la-moncloa.es/
http://www.spainun.org/pages/audio.cfm

President of France: text, audio, video
http://www.elysee.fr/president/accueil.1.html

President of Congo: French text
http://www.societecivile.cd/node.php?id=2710

French National Assembly
http://www.assemblee-nationale.fr/

French National Assembly, committee hearings: video
http://www.assemblee-nationale.tv/direct.html?flux=5

President of Lebanon: Spanish text
http://www.altapolitica.com/n109

President of Venezuela: Spanish text and video
http://www.rnv.gov.ve/noticias/index.php?act=ST&f=3&t=23495

US State Department video speeches
http://video.state.gov/

UK Prime Minister's speeches: texts
http://www.number10.gov.uk/news-type/speeches-and-transcripts/

Speeches of US presidents
http://cstl-cla.semo.edu/renka/modern_presidents/index.htm

Speech by President George Bush at UN: English text
http://www.un.org/webcast/summit2005/statements/usa050914.pdf
English video
http://www.un.org/webcast/summit2005/statements14.html

Speech by President Bill Clinton: English video
http://clinton4.nara.gov/WH/New/Europe-0005/speeches/20000602-1245.html

Speech by President Jimmy Carter: English video
http://www.youtube.com/watch?v=KCOd-qWZB_g

President Barack Obama speech in Berlin: English video
http://www.youtube.com/watch?v=Q-9ry38AhbU

President Barack Obama speech in Cairo: English video
http://www.youtube.com/watch?v=B_889oBKkNU

Text in other languages:
http://www.whitehouse.gov/blog/newbeginning/transcripts/

Language	Transcript
Arabic	Read
Chinese	Read
Dari	Read
French	Read
Hebrew	Read
Hindi	Read
Indonesian	Read
Malay	Read
Pashto	Read
Persian	Read
Portuguese	Read
Punjabi	Read
Russian	Read
Turkish	Read
Urdu	Read

President Barack Obama Nobel lecture: English video
http://www.youtube.com/watch?v=AORo-YEXxNQ&feature=related

President of Germany speech to Knesset
German video
http://www.ipernity.com/doc/fredw/2086966

Spanish text
http://www.raoulwallenberg.net/?es/interfe/interconf/100104.htm

European Commission webcast portal
http://webcast.ec.europa.eu/eutv/portal/index.html

President Nelson Mandela inaugural address: English video
http://www.youtube.com/watch?v=grh03-NjHzc

President Nestor Kirchner inaugural address: Spanish video
http://vimeo.com/22973522

President Alejandro Toledo: Spanish text
http://www.comunidadandina.org/prensa/discursos/toledo24-5-04.htm

Presidency of Mexico webcast
http://www.presidencia.gob.mx/multimedia/

Speech by President of Brazil: Portuguese video
http://www.youtube.com/watch?v=BkHzdx7KiUg

Speech by president of Central Bank of Brazil: Portuguese text
http://www.bcb.gov.br/pec/appron/apres/Febraban_Posse_Murilo_Portugal_17-03-11.pdf

President of China speech to UN World Summit: Chinese & English, video & text
http://www.un.org/webcast/summit2005/statements14.html

Emir of Qatar speech to UN World Summit: Arabic & English, video & text
http://www.un.org/webcast/summit2005/statements14.html

President of Brazil speech to UN World Summit: Portuguese video, English text
http://www.un.org/webcast/summit2005/statements14.html

President of Iran speech to UN World Summit: Farsi video, English text
http://www.un.org/webcast/summit2005/statements14.html

President of Korea speech to UN World Summit: Korean video, English text
http://www.un.org/webcast/summit2005/statements14.html

President of Russian Federation speech to UN World Summit: Russian & English video &
text
http://www.un.org/webcast/summit2005/statements15.html

Prime Minister of Turkey speech to UN World Summit: Turkish video, English text
http://www.un.org/webcast/summit2005/statements15.html

Prime Minister of Italy speech to UN World Summit: Italian video, English text
http://www.un.org/webcast/summit2005/statements15.html

Prime Minister of Israel speech to UN World Summit: Hebrew video, English text
http://www.un.org/webcast/summit2005/statements15.html

Foreign Minister of Serbia and Montenegro speech to UN World Summit: Serbian video,
English text
http://www.un.org/webcast/summit2005/statements15.html

Vice President of Vietnam speech to UN World Summit: Vietnamese video, English text
http://www.un.org/webcast/summit2005/statements15.html

Foreign Minister of Germany speech to UN World Summit: German video, English text
http://www.un.org/webcast/summit2005/statements15.html

President of Portugal speech to UN World Summit: Portuguese video, English text
http://www.un.org/webcast/summit2005/statements.html

Speech by President of Brazil: Portuguese video
http://www.youtube.com/watch?v=lY1KMrUMxKM&feature=related

President of Spain
Speech on G20 summit
http://www.youtube.com/watch?v=N1PIZZF0ALk
Speech to UN General Assembly
http://www.youtube.com/watch?v=SzCLwstqi3c
http://www.youtube.com/watch?v=vDPSeUQ4_70&feature=related

Dag Hammarskjold speech on UN Day 1954: English video
http://www.youtube.com/watch?v=HuppZpNG3kQ

Dag Hammarskjold interview: Swedish video
http://www.youtube.com/watch?v=m6JgVer7GD8&feature=related

Speeches of Margaret Thatcher: English texts, audio & video
http://www.margaretthatcher.org/speeches/default.asp

United Nations Webcast: current and archived audio & video speeches
http://www.unmultimedia.org/tv/webcast/

Press Conference by Russian Foreign Minister Lavrov – Russian video
http://www.blinkx.com/video/11-2008-part-2/NH9_IFUmbMieiMJQ8r5vvw

Speech by Russian President Medevedev – Russian video
http://www.blinkx.com/video/part-3/l-BouVxO7Sy6xvof9qpXBg

Press Conference by Russian Foreign Minister Lavrov – Russian video
http://www.blinkx.com/video/13-2008-part-1/85T3s4YayYsrD40ZuizkqQ

Famous speeches: audio
http://www.history.com/video.do?name=speeches

American Rhetoric speech bank: English audio & text
http://www.americanrhetoric.com/speechbank.htm

UCB Audio Speeches Library
http://www.lib.berkeley.edu/MRC/historicspeeches.html

Speeches in Urdu: video
http://www.google.com/search?q=speeches+in+urdu&tbo=p&tbm=vid&source=vgc
    &hl=en&aq=9&oq=+speeches

Speeches in Hindi: video
http://www.youtube.com/view_play_list?p=B060556A2D5CB96A

Speeches in Tamil: video
http://www.google.com/search?q=speeches+in+tamil&tbo=p&tbm=vid&source=vgc
    &hl=en&aq=6&oq=speeches+in+

Speech Tagalog: Benigno S. Aquino III, Third State of the Nation Address, July 23, 2012
    - Speech delivered at the Session Hall of the House of Representatives, Batasan
    Pambansa Complex, Quezon City
Audio:
http://www.youtube.com/watch?v=LtlS1Kp7aRM

UN Webcast, Human Rights Council: multilingual video
http://www.unmultimedia.org/tv/webcast/c/un-human-rights-council.html

World Economic Forum meeting in Dalian, 2011: video
http://www.weforum.org/events/annual-meeting-new-champions-2011

International Tribunal for the Law of the Sea webcast: video
http://www.itlos.org/index.php?id=39&L=1%2F

Consecutive interpretation by James Nolan of presentation by Dedé and Minou Mirabal at Middlebury College, Vermont, 6 November 2006: "Violence against Women and the Example of the Mirabal Sisters". Text and audio: http://middarchive.middlebury.edu/cdm4/item_viewer.php?CISOROOT=/diglectarc& CISOPTR=131&CISOBOX=1&REC=2

Interpreting Resources

Glendon School of Translation
http://www.glendon.yorku.ca/translation/
http://www.facebook.com/Glendon.School.of.Translation
http://www.glendon.yorku.ca/interpretation/

New York University Foreign Languages, Translation & Interpreting
http://www.scps.nyu.edu/areas-of-study/foreign-languages/

University of the Witwatersrand Language School
http://www.witslanguageschool.com/LanguageAreas/TranslationInterpreting.aspx

Nolan Seminars
http://www.facebook.com/media/set/?set=a.2580436870984.140280.1256307904& type=1&l=a6bd03a9a5

Association Internationale des Interprètes de Conférence
http://aiic.net/

Potail linguistique du Canada
http://www.noslangues-ourlanguages.gc.ca/truc-tip-fra.html

CTTIC
http://cttic.org/

CIUTI
http://www.ciuti.org/

European On-Line Language Observatory
http://www.poliglotti4.eu/en/index.php

ITI
http://www.iti.org.uk/indexMain.html

International T & I associations
http://www.kwintessential.co.uk/translation/associations.html

PROZ list of associations
http://www.proz.com/translator_associations

T & I Associations
http://www.letspeak.com/links/translatorsassociations.html

Links to resources
http://www.tau.ac.il/~toury/links.html

Translation resources
http://www.lai.com/edures.html

Speaking English
http://englishstudydirect.com/OSAC/langacls.htm

Speaking exercises
http://www.jem1.com/cx/speak.htm

Interpreter training resources
http://interpreters.free.fr/links.htm
http://perso.wanadoo.fr/e-weiser/index.htm

Cloze exercises (English)
http://grammar.ccc.commnet.edu/grammar/cgi-shl/quiz.pl/blanks1.htm
Proverbs
http://www.enchantedlearning.com/cloze/

Latin maxims, legal maxims
http://www.wagonerlaw.com/DKlegalquotes.html
http://www.giga-usa.com/gigaweb1/quotes2/qutoplegalmaximsx014.htm
http://www.willamette.edu/~blong/2006Words/LatinI.html

International courts & tribunals
http://www.pict-pcti.org/

Judicial interpreting blog
http://courtinterpreternews.blogspot.com/

Jergas de Habla Hispana
http://www.jergasdehablahispana.org/

Wikipedia
http://en.wikipedia.org/wiki/Main_Page

European Union portal
http://europa.eu/

European Parliament webcast: audio & video
http://www.europarl.europa.eu/en/see-and-hear

Canadian terminology data bank
http://www.granddictionnaire.com/btml/fra/r_motclef/index1024_1.asp

UN multilingual terminology database
http://unterm.un.org/

History of interpreting
http://lrc.wfu.edu/community_interpreting/pages/history.htm

Abbreviations and acronyms
http://www.acronymfinder.com/

United Nations
http://www.un.org

United Nations language outreach portal
http://www.unlanguage.org/default.aspx

United Nations examination announcements
http://www.un.org/Depts/OHRM/examin/exam.htm

United Nations interpreter examinations reference material
http://www.un.org/Depts/OHRM/examin/i-ref.htm

United Nations examinations for language positions
http://www.un.org/Depts/OHRM/examin/languageexam.htm

United Nations language services vacancy announcements
https://jobs.un.org/Galaxy/Release3/vacancy/Display_Vac_List.aspx?lang=1200&OCCG=18

United Nations employment conditions
http://www.un.org/Depts/OHRM/salaries_allowances/index.html

United Nations: a Day in the Life of Real Interpreters – video
http://www.youtube.com/watch?v=sUuliWL4LyI&feature=related

Europa: Interpreting for Europe
http://europa.eu/interpretation/index_en.htm

OAS Webcast
http://www.oas.org/en/media_center/videos.asp

OSCE Webcast
http://www.osce.org/mc/53135

OECD webcast
http://www.oecd.org/ict/4d/webcast.htm

Library of Congress webcasts
http://www.loc.gov/today/cyberlc/index.php

The Linguist List
http://linguistlist.org/

FBI Linguists
http://www.fbijobs.gov/124.asp

Académie française
http://www.academie-francaise.fr/

Real Academia Española
http://www.rae.es/rae.html

Academia Mexicana de la Lengua
http://www.academia.org.mx/

Office Québécois de la Langue Française
http://www.oqlf.gouv.qc.ca/ressources/bdl.html

Online Spanish Encyclopedia
http://www.enciclopedia-gratuita.com/

BBC World Service (news in several languages)
http://www.bbc.co.uk/worldservice/index.shtml?logo

World Press Review (news from newspapers around the world)
http://www.worldpress.org/

Courrier international (French news)
http://www.courrierinternational.com/gabarits/default_online.asp?ord_id=38

El Mundo (Spanish news)
http://www.elmundo.es/index.html?a=MAP9c6a011fff4b4bd3db12d0f473c6ec0a&t=
    1119232265

El País (Spanish news)
http://www.elpais.com/global/

Language and law
http://www.languageandlaw.org/

Legal Talk Network
http://www.legaltalknetwork.com/index.php

Bilingual topical guides from FITSPos at University of Alcalá
http://www2.uah.es/traduccion/publicaciones/materiales/materiales_2004_2007.html

AIIC Practical Guide for Professional Conference Interpreters
http://www.aiic.net/ViewPage.cfm/article21.htm

Iberian American Translation Portal
http://www.traduccionliteraria.org/

EMCI - European Masters in Conference Interpreting
http://www.emcinterpreting.org/
http://www.emcinterpreting.org/resources.php

Ethnologue: languages of the world
http://www.ethnologue.com/web.asp

English Spanish Translator Org
http://www.english-spanish-translator.org/

Spanish-English/English-Spanish Pocket Legal Dictionary
http://www.hippocrenebooks.com/book.aspx?id=1553

AIIC Tips for Beginners
http://www.aiic.net/ViewPage.cfm/article2305.htm

UNESCO World Digital Library
www.wdl.org

Resources for professional development of court interpreters
http://www.judiciary.state.nj.us/interpreters/resources.htm

Figures of Speech
http://en.wikipedia.org/wiki/Figure_of_speech

Trilingual (English/French/Spanish) index of expressions with equivalent meanings and illustrations
http://www.ccdmd.qc.ca/ri/expressions/index.html

US National Center for State Courts – court interpretation resources
http://www.ncsconline.org/D_Research/CourtInterp.html

Linguee: dictionary and translation search engine
http://www.linguee.com/

Centre National de Ressources Textuelles et Lexicales (French)
http://www.cnrtl.fr/definition/

French proverbs with English equivalents
http://www.e-frenchtranslation.com/fr/proverbes.htm

Institut National de l'Audiovisuel: French archives of radio and TV programs
http://www.ina.fr/

Radio France International
http://www.rfi.fr/

France 24
http://www.france24.com/fr/

Newspapers from around the world
http://en.kiosko.net/

United Nations Language Outreach Portal: list of selected translation & interpretation schools with programs in the UN official languages
http://www.unlanguage.org/UNTraining/Schools/default.aspx

Voces Hispanicas
http://cvc.cervantes.es/lengua/voces_hispanicas/

Yearbook of International Organizations
http://www.uia.be/yearbook

Index

Abbreviations & acronyms 39
Accuracy 3, 180
Adverbial clauses 53
Advocacy 8, 111
Allusion 205–210
Ambiguous syntactic links 25–26
Ambivalent conjunctions 30–32
Analogy 109–110
Anaphoric markers 39–40
Anticipating the speaker 17
Antonomasia 68, 90, 206, 210
Aphorism 66
Apostrophe 68
Apothegm 66
Argumentation 111
Assimilated latinism 262–264
Authority, argument from 111–114

Bilingual interpreter 6
Bromide 66
Business jargon 237–240

Catharsis 121
Chuchotage 4
Cliché 81–89
Clusters 44
Completeness 3, 180
Complex syntax 24
Compression 24, 38
Consecutive interpretation 3–4, 278
Context 56–58
Court interpreters 150
Critique 254–257

Decorum 122
De-verbalization 37–38

Diction 121, 162
Diplomacy 2
Drafting groups 121

Economic descriptors 255 *et seq.*
Economic discourse 225
Elegant variations 39
Emotion 63, 111, 117, 123
Endurance 180
Enumerations 32–37
Epigram 66
Errors in interpretation 26, 38, 253, 263
Euphemism 66, 125
Extended metaphor 67, 71–72

Fable 68, 206
Figures of speech 64–110
Fitness 17
Formal style 162

Humor 245
Hyperbole 66, 125–126

Idiom 65
Incongruity of register 123–124
Interpretation, defined 2
Intonation 20–21
Intuition 18
Inverted construction 164–167
Irony 253–254

Languages, official 5
Languages, relative importance 5
Latinisms 262–271

Legal terms 156–157
Length of speech 180 *et seq.*
Literary latinism 262
Logic 111
Logically necessary syntactic cues 26, 30–32

Maxim 66–67
Metaphor 67, 92–95, 159–161
Metonymy 68
Mission statement 180
Mixed metaphor 67
Moderation 121
Motto 66

Neologism 57
Note-taking 278
Noun–adjective clusters 44–50
Nuance 121–122, 127–128, 213–215,
    225–226
Numbers 272
Numerical expressions 108, 132–133,
    272–273

Official statement 180 *et seq.*
Oratory 163, 169 *et seq.*
Order of magnitude 272 *et seq.*
Overstatement by interpreter 246–247
Overstatement of case 118–119
Oxymoron 68

Parable 78, 81
Parallelism 32–37
Parenthetical phrases 42–43
Parody 66
Paronomasia 66
Parrhesia 66, 251–253
Pep talk 168–169
Personification 40
Petite équipe 4
Piece-by-piece strategy 25–26
Polemics 111
Policy address 180
Political correctness 121
Political discourse 211
Preparation 17
Professional requirements 6

Proverb 66, 74–81, 91
Puns 250–253

Quotations 205

Register 121
Relay interpretation 4, 92
Repartee 247
Re-translation 205

Sarcasm 247–250
Sense of occasion 162
Simile 65
Simplifying syntax 24
Simultaneous interpretation 3–4
Slang 156–157
Slogan 66
Social criticism 257–261
Speaking, public 8
Speeches, advance copies 17
Speed of delivery 24, 38, 247
Stage fright 8–9
Stereotype 158
Stress 7
Symbols in note-taking 278 *et seq.*
Symbols, sources of 281
Synecdoche 68
Synonyms 129–150

Taboos 150
Teams 4
Technical concepts 287
Technical latinism 262–265
Technical measurement 272 *et seq.*
Tone 162 *et seq.*
Translation, distinguished 2–3
Transposition 205–210

Units or meaning 44–45
Untranslatability 55 *et seq.*, 245 *et seq.*

Verb–object clusters 44–45
Voice, use of 8, 9, 16

Word order 44–45
Workload 7